COLOUR AND MEAN

The study of colour has become familiar territory in recent anthropology, linguistics, art history and archaeology. Classicists, however, have traditionally subordinated the study of colour to that of form. By drawing together evidence from contemporary philosophers, elegists, epic writers, historians and satirists, Mark Bradley reinstates colour as an essential informative unit for the classification and evaluation of the Roman world. He also demonstrates that the questions of what colour was and how it functioned – as well as how it could be misused and misunderstood – were topics of intellectual debate in early imperial Rome. Suggesting strategies for interpreting Roman expressions of colour in Latin texts, Dr Bradley offers new approaches to understanding the relationship between perception and knowledge in Roman elite thought. In doing so, he highlights the fundamental role that colour performed in the realms of communication and information, and its intellectual contribution to contemporary discussions of society, politics and morality.

MARK BRADLEY is Lecturer in Ancient History at the University of Nottingham. He is the author of a number of articles in the field of Roman visual culture, and has also worked on aspects of ancient approaches to pollution and cleanliness, as well as the reception of classical antiquity during the British Empire.

CAMBRIDGE CLASSICAL STUDIES

General editors

R. L. HUNTER, R. G. OSBORNE, M. MILLETT, D. N. SEDLEY, G. C. HORROCKS, S. P. OAKLEY, W. M. BEARD

COLOUR AND MEANING IN ANCIENT ROME

MARK BRADLEY
University of Nottingham

CAMBRIDGE
UNIVERSITY PRESS

CAMBRIDGE UNIVERSITY PRESS
Cambridge, New York, Melbourne, Madrid, Cape Town,
Singapore, São Paulo, Delhi, Tokyo, Mexico City

Cambridge University Press
The Edinburgh Building, Cambridge CB2 8RU, UK

Published in the United States of America by Cambridge University Press, New York

www.cambridge.org
Information on this title: www.cambridge.org/9780521291224

First published 2009
First paperback edition 2011

A catalogue record for this publication is available from the British Library

ISBN 978-0-521-11042-6 Hardback
ISBN 978-0-521-29122-4 Paperback

For Mary Beard

CONTENTS

PREFACE

This book revisits one of the oldest and most contested problems of classical philology – that of ancient colour perception and discrimination. The study of colour, and the senses in general, first attracted serious scholarly attention in the early nineteenth century with Goethe's theory of defective colour vision among the Greeks, an idea that was famously promoted in the wake of Darwinian theory by the British prime minister and Homeric scholar W. E. Gladstone and hotly debated by philologists and anthropologists well into the twentieth century. The issue of the poverty and imprecision of ancient colour vocabulary (or at least the difficulty in mapping it onto that of the modern West) has never been satisfactorily resolved, and the remainder of the twentieth century has continued to see a steady trickle of scholarship on the subject, mainly concerned with reinstating the perceptual sophistication of the ancients. In one of the most successful recent publications on the subject, Liz James (*Light and colour in Byzantine art*, 1995) drew together many of the ideas and approaches that had been adopted in the study of ancient colour and applied them to her own project on the interpretation of Byzantine art. The twenty-first century has thus far seen a modest revival of interest in ancient colour perception, with a spate of collaborative interdisciplinary conferences and publications concerned with the richness of Greco-Roman colour discrimination, the cultural specificity of ancient colour, and the complexity of literary and artistic engagement with vision and visual categories. In March 2001, M. Sassi (Pisa) organised a conference on *I colori nel mondo antico*, and in 2002, L. Villard (Rouen) edited a volume entitled *Couleurs et vision dans l'antiquité classique*. A major interdisciplinary conference on colour in the ancient world was hosted by Edinburgh University in September 2001, and was published as *Colour in the ancient Mediterranean world* by *BAR* in 2004 (edited by

L. Cleland and K. Stears). In May 2003, I co-organised the Cambridge Laurence Seminar on 'Sensory Perception' in the Classics, an interdisciplinary colloquium which drew attention to the diversity of traditions and registers concerned with the senses. More recently, A. Rouveret, S. Dubel and V. Naas published a volume entitled *Couleurs et matières dans l'antiquité* (2006, Paris), whose contributions laid emphasis on the use of contemporary ekphrasis to understand the classification and evaluation of ancient material culture. Since 2003 there have also been a number of high-profile exhibitions and conferences in Europe and America concerned with ancient sculptural polychromy, which have helped to reinstate colour as an essential component of classical art.

My work on concepts of colour in early imperial Rome targets something of an intellectual black hole in classical perception studies, bridging the gap between several important studies of colour in Classical Greece, and James' study of Byzantine perception. My book opens up a window onto elite uses of and debates about colour and perception in the early Empire, but it also operates as a critical response to other studies of perception in antiquity, and proposes an intellectual alternative to the traditional (and problematic) approach that favours the ancient prioritisation of light and luminosity over hue. My work develops as its central argument the line that Roman uses and discussions of *color* were principally concerned with the relationship between categories of visual perception and the inherent nature of the perceived object, and so between vision and knowledge. *Color* – the basic unit of perception into which the Romans divided the world – was a source of information and understanding, a tool for accurately understanding and evaluating the object of vision. Uses of *color* that seemed divorced from the material world, or phenomena that invited abstract categories (such as the rainbow), were often treated with considerable difficulty and caution by ancient thinkers. This basic principle of perception appears to have guided most Roman exploitation and interpretation of colour. As well as observing and exploring general patterns in the relationship between colour and meaning in Roman cultural history, this book will also argue that the discrimination and interpretation of colours could be formulated quite differently across the diverse registers and genres of the literate, highly educated male metropolitan perspectives that survive to us, and this study will explore several distinct but overlapping windows onto the deployment and evaluation of colour in early imperial Rome. Colour was not, and is not, a static, objective *thing*: it was a fluid, subjective, interactive unit of value and meaning.

It is no easy thing in the twenty-first century to find a book about colour that is not illuminated with page after page of colour illustration. *Colour and meaning in ancient Rome*, however, contains not a single image. For this I make no apologies: this book studies elite literary and philosophical perspectives about Roman visual culture, rather than Roman visual culture itself, and its emphasis is on the ancient classification, description and evaluation of colour. This is not to say that one cannot deploy classical art as a means of approaching ancient perception and theories of colour: I have attempted precisely this in two articles about classical marbles and sculpture, 'Colour and marble in early imperial Rome' (2006) and 'The importance of colour on ancient marble sculpture' (2009). Both of these articles were adapted from sections of my my doctoral thesis 'Concepts of colour in ancient Rome' (University of Cambridge, 1999–2004), which studied ancient discourses of colour in both literary and visual media, and which formed the intellectual platform for this book. The study of colour in classical literature (what the ancients themselves said about their visual culture) and the study of the visual culture itself, however, are rather different – if overlapping – exercises.

Just as colourful as the topic of this book have been the ten years of education and intellectual development that have led to its completion. Above all, I am indebted to my PhD supervisor, Mary Beard, for her intellectual and personal support, for her extraordinary patience, and for convincing me that a finished thesis was better than a good idea. I also owe thanks to Rolf Schneider, who supervised my thesis for a year and convinced me that visual arts had an important place in my work, and who has always been a source of support and inspiration. Along with Mary Beard, David Sedley was designated Cambridge University Press's reader for *Colour and meaning in ancient Rome*, and has been a mine of support in refining the philosophical sections of the book. I am also indebted in lots of different ways to Ashley Clements, Catharine Edwards, Christopher Kelly, Geoffrey Lloyd, Paul Millett, Robin Osborne, Emma Reisz, John Rich and Caroline Vout for their support and input during the long years that have led to the completion of this book. Financial assistance for the project was received from the Arts and Humanities Research Council, the Isaac Newton Trust, the Craven Studentship and the Jebb Fund. The Faculty of Classics at Cambridge and the University of Nottingham also provided funds to allow me to travel to and speak at various conferences and events.

Finally, it remains to thank my parents, who have always encouraged and supported me, Aidyn, Samuel and Ryan who helped me through the long months of work on this project, and all my friends who have helped keep life colourful and stimulating.

NOTE ON ABBREVIATIONS

Texts and periodicals are cited according to the abbreviations listed in the *Oxford Classical Dictionary* (3rd edition). All other references are listed in full.

hair that marked out the cheeks of adolescent boys. 'Blushing modesty' and the like, which had been proposed for *flauus pudor* by various translators, as well as the *Thesaurus* and Lewis and Short, was incorrect.[4] The *Thesaurus* had interpreted Ovid's *flaua ora* in the same way, by taking *flaua* proleptically after *tinxerat* (so the blush had 'tinged his face yellow'). Laughton's solution was to claim that the *Thesaurus* was wrong to connect *flauus* with the skin, and that the category primarily denoted (or suggested) blond hair.[5] This object-specific reading was, he argued, sustained by such examples as Virgil's Clytius whose cheeks are sprouting their first blond hairs ('*flauentem prima lanugine malas / ... Clytium*', *Aeneid* 10.324–5) and soldiers in Silius Italicus whose cheeks rub against helmets before they are even marked by the first blond down ('*galeaque teruntur / nondum signatae flaua lanugine malae*', *Punica* 2.318–19), where the connection with the blond *lanugo* is explicitly formulated. So deep-seated was this connection that the *Thesaurus*' other examples of alleged 'yellow skin' (*flaua cutis*) could not stand: thus, Valerius Maximus' description of *uir flaui coloris* (1.7.ext.6), Seneca's angry *flaui rubentesque* (*De Ira* 2.19.5) and his ethnic group *flaui* (*Epistle* 58.12) immediately evoke blond hair.[6] A further example (Ovid, *Amores* 2.4.39) compares a 'yellow girl' (*flaua puella*) to a 'pale girl' (*candida puella*) and girls who have a 'swarthy colour' (*fuscus color*): here too *flauus* must denote the 'blond'.[7] This could be corroborated by various examples of Greek 'yellow' (*xanthos*) from the *Greek Anthology*.[8] Although Laughton's correction of this linguistic

4 Lewis and Short (1879) s.v. *flauus*; *TLL* s.v. *flauus* 889 F '*de cutis humanae colore subrutilo*'. For translators, cf. Miller (1917) on *Hippolytus* (before the play was renamed *Phaedra*) 652 'blush of modesty'. Racine (1677), perhaps recognising the difficulty, had ignored it altogether (*Phèdre* 642 'Cette noble pudeur coloroit son visage'); similarly Harris (1904) 195 'the first bloom of youth'.

5 So, for example, '*Ganymede flauo*' (Hor. *Carm.* 4.4.4); '*flauis ... Britannis*' (Luc. 3.78). Laughton (1950) 88 suggests a similar model for *xanthos*, although he accepts the dubious LSJ line that *xanthos* could in later Greek denote complexion.

6 So too Claudianus Mamertus, *De Statu Animae* 1.20. At Festus p. 272 M/339.3L, however, *flauus* appears to be used to describe eyes.

7 The category, Laughton suggests, was perhaps institutionalised through the use of blond wigs in Roman comedy to mark out barbarian slaves; so Plaut. *Capt.* 648; *Mil.* 792; Ter. *Haut.* 1061. *Candidus* and *fuscus* typically referred to skin colour: further on Ov. *Am.* 2.4.39, see below pp. 138–40.

8 Laughton (1950) deals with two epigrams of Strato at 12.5.1–2 and 12.244.

mistake has been – with some exceptions – accepted and reflected in later translations, commentaries and dictionaries,[9] the important ramifications that his observations hold for the study of colour in Greco-Roman culture still remain, after sixty years, to be fully exploited.

In his 1950 article, Laughton posited that *flauus* should be understood as 'blond' because it (along with the Greek category *xanthos*) was a classic epithet of heroines and goddesses in Greek and Roman verse, as well as freshly bearded adolescent males.[10] This argument that it was the literary context that made *flauus* 'blond' was a diversion from his original, bolder, line that one should position this category linguistically and conceptually as a primary designator of blond hair. That original proposal had big implications: 'blond' should come first in our dictionaries – with 'yellow' as a secondary category whenever *flauus* was used to refer to something that was not hair, such as gold, corn or sand. Laughton had put his finger on an important cultural pattern. With this key semiotic rearrangement (rather than a mere literary conjecture), the Roman reader would have no doubt to what *flauus pudor*, *flaua ora* and *flaua puella* referred.

However, one would be wrong to claim that the simple rule *flauus* = blond would resolve all the difficulties surrounding this category. Although it seems certain that the *Thesaurus* incorrectly proposed 'skin colour' as one of the semiotic registers for *flauus*, there is an extensive and diverse list of physical contexts which employ *flauus*, where 'blond' does not appear to work. The *Thesaurus* finds two main areas for application of *flauus*: first,

[9] So Fitch's translation (2002, Loeb) of Sen. *Phaedra* 652 renders *flauus pudor* as 'golden modesty'; Boyle (1987) 83 'golden shame' (although he adds 'suffusing his gentle cheeks', suggesting he has not seen Laughton); *Oxford Latin Dictionary*, s.v. *flauus* cites this passage as an example of *flauus* = blond. André's work on colour (1949 – perhaps just missing Laughton's article) suggested that *flauus* at Ov. *Her.* 4.72 and Ov. *Am.* 2.4.39 refers (as part of its 'nuances brunes') to 'la couleur d'un teint hâlé par le soleil' (he misses the Seneca passage altogether). Giardina's edition (1966) 279 prefers an alternative manuscript edition replacing *flauus* with *flammis*, although he is aware of Laughton's suggestions. This change is unhelpful and should be dismissed. The Bristol Classical Press edition (Lawall, Kunkel and Lawall, 1982) copies this alteration. See Bremmer (1973) 180, suggesting *flauus rubor*. Coffey and Mayer (1990) revert to *flauus pudor* and accept Laughton's suggestion (albeit warning that 'behind the unusual phrase lies a complicated process of literary cross-reference').

[10] So Laughton (1950) 89.

of 'yellow' in the Roman wedding ceremony.[19] Ovid mentions *flaua pyrethra* (chamomile, *Ars Amatoria* 2.418) and *flaua liba* (wheatcakes, *Fasti* 4.476). Columella (4.30.4) talks of the Greek willow as possessing a *flauus color* (other types are *purpureus* and *rutilus*). Statius connects the category to clothes (*flaui amictus*, *Silvae* 2.3.16) and grapes (*Thebaid* 5.269 – but here as a wreath).[20] These examples demonstrate that *flauus* could be (with a certain amount of imaginative poetic flair) transferred to objects possessing broadly the same wavelength, where 'yellow' constitutes a more or less satisfactory translation. The same patterns occur with the use of the verbs *flaueo* and *flauesco* (particularly the participles *flauens* and *flauescens* which denote especially the *movement* of hair/corn/water).[21] However, the *Thesaurus*' category *de crinibus* (referring to hair) accounts for more than half the total references to *flauus* and – particularly when the skin category *de cutis humanae colore* has been correctly integrated into it – contains the large majority of all the direct prosaic uses of *flauus*.[22] This is evidence enough, it seems, both to reinstate 'blond' as the primary meaning of *flauus*, and to recognise that tentative efforts were in place in the educated metropolitan elite literature of the early Empire to extend this *color* beyond the blond. The issue that requires examination by both the philologist and the intellectual historian is the nature of this interface between the object and *how it looks*, and the question of when, how and why an object's natural *color* could be transferred to other objects outside the term's semantic range.

[19] Murgatroyd (1994) 77–8. Cf. Maltby (2002) 392 ('the chains are *flaua*, bright yellow or saffron, because this was the colour connected with the wedding ceremony'); Smith (1913) 413–14. The *color nuptialis* specified by Plin. *HN* 21.46 is in fact *luteum*, and Pliny implies this is reserved for the *flammeum*. It could be that *flaua uincula* is a corruption, and that one should substitute *laeta* (cf. Hor. *Carm*. 1.33.14).

[20] Cf. Columella, *Rust*. 3.21.3 on grape types '*uel generis albi uel flauentis uel rutili uel purpureo nitore micantis*'.

[21] *TLL* s.v. *flaueo* and *flauesco*. For the various nuances of these verb forms, see André (1949) 241–6. At 128 he claims that the *flauus* : *flauere* : *flauescere* frequency ratio is 75:13:10.

[22] André (1949) 128–9 recognises this ('L'emploi le plus caractéristique de *flauus* concerne les cheveux, représentant 66% des exemples du terme en prose, 45% des exemples poétiques'). André also points out that *flauus* can be used for the hair of animals, although he slots this under 'nuances brunes'.

Flauus is by no means an isolated case. The adjectives *uiridis* and *uirens* ('green') most commonly described the healthy crops and shrubs of Roman agriculture and horticulture, or the rich verdure of the Italian countryside.[23] Vitruvius, for example, discussing urban architectural design, advocates 'green spaces' (*uiridia*) because of the healthy sensation they bestow upon the viewer (5.9.5).[24] *Viridis*, however, is one of those Latin colour terms which stands in our dictionaries somewhat awkwardly on the line between representing our colour 'green' and the quality 'vigorous'. Most dictionaries aim to separate the two loosely: it seems incompatible with our idea of colour, for example, that Gellius could describe a strong and vigorous sound, such as the letter 'H', as *uiridis*.[25] Columella talks about the green *taste* of olives, and others describe the oil of the freshest varieties as *uiride*.[26] Pliny advises that seeds be sown under a 'green sky' (*uiride caelum*) – not literally 'green' of course, but clear and fresh and conducive to germination.[27] Similarly, it hardly seems plausible that Virgil's Euryalus, cut down in his '*uiridis*' youth was in any *real* sense 'green', nor the cheeks of children in Statius, nor the flame which Horace pictures

[23] Along with the substantives *uiridia, uirentia, uirecta, uiriditas* and the verbs *uireo, uiresco* and *uirido*; see André (1949) 184–94. For example, Cic. *Leg.* 1.5 *uiridis ripa*; Verg. *G.* 2.219 *uiride gramen*; 3.144; Hor. *Carm.* 1.25.17 *hedera uirens*; Columella, *Rust.* 1.5 *uirentia*; 12.57 *uiridia*; Apul. *Met.* 4.2 *uirecta*; Cic. *Sen.* 45 *herbescens uiriditas*; Verg. *Aen.* 6.206 *fronde uirere noua*; Sen. *Thyestes* 54 *uirescunt*. In Rome there was even a district called *uicus uiridiarius* (*CIL* 6.2225). The associations of ancient 'green' with health and vitality have been very thoroughly explored by Trinquier (2002), with critique by Bradley (2006b).

[24] Vitr. *De arch.* 5.9.5 'the subtle and rarefied air (*subtilis et extenuatus aer*) from the *uiridia*, flowing in on account of the movement of the body, clears the vision (*perlimat speciem*) and so carrying away the thick moisture (*umorem crassum*) from the eyes, leaves the gaze defined and the vision sharp (*aciem tenuem et acutam speciem relinquit*).'

[25] Gell. *NA* 2.3.1 (*H litteram ... inserebant ... uocibus uerborum firmandis ... ut sonus earum esset uiridior uegetior*; cf. 13.21.13 (*uiridior sonus*).

[26] Columella, *Rust.* 12.49.8 (*uiridem saporem oliuarum*); Suet. *Iul.* 53; cf. Quint. *Inst.* 12.6.3 (*fructum studiorum uiridem*); Cic. *Verr.* 1.45 on fresh/green firewood (*ignem ex lignis uiridibus*); Liv. 29.1.14; Ov. *Ib.* 235. In Columella, 42 out of 51 occurrences of *uiridis* constitute (in agricultural terms) the opposite of *aridus* – see André (1949) 187. Ov. *Hal.* 90 on shallows *verdant* with submarine plants (*num uada subnatis imo uiridentur ab herbis*); cf. Calp. *Ecl.* 2.57–8 describing a fertile river bank, *uirides qua gemmeus undas / fons agit*. The *Oxford Latin Dictionary* notes that uses of *uiridis* to denote the sea and streams 'may refer, in part at least, to the colour of surrounding vegetation'.

[27] Plin. *HN* 17.74; so also Calp. *Ecl.* 5.21 *tunc florent siluae uiridisque renascitur annus*.

spouting out of Mount Etna.[28] The blood of Seneca's Tiresias could be (figuratively speaking) *uiridis*, as could the 'ripe' old age of Virgil's Charon.[29] The list goes on, a series of colour puzzles that have caught the interest of generations of scholars. These examples, however, are not just anomalies: *uiridis* was 'verdant'. Just as *flauus* was the property of blond hair, *uiridis* was the property of plants and leaves, and much more than just what colour they were.[30] When Virgil described the growth of trees and grass (*arborei fetus alibi, atque iniussa uirescunt / gramina*), there was no sense in separating the 'green' and the 'grow'.[31] To describe, think of, experience *uiridis* for a Roman was to engage in a conceptual world of cultivation and growing.[32]

Like *flauus*, however, *uiridis* could break beyond the semantic range of 'verdant' (and so, in a sense, become a 'colour'). Outside verdure, *uiridis* was most commonly used to denote 'green' rocks, earths and minerals, particularly emeralds – presumably because

[28] Verg. *Aen.* 5.295; Stat. *Silv.* 3.3.125 (*uirides genae*); Hor. *Epod.* 17.33 (*uirens flamma*); cf. Manilius 2.941 on the rising sun (*uiridis ... Phoebus*). Cf. Stat. *Theb.* 4.98 on a snake emerging fresh in its new skin from hibernation, *laetisque minax interuiret herbis*.

[29] Sen. *Oedipus* 297; cf. Manilius 5.212 on the *uiridis sanguis* of sap. Verg. *Aen.* 6.304 *iam senior [Charon] sed cruda deo uiridisque senectus*; Sil. *Pun.* 5. 569 on the veteran Labicus as *uiridissimus irae*; Valerius Flaccus, *Argonautica* 1.77; Sen. *Ep.* 66.1 *senem ... uiridem animo ac uigentem*; Liv. 6.22.7 on the aged dictator Camillus in the Volscian wars: *sed uegetum ingenium in uiuido pectore uigebat uirebatque integris sensibus*; Columella, *Rust.* 1.pref.12 on the importance to farmhands of maintaining *uiridis aetas cum robore corporis*. Cf. Cic. *Tusc.* 3.75 on a prevalent evil possessed of *uiriditas*; *Rep.* 6.8 where Scipio advocates as rewards suited to *uirtus* not statues and triumphs, but *uiridiora praemiorum genera*.

[30] *Viridis* and its cognates may have belonged to a broad Latin semantic field that included such quintessential terms as *uir*, *uirtus* and *uis* – although the etymological relationship between these words is dubious; see Pokorny (1959) 1123–4 and 1133. Cf. also *Od.* 16.47, where a visitor in a poor man's cottage sleeps on a bed made up of χλωραὶ ῥῶπαι, boughs that possess a vital freshness and softness; see Clarke (2004) 135. Struycken (2003) 285–6 argues convincingly that uses of χλωρός by Democritus and other philosophers are emphatically phenomenological, evoking 'sprouting plants' and 'sap'.

[31] Verg. *G.* 1.55; cf. Ovid's description of Elysium at *Am.* 2.6.50 (*udaque perpetuo gramine terra uiret*). Cf. *Ecl.* 8.59; Columella, *Rust.* 11.2.67; Varro, *Ling.* 6.9 (etymologising '*uer*'); Apul. *Flor.* 10.4 (*uirores pratorum*); Plin. *HN* 16.88 on the underside of deciduous leaves, *pars inferior a terra herbido uiret colore*; André (1949) 186 does attempt a figurative – chromatic separation. Clarke (2004) 134–6 makes a similar point about the Greek category χλωρός, which (he argues) evokes 'kinetic' qualities such as 'fecund', 'oozing', 'vitality', and (in some cases) loses 'the chromatic aspect of the prototypical content'.

[32] Thus Cic. *Verr.* 3.47 on the *colles nitidissimi uiridissmique* of pre-Verrine Sicily; Lucr. 5.783–5 on the origins of the world herbaciously rooted in a *uiridis nitor* and *uiridans color*.

they had a similar wavelength.[33] A Roman could describe the parrot – something of a rare visual treat – as *uiridis*.[34] This category could also be used, with a certain degree of cultural sneering, to evoke the faces of woad-painted Britons,[35] madmen,[36] and those who were looking unwell or disorientated.[37] *Viridis*, then, could (like *flauus*) be extended beyond the object which it most properly described.

One final example: the category *caeruleus*, which evoked the appearance of deep sea or copious waters. One of Rome's biggest aqueducts, a great Claudian technical feat which brought thousands of gallons of fresh water into the capital from across Italy, brought water to the *fons Caerulea*, a deep reservoir so called (Frontinus tells us) from its *similitudo* – to the sea.[38] The *Thesaurus*, however, like other dictionaries, considers *caeruleus* to be derived from *caelum*, and sets 'sky-blue' as its first and primary meaning. Two early Latin verse fragments indeed appear to set this category in the

[33] Lucr. 4.1126 *uiridi cum luce zmaragdi*; Vitr. *De arch.* 7.7.4 *creta uiridis*; Prop. 3.3.27 *uirides lapilli*; Plin. *HN* 37.115; Sid. Apoll. *Carmina* 5.38–9, describing green *marmor Lacedaemonium* on the shield of Roma, is naturally drawn to the lively appearance of grass 'sprouting' out brightly to meet the gaze: *post caute Laconum / marmoris herbosi radians interuiret ordo*. For further discussion of emeralds in Pliny, see below pp. 102–3. For a comprehensive study of the therapeutic properties of green stones (especially emeralds) and animals (e.g. lizards and scarabs), situated in Egyptian ritual and iconography, see Trinquier (2002) 98–114.

[34] [Ov.] *Epistula Sapphus* 38.

[35] Ov. *Am.* 2.16.39 (*uirides Britanni*). On Britons and woad, see Carr (2005) and below pp. 175–6. *Caeruleus* could also be used to describe woad.

[36] Plaut. *Men.* 828, *uiden tu illi oculos uirere? ut uiridis exoritur colos / ex temporibus atque fronte, ut oculi scintillant, / uide*. Presumably, a green mask is being worn. The rendering of 'pale' and 'sickly' in the Gratwick commentary does not account for these nuances.

[37] Cf. Plaut. *Curc.* 22–3. on the sick pimp Cappadox: *quis hic est homo / cum collatiuo uentre atque oculis herbeis*?; *Ciris* 225, where the lovesick Scylla is afflicted by *uiridis pallor*; cf. Celsus, *Med.* 2.4.7 on green vomit. Faces are of course not usually 'green' by the standards of our colour charts (even though we still use the expression); one might argue that it is an appropriate category for sickness *because* it is so out-of-place. Artificial *uiridiaria* could incur the stigma of a natural colour unnaturally achieved – see Sen. *Controv.* 10.pref.9. Russian (for example) does not recognise the connection of green and sick faces. On χλωρός used for pale faces, see Clarke (2004) 133, 135 (where he curiously considers paleness to be 'chromatically green').

[38] Frontin. *Aq.* 13–14 (*a similitudine appellatus est*). Frontinus does not feel the need to spell out the object of this *similitudo* – commentators have noted 'The Blue' (Bennett) and 'la source bleu' (Grimal), although this is clearly unsatisfactory. Further on the *fons Caerulea*, see *CIL* 6.1257; Suet. *Claud.* 20.1. For a lexicographical synopsis of *caeruleus*, see André (1949) 162–75. Cf. Christol (2002) on 'Les Couleurs de la mer'.

qualifying sick faces, gems, marbles, parrots, dyes and cosmetics, and *caeruleus* describing the underworld, sapphires, woad, barbarian eyes and the like – giving a sense of 'yellow', 'green' and 'blue' that is familiar to modern western sensibilities. However, once one reinstates the significance of the object in ancient colour categories (hair, plant, water, etc.), a whole new playing field of literary and rhetorical allusion is opened up by these categories. The extension of these terms outside their usual range becomes a hallmark of such fundamental classical discourses as poetic metaphor, imperial cornucopia and philosophical epistemology. It is the character of such discourses that will form the subject of this book.

Modern literature

There have been several important efforts to deal with the challenge of understanding difficult Latin colour terms. The most comprehensive of these remains J. André's *Étude sur les termes de couleur dans la langue latine* (1949). The French philologist, who went on to conduct studies of Latin and Greek botanical categories, as well as Roman cooking and other comparative work, made this his first major attempt to classify and interpret a complex and awkward linguistic system so that it would make sense in the modern West.[57] The thorough and careful approach undertaken by the *Étude* was to a large extent undermined by the approach adopted in the first and main section – the 'Étude semantique' – to determine (in our terms) the precise shades denoted by individual Latin colour categories. Here, André forces the terms to match their closest modern equivalents, starting with what he considered to be the most important – le blanc, le noir, le gris, le rouge, le brun, le jaune, le bleu, le vert, le violet. Within each of these boxes, André oversimplifies the semantic range of the categories by insisting on sub-categories of shade (so, typically, *flauus* could denote 'nuances de jaune simple', 'nuances brunes' or 'nuances rouges' (129–30) or (at 101) *purpureus* used of the surface of the sea evoked 'un éclat, rose peut-être, effet d'un jeu de

[57] André (1955); (1956); (1958); (1967).

lumière'). A second section (an 'Étude Lexicologique') is concerned with the morphology and formation of various colour words (various adjectival usages, substantives and verb forms). Finally, in an 'Étude stylistique', he attempts to deal with broader topics such as basic colour symbolism, colour usages peculiar to each literary genre, differences between prosaic and verse uses of colour, epithets and formulae, as well as inter-textual imitation and idiosyncracy. This work elicited mixed responses from critics,[58] but it remains the only detailed sourcebook for Latin colour usage and is still widely cited. André reached some important conclusions: for example, some terms (such as *aerius*) may have emerged out of the specialist repertoires of 'les teinturiers' (182) and 'les produits de beauté' (292–3). His reliance on colour etymologies allowed for only a very superficial treatment of the literary contexts in which his colour terms occur – for example, his many verse examples are usually taken *prima facie* as evidence for colour meaning without considering the role of poetic creativity or literary context. Above all, André's bold attempt to catalogue both the differences and similarities of the Latin colour system was hamstrung by his failure to consider the important conceptual and philosophical principles at work in Greek and Roman theories of vision, and the position of colour within this system.

Less well known is N. Baran's ambitious and wide-ranging essay on 'Les Caractéristiques essentielles du vocabulaire chromatique latin' (1983) which explores cultural and stylistic trends and developments in Roman literature, art and society.[59] Baran provides a comprehensive *état de recherche* on the subject, and makes some useful observations about developments in colour usage from Homeric to Classical Greek through to various Latin literary and historical contexts, and draws some interesting comparative connections with Baran's native tongue, Romanian. In particular, Baran endorses the idea of the gradual enrichment of colour vocabulary over time, and identifies (p. 325) a development from 'sens matériel-concret' to 'sens figuré-abstrait' in patterns of colour

[58] The most visceral response came from Laughton (1951). For a more favourable review, see Messing (1955).

[59] This study expanded out of Baran's earlier article (with M. Chişleag, 1968) on the sophistication of colour terminology in Lucretian verse.

usage.[60] Baran offers a much more sensitive treatment than André of different genres and registers in which colour is employed, although some of his literary and historical conclusions are optimistic and over-generalised (for example, that Augustan literature represented a 'peak' in Latin colour terminology or that Latin colour vocabulary was 'richer' than Greek).[61] More recently, these detailed treatments of Latin colours have been complemented by C. Abellàn's more focused *Estructura semàntica de los adjetivos de color en los tratadistas Latinos de Agricultura y parte de la Enciclopedia de Plinio* (1994) which reaches similar conclusions to those of André but which explores in detail the thematic position of colour categories in Latin agricultural texts.

Greek colour usage has generated the greatest difficulties for translators and visual historians, and has consequently offered the most fertile ground for study. Interest in the nature of Greek colour vision first attracted serious scholarly attention with Goethe's theory of defective colour vision among the Greeks, an idea that was famously promoted in the wake of Darwinian theory by the British prime minister and Homeric scholar W. E. Gladstone. Gladstone claimed that the Homeric colour system was founded upon light and darkness, and that the organ of vision 'was but partially developed among Greeks of his age' and had not developed much further by the time of Aristotle.[62] This was connected to the material poverty of colour in their natural environment, the paucity of dyes, paints and flower varieties and the relative uniformity of somatic colours. More detailed research into Greek colour terminology supported Gladstone's claim, its arguments focusing in particular on the linguistic ignorance of a green-yellow distinction, and the newly investigated phenomenon of colour-blindness was famously invoked to explain this cultural deficiency.[63]

[60] He also draws (and overstates) a sharp contrast between modern and ancient colour usage (p. 404): 'Notre système chromatique (très riche et nuance) est axé sur l'interprétation des couleurs du spectre solaire, tandis que celuis des Anciens avait une base essentiellement naturiste'.

[61] Baran (1983) 350; cf. 365 'ils étaient plutôt des gens pratiques, poursuivant les avantages immédiats'.

[62] Gladstone (1858) 488 'Homer's perceptions and uses of colour', expanded in Gladstone (1877). Gladstone's claim is discussed by Irwin (1974) 6–7.

[63] Esp. Schultz (1904) 187–8.

Another solution (which became a premise for Berlin and Kay's *Basic color terms* (1969)) was to propose a biological evolutionary view of colour designation.[64] Others, led by K. Müller-Boré (1922), argued on the other hand that the lack of emphasis on colour was characteristic of epic style.[65]

Studies of Greek colour across the next hundred years or so were dominated, on the whole, by efforts to demonstrate that (contrary to Gladstone *et al.*) the Greeks employed a highly sophisticated and subtle colour system.[66] Prominent in these studies was the notion that Greek colour terms denoted more than simply (in our terms) 'colour': luminosity, saturation, texture, smell and even things that had nothing to do with colour such as 'agitation' and 'liquidity' were highlighted and explored by these surveys.[67] Much was made of the central position of *leukos* and *melas* as expressions of brightness and darkness, and other 'intermediate' colours as subtle configurations of these two. This revision of ancient colour perception even found some space for the contemplation of colours as objects.[68]

[64] This line was later applied to Hebrew and Norse – see Brenner (1982) esp. ch. 1.

[65] Müller-Boré (1922) esp. 43–4. Rowe (1972) 330–1 prefers to envisage Homeric colour vocabulary as representative of contemporary colour perception. Smyshliaeva [Смышляева] (2002) constructs a similar argument about the paucity of 'blue' in Latin elegy which (she argues) is due to the influence of epic which favours a 'red-white-yellow' triad.

[66] For opposition to Gladstone's view, see Hochegger (1884) esp. 38–41; Veckenstedt (1888); Platnauer (1921) 162 (Platnauer, in spite of his impressive demonstration of the subtelties of colour-categories, finishes by endorsing the notion of Greek colour-blindness); Müller-Boré (1922); Wallace (1927); Kober (1932); André (1949) 12; Gernot (1957); Mugler (1960); Reiter (1962); Young (1964); Osborne (1968); Dürbeck (1977). Kranz (1912) aimed to connect the interest in luminosity with Greek theories of colour. For a reasonably up-to-date survey of the question, see Grossman (1988). For a synopsis of the problems from a linguistic point of view, see Lyons (1999). According to Pollitt (2002) 8, recent studies of Greek colour have preserved an assumption about primitive ancient colour vision. For an approach to Greek colour terminology within the framework laid down by Berlin and Kay, see Moonwomon (1994).

[67] Suggestions persisted that one could restore hue as a primary quality of Greek and (particularly) Latin colour terms; for example, Rowe (1972) suggested that even in Homer one could detect up to thirty hue-words. However (p. 329), luminosity was prominent: 'Homer's world is a world of brightness and darkness, of the gleam of weapons and the dark lustre of a swelling sea … a different kind of sensitivity to visual stimuli'. More recently, Dowden (2005) has attempted to embed Heliodorus' *Aethiopica* in a literary and cultural tradition that privileges light and luminosity over colour.

[68] Rowe (1972) 333–5 considers *leukos* and *melas* (along with *eruthros*) as the first of antiquity's 'abstract' colours (so following the research of Berlin and Kay (1969): 'the process of abstraction, of the grouping of the infinitely varied colours of the environment under a limited number of general terms, had as yet only begun'). He argues that other early Greek colour terms were principally associative (for example p. 343 on *phaios* as a

(clusters of colour for dramatic purposes); and associative (linking one scene with another). Edgeworth emphasised the importance of individual subtlety and stylistic and functional fluctuation, although the connections he makes sometimes seem a little contrived (so *purpureus* = Roman death-rites, pp. 29, 53) and his recourse to psychological interpretation (particularly at pp. 43–52 – e.g. green + white = release of tension) can seem somewhat tenuous. Edgeworth also seems uninterested in the use of verb forms as expressions of colour. The alphabetical catalogue of seventy-eight colour terms in the *Aeneid* (pp. 65–168) alerts the reader to the blur between conventional colour terms and objects (e.g. *lilium, nix, trabea, uiola*), but the implications at work here are not developed. *The colors of the Aeneid* usefully appended Edgeworth's earlier articles on Latin colour, the most important of which ('Does *purpureus* mean "bright"?') aimed methodically to demonstrate that all the difficult uses of this term can be explained away as Homeric *formulae* or allusions, and that it always approached something akin to 'red'.[74]

This interest in the stylistic 'mood' and emotion of poetic colour usage has fuelled, most recently, the work of J. Clarke (2002) *Imagery of colour and shining in Catullus, Propertius and Horace*, which explores the role of colour as part of the *enargeia* and *ekphrasis* in selected passages of Latin verse. This monograph grew out of Clarke's earlier article 'Colours in conflict: Catullus' use of colour imagery in c. 63' (2001), where she offered an acute analysis of colour usage in Catullus 63.[75] Clarke's work is an important contribution to literary criticism, but the ease with which she translates Latin colour terms into modern abstract colours (red, white, green), her simple schemes for colour contrast (dark-light, white-red etc.), her indulgence in abstract qualities of colour symbolism (madness, death, beauty, softness), and the casual employment of such difficult terms as 'synaesthesia' reflect a number of methodological shortcomings for this study of colour, and Clarke's project makes little headway in resolving the

[74] For an early study of light symbolism and colours in the *Aeneid*, see Schulbaum (1930–1). Cf. Baran and Chişleag (1968) for a philological survey of chromatic aesthetics and colour symbolism in Lucretius (with an emphasis on luminosity).

[75] Cf. also Clarke (2004) on colour sequences in Catullus' long poems, reaching similar conclusions.

traditional difficulties of translating and understanding ancient colour usage. Other literary studies have also tended to skate around the importance of basic cultural and conceptual differences in perception and categorisation. P. Barolsky's 'Ovid's colors' (2003), for example, is more concerned with demonstrating that Ovid's *Metamorphoses* exploited rich and diverse colour motifs and contrasts than exploring the broader cultural patterns or ramifications of the connections Ovid draws between colours and objects.[76] The use of colour in later Latin literature has received some attention, stressing particularly the flexibility of categories, although this material can be misleading for the interpretation of earlier literature where (I will argue) significant conceptual changes in the use of colour were taking place.[77]

The most difficult colour of all, *porphura/purpura*, has received attention from a number of directions. M. Reinhold's *The history of purple as a status symbol in antiquity* (1976) is a useful account of the exploitation of sea-purple dye (and imitation purples) from the Assyrians through to the late Roman Empire, but although it draws attention to the political, social and economic dimensions of the actual dye and its manufacture, it is only superficially concerned with the semiotics of purple as a colour.[78] Some gaps in Reinhold's work are partially filled by H. Stulz's thorough *Die Farbe Purpur im frühen Griechentum* (1990) which catalogues Greek terms for 'purple' and 'red' in great detail and offers a more sensitive analysis than did Edgeworth's 'Does *purpureus* mean "bright"?'. More recently, O. Longo (1998a) edited a collection of short essays on the literature, art and science of purple from antiquity through to the early modern period, opening some important windows onto the cultural and technological evolution of the dye as a status symbol in the Mediterranean world, as well as literary and artistic associations of 'purple' as a category of colour. There have also been several significant discussions of the social relationship

[76] This preoccupation with 'colour symbolism' also dominates Thomas (1979); cf. also Grant (2004) on colour and characterisation in Petronius.

[77] For example, Newbold (1981–2); Roberts (1989) 72, 76, 78 on the diverse nature of colour terms in late antique poetry.

[78] See also Doumet (1980). More recently, Edmonds (2000) has discussed the technical history of the production of purple dye. Cf. also Spanier (1987) on the relationship between 'royal purple' and 'biblical blue'.

between material colours (particularly purple and gold) and Roman *luxuria*, and of attempts by the state to police and control them.[79]

Running parallel to the developing linguistic and literary analyses of Greco-Roman colour terms was a rich scholarly interest in the use of colour in classical art. This emerged in the late eighteenth century, when it became clear that a significant proportion of Greek and Roman sculpture and architectural elements was richly coloured. This proposal goaded proponents of a pure, ideologically and physically monochrome antiquity into a sometimes fiery debate (particularly over the Parthenon frieze) that lasted throughout the nineteenth century and well into the twentieth.[80] This debate intersected only superficially with the ongoing linguistic-literary debate, although the notion of a rich polychrome material world was occasionally invoked by those who wished to restore colour sensitivity to the ancients.[81] Even more so than the linguistic material, this research focused predominantly on the art of Classical Greece, with only a few important treatments of the Roman material. The fullest and most up-to-date consideration of polychromy in early Greek sculpture is V. Brinkmann's *Die Polychromie der archaischen und frühklassischen Skulpturen* (2003a) which relays and interprets the latest findings of scientific research into pigments on marble statuary. Both this and V. Manzelli's *La policromia nella statuaria greca arcaica* (1994) work on the principle that ideas of monochrome white marble sculpture should be regarded as a neo-classical dogma.[82]

The most comprehensive study of colour in Roman sculpture remains P. Reuterswärd's thorough *Studien zur Polychromie der Plastik: Griechenland und Rom* (1960).[83] Reutersward laid

[79] For example, Culham (1986) on the *lex Oppia*; cf. Barker (1996) on the ethical ambiguities of gold and goldenness in Augustan Rome; Jones (1999) on Greco-Roman processional colours, 200 BC–AD 200.

[80] For some aspects of responses to colour on sculpture over the last two centuries (particularly in reconstructions), see Kader (2003); Prater (2003); on the reconstruction of the Cambridge Peplos Kore, see Cook (1978).

[81] For details, see Gage (1993) 11; Bruno (1977) esp. 47–51.

[82] Cf. also Brinkmann (1987); (1994) on the Siphnian treasury. For a full bibliography, see Brinkmann and Wünsche (2003) 268–71. Some important recent work has been done on the chromatic effects of bronze sculpture, as well as the description of different types of bronze alloys in literary ekphrasis: see in particular Descamps-Lequime (2006) and esp. Muller-Dufeu (2006), complemented by Dubel's 2006 study of the relationship between materiality and colour in ancient descriptions of metal artefacts.

[83] For an earlier account, see Phelps (1930).

emphasis on the diversity and sophistication of patterns of polychromy across Greco-Roman antiquity and across artistic genres, and argued for a general evolution towards lighter colour-schemes in finer portraits and reliefs particularly later in the Empire, suggesting an increasing artistic concern for 'naturalism'. He drew together all the available archaeological evidence for colour traces to demonstrate that the original sculptural material (marble or bronze, for example) played a more or less central visual role in the finished product (with any pigments/patinas/glazes often discreetly enhancing the underlying colour rather than simply creating a new one). This draws the art historian's attention to the essential interaction of colour and form in classical art (rather than systems of colour *qua* colour). Since 2003, Brinkmann and other archaeologists and art historians around Europe have put together exhibitions of painted Greek and Roman casts at more than ten international venues, and an exhibition at the J. Paul Getty Museum in Malibu in 2008 (*The color of life: polychromy in sculpture from antiquity to the present*) integrated the work on ancient sculptural polychromy with current research into polychrome sculpture in medieval and modern western art, with some highly significant findings. Aspects of the history, archaeology, literature and science of colour and pigmentation on Greco-Roman sculpture have been discussed in detail in my article 'The importance of colour on ancient marble sculpture' (2009a).[84] The art-historical study of pigments on Roman sculpture is less advanced than that of its archaic and early classical Greek counterparts, although J. S. Østergaard (Curator of Ancient Art, Ny Carlsberg Glyptotek) has established the interdisciplinary 'Copenhagen Polychromy Network Project' (2008–10) in order to analyse a representative selection of classical sculptures in the Glyptotek with a view to redressing this imbalance. Studies of the relationship between sculptural/architectural material and colour in Rome, on the other hand, are well represented: in particular, R. Schneider's seminal *Bunte Barbaren* (1986) on coloured marbles, M. De Nuccio and L. Ungaro's

[84] For details about these exhibitions, and their accompanying catalogues, see Bradley (2009a) 427. For a review of R. Panzanelli's accompanying catalogue to *The color of life* (2008), see Bradley (2009b).

exhibition catalogue *I marmi colorati nella Roma imperiale* (2002), and my own article 'Colour and marble in early imperial Rome' (2006a), which focuses on the relationship between colour and stone in ancient ekphrasis. Important research has also been conducted on Pompeian paints as well as polychromy in ancient art and restoration techniques.[85]

The ramifications of such research in ancient art for the study of ancient colour systems have been acutely demonstrated by E. James' *Light and colour in Byzantine art* (1995), which explored the rich extant material of Byzantine church art against the background of Greco-Roman theories of colour.[86] This work is one of the clearest and most important contributions in recent years to the study of classical colour theory. James' subtle art-historical account of light and colour in several important Byzantine mosaics is qualified and enriched by a synopsis of modern approaches to colour perception in various disciplines.[87] James decided to exclude Latin linguistics and theory from her work on the grounds that the Byzantines used Greek and not Latin (p. 47), a reminder that important work on the contribution of Roman/Latin colour theory to the study of ancient perception still remains to be done. Her glossary of fifteen Greek colour terms, a judicious summary of their nuances and uses, claims to avoid offering English hue-equivalents (p. 49) but still subscribes to abstract parallels (e.g. *ōchros* = 'another of the less than precise shades of the green-yellow band'). Furthermore, James extracts terms and ideas from Platonic and Aristotelian discussions of colour in order to enrich her interpretation of Byzantine art without full consideration of the cultural changes that took place in the intervening period, or the generic differences between classical philosophy and early Christian art. James' principal conclusion (corroborated by her discussion of pigments and the four-colour palette in ancient art) that Greek colour words were principally concerned with dark–light opposition is important for her evaluation of Byzantine art,

[85] See Augusti (1967); Béarat *et al.* (1997); Brinkmann (2003a); Jenkins and Middleton (1988); Jenkins (2001). Important work has been conducted on Egyptian pigments and colour-schemes – in particular, see Baines (1985) and (2001).

[86] And more recently, see James (2003).

[87] See esp. Chapter 1. Cf. Schwarzenberg (2000).

but its prominence obscures other significant patterns that emerge from her work, such as the connection between artistic *mimesis* and philosophical epistemology. Nevertheless, her treatment of colour in Byzantine art and literature (chapter 4) demonstrates that light and luminosity, as well as ontology (i.e. colour as an inherent property of an object; 'definition of being', p. 80) were still high on the artistic agenda. Through a study of the rainbow, James demonstrates that an organised system of colour (hue) 'symbolism' appears not to have existed in the Classical and Byzantine world. Her chapter on 'The rhetoric of colour' then underlines the fundamental imagination and flexibility of Byzantine colours in both literature and art, although this flexibility sits uneasily with the conclusion of her final chapter that colour defined form and therefore reality, a 'true' property of the object or phenomenon it represented (p. 138). James' *Light and colour* is a highly successful and carefully formed thesis on the role of colour in antiquity and its expression in art, and offers one of the most promising methodologies in the pursuit of ancient colour theory. *Colour and meaning in ancient Rome* aims to fill the scholarly blind spot towards Roman ideas about colour, which will help to create a bridge between studies of classical Greek colour vision and James' Byzantine material and will also develop a more sophisticated interpretation of the ethical and philosophical debates about colour, perception and knowledge that dominated intellectual discussions of the subject in antiquity.

The twenty-first century has thus far seen a spate of interdisciplinary conferences and edited volumes dedicated to demonstrating the richness of Greco-Roman colour discrimination, the cultural specificity of ancient colour, and the complexity of literary and artistic engagement with vision and visual categories. One of the first, and most successful, of these is L. Villard's *Couleurs et vision dans l'antiquité* (2002), a collection of ten short essays by French philologists representing a wide range of expertise in (mainly Greek) linguistics and literature from the Hippocratic corpus through to Lucian.[88] Villard's volume lays particular focus on ancient medical texts and Greek literature of the second century AD and

[88] For a detailed review, see Bradley (2006b).

contains some important new observations about the deployment of colour as an epistemological tool in medical texts, as well as exploring the relationship between the ancient philosophy of perception and the formulation of colour experiences in Greek literature. While Villard's volume concentrated primarily on Greek linguistics and literature, A. Rouveret, S. Dubel and V. Naas' *Couleurs et matières dans l'antiquité* (2006) takes as its main focus material culture and ancient literary ekphrasis, and deals predominantly with Rome.[89] This volume lays emphasis on the importance of exploring material culture from the perspective of artistic ekphrasis, and underlines the significance of evaluating ancient art through its contemporary literary and linguistic culture. Its contributors are committed to the idea that it is in the field of art that we can find some of the most sensitive and sophisticated ancient approaches to colour, and of particular importance is the volume's emphasis on associating colours with particular materials or phenomena rather than simply (as philologists such as André or Maxwell-Stuart have done) a set of abstract lightwaves. Rouveret *et al.* also do a commendable job of reinstating the significance of colour in moral and philosophical debates about artistic mimesis and the function of art. Much more ambitious (and so less coherent as a whole than the volumes mentioned above) is L. Cleland and K. Stears' edited conference volume *Colour in the ancient Mediterranean world* (2004), a collection of twenty-five essays on wide-ranging themes and periods by philologists, archaeologists, art historians and literature scholars which delve into anthropology and sociology, as well as Egyptology and Biblical Studies, among other things.[90] These interdisciplinary approaches to colour in the ancient world, although sometimes a little fragmentary, nevertheless draw attention to important overlaps and continuities between different literary and artistic registers that have previously, on the whole, been considered in isolation. Others have also undertaken

[89] For a review of Rouveret *et al.* (2006), see Bradley (2007). This volume also complements Tiverios and Tsiafikis' conference volume (2002) on the role of colour in Greek art and architecture.

[90] Developed out of a conference held in Edinburgh in 2001 ('Colours in Antiquity'). For a review, see Arkins (2005), who simplifies his analysis by considering what papers can tell us about 'white', 'red', 'black', brown' and 'violet/purple'.

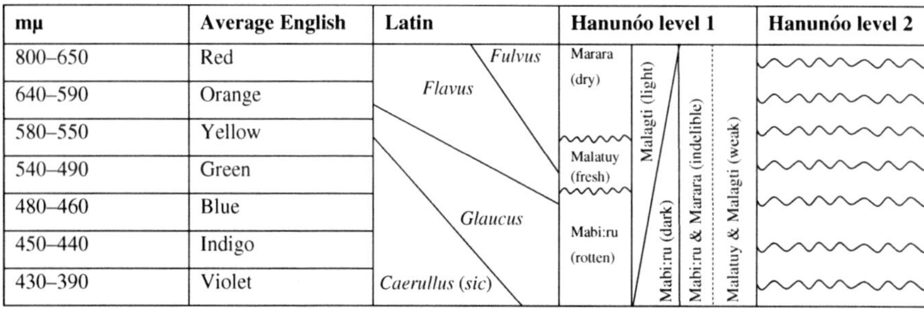

Fig. 1. A comparative diagram of colour categories in English, Latin and Hanunóo, with lightwave estimates, after U. Eco (1985) fig. 8.

important interdisciplinary studies of the subject: in particular, M. M. Sassi has made a valuable and wide-ranging contribution to the understanding of the symbolic role of colour in ancient thought and culture.[91]

The general treatments of colour not restricted to antiquity are too extensive to mention in full here, save to say that the following have been important for the development of my ideas about colour in ancient Rome. Newton's *Opticks* (1704) set the agenda (as well as the terminology) for most modern studies of colour, as well as sparking adversarial responses from the likes of Goethe (*Zur Farbenlehre*, 1810), who redirected the study of colour away from the purely physical towards the mechanics of human perception and artistic aesthetics.[92] This latter position (which was primarily concerned with colour *categories*) in the psychology of colour perception was developed in the twentieth century most

[91] See esp. the conference volume *I colori nel mondo antico: esperienze linguistiche e quadri simbolici* edited by S. Beta and M. Sassi (2003) and Sassi's monograph *The science of man in ancient Greece* (tr. Chicago University Press, 2001) which begins with the vocabulary of skin colours to explore a chain of arguments about ancient physiognomy, medicine and ethnography; Sassi (1993) on Greek physiognomics; Sassi (1994) on the question of imperfect Greek colour vision; most recently, Sassi (2005). Cf. also the Laurence Seminar 'Sensory Perceptions' held at the Faculty of Classics, Cambridge in May 2003 (co-organised by M. Bradley and A. Clements) with a similarly ambitious disciplinary and chronological scope.

[92] On Goethe's theory of colours, see Schindler (1964).

coherently by L. Wittgenstein (*Bemerkungen über die Farben*, published 1977). This worked hand-in-hand with studies of basic/primary colour categories, of which the most influential had been that of the physiologist E. Hering (*Zur Lehre vom Lichtsinn*, 1878). J. Itten's *Kunst der Farbe* (1961) – attempting to forestall criticism about the difficulties of defining colour – drew an important distinction between pigments as chromatic reality and our perceptual response as chromatic effect. Thinkers from many different disciplines have recognised that colour is no easy matter: one critic argued that 'the meaning of the term colour is one of the worst muddles in the history of science'.[93] These difficulties are extensively represented by anthropological studies of colour usage: the Hanunóo, the Dani of Papua New Guinea, the Irish and Russian are just a few well-documented examples of cultures which use colours in ways that to us are strange or incongruous.[94] Others, such as S. Pinker, have adopted a squarely universalist paradigm of colour usage.[95] U. Eco's 'How culture conditions the colours we see' (1985) clearly articulates many of the linguistic and conceptual issues at stake in the process of colour perception, and relates this process both to cultural pertinence or functionality (a skier can recognise different qualities of snow etc.) and the relative position of a colour within the system.[96] His comparative table (fig. 1) of colour categories in English, Latin and Hanunóo alongside lightwaves demonstrates some of the possible differences in systems of

[93] Gibson (1968); cf. Sahlins (1976) 1, 22 which asserts that colour is a cultural matter, and remarks that every test of colour discrimination is rooted in a sort of referential fallacy.

[94] The most widely cited example of chromatic difference is the Hanunóo, who appear to have a subtle vocabulary for colour contrasts but no distinct categories for absolute values of hue; for a first-hand report, see Conklin (1955). Another is that of the Dani of Papua New Guinea, who use terms for 'cool' (*mola*) and 'warm' (*mili*), but have no other colour words at all: see Heider (1972), simplified by Berlin *et al.* (1997) 21. On distinct categories for 'green' in Irish, see Clarke (2004) 131. For Russian 'light blue' (*goluboj*) and 'dark blue' (*sinij*) as distinct categories, see Corbett and Davies (1997) 205–7.

[95] Pinker (1994) 62–3, 'Humans the world over colour their perceptual worlds using the same palette, and this constrains the vocabularies they develop ... The way we see colours determines the way we learn words for them, and not vice versa'. This idea is copied by Duranti (1997) 65–7. *Contra*, see Lucy (1992) 127–87; Lucy (1997).

[96] Eco (1985). This article considers Gell. *NA* 2.26 as part of his material for colours as semiotic codes in systems of communication. Eco distinguishes 'elaborated codes' (e.g. heraldic colours, recognised by a cultivated minority) and 'restricted codes' (a simpler universal system, such as 'red = blood', 'white = peace').

classification (as well as the shortcomings of such linear measures of perception: *flauus* and *caeruleus*, as we have seen, can hardly be made to fit such a model). There are several important works on colours as semiotic codes or informational systems. The standard structuralist approach (proposed Lévi-Strauss and Turner, among others) holds that colours are signifiers and are closely associated with the object or idea that is signified.[97] Others have offered more flexible models of improvisation and contextualisation.[98] Both approaches have informed my ideas about colour in the Roman world.

No study of colour would be complete without mention of J. Gage's seminal *Colour and culture* (1993) and the shorter *Colour and meaning* (1999) which chart (from a principally art-historical perspective) the history of colour from Classical Greece through to the twentieth century. *Colour and culture*, particularly the sections 'Classical inheritance', 'Unweaving the rainbow' and the chapters on Newton and Goethe, have proven an invaluable source of ideas and references in the initial stages of my research. Essential reading also includes Berlin and Kay's hugely influential – and now universally criticised – *Basic color terms* (1969), which argued for an evolutionary system of colour discrimination based on cultural advancement (evidence included that of Homeric Greece).[99] There have been various attempts to bridge the disciplinary crevices between scientific, anthropological, linguistic, psychological and scientific treatments of colour, but these studies have drawn attention to the differences, rather than the common ground between these accounts (see, for example, T. Lamb and J. Bourriau, *Colour: art and science*, 1995 or C. Riley, *Color*

[97] Lévi-Strauss (1970) 322–5; Turner (1967) 59–91; cf. also Sahlins (1976).

[98] For example, Sperber (1975) chapter 5 on smells (with colours as parallels); Linksz (1952) 52–178 considers the flexibility of semiotic codes for colour-blind individuals; Gombrich and Riley (1994) considers the versatility of colour perception in artistic experience.

[99] On the current state of the debate about basic colour terms, see Berlin *et al.* (1997). Kay and McDaniel (1978) reformulated the basic colour term as a 'fuzzy set' rather than a distinctive category of colour, with the result that colour has become a key example for prototype theorists: see Lakoff (1987) 26–30; Wierzbicka (1990); MacLaury (1991). For a critique of Berlin and Kay, see Clarke (2004) 132–3.

codes: modern theories of color in philosophy, painting and architecture, literature, music, and psychology, 1996).[100]

Recent years have produced several important works on the archaeology of colour, particularly elements of the 1998 volume on *The archaeology of perception and the senses* (*Archaeological Review from Cambridge* 15:1), and A. Jones and G. MacGregor, (2002) *Colouring the past: the significance of colour in archaeological research*, which direct attention to the importance of colour as an expression of materiality in historical landscapes. The archaeology of the senses has been principally concerned with the relationship between the perceiver and the environment. Some have adopted a *phenomenological* view of the world – where perception is the act of receiving stimuli through the senses, from a world outside the body, and where the perceiver is the passive recipient;[101] others have claimed that perception is the result of an attempt to impose ideas on the external world which began as concepts in the individual's mind – a 'mental map' or 'mental template'.[102] Recently, archaeologists have favoured a middle line, a 'perceptual framework', which mediates between the individual and the environment and is influenced by memories, foreknowledge and preconceptions.[103]

The nature and history of colour have in recent years received extensive treatment in more popular academic literature. F. Delamare and B. Guineau's New Horizons publication *Colour: making and using dyes and pigments* (1999), for example, is an excellent and

[100] For a more recent set of papers on the philosophy and psychobiology of colour (from a conference held in 1996), see Mausfield and Heyer (2005).

[101] So Tilley (1994), who takes the world as real, natural, material; a 'given', existing outside of history. For a critique of Tilley's approach, see Brück (1998) 34 'perception is not simply a physical process but is a deeply cultural phenomenon'. Also taking the phenomenological approach, see Tuan (1977); cf. Ingold (1992) 46 'the structures and meanings that we find in the world are *already there* in the information that we extract in the act of perception; their source lies in the objects we perceive, they are not added on by the perceiver'.

[102] For example, Renfrew (1987). Cf. Appleton (1980) 9.

[103] For a useful summary of the issues of 'perceptual framework', see Jones (1998) esp. 8. Useful for this approach is Bourdieu's (1977) concept of a cultural 'habitus' in perception. Warburton (2004) discusses the complex technological, intellectual, economic and political influences on the development of colour categories, in a concise study of the Egyptian colour system. On various aspects of chromatic developments in the Mediterranean World, see the edited volume by Borg (1999).

well-illustrated account of the history of paints, dyes, inks, earths and coloured materials, and brings out some important themes for the evolution of colour concepts over time.[104] S. Garfield's *Mauve* (2000) gives a more focused account of the invention of synthetic chemical dyes in the nineteenth century, and the impact this innovation had for the distribution and diversity of colour in the modern West.[105] Targeted at a more popular readership, D. Batchelor's *Chromophobia* (2000) adapts Pastoureau's more scholarly *Figures et couleurs* (1986) – a work that tabulated colour references in Western literature with virtues and vices) and argued that one can identify a universal binary interpretation (positive and negative) of colour across different cultures. Furthermore, D. Jarman's *Chroma* (1995) provides a moving account of the subjectivities of colour in the face of a rigid and institutionalised colour system. In recent years, this flexible approach to colour aesthetics has found a rich home in scientific research concerned with the challenges of developing a world scale of colour measurement for purposes of global marketing and e-commerce. Its results have been disappointing.[106]

Finally, it remains to mention that there have been several important anthropological studies of colour and modes of perception, and since one objective of this book is to situate ancient Rome within the anthropology of perception, it is necessary to say a few words about the methodological contribution of this discipline to the present study. One study in particular that can help shape our understanding of the relationship between colour and culture is that of the nomadic Dinka tribe of the Southern Sudan. This primitive community used to be credited (rather like the eskimoes with their plethora of snowflakes) with distinguishing dozens of colour terms within the yellow-brown range.[107] It was this rich deployment of perceptual categories that led Berlin and Kay to elevate the Dinka to the dizzy heights of stage VII of their evolutionary colour chart

[104] On some aspects of ancient pigments and their application, see Salvetti (1998); Brinkmann (2003b).

[105] See also Chenciner (2000); Butler Greenfield (2005).

[106] These efforts were usefully summarised by Sebba in *The Times Higher Education Supplement*, 27 October 2000: 18–19.

[107] For this myth, see Lienhardt (1960) 12–16; Beard (2002) 47.

alongside English, Russian and Japanese.[108] More recently, however, anthropologists have observed that many of these categories allude to the colours of their *cows*.[109] Dinka 'blue', for example, has been identified as the category *majok*, a notable pattern of bovine marking which was reproduced locally on painted branches, pots and other artefacts. Another highly prized category is *marial*, possessed by Dinka 'personality cows', animals that are ritually castrated to preserve their exclusiveness (and make them bigger and glossier), then richly fed, groomed, sharpened, trained, decorated and paraded endlessly around the community. A *marial* cow is a work of art, its appearance idolized by the tribal song, and its owners sounding more like art critics than stockbreeders. For the Dinka, then, the visual patterns and categories of their cattle are embedded in the society's memory, experiences and mode of communication. The Dinka provide a useful example of how comparative anthropology can elucidate cultural patterns in colour usage: they help us to understand the relationship between a community's colour categories and its value systems, and they also highlight the importance of the various types of discourse in which these categories are deployed.

Colour and meaning in ancient Rome: objectives and methods

Colour and meaning in ancient Rome attempts to understand how Romans of the early Empire categorised, organised and applied colours, and outlines the differences and similarities between ancient and modern concepts of colour. By drawing together evidence and ideas floated by contemporary philosophers, elegists, epic writers, historians and satirists, this research reinstates colour as an essential informative unit for the classification and evaluation of the Roman world. It also demonstrates that the questions of what

[108] Although Berlin and Kay normally marginalised any terms seen to be derived from other vocabulary items; see Clarke (2004) 132.

[109] On this famous anthropological puzzle, see Coote (1992) 250, following Deng (1972) and (1973). This prompted a critical response from Gell (1995), who situates the aesthetic of the ox in the competitive discourse of the Dinka poet.

colour is and how it functions – as well as how it could abuse the senses – were high on the Roman intellectual agenda. It sets out to offer strategies for understanding and translating Roman expressions of colour in Latin texts, and to suggest new models for understanding fabrics and materials in Roman visual culture. For the cultural historian, it highlights the central role that colour – the concept of *color* and all the categories that constituted it – performed in the realms of communication and information, the intellectual currency that was attached to maintaining solid ties between colour and object, as well as the ethical and philosophical problems generated by the use of what one might term 'abstract' colours.

By focusing primarily on early imperial Rome, this book engages with a period that has received little attention in studies of ancient perception. In doing so, it aims to connect research by M. Clarke, E. Irwin, P. G. Maxwell-Stuart and others on Greek colour perception to James' work on Byzantine colours, as well as to integrate a number of disparate studies of colour in Roman literary and artistic culture. It explores discourses and debates about the role of colour and perception in Rome under the early Empire, and at the same time offers a critical response to various modern theories about ancient perception by suggesting a number of alternative approaches to understanding colour in antiquity. *Colour and meaning in ancient Rome* develops two central arguments: (1) that a prevailing concern in Roman treatments of colour was the capacity (or incapacity) of the senses to derive knowledge about the world, (2) that the moral, ethical and philosophical dangers of using colour in a misleading or abstract way dominated Roman discussion and debate about perception.

This book is structured into seven chapters, each dealing with a specific aspect or register of colour-use which feeds into an overall argument about the dialogic relationship between perception and knowledge. It is a recurring temptation when undertaking a study of the relationship between colour and culture to seek a generalised or structuralist interpretation, and to pay too little attention to the semiotic and discursive differences that exist between different genres of thought, different areas of life, and different historical contexts. *Colour and meaning in ancient Rome* will attempt both to identify distinct ways of formulating and intepreting colour in a range of Roman discourses and contexts, and to observe patterns that cut across all these contexts. By doing so, this book aims to write a cultural history of Roman colour that is sensitive to the different registers and nuances of perception that were formulated in the highly educated male elite metropolitan discourses of early imperial Rome.

Chapter 1 examines discussions by Seneca and other Latin writers of the *locus classicus* of colour discrimination, the rainbow. The rainbow is one phenomenon that looked the same in the ancient Mediterranean as it does in the modern West, and yet strategies for classifying and understanding it differ widely not only between cultures but also significantly from viewer to viewer. The rainbow was a giant problem for ancient perception, and this chapter studies the Roman contributions to this perceptual debate, as well as setting them against the background of Greek accounts of the rainbow. This chapter introduces the idea that Roman thinkers, in contexts that to us invite abstract uses of colour, could go to great lengths to establish connections between the colour perceived and the phenomenon that was thought to be responsible for that colour. The chapter closes by examining Newton's efforts to resolve these difficulties, and modern resistance to Newton's ideas of a tidy spectrum, and so illustrates some of the differences between modern and ancient approaches to colour (as well as the continuity of some of the key debates).

The second chapter situates the questions, debates and problems concerning the rainbow within a larger philosophical debate about the epistemology of vision. It first assesses the role of colour and perception in various strands of classical Greek and Hellenistic philosophy and explores differences and debates between these schools concerning the formulation, function and evaluation of colour. It also highlights the importance of the hotly contested relationship between perception and knowledge in philosophical discussions of colour. Against this background, this chapter revisits Lucretius' detailed discussion of colour in *De Rerum Natura* book 2, and explores how Lucretius related colour to the ethics and morals of perception in attempting to teach the correct way to 'view and understand'.

Chapter 3, on the 'unnatural history' of *color*, engages in a detailed study of the role of *color* in key sections of Pliny's

Natural History, situating his commentaries against the background of his bigger moral and philosophical project about the values of the early Empire. Pliny has always been a rich source for the use and interpretation of Latin categories of colour in Roman material culture; this chapter argues that he too was participating in the traditional moral and philosophical debates about the relationship between perception and knowledge. It explores the use of *color* as a tool of classification and evaluation in Pliny's discussion of three key elements of Roman material culture: marbles (book 36), pigments (book 35) and gems (book 37). This chapter examines the troublesome relationship between the identity/provenance of these materials, and the categories of colour with which they were described. It argues that one can detect a great deal of philosophical frustration underlying the text concerning the misuse of colour as a tool of classification in contemporary material culture. In doing so, the chapter offers an original interpretation of the relationship between early imperial aesthetics and *luxuria*, a theme that is now well established in Plinian studies.

Chapter 4, '*Color* and rhetoric', studies the development of the category *color* in Latin rhetorical circles, its relationship to physical and material *color*, and the ethical values and ambiguities implicated in the exercise of *color* in oratory. The same questions about appearance, nature and classification that so bothered Pliny in his account of *color* also underpinned Roman debates about the *color* of oratory, and the relationship of that *color* to the character of the speaker. This chapter examines sections of Cicero's rhetorical works, as well as discussions of *color* in the works of the Elder Seneca and Quintilian, and also explores the role of rhetorical *color* in Roman drama. It also studies similarities and differences in uses of the Greek *chroma*, and considers how and why *color* became such a key category of rhetorical personality in the late Republic and early Empire. This chapter, then, sets the scene for a detailed study of the description and evaluation of *color* on the Roman body.

Chapter 5 forms the first of two chapters on the classification and evaluation of colour on the body, and complements the previous chapter's focus on rhetorical *color* and personality by studying the range of natural skin, hair and eye colours that were connected to an individual's ethnicity, profession and behaviour, both in medical and physiognomic texts, and in a broader range of Latin literature concerned with personal appearance. In these contexts, *color* was a basic index of information about the individual's character and background. This chapter also examines interpretations of blushing and blanching, and considers how these spontaneous changes in colour were connected to morals, behaviour and character. This study draws upon a range of elite texts (especially Latin elegy) which derive social, cultural and political meaning from natural bodily appearances and insert that meaning into the centre of contemporary racial, economic and ethical debates. In particular, it draws attention to the emphasis on colour *change* in these debates, and the ramifications that such change held for visual cognition and social understanding.

Chapter 6 pursues the study of colour manipulation to its next logical stage by examining the interpretation and evaluation of artificial and cosmetic schemes of colour on the Roman body. In particular, it demonstrates that the manipulation of those colours explored in Chapter 5 was a subject high on the moral agenda of the Roman literary elite, and that what was at stake was precisely this relationship between perception and knowledge. The best-documented area of study is the use of make-up by Roman ladies, which several of Ovid's poems make one of their central themes. By endowing the wearer with different/unnatural *colores*, cosmetics interfered with the correct understanding of the individual's personality and character, and were therefore a long-standing site for ambiguity and controversy, linked to traditional discourses of feminine deceit and entrapment. This chapter will also consider, to similar ends, accounts of the use of hair dyes and wigs, and the impact of diverse and exotic cloth-dyes on the understanding and interpretation of the Roman body.

The final chapter concentrates on the most controversial and well-studied of Roman colours: *purpura* (the 'murex snail' aka 'sea-purple dye' aka 'purple'). As the most historically significant of the artificial colours discussed in Chapter 6, *purpura* developed the most complex and multifarious set of meanings and associations, and its role on the body was a popular topic of social, political and moral debate. This chapter considers the position of *purpura* in the context of ideas raised by earlier chapters (particularly Chapter 3 on the classification of material culture and Chapter 6 on colour/identity manipulation). It argues that sea-purple, with its flexible and negotiable associations with luxury, autocracy and decadence, was a paradigm for the development of abstract colours in antiquity (that is, colours that lose their association with the objects to which they properly belong). This chapter also represents the book's boldest attempt to historicise Roman colour, by exploring shifts in the categorisation and evaluation of *purpura* from the mid Republic through to the late Empire.

The conclusion identifies cultural patterns in colour usage that cut across the various genres and contexts examined within the book. In particular, it returns to the ancient preoccupation with the relationship between perception and knowledge, and considers Rome's historical contribution to this trend as part of a broader history of ideas. In addition, it identifies the major differences and similarities between modern and ancient Roman systems of colour, and suggests ways that an appreciation of these differences can aid textual interpretation and artistic ekphrasis. As a concluding motif, the book compares descriptions of Queen Elizabeth II's Coronation with ancient descriptions of the Roman triumph, and, by examining these two distinctive spectacles side-by-side, highlights some of the key differences between modern and ancient uses of colour.

One of the most extensively cited, and least understood, ancient discussions of colour is Aulus Gellius' *Attic Nights* 2.26, a debate about the relative richness of Greek and Latin colour terms produced within the bilingual elite culture of second-century Rome. The book closes with an *Envoi* that applies some of the approaches, ideas and patterns observed in other contexts of Roman colour usage as a test-case for reinterpreting this difficult text. In doing so, it is hoped that the final section can operate as a pilot for the practical application of findings from this research to reach a greater understanding of the role of colour within Roman literature.

I

THE RAINBOW

ingens enim uariumque corpus intra momentum subtexitur caelo et aeque celeriter aboletur.

In a moment the huge and varied form is woven in the sky, and just as quickly it vanishes.

Seneca, *Natural Questions* 1.4.2

Since Newton, everyone – in the West at least – has always known there are seven colours in the rainbow.[1] Red, orange, yellow, green, blue, indigo and violet are the colours we seek and (if we look hard enough) find in the modern spectrum. Newtonian optics had solved colour's oldest problem. Greeks and Romans had no such institutionalised colour spectrum; ancient writers from Homer to Isidore offered versions of a rainbow ranging from one to six chromatic divisions. Poetic imagination prompted Ovid and Virgil to suggest a thousand. Sometimes one could even describe the spectrum using Greek *porphureos* or Latin *purpureus*, a single term we normally translate as 'purple'. The rainbow – what it was made of and what created its medley of colour – elicited little agreement among the ancients.[2] This chapter, therefore, will explore one the greatest challenges to visual perception in antiquity, and will operate as a pilot for discussing the representation and evaluation of colour among the intellectual *cognoscenti* of early imperial Rome. It will also expose some of the underlying differences in the formulation and discussion of colour across different texts and genres.

Greek philosophy

[The colours of the rainbow] are almost the only ones which painters are not able to manufacture. For they produce some colours by mixing, but shades of 'scarlet'

[1] For a comprehensive account of the history of the rainbow, see Gage (1993) ch. 6.

[2] On the ancient rainbow, see Dürbeck (1977) 42–9. On the Byzantine rainbow and its relationship to earlier accounts, see James (1995) ch. 5.

(*phoinikoun*), 'grass-green' (*prasinon*) and 'sea-purple' (*halourgon*) are not formed as mixtures. These are the colours the rainbow has – but between 'scarlet' and 'grass-green', 'yellow' (*xanthon*) is often seen. (Aristotle, *Meteorologica* 372a)

Aristotle's rainbow consisted of three colours (*trichrōs*).[3] This trichromatic model was highly influential for subsequent philosophers, particularly in the late antique and early Byzantine period, with the result that Aristotle could be described as 'the Byzantine world's Newton'.[4] J. André considered this scheme of basic colours so important in antiquity that he introduced his study of Latin colour terms with a diagram of the Aristotelian rainbow, in which he distinguished three basic colours – 'violet' (*porphurous* or *halourgēs*), 'vert-jaune' (*prasinos* or *kuanous*) and 'rouge' (*phoinikous* or *eruthros*), which corresponded to three of the main categories for his *Étude*.[5]

Aristotle's treatment of the rainbow, however, is (surprisingly) brief and, unlike Roman thinkers, makes no explicit connection between the colours and the phenomena behind them. This rainbow is simple and categorical: these are 'primary colours' on mystical, philosophical, arithmetical and experimental grounds.[6] Aristotle also compares and contrasts this abstract scheme with that other major site for colour discourse, the artist's palette.[7] In his work on the sensible world, Aristotle claimed that qualities such as colour were real and existed in their own right. Aristotle did not attempt to account for the provenance of these rainbow colours, although he does indicate by his choice of language (τὸ ξανθὸν φαίνεται) that colour discrimination in the rainbow was subject to a degree of interpretation. Aristotle's rainbow was not evidence for a schematic

[3] Cf. Gilbert (1907) 610.

[4] James (1995) 95. Poseidonius describes the same three colours, and adds *kuaneos*. Cf. Diog. Laert. 7.152; Aëtius, *Compendium* in Reinhardt (1921) 165 n. 2 and Gilbert (1907) 604–18; Stobaeus in Wachsmuth (1884) 30.6.238–42, who stresses that the colours are products of sunlight and rain. Alexander of Aphrodisias (*Mete.* 139:33–5) was key to the transmission of Aristotle's three colours as the orthodox view in the late antique and early Byzantine period; on Alexander's interpretation of the role of colour appearances in Aristotelian theory, see Ganson (2003). For Byzantine references, see James (1995) 95 n. 26.

[5] André (1949) 13; cf. Dürbeck (1977) 42–9; Diels, *Dox. Graec.* p. 372.33–4.

[6] So *Sens.* 439b21–440a6; *Mete.* 375a4–20; *Cael.* 268a7–23.

[7] On this idea, see Struycken (2003) 292–3, who provides a compelling argument against using the artist's palette as a rationale for interpreting various philosophical colour blends.

system of abstract colours in the Greco-Roman world; on the contrary, he was participating in a heated philosophical debate on the nature of colour and the relationship between vision and knowledge that had preoccupied some of the earliest extant Greek philosophers, and which continued long after Aristotle. Not only were the precise colours of the rainbow up for dispute (even for Aristotle himself), but it was also clear that intellectual ownership of the rainbow – and what it meant – was contested between different genres of thought. A fragment of Xenophanes (c. 530 BC), for example, had also described a trichromatic division of the rainbow, although with slightly different categories: ἥν τ' Ἶριν καλέουσι, νέφος καὶ τοῦτο πέφυκε, / πορφύρεον καὶ φοινίκεον και χλωρὸν ἰδέσθαι (she whom they call Iris, this too is by nature a cloud, 'purple', 'scarlet' and 'green' to behold).[8] This is not evidence for philosophical consensus on the spectrum: Xenophanes was wresting ownership of the rainbow from the mythical aetiology of the poets (the unspecified subject of καλέουσι) who had equated the rainbow with Iris. This fragment perhaps anticipates scepticism about the rainbow's colours: although it might be by nature (πέφυκε) a cloud, its colours are the subjective categories of human vision (ἰδέσθαι), and ones that, by implication, were most at home in the creative domain of poetic ekphrasis. This is perhaps the earliest surviving example of philosophical frustration towards prevailing systems of colour classification, and the epistemological tensions that could emerge when the worlds of poetry and philosophy met. It would be several hundred years before any philosopher that we know about sought a sustained rationale behind the colours of the rainbow.

Latin prose

The younger Seneca produced in the first book of his *Natural Questions* one of antiquity's longest and most detailed discussions of the rainbow (1.3–15).[9] This is a valuable document for assessing

[8] Xenophanes 21b32 = DK 1.136.14–15; cf. Anaximenes 13 A 18 = DK 1.94.13 (αὐτοῦ τοῦ ἡλίου φοινικοῦν φαίνεται). I thank Jenny Bryan for drawing my attention to the difficult philosophical subtext of this line.

[9] For an overview of the complexity of the *Quaestiones Naturales*, see Gross (1988). The precise ordering of the books is disputed.

the thinking behind Roman colour discrimination, as well as understanding the Latin concept of *color*.

Seneca was interested in the constituent materials of the rainbow and the relationship between the clouds and the sun. The rainbow – a familiar feature of myth and metaphor – was a philosophical enigma that deserved pride of place early on in Seneca's study of the puzzles of nature. His synopsis offers a critical account of different theories of rainbow production, and his own thoughts are complex and difficult. One of his guiding principles was that the *colores* of the rainbow were its 'reflections' (*imagines*), but not (as some thought) its ingredients.[10] Nevertheless, Seneca's rainbow had colour as its defining – and most interesting (*mirabilis*) – feature.

His rainbow is produced when the rays of the sun penetrate clouds. This, he says, is what generates colour (*illis colorem suffundat*), and creates the shape of a variegated rainbow (*discolor arcus*, 1.3.1). Variegation – *discolor* or *uarietas* – is a recurring label for the rainbow in Seneca's account, and it is the phenomenon of this shift, this flux in *color* which attracts Seneca's attention. Commenting on a theory that rainbows were formed out of tiny droplets varying in translucency, Seneca responds that this might be feasible, *if* the rainbow consisted of just two *colores*, light and shade (*ex lumine umbraque*).[11] As it is, he employs a poetic cliché (Ovid *Metamorphoses* 6.65–7[12]) to argue that a rainbow's *colores* are countless (*mille*) – 1.3.4:

> 'diuersi niteant cum mille colores,
> transitus ipse tamen spectantia lumina fallit:
> usque adeo quod tangit idem est, tamen ultima distant.'

uidemus in eo aliquid flammei, aliquid lutei, aliquid caerulei et alia in picturae modum subtilibus lineis ducta. ut ait poeta, an dissimiles colores sint, scire non possis, nisi cum primis extrema contuleris. nam commissura decipit, usque eo mira arte naturae: quod a simillimo coepit, in dissimillimo desinit. quid ergo istic duo colores faciunt lucis atque umbrae, cum innumerabilium ratio reddenda sit?

10 He later claims that the spectrum is not a reflection of the sun so much as a reflection of its *color* (1.7.1, *non imaginem hic solis esse, sed coloris imitationem ex repercussu*).

11 I have chosen to use '*color*' rather than 'colour' where the text or context implies a sense that may not be straightforwardly translatable.

12 See below pp. 47–8.

'Although a thousand different *colores* gleam, / yet their very transition escapes the watching eye. / Just as far as that which touches is the same, yet things far-parted are distinct.'

In the [rainbow] we see some *flammeus*, some *luteus*, some *caeruleus* and other *colores*, as in a painting, drawn in subtle bands. As the poet said, you cannot know whether the *colores* are dissimilar unless you have compared the first with the last. For the point of transition is deceptive, in keeping with the marvellous art of nature, which starts from the most similar and ends with the least similar. Therefore what do the two *colores* of light and shade do there, when a reason must be given for innumerable ones?

For us, the bands of the rainbow are fairly simple, if we know and accept the colours we are looking for. For Seneca, the colour transition is problematic, the divisions (*lineae*) so subtle that the observer is faced with a continuum rather than separate discernible colours. The result is deceptive (*decipit*). For Seneca, the transition from like to unlike is what makes the rainbow intrinsically *discolor*.[13] Not only is it 'variegated' but the rainbow, under close scrutiny, lacks any coherent *color*. Poetic *mille* was normally a hyperbole, shorthand for a number that was beyond precise human analysis.[14] The problem Seneca faces, then, is how to manage the transition from the two *colores* of light and shade onto the *mille colores* that his highly educated literate readers are used to.

Seneca describes three key *colores* in the rainbow – *flammeus*, *luteus* and *caeruleus*. These bands are colours seen (*uidemus*), not necessarily there – but they are properties of something (*aliquid*). For Seneca, the divisions are on some level artificial, like a painting (*in picturae modum*). The untrained eye can visualise and schematise the rainbow incorrectly; Seneca, however, will strive to find a rationale (*ratio*). 'Red', 'yellow' and 'blue' (as the Loeb translates these categories) might appear to be convenient translations for *flammeus*, *luteus* and *caeruleus*, but (as we find out) the Latin terms themselves contain clues as to where the colours came from. *Flammeus* is the visual property of the sun's rays; *caeruleus* that of the water droplets; mixed together they generate the diluted

[13] Cf. 1.3.9, where Seneca suggests the sun displays *unus color*, but its reflections (*imagines*) display *diuersus color*.

[14] *Oxford Latin Dictionary*, s.v. *mille* 1b.

luteus. Elsewhere, Seneca lays claim more explicitly to this idea: 'its fiery colour comes from the sun, its watery colour from the cloud, and the other colours are mixtures of the two' (*color illi igneus a sole est, caeruleus a nube, ceteri utriusque mixturae*, 1.4.3). Seneca goes on to develop this idea in a later section (1.3.12–13):

> The variety occurs for no other reason than that a part of the *color* comes from the sun, and a part from that particular cloud. The moisture produces now bands of blue (*caeruleus*), now bands of green (*uiridis*), now ones resembling sea-purple dye (*purpura*), and bands of yellow (*luteus*) or fiery (*igneus*), with two *colores* – subdued (*remissus*) and intense (*intentus*) – creating this variety. So purple dye (*purpura*) from the same shell does not come out in one type; it makes a difference how long it has been soaked, whether it has taken on a thicker application or a more diluted one, whether it has been dipped and boiled once or more often. Since there are two things, the sun and the clouds, that is, the object and the mirror, it is no surprise that as many types of *colores* are produced as can be intensified or subdued in many ways. For one *color* comes from a fiery (*igneus*) light, another from a duller (*obtunsus*) and softer (*lenior*) light.

This passage is not easy. Seneca appears to be claiming that *uarietas*, namely the bands of *caeruleus, uiridis, purpurae similis* and *luteus/igneus* (presumably categories of linguistic convenience, as above), are produced by an antagonistic system of two distinct *colores* – one from the cloud that is subdued (*remissus*) and one from the sun that is intense (*intentus*). Seneca's descriptive bands, then, owe as much to the creative world of painting or dyeing as to the world of physics.[15] So it is that sea-purple garments from the same ink can look very different depending on their preparation. Seneca seems to be saying that there are two primary generative *colores* from two very different sources which combine to produce the secondary *uarietas colorum* by which we recognise the rainbow. The model is a mixture theory, although the constituent colours have little in common with the artist's palette or Aristotelian ideas about primary and secondary colours (see below pp. 64–5). Unlike Seneca's arbitrary bands, these two primary *colores* are real visual properties of two physical phenomena. By

[15] Cf. 1.6.3 '*denique inter me teque conuenit colores illos quibus caeli regio depingitur a sole esse*'.

our standards, of course, *remissus* and *intentus* are hardly 'colours', but they are nevertheless the visible manifestation of two definable phenomena – clouds and sun. A second thing this passage shows us is that the colouring of cloth provided a convenient metaphor for the conceptualisation of colour physics. Later, he claims that the clouds are 'dyed' (*infici*) by the sun (1.5.9; cf. 1.8.2 *tingit*). Whether it was painting, weaving or dyeing, the rainbow prompted Seneca to resort to metaphor and artifice in order to reach a sensible explanation of its colours.

Later, commenting on the difference in shape (*figura*), *color* and scale (*magnitudo*) between the sun and the rainbow, Seneca says that 'the rainbow is far larger and, in the part that gleams (*fulget*), far redder (*rubicundior*) than the sun, and in fact different in its other colours too' (1.5.2). Here, he draws attention to the part of the rainbow which finds its *color* in the sun, the part which *gleams*, and says even this is 'redder' than you would find in the sun, thus connecting the colour 'red' to the intense light of part of the rainbow. Seneca does a similar thing with the sky at sunrise: furthermore we see, when the sun rises, a certain part of the sky turn red, and sometimes we see clouds that are fiery in colour (*praeterea uidemus ortu solis partem quandam caeli rubere, uidemus nubes aliquando ignei coloris*, 1.5.8). The colours of the rainbow, then, were reflections (*imagines*) of natural phenomena ranging from direct sunlight to the dullness of rainclouds. The hard work that Seneca makes of the relationship between perception and physics in the rainbow, therefore, is revealing about the nature and function of *color* in contemporary thought. It was imperative, even for the most complex visual phenomena, to connect *color* to the realia of the natural world.

One of Seneca's pivotal lines in discussing colour perception is that colours are in some sense insubstantial, and illusive. He goes on to say that 'nothing is more deceiving than our eyesight' (*nihil esse acie nostra fallacius*, 1.3.9). The *colores* 'appear' (*apparent*) to an observer; as such, they rely on an observer for their existence. Later, Seneca compares the rainbow to water sprinkled from a burst pipe, the artificial spectrum produced by a glass rod, the neck of a dove,[16] and the neck of a peacock in movement

[16] Here he cites Nero's verse '*colla Cytheriacae splendent agitata columbae*'.

(1.5.6).[17] The idea is that movement manipulates *color*. However, Seneca draws a middle line between rainbow colour as a construct in the eye of the observer, and as a phenomenon physically rooted in the rainbow. The former was a theory postulated by the late Republican Stoic Posidonius, who had insisted that a cloud merely *seemed* to be coloured (*colorari*): 'if there were any *color* in the rainbow, it would remain and be seen all the more clearly the closer it is; as it is, the image (*imago*) of the rainbow, clear at a distance, fades away when you come close to it' (1.5.10). Seneca responds by suggesting that the cloud *is* actually coloured, but that its *color* is not apparent from all sides. Seneca would agree that *color* is misleading, but not counterfeit (*ita non est argumentum falsi coloris*).[18] *Color* is not a static objective *thing*, but is negotiated in the interface between the viewer and the viewed (1.5.12).

> Besides, when you are told that a cloud is tinted (*suffecta*) by the sun, you are not being told that the *color* is being branded (*inustus*), as it were, into a hard, stable and enduring body, but into a fluid, wandering body receiving nothing more than a brief appearance (*species*). There are also certain *colores* which show their properties (*uis*) best at a distance: for example, Tyrian purple – the better and richer (*saturior*) it is, the higher you ought to hold it to show its gleam (*fulgor*). However, because a cloth which has the best *color* does not show it in all the ways it is folded, does not mean it does not have that *color*.

Color for Seneca, then, is not a hard and fast phenomenon (a '*durum corpus*', as he puts it). It is not simply *there*. Instead, he argues it is a fluid, interactive appearance – something to be *seen*. Later, arguing with an unnamed theorist who claims quite the opposite of Posidonius, he sums up: 'you say that *color* is real, I say it is only apparent (*tu dicis illum colorem esse, ego uideri*)'. Again, Seneca draws a middle line, arguing that the perceiver is the crucial player in the conceptualisation of reality. Secondly, the *colores* of the rainbow can look different depending on how close you are to them; their *uis*, their visual force, is best viewed at a particular

[17] These were among the classic examples of sceptical discussions of perception: see below pp. 79–80.

[18] He later appears to claim the opposite (1.7.2): *apparet non fieri ullum colorem sed speciem falsi coloris*. He uses the mirror as an example of something that produces only *simulatio quaedam coloris alieni*.

distance. Thirdly, Tyrian purple is again evoked as an analogy to the rainbow. 'Sea-purple' is a real, tangible, visible thing – but one whose *color* is not static and not stable.

Seneca concludes (1.15.7), that a rainbow reproduces the deception of a mirror (*fallacia speculi*), in that it counterfeits (*mentientis*) something outside itself. Then he digresses: 'those sorts of things are illusions (*simulacra*) and the insubstantial imitations of real objects (*inanis uerorum corporum imitatio*)'. The rainbow is a smart example of the visual trickery to which Roman eyes could be exposed. Seneca likens this, in a strange simile, to a *cinaedus* who used misshapen mirrors to distort the size of the men whom he was fellating. One has to train and teach the senses to perceive correctly, to resist the temptation to let perception slide away from reality. Therefore, one can accurately discern *color igneus* and *color caeruleus*, because they are expressions of their proper material provenance, the fire of the sun and water of the clouds. Further *colores* are the product of poetic and artistic imagination, only apparent to an observer (as in the case of a mirror, or the unstable surface of sea-purple cloth). For Seneca, the *discolor arcus* is an epistemological puzzle, a giant test of perceptual intelligence, and a demonstration that Stoic philosophy performs an important role in re-educating perception and understanding in the early Empire.

Later prose accounts of the rainbow followed Seneca's lead in recognising the epistemological difficulties the rainbow posed, and attempting (and competing) to find a satisfactory interpretation. The most interesting of these is the description of a prodigious rainbow in the Persian expedition of Constantius II by the fourth-century *protector domesticus* Ammianus Marcellinus (20.11.27–9).[19] Ammianus simplified the rainbow into five bands – *luteus*, *flauescens-fuluus*, *puniceus*, *purpureus*, and *caeruleus-uiridis* – but added that further explanation was needed. Ammianus first invents an etymology for the initial 'yellow', *luteus*: it is, he claims, diluted (*dilutior*) by the surrounding air.[20] He goes on to explain

[19] See Den Boeft *et al.* (1987) 280–91.

[20] Den Boeft *et al.* (1987) 287, suggests that *concolor* here refers to the whiteness of the air, which blended into *luteus*, but this seems unsatisfactory; Szidat (1996) sees in *dilutior* a reference to the transparence of the cloud. Cf. *De Coloribus* 791.2–3. For *concolor*, see Hagendahl (1921) 52.

that the other colours are generated by the interaction of the sun's rays (*radii*) and rain-showers (*aspergines*). This elemental shift is reinforced in Ammianus' account by his use of verb forms (*purpurat*) and participles (*uirentem*). Furthermore, he stresses that the categories he has chosen are 'appearances' (*species*) rather than inherently existing things: 'whatever mortal eyes capture, that is what earthly minds think' (*quantum mortalis oculus contuetur ... ut terrenae existimant mentes*). Ammianus then offers an alternative version of rainbow formation (20.11.29) with the same mixture theory of sunlight and rainclouds, but with *albus* at one end and *subuirides* at the other, and compares this colour flux with the appearance of the sea. Ammianus' digression was an ostentatious display, in the middle of his historical narrative, of his acquaintance with scientific and philosophical debates, as well as a shrewd comment on the state of human misunderstanding. It also demonstrated a continuing effort to ground the colours of the rainbow in the material phenomena that produced them. Even later, in the early seventh century, Isidore of Seville (*De Rerum Natura* 31.2) found in the rainbow a pertinent slice of Christian symbolism, but still grounded its *colores* in elements: most notable was his identification of a 'fiery colour' (*color igneus*) and a 'watery colour' (*color aquosus*), the manifestations of Hell and the Flood. Elsewhere (*Etymologia* 13.10.1) he points out that its varying colours (*uarii colores*) were appearances (*species*) formed from a combination of 'thin air' (*aqua tenuis*), 'bright air' (*aer lucidus*) and 'dark clouds' (*nubes caligantes*). The rainbow, then, offered these writers an opportunity to ponder various layers of cosmic symbolism, but above all it offered them a philosophical challenge. The rational solution to this puzzle was to relate the diverse colours of the rainbow to the various mixtures of sun and rain that had produced it, and the (sometimes strange) categories employed and associations made pointed towards a highly phenomenological system of colour usage. The alternative to this rationalising approach, an alternative that had long been popular in the world of epic verse, was to attribute the rainbow and its complex colours to the supernatural realm of divine agency where both chromatic discrimination and chromatic explanation were beyond human reasoning.

Latin verse

In his account of the death of Dido in *Aeneid* 4, Virgil describes the appearance of Iris:

> ergo Iris croceis per caelum roscida pinnis,
> mille trahens uarios aduerso sole colores,
> deuolat.

So Iris, covered in dew on her wings of saffron (*croceis*), flies down through the sky, dragging a thousand *colores* shimmering in the facing sun.

(Virgil, *Aeneid* 4.700–2)

It is unsurprising that epic verse should find the rainbow an evocative site for divine personification. The association of Iris and the rainbow was a tradition that dated at least as far back as Hesiod.[21] Two things emerge from Virgil's lines: first, the rainbow exceeds the capacities of human perception (poetic *mille*, as we have seen, suggested a challenge to the senses). Here too, *uarios* refers not to 'varied' (this is normally rendered in Latin by *diuersus*), but 'varying' – the rainbow is a fluctuating and difficult medium for perception. The rainbow, therefore, is constructed as the home, and trademark, of the divine, the expression of a phenomenon that defied the physics and logic of *color*. Nevertheless, there is a hint of the blend of familiar elements of the material world by the divine: the opposing sun (*diuerso sole*) and water droplets (*roscida*) evoke the same mixture theory described by Seneca, even if the agency (and method) of the mixture is beyond human understanding. This latter enigma is emblematised by Iris' *croceae pinnae*: the cloth-dye 'saffron' taps into the metaphorical world of dyeing that later provided such a convenient (and provocative) point of comparison for Seneca's rainbow.

Elsewhere in the *Aeneid* (5.87–9), a prophetic serpent emerges from Anchises' burial mound with 'water-blue marks' (*caeruleae notae*) dotting its back and a golden gleam (*auro ... fulgor*) firing up its scales, like a rainbow facing the sun that casts a thousand

[21] Austin (1955) 201–2.

varying colours (*mille uarii colores*) on the rain-clouds.[22] Here again, Virgil represents a coalition of the sun and the rainclouds, both within the rainbow metaphor and in the physical appearance of the serpent (*caeruleus* and *fulgor*, as we have seen, evoke water and sun respectively). Virgil's choice of categories (which frame the clause as they frame the rainbow) stages the metaphor which follows. Even this imaginative hexameter account of the rainbow, where the divisions are (pointedly) beyond human comprehension, weaves a connection between its colours and the phenomena that produce it.

Ovid's *Metamorphoses* pictures Iris donning veils of a thousand colours (*uelamina mille colorum*), before marking the sky with her bow (11.589–91). Iris' technicolor dreamcoat is a convenient poetic metaphor for interpreting the rainbow. It implies a sensational, supernatural surface that marks (*signans*) the sky, and offers Ovid a way of transforming a familiar phenomenon into a poetic artefact. For more on the embroidery of the rainbow, we might turn to Ovid's account of the weaving contest between Pallas and Arachne (*Metamorphoses* 6.61–9):

> illic et Tyrium quae purpura sensit aenum
> texitur et tenues parui discriminis umbrae;
> qualis ab imbre solent percussis solibus arcus
> inficere ingenti longum curuamine caelum;
> in quo diuersi niteant cum mille colores,
> transitus ipse tamen spectantia lumina fallit:
> usque adeo, quod tangit, idem est; tamen ultima distant.
> illic et lentum filis inmittitur aurum
> et uetus in tela deducitur argumentum.

There is interwoven the purple cloth (*purpura*) which had experienced the Tyrian kettle,[23] and lighter shades with little to tell between them; as when, after a rainstorm when the sun's rays have struck through, the rainbow is accustomed to paint the wide sky with its huge arc. Although a thousand different *colores* gleam in it, yet their very transition escapes the watching eye. Just as far as that which touches is the same, yet things far-parted are distinct. There too pliant gold was worked in with the threads, and an old story was spun out on the loom.

[22] Cf. 5.609 on Iris, '*illa uiam celerans per mille coloribus arcum*'.
[23] In which the garment was dyed.

The opening description of the colours of the woven cloth sets the scene for a rainbow simile. Once again (as in Seneca) we see *purpura* and various subtle cognate shades (*parui discriminis umbrae*) of woven cloth as a useful point of reference for understanding the rainbow. Then the simile: rain and sun collide and paint (*inficere*) the sky on which the rainbow appears. The *colores* 'gleam' (*niteant*); they are, paradoxically, countless (*mille*) and different (*diuersi*). They deceive eyesight in that one can tell that they differ, but not *where* they differ. The rainbow, like the mythical woven cloth, is paradigmatically supernatural.

Virgil and Ovid both exploit the problematics of rainbow colours. The poetic formula *mille colores* underlines this difficulty, and the association of the rainbow with the divine and the sensational (Iris, Anchises' serpent, mythical woven cloth, sea-purple) offers a convenient solution to the visual and epistemological challenges it poses. While we simplify the rainbow using Newtonian optics, Latin verse made the most of the problems, institutionalising the rainbow as a poetic – and cultural – artefact. This said, the two poets concurred with the physicists in recognising the basic interaction of elements of sun and water in generating the rainbow. For the poet, however, there was magic in the making, and the inscrutability of its colours was the essence of that magic.

One imaginative solution was to draw upon chromatic categories that carried the rainbow into other areas of Roman life. So Propertius, exploring various quirks of nature, labels the rainbow with just one colour: why does the *purpureus* rainbow drink up the rain-water (*purpureus pluuias cur bibit arcus aquas*)?[24]

Propertius' one-line mention of the rainbow has become a classic in the list of odd and frustratingly untranslatable uses of *purpureus*. The Penguin translation renders it 'bright-hued', the Loeb 'coloured'. Guy Lee chooses 'radiant'. Tremenheere opts for 'brilliant bow'. Other translators have tried 'purpurfarbener Bogen', 'l'arco baleno ('flashing')', and 'der Bogen so bunt'.[25] One missed it out altogether.[26] Commentators have incessantly ignored the problem.[27] Rothstein's edition prefers to change *purpureus* to

[24] Prop. 3.5.32. [25] Luck (1964); Bonazzi (1939); Helm (1965). [26] Paganelli (1929).
[27] For example, Butler and Barber (1933); Shackleton Bailey (1956); Camps (1966).

purpureas and attach it to the rainwater.[28] Earlier commentators had advised *caeruleus*, presumably on the grounds that it might be more appropriate in this watery context.[29]

As we have seen above in Seneca's description, the cloth-dye *purpura* was a complex *color*, difficult to pin down in any colour chart. *Purpureus arcus* (as far as we can tell) was not a commonplace formula in extant Latin literature; only Propertius used it.[30] Propertius was presumably echoing Homer's formula *porphureēn irin* (*Il.* 17.547) a connection that has prompted some to interpret Propertius' description as archaic and deliberately obsolete. However, Latin literature is riddled with uses of *purpureus* that are just as unlikely. *Purpureus* has been used to describe the sun, its light, and its chariot and horses.[31] We see 'purple swans', 'purple snow' and 'purple salt'.[32] *Amor* could carry the epithet *purpureus* (as could his wings).[33] The sea (particularly in verse) was stereotypically *purpureus*.[34] Spring too could carry this label.[35] There are other examples.[36]

Edgeworth (1979) has little sympathy with daring interpretations and translations of *purpureus*, and re-interprets a large handful of these examples to make them map onto 'red'. He argues that interpretations such as 'bright', 'gleaming', 'fluctuating' etc. are the result of a century-old fad for re-readings in Greek and Roman colour terms.[37] Edgeworth's hues do away with elaborate

[28] Rothstein (1966) 39 n. 32 appears to suggest that it can, however, attach to *arcus*.

[29] As Smyth (1970) 94.

[30] Edgeworth (1979) 289 contradicts André (1949) 100, by suggesting either that it is purely a literary allusion to Homer, or that the bright 'red' band of the rainbow is a synecdoche for the whole thing.

[31] *Ciris* 37; Verg. *Aen.* 6.641; Sen. *Hercules Oetaeus* 1838; Ov. *Fast.* 3.518; 2.74; *Her.* 4.160; 21.88.

[32] Hor. *Carm.* 4.1.10 (*purpureis ... oloribus*); *Elegia in Maecenatem* 1.62 (*purpurea ... niue*) – Edgeworth (1979) 282 ascribes this to a manuscript error. Cf. Valerius Flaccus, *Argonautica* 3.422 (*sale purpureo*) – Edgeworth (1979) 283 argues that this is a metonym for the sea, and (following Irwin (1974) 18) is not necessarily 'chromatic'.

[33] Ov. *Am.* 2.1.38 (*purpureus ... Amor*). On his wings, see Ov. *Rem. am.* 701.

[34] Cic. *Acad.* 2.33.105; Prop. 2.26.5; Catull. 64.275; Verg. *G.* 4.373.

[35] Verg. *Ecl.* 9.40 (*uer purpureum*); Columella, *Rust.* 10.256; Stat. *Silv.* 3.3.130 (*purpurea uerna*).

[36] André (1949) 96–102; Edgeworth (1979).

[37] Edgeworth (1979) 291; Forcellini's *Totius Latinitas Lexicon* (1865) s. v. *purpureus* had described this category as '*poetice purpureus est nitidus, purus, splendidus, aspectu pulcher, cuiuscumque coloris sit*'. The *Oxford Latin Dictionary* offers a similar description (s.v. *purpureus* §3) 'stress partly or wholly on sheen rather than actual colour'.

renderings of *purpureus*, but 'red' seems even less satisfactory. The sea-purple dye on which this category was primarily based is known to have had unique physical properties, sitting on the surface of garments rather than within the fabric and reflecting and manipulating sunlight in a similar fashion to oil floating on water.[38] Some have argued that many of these difficult uses of 'purple' belong to a pervasive intertextual poetic register in which *purpureus/porphureos* evokes water: swelling seas, stormy skies and watery rainbows.[39] Edgeworth rightly draws attention to the futility of denying what we call 'colour' content in this category. *Purpureus* does not mean 'bright'. Nor does it make sense (in our terms) as 'red' or 'purple'. To solve the riddle we must seek different visual co-ordinates.

The *purpureus arcus* helps us to do this. We have seen that the *colores* of the rainbow could be freely negotiated, and cultural divisons varied from two to infinity. The idea that *purpureus* is synecdochic is unconvincing: one colour taking the place of a spectrum makes little sense. If one were to choose one category to represent the rainbow, sea-purple dye with its unstable and heterogeneous surfaces could be made to fit. At the same time, *purpura* was the quintessential cultural artefact, a colour that was really prestige cloth. Horace's 'purple' swans, Ovid's 'purple' sun, Catullus' 'purple' sea, and Propertius 'purple' rainbow, therefore, were expressions of highly skilled poetic embroidery, rather than just indices of a particular part of the spectrum. To this one might also connect James' distinction between 'naturalistic' and 'non-naturalistic' rainbows in Byzantine art: the former were bows represented by several colour bands, the latter by a single or double band of basic colour in the shape of an arc (normally red, sometimes blue).[40] For us, the monochromatic non-naturalistic rainbow

38 See below p. 189.

39 This is the emphasis of Soverini (1998), esp. 112–13 on 'πορφυρέην ἶριν' and p. 116 on the watery sky as 'una situazione di porpora'. Soverini observes a recurring literary analogy between angry seas, stormy skies and features of war (blood and cloaks) in which 'purple' is a common denominator, although his connections are sometimes a little forced.

40 James (1995) 105–9 goes on to argue that in the naturalistic rainbow, bands of red, blue, grey/silver and gold are all (generally) symbolic of divine light, thus reinforcing her central thesis of 'a fundamental element of colour being its light-bearing quality' (99).

is an anathema. For the Byzantines, the rainbow could be a festival of light as the expression of divinity.[41] For others, such as the first-century Jewish philosopher Philo, the biblical bow is 'the unobservable power of God', and a quite different thing from the earthly bow which confounds mortal vision.[42] Both in theological circles and in the imaginative traditions of high art and literature, then, the rainbow could be conceptualised and simplified as a single phenomenon (divine light, exquisite cloth, etc.) that evoked one distinctive visual category rather than separate colour bands.

One encounters a similar difficulty in Lucretius' short description of the rainbow (*De Rerum Natura* 6.524–6): 'In these circumstances, when the sun with its rays shines (*fulsit*) amid the dark storm (*opaca tempestas*) and against the spray of the clouds which faces it, then there stands out in the black clouds (*nigrae nubes*) the 'colour of the rainbow (*color arqui*)'. Surprisingly, the formula *color arqui* has not been queried by any editor or commentator (as was Seneca's less difficult *color ignis*, see below p. 56). What it shows us, however, is that the compartmentalisation of the rainbow into blocks of colour could be secondary to the formulation of the rainbow as a phenomenological whole, a whole which had its own characteristic *color* (if not a single characteristic 'colour').

Conclusion: the rainbow from antiquity to modernity

'Red, orange, yellow, blue and green, Indigo and violet the prettiest I've seen'; 'Richard Of York Gave Battle In Vain'; French 'Vous Inventez Bien, Vous, Jeune Oisif Ridicule'; Italian 'RoAranGiVerTurInVio'; Russian 'каждый охотник желает знать где сидит фазан'. The schools of the modern world have no dearth of mnemonics to remind the young learner which colours to look for, and expect to find, in the rainbow. These didactic drills are symptomatic of attempts to standardise, systematise and

[41] An echo of the four biblical descriptions of the brilliance (rather than polychromy) of the rainbow: *Genesis* 9.13; *Ezekiel* 1.28; *Revelations* 4.3; 10.1; *Ecclesiastes* 43.11–12; 50.7.

[42] Philo, *Questions and answers on Genesis* 2.64; cf. Basil, *Letter 38 PG* 32, 333C–335C; Arethas, *Commentary on the Apocalypse PG* 106, 568D, who both expand upon this theme.

categorise what had long been one of the most difficult and elusive sites for exploring colour discrimination.

Early in 1666, Isaac Newton performed his famous *experimentum crucis*. In a darkened room, he projected a beam of sunlight through a prism onto a white wall about twenty-two feet away. He observed not a curved rainbow (as earlier colour theorists had recorded) but a long oblong spectrum of seven distinct colours: red, orange, yellow, green, blue, indigo and violet.[43] From this, he concluded that 'light consists of rays differently refrangible [refractable]': 'to the same degree of refrangibility ever belongs the same colour, and to the same colour ever belongs the same degree of refrangibility'. Newton's *New theory about light and colours* (1671–72) transformed the spectrum into a standard for the science of colour.[44] Nevertheless, Newton's division of the prismatic spectrum into seven chromatic areas, announced so casually in a letter to the Royal Society of 1675, reflected his interest in the eternally stimulating search for objective principles of visual colour-harmony. It was the analogy with the seven notes of the musical octave – with its corollary that colour-harmony might be established on the same proportional basis as musical harmony – that accounts for the remarkable persistence of the seven-colour scheme in his optical writings.[45] In fact, Newton was hampered by the lack of standard colour-nomenclature; even he was to divide his visible spectrum into as many as eleven colours, and as few as five, before finally settling on seven.[46] The number of 'primary' colours proved even more perplexing.[47]

43 For a catalogue of diverse pre-Newtonian attempts to enumerate the colours of the rainbow, see Gage (1999) 132.

44 For a detailed account of Newton and his influence, see Gage (1999) 133–43. Bartholin's *Specimen Philosophiae Naturalis* (1703) was one of the earliest textbooks to accept Newton's simple theories, marking a big shift in colour concepts from the complex theories suggested (for example) by Goclenius (1613).

45 For further discussion of the theoretical basis for the analogy, see Gage (1999) 55–6, 139–43; Shapiro (1993) 99–101.

46 Gage (1993) 232. Newton's *Opticks* (1704) had already swapped the term for the most refrangible colour from purple to violet. For some idea of the complexities of seventeenth-century colour categories, see. Gage (1999) 26.

47 Newton (1704) I, ii, prop. V, theor. iv, Experiment 15 proposed 3 primaries. In Experiment 9, however, at least 5 primaries are implied. Cf. Field (1845) 182–5 on just one.

Nevertheless, Newton's scheme for the most part tidied up the categorical confusion of the spectrum, and was embraced in fields much broader than (what we now call) 'classical optics'. He offered an answer to the concerns of painters, especially in Rome and Paris, who were seeking some firmer theoretical basis for the study of colour in art.[48] Poetry, mathematics, even entomology had also abundantly embraced the *Opticks* and its neat schematisation of colour.[49] Joseph Priestley in his *History and present state of discoveries relating to vision, light and colours* (1772) claimed that the *Opticks* were Newton's greatest mathematical achievement, although he referred to the Platonic maxim that 'to pry into the mysteries of light was to encroach upon the prerogatives of divinity'. By the middle of the eighteenth century, however, some writers (such as Castel and Gautier d'Agoty) sought to drive a wedge between the quantitative study of the colours of light and the qualitative study of artistic colorants, a tension much exploited by Goethe (1810). This century gave birth to a generation of anti-Newtonians, among them Keats, Wordsworth and Charles Lamb who were eager to preserve the poetic and artistic integrity of the rainbow.[50] Even in the twentieth century, the more straightforward spectrum of white light has presented difficulties to spectators in laboratory experiments.[51] The inheritors of Newtonian optics did not take long to realise that colour perception and colour categories did not form such a coherent couple. It became once again clear that it was not possible to interpret the universe of colour under one all-enveloping theory.

San Francisco of 1978 witnessed the genesis of the Rainbow Flag, an icon destined to become recognised across the Western world as a global symbol of the gay community. To the original seven-colour scheme, the designers had added an eighth colour – pink. This was a bold cultural demonstration against the rigidity of Newtonian optics that the world needed to be more flexible in its

[48] For Boutet's painter's circle of 1708, see Gage (1993) 171–2; On Blake's Newtonian rainbows, see Gage (1999) fig. 48 and pp. 144–52. Cf. Harris (c. 1766), describing the first completely symmetrical and complementary colour-system.

[49] Gage (1999) 134. Taylor (1719) for Newtonian colour mixture systematically applied to Mathematics; Denis and Schiffermüller (1775) on the identification of butterflies.

[50] Gage (1999) 150–1 on the preference for a 'materialistic' rainbow.

[51] Boigey (1923) 18–19; Beare (1963).

classifications. The Rainbow Flag, of course, made no big claims that the rainbow contained a pink band. This rainbow was culturally constructed, its extra colour artificially sewn on, the flag a powerfully symbolic renegotiation of a conservative and outmoded perceptual framework.

Since the Greeks and Romans did not need it, there was no 'pink' in antiquity's rainbows. However, the ancient rainbow was a cultural enigma for colour perception. Try as they might to work up a coherent spectrum, ancient commentators from Xenophanes to Aristotle, to Ovid, Virgil and Seneca, right through to Ammianus and Isidore, found in the rainbow a renegotiable site for colour optics. There was little agreement over the number of colours in the rainbow, or even over what constituted a rainbow '*color*'. How one evaluated the rainbow, then, was hotly contested and the stuff of literary imagination: for some, its appearance was incomprehensible (hence *discolor* and *uarius*); for others, it was a site for divine activity (Iris, Isidore) or sensory deceptiveness (Seneca). On the other hand, most discussions of the rainbow – even in verse – agreed that its colours were created by complex combinations of sunlight, air and moisture. These colours were the product of ancient mixture theories, and were grounded phenomenologically in the elements that produced them (Seneca considered them to be images or mirrors – *species* or *aspectus* – of these mixtures). While it is indeed true that descriptions of the rainbow highlight the importance of different effects or intensities of light (*splendor*, *fulgor*, *intermicans*, *lux*), and that the colour categories employed – *luteus*, *puniceus*, *purpureus*, *igneus*, *flammeus* – also evoked light, we should remember that this has a lot to do with the position of light as a key constituent of the phenomenon described, and was not straightforwardly because luminosity was more central than 'hue' in ancient systems of colour (as some have argued).

Another solution was to resort to metaphor and transform the rainbow into a cultural artefact derived from paints or dyed fabrics. Prose and verse accounts alike found it convenient to draw upon these metaphors, and these were the connections that generated such difficult-to-translate expressions as *arcus purpureus*. By forming these connections, the writer could also suggest (or perhaps parody) the idea of skilled agency in the production and expression of the rainbow, whether this be divine craftsmanship or poetic creativity. The ancient rainbow, then, was a complex and provocative phenomenon that pushed the intellectual infrastructure of Roman colour vision to its limits. Contemporary discussions and interpretations reveal a great deal about how ancient colours were thought to originate and function.

2

LUCRETIUS AND THE PHILOSOPHY OF *COLOR*

After making such hard work of the Roman rainbow, Seneca proceeds in book 2 of the *Natural Questions* to discuss lightning, which he describes as fire in rapid motion (with '*impetus*'). You can tell, he says, by its *color*: 'its *color* shows that it is fire, since such *color* only comes from fire' (*esse illum ignem color ostendit, qui non est nisi ex eo*, 2.21.2).

This line is not easy. Generations of Senecan commentators have wrestled with Seneca's claim, replacing *color* with *calor* ('heat'), inserting *ictorum* after *color* to refer to the soot left by the lightning strike, and the like.[1] The objection was that one cannot map 'colour' onto a lightning bolt. Even if this were possible, the resulting colour would have little in common with a regular flame. '*Splendor*' or '*fulgor*' would perhaps be more natural.

Hine, commentating on Seneca's passage, accepts *color*, but with the caveat that Seneca tends sometimes to be a little lax – a laxness which (he adds) might on occasions prompt the modern Westerner to talk of 'flame red' or 'fiery coloured'. In fact, Seneca was echoing a formulation already made by Aristotle.[2] In addition, Latin literature, prose and verse, was riddled with such configurations as the *color* of flames, light and stars (*color flammae*, *color lucis*, *color siderum*, *color ardens, color igneus*).[3] Such uses of *color* cannot be explained away as examples of authorial laziness.

This is a short and relatively simple example of the difficulties encountered in the translation and interpretation of Latin *color*. Studies of colour have been principally concerned with the nuances

[1] See Hine (1981) 287–8 for a detailed review.

[2] Arist. *Phys*. fr. 3, p. 188.2–3; cf. Cic. *Nat. D*. 2.40. See also Clarke (2004) 136 on the Greek term ἀργός evoking both the colour and the flash of lightning.

[3] Lucr. 6.213; Sen. *Agamemnon* 862; Lucr. 6.828; Plin. *HN* 33.58; 21.16; Sen. *QNat*. 1.44; 5.8. It has also been noted (above p. 51) that one could conceive of the rainbow as possessing one distinctive *color*.

of specific colour categories (a pattern I have followed with the survey of *flauus, uiridis* and *caeruleus* in the introduction, above pp. 1–12); this chapter, however, will concentrate on the phenomenon of *color* itself, and explore its role and evaluation within philosophical theories of perception. It will first outline the prevalent Greek and Hellenistic philosophies of colour vision (as well as the function of *chrōma* in discussions of Greek rhetoric, music and art), and will then apply this intellectual background in order to undertake a more sophisticated reinterpretation of Lucretius' extended discussion of colour in book 2 of the *De Rerum Natura*. The aim of this chapter, then, is to identify some of the key approaches to colour and colour perception that were transmitted to and exploited by the educated literary elite of early imperial Rome.

Greek theories of colour

Lucretius' ideas about colour grew out of and engaged with a complex and diverse set of Greek and Hellenistic theories about perception. Thinkers from Parmenides to Theophrastus and a welter of Stoic and Epicurean philosophers debated at great length the connection between the perceiving eye and the object perceived, the precise route taken by vision, and the relationship of perception, categorisation and thought.[4] All appear to have agreed that colour was the primary sense object for sight (as sound is for hearing and odours for smell), and therefore a principal index of knowledge and understanding. To what extent the human senses could succeed in achieving knowledge and understanding from the perceptible world, however, was hotly contested and debated.

Pre-Socratics

The relationship between perception and knowledge was a pivotal question for Pre-Socratic philosophy. One of the earliest theorists, the natural philosopher and physician Alcmaeon, argued that humans (unlike gods) have an understanding of the world that

[4] In general on this theme, see Manetti (1996).

allows only *conjecture* from signs (τεκμαίρεσθαι).[5] He became one of the earliest philosophers to draw a sharp distinction between sense perception and higher cognitive functions such as thought. A generation later, Parmenides, though committed to the idea that thought could yield truth, argued that the world grasped by the senses is not Truth but Doxai, appearances, and that these can be delusional.[6] This argument that the senses could be unreliable also found a home in the work of Anaxagoras, who claimed that the diversified *kosmos* is derived from an original mixture of basic constituents (black and white, along with hot/cold, heavy/light etc.) by the action of the mind.[7]

This realist view of the perceptibles in the world was taken up by Empedocles. Within the framework of a cyclical cosmology, he undertook a materialistic explanation of sense perception using a theory of matter that relied on a mixture of elements.[8] Empedocles accordingly appears to have envisaged four primary colours – *leukon, melan, eruthron* and *ōchron* – which were properties of fire, water, earth and air respectively, with intermediate colours produced by various mixtures of elements.[9] The eye was composed of all four elements, and sense perception occurred when material effluences from the surfaces of physical objects entered the sense organs through pores in the body. Colour effluences from objects fitted particular pores in the body.[10]

For others, colour was a subjective and secondary quality. The atomists Leucippus and Democritus claimed that atoms have only the primary qualities of shape, size and solidity; secondary qualities like sweetness, heat and colour existed only 'by convention'

5 For a discussion of Alcmaeon, see Lloyd (1991) ch. 8.

6 Following the argument of Mourelatos (1970).

7 Arist. *Phys.* 187a36–b7; Theophr. *Sens.* 27–8.

8 On Empedoclean theory and its transmission through Theophrastus, see Sedley (1992) 20–31; Long (1966). On colours and elements in Empedocles, see Ierodiakonou (2005).

9 According to Aëtius (DK 307 A92). Theophr. *Sens.* 37 cites only *melas* and *leukos*, and their connection to water and fire. Cf. Siegel (1959) 152, who pointed out that 'colour' was not yet separated from the object which carried it. On Empedoclean colours and their relationship to the artist's palette, see Ierodiakonou (2004).

10 The theory is described at Arist. *De an.* 419a17. Cf. [Plut.] *Epit.* 1.15.3: Ἐμπεδοκλῆς τὸ τοῖς πόροις τῆς ὄψεως ἐναρμόττον. On the idea of a 'double movement' in Empedocles (where the eye both emits and receives light), see Svenbro (2004).

(*nomōi*).[11] Colour sensations were generated from atomic shape, and so related to touch.[12] The second part of the sensation theory had it that, in the case of vision, material 'films' or replicas (*eidōla*), having the shape of the object from which they flow, enter the eye and stamp an image onto it.[13] Democritus contrasted the mind's 'legitimate' judgment with the senses' 'bastard' judgment, and formulated the idea that the senses had persuasive powers (*pistis*), which could lead untrained individuals to see things in a certain way.[14] Democritus' most important influence was on Epicurus and his atomist school.

The Pre-Socratics, so far as we can tell, were interested principally in enquiries of a physical or physiological nature. Most were concerned with the mechanics of perception and the phenomenology of colour, sound, heat and so on. Sensory perception as a factor in epistemology was at an early stage of philosophical development; very few were interested in the question of how one reaches the truth. The noun *aisthēsis* appears first to have loomed large in discussion by the sophists of the late fifth century, and finds a rich home in the works of Plato and Aristotle. Here, attention was drawn away from the nature of the world to the perceptions and thoughts of man.

Plato

Plato offers us our first complete ancient discussion of colour and sensory perception.[15] It has been argued that Plato's primary

[11] Sext. Emp. *M.* 1.135 on fr. B9 of Democritus: 'Sweet by convention (νόμῳ) and bitter by convention, hot by convention, cold by convention, colour by convention. Atoms and void by nature (φύσει)'. The crucial meaning of *nomos* here is debated – see Lee (2005) 221–6; Galen, *Elements according to Hippocrates* 1.417–418K (= DK 68 A49). Cf. Theophr. *Sens.* 50–4; 73–82 on Democritus' theory of colour. On Democritus' primary colours, see O'Brien (1970) 164; Siegel (1959) 153; James (1995) 53, who is principally concerned with relative light-darkness in Democritus. For a detailed recent study of Democritean approaches to colour and colour mixtures, see Struycken (2003) esp. 278, 283–6.

[12] Arist. *Sens.* 442a29–b3; cf. Hahm (1978) esp. 70.

[13] Struycken (2003) 286 argues that one should understand Democritean basic colours (ἐρυθρόν, λευκόν, μέλαν and χλωρόν) as being related to, or grounded in, specific phenomena (radiant heat/ fire; light; darkness/ air; sprouting plants/ sap/ water).

[14] Lee (2005) 235–6. Cf. Cic. *Acad. post.* 1.12.44 for a sceptical interpretation.

[15] On the difficulties of Platonic colour theory, see Gaiser (1965).

concern with the soul and moral qualities led to a neglect of what we might describe as sensory perception in his works. The ephemeral and the experimental were generally unpopular subjects for Plato.[16] Metaphysical and epistemological interests, particularly in his middle and later works, are often background material for moral discussion. Nevertheless, one important development – although there is debate over its originality – seems to have been that Plato extended Empedocles' theory of effluences from the object entering the eye to incorporate a theory of vision with outward-flowing fire from the eye. With this adjustment, accounts of the senses could divert more attention to the observer as a protagonist in the process of perception.[17]

In numerous dialogues, Plato contrasts the permanence and changelessness of the Forms with the constant flux (*to rheon*) of the sensible world, characterised by shapes (*schēmata*) and colours (*chrōmata*).[18] The *Theaetetus* further develops a case for the insufficiency of the senses by arguing against the Protagorean doctrine that perception *per se* constitutes knowledge and that everything that appears to us is true.[19] The *Theaetetus* also posits an argument (182d) that, because the sensible world is so fluid and flexible, each individual's perceptual framework plays a significant part in the interpretation of sensation. Different perceivers *see* differently (153a–154a). Also, nothing is coloured unless it appears so to someone (160b6–7).[20] The *Theaetetus*' arguments are principally dialectical, but Socrates' criticism of various stances about the connection of perception and knowledge in this dialogue suggests an underlying commitment to the fluidity and unreliability of

[16] Siegel (1959) 154. Nevertheless, see Nakhnikian (1955).

[17] Siegel (1959) goes as far as suggesting that this may be the equivalent of 'throwing a glance' at something. The theory is difficult: see O'Brien (1970) esp. 157–9; cf. Gell. *NA* 5.16; Calcidius, *In Tim.* 236, 243 on Stoic, Epicurean and Platonic theories of vision. Svenbro (2004) attributes this idea of a double movement in vision to Empedocles.

[18] For the formula χρώματα καὶ σχήματα used to describe the world of sense perception as opposed to that of the ideal Forms, see *Resp.* 373b6, 601a2; *Leg.* 668e3. Cf. *Resp.* 479a–d; *Phd.* 78d–79a; *Cra.* 439c–e; *Symp.* 211a–b; *Ti.* 49c–d, 51e–52a. Arist. *Mete.* 987b2–3 describes Plato's ideas as schemata of absolutes and universals.

[19] Day (1997); Cooper (1970); Lee (2005) 78–9.

[20] Socrates' final refutation is that we should talk about perceiving objects *through* the senses, but *with* the mind. For a lucid interpretation of the Secret Doctrine (*Tht.* 153–60), see Lee (2005) 93–111.

human perception.[21] Nonetheless, Plato did not maintain that colours did not exist.[22] In the *Meno*, shape and colour are essentially co-existing entities (ἔστω γὰρ δὴ ἡμῖν τοῦτο σχῆμα, ὃ μόνον τῶν ὄντων τυγχάνει χρώματι ἀεὶ ἑπόμενον, 75b), and Socrates cites Gorgias' definition, following Empedocles, that colour is an effluence from shapes, which is commensurate with sight and perceptible by it (ἔστι γὰρ χρόα ἀπορροὴ σχημάτων ὄψει σύμμετρος καὶ αἰσθητός, 76d) – in other words that colour is what is visible of an object. In the *Philebus*, Socrates describes as 'true pleasures' (ἀληθεῖς ἡδοναι) those taken in the basic forms, as well as so-called 'beautiful colours' (τὰ καλὰ λεγόμενα χρώματα, 51b) such as *ostreon* ('sea purple'). Even these, however, can be misleading: the *Republic*, for example, attacks errors of vision caused by colours (πλάνη τῆς ὄψεως περὶ τὰ χρώματα, 602c) and criticises forms of art that exploit these weaknesses as a type of witchcraft.

Plato's philosophy of the natural world is most coherently presented in the *Timaeus*, where he depicts a divine craftsman who looked to the Forms and transformed disorderly moving bodies into a beautiful and measured cosmos. In this fanciful 'living' world colours are perfectly produced and mixed by the 'divine craftsman' in a way that cannot be reproduced by human experiment.[23] The abstract colours described are *leukos*, *melas*, *eruthros* (this is described as 'blood-coloured', *chrōma enaimon*), *lampros* ('shining'), *xanthos, halourgos, orphninos*,[24] *purros*,[25] *phaios, ōchron, kuanous, glaukos* and *prasios*. The first four of these are to be understood as 'primary' colours out of which the others are mixed.[26] All of these, the speaker stresses, are necessary linguistic

[21] On the *Theaetetus*' dialectical approach, see Burnyeat (1990) 2; cf. 10–19 on the three theses about knowledge and perception.

[22] See Theophr. *Sens.* 60, comparing Democritus and Plato. At Pl. *Chrm.* 167c–d, *chrōma* is specified as the primary object of vision.

[23] *Ti.* 67c–68d. This idea complements that of the *Phaedo*, where human senses obstruct reason, and understanding can only be achieved after the soul leaves the body.

[24] An expensive and elegant dye; cf. *De Coloribus* 2.792a 25; 4.794b 5; Xen. *Cyr.* 8.3.3 ('red sauce coloured').

[25] See Sassi (1982).

[26] Plato's mixing process has baffled modern commentators: see, for example, Taylor (1928) 276. For an interpretation of the mixtures within a brightness-darkness scale, see James (1995) 56–8. On ancient approaches to the *Timaeus*, see Sharples and Sheppard (2003).

categories, things *spoken* of (*prosrēteon*), since he claims (68b) that we are fundamentally unable to appreciate the proportions involved – that is the prerogative of the divine. Most of the categories presented here are therefore ones normally found in human and cultural spheres, such as blood (*haima*), vegetables (*prasios*) and blond hair (*xanthos*). Plato's elaborate recipes for colour mixtures (68a–d) are, it might follow, deliberately riddled with incongruities, a riddle that can be solved neither by considering the categories to be abstract, nor by substituting them with the painter's pigments.[27] Timaeus describes the sensation of *seeing* by presenting '*chroai*' – a word we translate as both 'surface' and 'colour' – as the means by which varieties (*poikilmata*) are perceived (67c). These consist of a flame (*phlox*) of particles (*moria*) of different shapes and sizes which strike the visual stream and produce different sensations, a theory very similar to that of Empedocles and Democritus.[28] Timaeus also goes (68a) on to say that the effect of a dazzling object on a teary eye produces colours of all kinds (παντοδαπῶν ἐν τῇ κυκήσει ταύτῃ γιγνομένων χρωμάτων), a sensation called 'marbled' (μαρμαρυγὰς μὲν τὸ πάθος προσείπομεν).[29] As far as colour was concerned, human perception and human classification offered no easy route to enlightenment.

Aristotle

Aristotle produced a very different treatment of the senses. This was a topic that cut across several important works. The *De Caelo* and the *Meteorologica* treated form and colour in celestial phenomena. The *De Anima* gave a general account of the nature of the soul and its various capacities, including sensory perception. The short treatise *De Sensu et Sensibilibus* covered this ground in more

[27] As does Bruno (1977) 89–95; cf. Westerink (1962) 13–15 for the apocryphal tradition of Plato's experience as a painter; on the shortcomings of this explanation, see James (1995) 55. For more on the problems of using the artist's palette as a rationale for understanding Platonic colour mixtures, see Struycken (2003) 296–303.

[28] Taylor (1928) 278–82 supposes that effluences and pores were used to explain the perception of colours, while the visual ray issuing from the eye was used to explain vision more generally. For more on Plato's definition of colour, see Wright (1920).

[29] This category is not easy to translate; it was traditionally used of shiny stones, and the surface of the sea. See Bradley (2006a) 5–8.

detail, examining the perceptive faculties of the body. Aristotle's theory of colour, however, could be very inconsistent.[30]

Aristotle shifted the dynamics of epistemology far away from the abstract intellectualism of Platonic theory. His basic thesis was that our knowledge of first principles arises out of *experience*, that experience arises out of numerous and repeated *memories*, and those memories result from numerous and repeated *perceptions*. Perception forms the ultimate inductive basis for epistemology. Qualities, including sensible qualities, actually exist, albeit parasitically on a substance. Colours are *at* the surface of physical bodies.[31] This meant that, according to Aristotle, colours were static – an object's colour was fixed and there was no place for perceptual relativism. He even went so far in the *De Sensu* as claiming that the sense and the object were essentially one and the same, since it was not possible to have sight without there being a colour there to see.[32] In the *De Anima*, he asserted that colour is that which is seen (τὸ γὰρ ὁρατόν ἐστι χρῶμα).[33] Colour is an active capacity of physical bodies to change a transparent medium such as air or water (κινητικὸν τοῦ κατ' ἐνέργειαν διαφανοῦς), in such a way that 'seeing' occurs when that medium is continuous between the eye and the visible object. Aristotle's idea of *pathos* was the experience and quality of the object experienced (a definition which made perception very passive), whereas Plato has *pathos* as just the 'impression' given by the active sense. For

[30] Gottschalk (1964) 78–82; Broackes (1999) 108–13; Hamlyn (1961) 23–4. At *De Caelo* 290a, vision is due to rays emanating *from* the eye and reflected back from the object, a theory incompatible with the doctrine of the *De Anima* and *De Sensu*. For a discussion of the differences between the approaches of Plato and Aristotle to perception, see Lycos (1964).

[31] On this emphasis in Aristotle, see Machamer and Turnbull (1978) ch. 1, esp. 4: 'Colours ... are not ideas in the mind, sense-data, sensibilia, sentiments, or any other members of the general family of modern philosophical inventions'; cf. Silverman (1989) 288: 'The physical objects of Aristotle's world actually are colored. And they would be colored even if there were no Aristotles to perceive them'.

[32] *Sens*. 425b26; cf. *Metaph*. 1010b35; 1051b7 (cf. *Int*. 9.19a32). Cf. Broackes (1999) 62 'colours are powers to produce perceptions of colour'. On the object of perception in the *De sensu*, see Johansen (2006) 152–4.

[33] 418a27 – just as heat, cold, moist and dry are intrinsic objects of touch. On colour perception in the *De Anima*, see Silverman (1989). On the demarcation of the five senses, Sorabji (1971).

Aristotle, the world of sensory perception provided the cornerstone of his works on ontology and epistemology.[34]

Critics have objected to Aristotle's statement that colour is the primary object of sight.[35] This appears to ignore other visual factors, such as size, shape, motion, rest, texture, depth or the location of things; these, however, are for Aristotle 'common sensibles', which are not peculiar to one sense and so do not fall into the category of 'special sensibles'. In the *De Sensu* (439a6–440b25), Aristotle argues that the colour of a visible object is the 'surface' of the transparent in that object, that it arises at the extremity of a body. Aristotle claimed colour was only visible at the surface (ἧπερ καὶ ἔξω χρωματίζεται).[36] The evaluation of colour as 'surface' is important. It meant that one could consider colour, in very broad terms, to be the visible property of an object and therefore to incorporate other visual factors that we would not classify as 'colours'.

There was still room in this definition for a theory of 'basic units'. Aristotle thought that colour was composed of tiny bits of black and white juxtaposed, the perceived colour of the whole dependent on the numerical ratio.[37] Red, green, blue and other colours, therefore, were intermediate between white and black, each produced by a mixture of those extremes (440b1–17). These gradations were in some ways analogous to melodic progressions, with attractive colours such as *halourgon* and *phoinikoun* resembling musical intervals (439b31) and other colours with no definite ratio analogous to a mere noise, although Aristotle is sceptical that

[34] The *Metaphysics* argues that Platonic Forms do not actually exist (even though Aristotle's ideal of knowledge is a god who is pure intellect with no sensory apparatus at all). In spite of this, there is still debate over whether Aristotelian colours were fundamental in the same way as hot, cold, wet and dry – or in some way derivative; see particularly Broackes (1999) 57–9; cf. Broadie (1993).

[35] Sorabji (1971) 79–80; Hamlyn (1961) 24: 'Each individual sense has a special sense object which is connected essentially with it; hearing has sound, smell odours, and sight, though Aristotle is wrong about this, colour'. The principle that colour was the primary object of vision had already been asserted by Plato at *Chrm.* 167c–d.

[36] Zabarella, *In De Anima* 2.132 concludes that Aristotle meant that colour is *in act* only when it is 'able to perform its task' (an aid to acquiring knowledge, or for the preservation of life), hence when it is visible at the surface (*ille solus est actu color, qui aptus est per se operam suam praestare, hic autem est ille solum, qui in superficie est.*); cf. Broackes (1999) 59–69.

[37] Cf. Siegel (1959) 158, who attributes this to the confusion of luminosity and colour.

there is such a simple *logos*.[38] He also suggests the possibility that colours might appear through one another, resorting to the analogy of the painter laying pigments over each other to show the effects of fog or smoke (440a7–15).[39] Nevertheless, Aristotle identifies seven 'basic' natural colours (*De Sensu* 442a21): *melas, leukos, prasinos, kuaneos, phoenix, halourgos* and either *xanthos* or *phaios*.[40] But rather than being (in our terms) 'abstract' colours, these 'building blocks' were distinctive observable phenomena in Aristotle's world, and therefore practical models of vision with which his readers could measure that physical world and derive knowledge.

Theophrastus and the De Coloribus

Aristotle's Peripatetic successor Theophrastus was the author of an important doxographical work, the *De Sensibus*, which catalogued many earlier views on sense perception, and (some have argued) the author of – or at least the mind behind – the anonymous *De Coloribus*.[41] He was heavily influenced by his mentor Aristotle, and developed many of his ideas by using methods that were highly empirical.[42] Like Aristotle, he investigated the relationship between sense perception and intellectual activity and dealt in depth with the physiological aspects of sensation, emphasising the blending of the four fundamental qualities of hot, dry, cold and moist in physiological processes. Like Aristotle, he argues that colour was the specific object of sight, carried to the eye by light. His phenomenological approach had it that perception occurs when the visible reaches the eye and produces a qualitative change. He held that colours themselves are a cause of seeing colour and that a colourless object cannot be seen – so implying that form is defined by colour.

[38] Cf. Burnyeat (1996). Further on colour mixture as an alternative to colour juxtaposition, see Sorabji (1972).

[39] The word he uses is *chroai*, contrasting with the *chrōmata* of the general discussion.

[40] On colour ratios in the *De Sensu*, see Johansen (2006) 154–5.

[41] So Gottschalk (1964) 82–5.

[42] Capelle (1958); Siegel (1959) 152; Long (1996b). For more on the much-debated objectives of Theophratus' thesis, see Baltussen (1998).

The Peripatetic tract *De Coloribus* is a collection of observed facts about the physical basis of colour in plants and animals, and the position of heat and moisture in producing this colour.[43] It begins by asserting that there are two primary colours, *leukos* and *xanthos*, the former the natural colour of the earth, air and water, the latter of fire and sunlight. A third, *melas*, is presented as the colour of every 'element' in the process of transmutation into another. The *De Coloribus* stresses that colours are fundamental properties of substances, and concludes that what reaches the eye is a complex mixture of primary colours, called by the name of the primary or compound that predominates. No colour seen is absolutely pure. He remarks (perhaps echoing the sentiments of Plato's *Timaeus*) that one should not base theories on the way in which pigments are mixed but on the observed effects of different illuminations on the colour of the same object (792b16). The *De Coloribus* therefore connects knowledge with empirical observations: the way vegetation changes its colour as it ripens, for example, or the relationship of the colouring of hair and feathers to the general physiology of the organism. In describing human body colour, the *De Coloribus* employs similar tactics to the discipline of physiognomics, attributing (for example) reddish hair to a lack of moisture and nourishment and albinism to an excess of these things; such physiological foundations for colour would later be used to explain character and behaviour (see pp. 135–7). What emerges is a firm reliance on the idea of a physical, material origin for colour – sometimes expressed as 'dye' (*baphē*).[44] The experimental, empirical focus of this work, and its emphasis upon observable nature (*phusis*) became an important model for Pliny the Elder's *Natural History*.

Hellenistic theories

Hellenistic philosophy is marked by the formation of two philosophical traditions that became the most influential schools in the Roman world until the later Empire – Stoicism and Epicureanism.

43 For a lucid summary of the *De Coloribus*, see Struycken (2003) 282–3.

44 Cf. Machamer and Turnbull (1978) 75–8. Natural colouring agents described in the *De Coloribus* include sea-water, lye, orpiment and dust. The work contains a chapter on artificial dyeing, focusing particularly on the production of the *murex* dye.

Stoicism was chiefly concerned with the relationship between nature and virtue, advocating a didactic and moral system of life in which truth and the soul were at the top of the philosophical agenda. Stoics clashed with followers of the Academy in claiming that colour existed objectively, and that colour perception could yield trustworthy information about the world. A fragment of Zeno asserts (contrary to the Epicurean line) that *chrōma* is an actual attribute of matter, 'surface coloration' (*epichrōsis*) being the first or most basic part of the formation of the initial appearance of things (*prōtoi schēmatismoi*) by the divine.[45] Chrysippus held that colour is seen when the air between the eye and the object experiences a change of state induced by the object, which then imprints its colour on the soul.[46] The Stoic approach to perception was a very rational one working from the top down, whereas the Epicureans engaged in a more mechanical conception of the universe, a bottom-up approach working from the atomic level up to all the phenomenal features of the world.[47]

Epicurus was heavily influenced by the atomist theories of Democritus, and claimed that *aisthēsis* is the ultimate standard to which we must refer our judgment.[48] Sensory perception is formed of true impressions from outside – sensations which are *alogoi* – to which are added a true or false opinion 'from within ourselves'.[49] According to Epicurus' physical theory, every sensory impression corresponds to a configuration of atoms which makes an impact on the sensory organ. These sensory impressions serve as the foundation of knowledge. Perception occurs when these atoms make contact with the atoms of the soul. The streams of images (*eidōla* = Latin *simulacra*) are composed of atoms that have only shape, size and weight; secondary qualities, such as colours, flavours and

45 See Pearson (1891) 131–2, Ζήνων ὁ Στωικὸς τὰ χρώματα πρώτους εἶναι σχηματισμοὺς τῆς ὕλης; *SVF* 1.91: Aët. 1.15.6. Cf. Gal. *Philosophus Historia* 27. On some aspects of Stoic epistemology and the senses, see Hankinson (2003) esp. 82–4.

46 Cited by Aetius 4.15.3 (*SVF* 2.866, 869).

47 A contrast outlined by Sedley (1988) 298. See also Lapidge (1978); Long (1996a). Inwood (2007) 363–67 offers a good synopsis of approaches to perception in different philosophical schools in his analysis of Sen. *Ep.* 124.

48 Quoted by Diog. Laert. 10.31–2; cf. Harry (1970); Asmis (1999); Solmsen (1961).

49 *Ep. Hdt.* 50–1; further on this, see Striker (1977). On the relationship between perception, dreams and desire, see Balaudé (2004).

sound are perceived when atoms from outside collide with the sensory organ. These qualities therefore are not integral to the atoms, but products of configurations (*theseis*) of atoms of different shapes and sizes.

A third position one could adopt for the interpretation of colour was a sceptical one. What counted as 'scepticism' ranged from the claim that one should suspend judgment since we cannot know how things are by nature (Sextus Empiricus) to a quite different assertion that things are by nature radically indeterminate (probably the line originally adopted by Pyrrho). What we call 'Academic scepticism' (esp. that of Arcesilaus and Carneades) was particularly influential in Roman circles from the late second century BC onwards. This did not constitute a conclusion; rather, it was an attitude of mind which led thinkers to question theories of colour and sensory perception. This attitude formed the intellectual background to the scepticism of Sextus Empiricus in the second century, which argued that humans and animals could inherently possess very different modes of colour perception (διάφορον αὐτοῖς τὴν χρωμάτων ἀντίληψιν).[50] Habits such as staring at the sun, this line of argument maintained, could also change the colours that we see. Sextus employed a range of empirical tests to demonstrate that it was impossible to draw universal truths about colour vision, as some had done in the past.[51]

Chrōma *in rhetoric, music and art*

Ancient philosophical discussions of colour perception frequently exploited and engaged with discourses of colour in the worlds of rhetoric, music and art, with the result that these activities offered thinkers a useful point of reference for the formulation and understanding of colour and colour vision across antiquity. In Greek, there were two expressions for 'colour': the first, and most familiar was *chrōma*, the second – and more difficult – *chroia* (and, to a

[50] See Sext. Emp. 1.44–5; House (1980). On some aspects of sceptic optics, see Betts (2007). On Aristotelian epistemology as a defence against the arguments of Greek scepticism about the senses, see Long (2006a) esp. 51–3, 60–3.

[51] On Cyrenaic scepticism and its relationship to Epicurean doctrine about *aisthēsis*, see Tsouna (1998), esp. 115–21; cf. 39 on the fallibility of the senses.

lesser extent, *chrōs* – 'skin'/'flesh'). Both appear to have approximated to our sense of 'colour' through primary reference to surface, particularly the skin of the body or face. Through into the fourth century, these terms appear to have been used to describe such surfaces often without referring to anything which we might consider to be 'colour'.[52] *Chroia*, even when it was used in contexts where it could map onto our 'colour', seldom escaped its attachment to skin complexion (*chrōs* at its most colourful described the skin of a chameleon).[53] Where it did (principally in philosophical treatises), it still denoted superficial surfaces, of such things as atoms or natural phenomena such as light or water. *Chrōma* had a similar history, but came also to be attached to things like paints, dyes and cosmetics.[54] Even so, the word was inextricably bound up with the external and the superficial.[55]

Connected to this principle of 'appearance', and foreshadowing similar connotations of Latin *color* (see Chapter 4), *chrōma* could also be used to refer to the complexion or character of writing styles, particularly in terms of ornament and embellishment, and later was used alongside *color* to denote rhetorical fabrication.[56] In Plato's *Gorgias*, Socrates, arguing that political oratory is little more than a form of flattery, observes that its function in proper statesmanship is as inappropriate as that of cosmetics in gymnastics, and describes it as an illiberal art that deceives men with shapes (*schēmata*) and colours (*chrōmata*).[57] Even more characteristic of classical Greek usage was a connection that seems not to have been integrated into Latin: that of a musical scale or nuance. Plato's *Republic* (601b) discusses the superficial practices of poets, using words and phrases

[52] Hippoc. *De Insomniis*. 89 (κάθαρσις διὰ τοῦ χρώματος); Hom. *Il*. 14.163 (παραδραθέει φιλότητι ἠ̣ χροιῇ); Ar. *Pl*. 1020 (ὄζειν … τῆς χρόας ἔφασκεν ἡδύ μου). For further references, see *TLG* and LSJ s.v. χροιά. Further on the blurry distinction between 'skin' and 'colour' in early Greek philosophy and medicine, see Villard (2002b) esp. 46–7.

[53] [Arist.] *Mir. ausc*. 832b14 (τὸν χρῶτα [μεταβάλλει] ὁ χαμαιλέων). On the Pythagoreans and *chroiē*, see Arist. *Sens*. 439a31 (διὸ καὶ οἱ Πυθαγόρειοι τὴν ἐπιφάνειαν χροιὰν ἐκάλουν).

[54] Pl. *Resp*. 429e; Xen. *Cyr*. 1.3.2; Arist. *Gen. an*. 747a10.

[55] So Pl. *Resp*. 601a on the habit of looking only to the outside of things, ἐκ τῶν χρωμάτων καὶ σχημάτων θεωρεῖν; *Cratylus* 394a on the folly of judging *pharmaka* purely on the basis of their external appearance – *chrōmata*).

[56] For example, Pl. *Phdr*. 239d; Dion. Hal. *Comp*. 20; Hermog. *Stat*. 1.3; Phld. p. 84K.

[57] Pl. *Grg*. 465b.

(ὀνόματα καὶ ῥήματα) to colour (ἐπιχρωματίζειν) the arts he describes and beguile the listener into thinking that these arts are accurately depicted: 'so mighty is the spell that these adornments naturally exercise – but when they are stripped bare of their musical colouring (τὰ τῆς μουσικῆς χρώματα), we all know what they stand for'. Rhetorical *chrōma* was an idea, some have argued, rooted in early Greek musical theory.[58] Musical *chrōmata* could constitute a simple modification or embellishment,[59] but they also formed categories in a technical repertoire of musical scale.[60] The 'movable' notes within the tetrachord were categorised as 'enharmonic', 'diatonic', and 'chromatic', the latter called so because it lent itself most readily to adjustment or 'colouring' (aside from this, stringed instruments were tuned to manipulate the *chroai* or 'spin' of the musical effect).[61] In the late fifth century, Damon and his successors were arguing a case later taken up by Plato and Aristotle that different types of musical *chrōmata* imitated particular characteristics in the soul, and could evoke corresponding virtues and vices in the hearer.[62] The chromatic genus was sometimes thought to make men cowardly, and it seems likely that musical colour was easily associated with colour in cosmetics, and all the connotations of effeminacy and beguilement that it brought with it.[63] Plato likewise objected to the poet's employment of stylistic devices, describing the activity as 'colouring in' (*epichrōmatizein*).[64] Colour intersected with music both as a technical category and as a metaphor for moral and ethical evaluation.[65]

58 Wiseman (1979) 3–4. See Plut. *Mor.* 645e on Agathon as the creator of the chromatic *genus*; Antiphanes ap. Ath. 14.643d on χρώματα in the music of Philoexus.

59 Antiph. 209; Philoch. 66.

60 Anon. in *PHib.* 1.13.22; cf. Cleonides, *Introductio Harmonica* 3, 7; Bacchyl. *Harm.* 23; Dion. Hal. *Comp.* 19; Alciphro 1.18; Plut. *Mor.* 744c; Phld. *Mus.* p. 63K.

61 As Aristox. 50.25–7. See Landels (1999) 90–2; Barker (1984) esp. 225–7.

62 In Ath. 628c; Pl. *Resp.* 4.424c6; Aristid. Quint. 2.14; cf. Arist. *Pol.* 8.1339a–1342b, esp. 1340a; Anderson (1966) 38–42

63 *PHib.* 1.13.15–23; cf. Aristoph. *Thesm.* 130–72, mocking the effeminacy of Agathon and his musical style. On cosmetic colours and effeminacy, see Pl. *Phdr.* 239c–d where the unmanly lover is ἀλλοτρίοις χρώμασι καὶ κόσμοις ... κοσμούμενον.

64 He toys with the metaphor of musical 'colour' at *Leg.* 655a; cf. Ath. 638a on Lysander (a kitharist from Sicyon) who played the kithara with unconventional 'colourful shadings' (χρώματα εὔχρόα); cf. 643d.

65 Arist. *Top.* 106a–b, 107a points out that *leukos* is used to denote both skin colour (χρῶμα σώματος) and a note which is clearly heard. Cf. Arist. *Pol.* 1342a26 on irregular melodies as παρακεχρωσμένα.

Colour in Greek art has received some detailed treatment.[66] For contemporary philosophers, paints were symptomatic of the disjunction that could exist between perception and understanding. Paints were artificial surfaces, and therefore any connection with the underlying object was arbitrary.[67] Artistic and poetic colours were sometimes considered incompatible: qualities of colour in Greek verse such as 'rosy-fingered' (*rhododaktulos*) could hardly be reproduced on the painter's canvas with 'rose' dye.[68] One solution to the logical problem posed by paints was to aim to use the 'correct' colour (so, in crude terms, make art 'veristic'). Thus Plato, in a section of the *Republic* (420c) comparing the correctly painted statue to the correctly organised state, draws attention to the role of colour in achieving mimesis, and the importance of applying the correct colours to the correct parts of the image: 'by assigning what is appropriate to each part, we make the whole beautiful' (τὰ προσήκοντα ἑκάστοις ἀποδιδόντες τὸ ὅλον καλὸν ποιοῦμεν).[69] This emphasis on using the proper colours in art, on imitating, copying and reproducing visible physical objects, goes some way to explaining the intensity of the Greco-Roman debate on mixing and on using pure colours (below pp. 94–101).[70] It also finds expression in the paint- and colour-systems of Greco-Roman architecture.[71] The ethical dangers of being carried away by the sheer diversity of artificial paints, pigments and dyes are neatly represented by the pervasiveness of the simple 'four-colour palette' (described by Pliny) which some have connected to the

66 Most notably Bruno (1977); James (1995) 62–8; cf. Keuls (1978); Lodge (1975); Rouveret (2006) 23. More recently, Rouveret *et al.* (2006) collected essays exploring various aspects of ekphrasis as a point-of-entry into understanding the use of colour in Greco-Roman art. I have examined the significance of paint and surface colorations in Greco-Roman sculpture in Bradley (2009a), esp. 440–1 on philosophical difficulties with artistic colour.

67 For an excellent and concise study of the role of colour in Classical Greek artistic culture and its moral and intellectual ambiguities, see Duigan (2004).

68 So Ion of Chios (at Ath. 604b): εἰ γάρ τις ῥόδεον χρῶμα βάψειε τοὺς δακτύλους, πορφυροβάφου χεῖρας καὶ οὐ γυναικὸς καλῆς ποιήσειε. Further on this poetic-artistic distinction, see James (1995) 62–3.

69 On this passage, see Rouveret (2006) 23. This idea recurs at *Resp.* 2.377E; 586B–C; cf. *Cra.* 424E–425B.

70 Philostr. *Imag.* 1.2, who asserts: ζωγραφία δὲ ξυμβέβληται μὲν ἐκ χρωμάτων; cf. Plut. *Quaest. conv.* 725C.

71 The architectural distribution of coloured marbles is discussed in Bradley (2006a). On the use of paint on Greco-Roman sculpture, see Bradley (2009a).

elemental tetrads of early Greek philosophy.[72] The dynamics of colour in Greek art are of course highly complex, and not the subject of this present study. However, two significant themes appear to have dominated discussion of colour in painting: first, paints (like rhetorical and musical *chrōmata*) posed an inherent problem for the understanding of how colour functioned in perception; second, this cultural tension could be resolved by laying emphasis on the controlled and sober use of 'correct' pigments for imitation and representation.[73]

The philosophical debates out of which Lucretius' discussion of colour emerged, then, were diverse, complex and hotly contested. They appear to have grown out of interests in natural philosophy and the primary features of the natural world. Discussions of the senses in moral, ethical and cognitive philosophy therefore toed a difficult line between the physical world and thought. For this reason, some thinkers (particularly Democritus and Plato) were sceptical about how far the senses could reach a true understanding of the world. Others (especially Aristotle) argued that knowledge and perception were fundamentally connected. The debates between these stances formed the basis of most of the philosophical discussions of colour.

Greek philosophers appear to have agreed in considering colour (*chrōma*) to be the primary object of sight (a concept which some have found difficult), rather than other characteristics such as size, shape, motion, rest, location, texture or depth. *Chrōma* and particularly *chroia* ('skin') were often represented as the surface (or 'what is visible') of an object, rather than as entities in their own

[72] Plin. *HN* 35.50. On the four-colour palette, see Gage (1981); James (1995) 67–68. Most recently Brécoulaki (2006) argues that the four-colour palette was a highly subjective phenomenon, and that – although one can trace a progression over time towards more sophisticated techniques and complex colours – there remained a stubborn preoccupation with mimesis and artistic conservatism. For an interesting discussion of philosophical resentment towards extravagant uses of colour, and the continuity of these ideas through into second-century literature, see Rouveret (2006).

[73] The significance of this principle, as well as the intellectual complexities generated by integrating artistic, poetic and philosophical discourses of colour, are the subject of a well-known section of Lucian's *Imagines* (7–8). For a commentary on this passage, see Bradley (2006a) 17–18. On Lucian's subversion of the traditional philosophical doctrines about sight and knowedge, see Gassino (2002).

right. Nevertheless, most thinkers (including Plato) accepted that a schematic and objective system of colours existed in the world, even if human perception was not up to the job of perceiving them accurately. Empedocles appears to have adopted a materialistic approach to colour, considering colours (among other things) to be relative configurations of earth, fire, air and water. This connection was embellished by later theorists such as Theophrastus and (more explicitly) by the author of the *De Coloribus*, who describes colour as a sort of 'dye'. Such colour theories may have grown out of experimentation and empirical observation (particularly the artist's palette and dye mixtures).

Greek optics offered one significant way of negotiating the perception of colour in relation to the physical world. The most pervasive approach was to consider colours as effluences from the object that produced them. For most (starting with Empedocles), the eye was a passive recipient of these effluences. Plato appears to have developed the notion of an outward-flowing fire from the eye, an optical theory in which the perceiver and the soul could perform a more active role in perception. This principle in some ways picked up Democritus' idea that individuals had different receiving 'pores' in the sense organs so that different atomic configurations and shapes – the basis of colour – penetrated different people, leading to different perceptions of reality.

Hellenistic approaches to sensory perception, the most immediate background to Lucretius' *De Rerum Natura*, were influenced by two prevailing doctrines: that of the Stoics who claimed that sensation (*aisthēsis*) often yielded true information about the world (colour being a primary feature of matter); and that of the Epicureans who saw colour as a secondary feature of objects generated by the shape and arrangement of atoms; although colours are real, the untrained eye could misinterpret them. A third, one we loosely term 'scepticism', questioned theories of colour and sensory perception, and advocated suspension of judgment on such matters. These schools of thought also found recourse to other registers in which 'colour' was integral, such as rhetoric, music and art. These registers, which would be exploited and developed more fully in Roman literature, introduced a moral and ethical dimension to the theme of colour vision.

Lucretius

The philosophical atmosphere of mid first-century BC Italy, when Lucretius linked the world of Latin verse to the philosophy of vision, was highly charged. This was a period of unsurpassed philosophical upheaval in the Greco-Roman world, in which the centre of philosophical gravity was shifting away from Athens and finding expression on the Italian mainland. The various philosophical schools – representatives of the Old and New Academies, Pythagoreanism and Peripatetic philosophy, as well as Stoicism, Epicureanism and Scepticism – began to exert their influence on the philosophical intelligentsia of Rome.[74] Cicero's correspondence with a range of influential Roman contemporaries shows them to be remarkably well-attuned to live philosophical issues and inter-school debates.[75]

De Rerum Natura *2.730–841*

Titus Lucretius Carus' *De Rerum Natura* adapted into Latin hexameter Epicurus' didactic prose monologue *Peri Phuseōs*, and appears to be faithful to orthodox Epicureanism, although its source material is drawn from a fairly wide range of Roman social, literary and artistic experiences.[76] Following the pattern of didactic poems by Parmenides and Empedocles, Lucretius is notable for his exploitation of poetic ekphrasis, metaphor and simile and forges a philosophic vocabulary out of largely untechnical Latin verse.[77]

[74] For a philosophical contextualisation of Lucretius, see Sedley (1998) ch. 3. See also Jocelyn (1977); Barnes and Griffin (1997). For Peripatetic rebirth, see Sandbach (1985) esp. 14, 48; Sedley (1998) 64. On Epicureanism in the late Republic, see Castner (1998). On Scepticism, see Schrivers (1992).

[75] See esp. Griffin (1995); Sedley (1989).

[76] On fundamentalism/innovation in Lucretian ethics, see Furley (1966) and Sedley (1998) 75–8.

[77] See esp. the proem to book 4 (repeated almost verbatim from 1.921–50), with its stress on Lucretius' role as a poet-cum-philosopher and its Callimachean imagery. On Lucretius and Empedocles, see Kranz (1943); Gale (1994) 59–75. Lucretius' stance as saviour of humanity is evoked at 2.1–61; 3.59–93; 5.43–54. On the richness of colour vocabulary and imagery in Lucretian verse, see Baran and Chişleag (1968), who credit Lucretius with a formative role in the development of Latin colours. On poetic imagery in Lucretius, see West (1969); on puns and poetry, see Snyder (1980), whose basic thesis argues that Lucretius' poetry and his philosophy were fundamentally intertwined.

These innovations were particularly pertinent for the discussion of colour, where (as we have seen) linguistic categories and literary registers had a significant effect on the way it was formulated. In spite of this, Lucretian ethics was principally a matter of breaching the epistemological barriers of language and modes of expression and seeing the truth about the world, and so attached special importance to instruction in the physics of the senses. The aesthetic appreciation of the spectacle – standing back, observing, interpreting – is recommended as the ethically correct way to live.[78]

Lucretius' discussion of colour in the second half of book 2 follows an extensive treatment of atomic forms and their effects.[79] He ends this section with a general proposition that atoms have different shapes, and these shapes account for different species, as well as qualities such as colour, taste and smell.[80] These qualities touch the senses in different ways, and therefore the bodies which carry them must vary in their atomic shapes (661–99). Lucretius also maintains that not every combination is possible, and that things must remain true to their species (700–29). Lucretius deals explicitly and separately with all the individual qualities (*euenta*) of things perceptible to the senses, taking colour as his chief example (730–841), and treats the other qualities of heat, sound, taste and smell more briefly (842–64). Lucretius then discusses 'sensation' (*sensus*), an active power of animate beings rather than a passive quality, such as colour, sound or taste, but which is still dependent on size, shape, position and movement of atoms. His central project in this section is to argue that individual atoms *lack* such qualities, and so to underwrite their secondariness.

Epicurean *color* was a quality produced by atomic arrangement and position on the surface, and one which was conveyed to the perceiver by means of a film with the same atomic configuration as the original object. One important difference between the doctrine of Epicurus and that of (for example) Democritus is that the former did not regard 'secondary qualities' as purely subjective, but as real qualities or 'accidents' of atom position and location which have an

78 For this theme, see esp. Lucr. 2.112–41; Schiesaro (1990); Godwin (1998).
79 A lucid treatment of Lucretius' atomic theory is presented by Wardy (1988).
80 For more on this, see Ernout and Robin (1962) I.305; Bailey (1947) 910.

existence independent of their perception. Nevertheless, the interpretation that follows, building upon the work of D. West (1969) and J. Snyder (1980) on the complexity of Lucretius' poetic imagery and its relationship to Epicurean doctrine, suggests ways of approaching Lucretius' theories of colour perception through his creative use of language and descriptive imagery.[81]

Lucretius' argument in this section is structured as follows:[82]

Introduction. 730–47

We must not consider that white things are made of white atoms, black of black, or so on. In the former example, Lucretius switches between *albus* ('white') and *candidus* ('shining') – a form of poetic *variatio* that itself alludes to the transitory nature of colour discrimination.[83] Similarly, for black, he invents an intransitive verb *nigrare* ('to blacken'). Lucretius' poetic creativity in the domain of colour is underpinned by the recurrent metaphors of dyeing employed within the passage: Lucretius asks us to imagine a world in which 'bodies of matter' (*corpora materiai*) are 'dyed' (*tincta*, 736, 747) with some fundamental colour or made-up with cosmetics (*circumlita fuco*, 745). This line of argument reminds us of the doctrine of Theophrastus and the *De Coloribus*, for whom a material's colour could helpfully be conceptualised as a dye, or of Plato's *Timaeus* which imagined a world divinely painted with colour. However, Lucretius' claim is a clear one: 'there is no colour at all in the elements of matter, neither monochrome atoms nor varicoloured ones (*nullus enim color est omnino materiai / corporibus, neque par rebus neque denique dispar*, 737–8)'. At the atomic level, colour is not an integral part of the world, and so

[81] More recently, O'Hara (2007) ch. 3 has argued that inconsistency and fluidity of language and content in Lucretius is characteristic of epic tradition, and an intentionally provocative part of his Epicurean doctrine.

[82] Following the structural breakdown suggested by Bailey (1947).

[83] On the characteristic fluidity of poetic language and imagery in Lucretius, see West (1969) 79–93. Snyder (1980) 11–30 argues that, since Epicurean doctrine considered the nature of language as a kind of mirror of reality, verbal play was as integral to his philosophy as to his poetry. More recently on fluidity and inconsistency, see O'Hara (2007) ch. 3.

provides an unsteady platform for understanding the basic constituents of that world.

Proof 1. 748–56

All colours change, but atoms that change their colour would not be permanent foundations of things.[84] Line 749 appears to claim (although this is part of a damaged manuscript[85]) that any colour at all can change into any other (*omnis enim color omnino mutatur in omnis*). Colour, then, is fluid and transitory. Lucretius ends with a warning: take care not to steep in colour (*colore ... contingas*) the seeds of things, lest all things come back utterly to nothing – an assertion that colour is not the most reliable indicator or measure of the world. Lucretius' choice of the verb *contingo* – a word which is sometimes used in the sense of 'contaminate' – implies a relationship between the art of dyeing (an activity attached to a long-established tradition of deceit and cosmetic trickery: see Chapter 6) and the creative use of colour in descriptive verse.[86] Later, at 797, Lucretius asserts that atoms are not 'veiled' (*uelata*) with colour, further alluding to the epistemological limitations of 'dressing up' matter with colour.

Proof 2. 757–94

Change of colour is better explained by colourless rather than coloured atoms. Colour is produced by variety of shapes and arrangements of atoms, the result of an external blow such as light, or the effect of wind on waves. This makes it easier to explain how black things might become white (like the sea when it is churned by wind). Once again, the poet is creative in his choice of colour categories (763–75):

> [If atoms are colourless, and colour derives from shape and arrangement], you could very easily explain instantly why those things which were of a black (*niger*)

[84] This is almost a translation of Epicurus, *Ep. Hdt.* 54.

[85] For details, Bailey (1947) 922. The *De Coloribus* had argued that materials could undergo comprehensive changes of colour.

[86] For the use of *contingo* elsewhere in this sense, see Lucr. 1.934 (*musaeo contingens cuncta lepore*) and 6.1188 (*croci contacta colore*).

colour just recently can suddenly take on a marbled gleam (*marmoreus candor*), as the sea when great winds have stirred up the surface is transformed into hoary (*canus*) waves with gleaming marble (*candens marmor*). For you could say that what we often see as black (*niger*), when its matter is mixed up and the order of its first beginnings changed, some being added, some taken away, immediately that is seen to be gleaming (*candens*) and white (*albus*). But if the surface of the sea were composed of blue seeds (*caerulea semina*), in no way could it become white (*albescere*). For however you may jumble up things that are blue (*caerulea*), they can never change into a marbled colour (*marmoreus color*).

'*Marmoreus*' is a category of colour applied to the sea and to human skin as a metaphor in verse.[87] Its use here by Lucretius, for a number of reasons, is innovative and bold, as is the transposition of substantive and adjective in 765 and 767. '*Caeruleus*' too is an almost exclusively poetic category, a colour denoting the deep blue sea (see above pp. 9–11). '*Canus*' – a word normally found describing grey or white hair – is likewise a creative poetic category, traditionally used to evoke the age or timelessness of the sea.[88] Lucretius plays a language game with his reader, his loose and versatile employment of colour categories (*niger, caeruleus, albus, marmoreus, candens, marmor, candor*) a smart and provocative demonstration of the transitory nature of colours. The passage is imbued with a certain amount of philosophical tension: colours do exist and are produced and changed by specific arrangements and movements of atoms, but they are a by-product rather than an inherent property of these atoms, which is why their recognition and classification on particular objects or phenomena can be inconsistent. Unlike Aristotle, Lucretius proposes no neat formulae for working out colours; they are well-suited to verse description, but not the tidy world of Epicurean atomism. Poetic ekphrasis, then, is exploited to underwrite the unstable and transitory nature of colour as a basic index of matter.

Having demonstrated that the atoms of any given thing cannot all be of one colour, Lucretius then investigates the possibility that they are of many different colours (again, *semina tincta colore*,

[87] Bradley (2006a) 5–8. For a philological interpretation of this passage and its colour categories, see Baran and Chişleag (1968) 162.

[88] See Christol (2002) 37–44, who is more concerned with identifying a precise hue equivalent for this category.

776). This theory would have it that all things contain within themselves atoms of many colours, but the colour of the whole is that of the *predominant* coloured atoms.[89] Lucretius, deploying the same experimental empiricism as that found in Theophrastus and the *De Coloribus*, suggests that – if this were the case – we ought to be able to see on the surface patches of different colour within the uniform colour of the whole.

Proof 3. 795–809

Colour cannot exist without light. Atoms never appear in light, and therefore cannot have colour.[90] Colour is created and changed as light strikes straight or slantwise (*recta aut obliqua*), which – Lucretius appears to be claiming – rearranges the surface atoms. One only has to look at the feathers on a dove's neck and the peacock's tail (801–9):[91]

> In this way the plumage of doves shows itself in the sun, which lies about the nape and makes a ring round the neck; for at times it becomes red (*rubra*) like the bright garnet (*clarus pyropus*), sometimes, under certain conditions of perception (*sensus*), it comes to appear a blend of blue (*caeruleum*) and green emeralds (*uirides zmaragdi*). And the tail of a peacock, when it is suffused with plentiful light, in a similar vein changes its *colores* as it turns to the light. Since these *colores* are caused by a certain impact of light (*ictus luminis*), you must not think that they can be produced without it.

Again, Lucretius exploits rich poetic ekphrasis and similes that combine visual comparison alongside associations of material splendour. References to the garnet, the emerald (and perhaps to the implied lapis lazuli of *caeruleum*) could have been drawn straight from the pages of Theophrastus.[92] Lucretius' example, however, cleverly undermines attempts by Theophrastus (and coincidentally by Pliny a hundred years later) to pin down colours and

[89] This may have been a theory proposed by Anaxagoras: τὴν χρόαν τὴν κρατοῦσαν (Theophr. *Sens.* 27, DK A. 92).

[90] So Epicurus in Plut. *Adv. Col.* 7.1110c.

[91] These were classic points of debate in visual epistemology: Cic. *Acad. Pr.* 2.7.19; 25.79; Plin. *HN* 37.72 (discussed below pp. 113–14); cf. Sen. *QNat.* 1.7.2 (above pp. 42–3).

[92] See Bailey (1947) 929. Plin. *HN* 34.94 on the *pyropus* (cf. Ov. *Met.* 2.2 *flammasque imitante pyropo*).

connect them fundamentally to material objects. The colour categories themselves are features of creative poetic ekphrasis: *ruber* finds its primary referent in the redness of the face, *caeruleus* in the deep blue sea; the similes offer further detachment from the physics of colour perception, but are not unfamiliar in hexameter verse.[93] Herein lies the *ratio* (807) of dove and peacock colours – fluid, unstable, transitory.

Nevertheless, atomic shapes and configurations are finite, as Lucretius earlier claimed (478–521). If they were infinite, all that is now beautiful in colour would be far surpassed by new colours – 'for then you would see barbarian clothes and gleaming Meliboean purple (*purpura*), dyed (*tacta*) with the *color* of Thessalian conches, and the golden generations (*aurea saecla*) of peacocks steeped in smiling beauty, lie outdone by some new colour of things (*nouus color rerum*, 500–3)'. Same for smells, tastes and sounds. This connects to Lucretius' idea that some *colores* are objectively attractive (see below).

Proof 4. 810–16

Different films impact on the pupil of the eye and produce the sensation of different colours. Touch or contact depends on form not on colour, so first-beginnings (*principia*) have no need of colours. Primary physical shape of atoms is what matters in all cases. Here, Lucretius is drawing upon a principle maintained by Democritus and developed by Aristotle that all the senses can be reduced to *touch*. Atomic films *touch* the eye, and produce the sensation of colour dependent on the shape of those atoms.

This argument recalls a short section on the aesthetics of sensation earlier in book 2, where Lucretius explains that some things please the taste buds, ear drums and eyes, and others displease, because of the shapes of the atoms which penetrate (*penetrare*) the sense organs: on colour, 'do not suppose that good colours (*boni colores*) which are able to feed our eyes consist of the same seed as those which sting the gaze (*acies*) and force tears, or look dreadful and vile in their foul appearance (*foeda species*)' (418–21). Some

[93] On *rubor* as 'blush', see Bradley (2004).

colours are by nature pleasing, others displeasing – depending on how offensive the shape of the atoms is. A little later (679–87) Lucretius argues that any one object must *per se* be composed of different shapes, because things can possess colour (here, *fucus*), taste and smell simultaneously, but they reach the senses in different ways: *nidor enim penetrat qua fucus non it in artus, / fucus item sorsum, sorsum sapor insinuatur / sensibus* (683–6).

Moreover, in his last reference to *color* in book 4 (706–21), Lucretius argues that sight, like all the other senses, can affect different creatures in different ways: *species rerum atque colores / non ita conueniunt ad sensus omnibus omnes* (707–8).[94] This is why certain *colores* can be stinging (*acria*) for some, but not for others. Lucretius goes on to qualify his point by using the example of the cock (*gallus*) which strikes fear into the eyes of lions, because there are seeds (*semina*) on the bodies of cocks which penetrate (*interfodiunt*) the eyes of lions and cause stinging pain (*acer dolor*), although they do not penetrate and sting human eyes (715–17). The theory is not extended to engage in the idea explored by Parmenides and Anaxagoras, and developed by Protagoras and certain Platonic dialogues, that different human perceivers experience the world in different ways, but Lucretius does make an important contribution to the theories of the continuity of perception between humans and animals.[95] Animals carried no less capacity for sensory perception than humans, although the receiving pores could be very different, allowing evaluations of the world to differ considerably between species.

Proof 5. 817–25

Since no definite colour is allotted to each fixed atomic shape, and all kinds of atomic configurations may be found in things of every colour, why are there no examples of every colour in each species of creature, such as white crows or black swans?

[94] By *colores*, Lucretius refers to the films that give the primary experience of an object to the eye (*species atque colores* can be read as hendiadys).

[95] Though see 4.332–6, which argues that seeds of yellow from the bodies of jaundiced individuals cause them to see everything yellow.

This is a condensed and consequently difficult proof. Lucretius does not suggest that atoms of a certain shape (*figura*) give off a certain *color* (e.g. square atoms were always red), but his point is that if atoms were themselves coloured, there is no reason why in any given species there should not be every variety of colour. No answer is offered.

Proof 6. 826–33

The smaller the pieces into which a thing is separated, the more its *color* is seen to disappear. To illustrate this, he takes the example of sea-purple cloth (*purpura*) and 'scarlet' (*poeniceus*), the brightest colour of all (*color clarissimu' multo*, 830). A piece of purple cloth (*austrum*) torn up thread by thread (*filatim*) loses all its colour; particles would breathe away (*efflare*) all their *color* before the 'seeds of things' (*semina rerum*) were reached. The purple, then, is the characteristic *color* and the material becomes 'colourless' when *color purpureus* is no longer there. This would presumably be true also of the white swan. As before, the dye analogy reinforces the idea that *color* is an incidental and transitory property, rather than a fixed property of atoms.

Proof 7. 834–41

Things may be without colour just as much as they can be without sound or smell. The intelligent mind can recognise the former as it can the latter. A final empirical proof: silent things have no sound, unscented have no smell, and invisible have no colour. Lucretius, then, was still embracing the assumption that colour is the first condition of visibility.

Lucretius then moves on to a very short section summarising how the atoms are without other secondary qualities: heat, sound, moisture or smell. He ends with a six-line aphorism (859–64) that secondary qualities – heat, sound, smell, taste, moisture and colour – are perishable (*mortalia*). They must be separated from first-beginnings (*principia*), so that you do not find all things passing back utterly to nothing (*ne tibi res redeant ad nilum funditus omnes*, 864).

Lucretius picks up colour once again in the *De Rerum Natura*, in a discussion of films (*simulacra*) in book 4, thrown off the surface of things to produce vision.[96] Lucretius argues that heat and smoke discharged from certain objects are evidence of *simulacra*, like the skins shed by crickets and snakes. On the evidence of colour, Lucretius chooses a familiar and vivid example from Roman public life (72–89):

> For certainly we see many things casting off particles in abundance, not only from the depths and deep within, as we said before [about smoke and heat], but also often *color* from the outermost surface (*de summis*). Commonly, awnings of yellow (*lutea*) and red (*russa*) and rusty colours (*ferrugina*) do this, when spread out over great theatres and stretched for the folk (*uolgata*) they flutter (*fluitant*) trembling over posts and beams. For there the assembly of the hollow below and the whole appearance (*species*) of the stage and the distinguished throng of the senators, they dye (*inficiunt*) and force to flutter (*fluitare*) in their own *color*. The more closely the walls of the theatre are shut in all round, the more everything within laughs drenched with beauty (*perfusa lepore*), when the daylight has been shut out. Therefore, since canvas radiates colour (*fucus*) from its outermost surface (*de summo*), everything else must also throw off thin films (*effigiae*), since in either case they cast off from the surface (*ex summo*). There are therefore specific traces of shapes (*certa uestigia formarum*) which flit about everywhere (*uolgo*), made up of fine texture, but singly and separately cannot be seen.

It can be no accident that Lucretius has selected a theatrical setting to illustrate the phenomenon of colour films. Lucretius spells out with sometimes awkward lexemes the connection of colour sensationalism and the crowd: *uolgo* (75), *uolgata* (77), *uolgo* (88).[97] Once again, the metaphor of dyeing is prevalent: *inficiunt* (80), *perfusa* (82) and the choice of *fucus* (84) to denote *color*. The verb *fluitare*, normally used to refer to flowing water, also underpins the transitive force of the colour spectacle.[98] The effect of the coloured

[96] Book 2 deals generally with the motion and shape of atoms up to the level of the compound; book 4 discusses (by taking the atomic phenomena up to the level of the human) a variety of psychological phenomena, including perception, and is a pointed attack on scepticism. For a critical analysis of Lucretius' account of vision in book 4, see Sharples (2002).

[97] The imagery of the theatre in Lucretius is discussed by West (1969) 35–48; on this particular passage, see 38–41 ('the man who is mad on the theatre, so mad that not just his dreams, but even his waking after-images visual and aural, are full of its glitter and excitement').

[98] On the transfusion of terms in Lucretius (as well as dyeing metaphors), see West (1969) 43–8.

awnings, then, is described from the perspective of the uneducated crowd and glamourised in hexameter verse. As Epicurus put it, what the eye perceives is not the individual image (*eidōlon*), but the impression (*phantasia*) produced by the quick succession of many *eidōla*.[99] Colours migrate, and the language and setting that Lucretius chooses to illustrate this principle underpin the idea that colour is a secondary, transitory feature of the world.

Lucretius goes on to explain that smell, smoke and heat are diffused since they come from the interior of things and are therefore torn apart in their route to the outside. When a thin film of colour comes off the surface (*tenuis summi membrana coloris*, 95), on the other hand, there is nothing to tear it. Colour is an image (*simulacrum*) of the surface: *de summis* (74), *de summo* (84), *ex summo* (86) etc. It lies 'in front and on the very outside (*in promptu quoniam est in prima fronte locata*)', 97. Following the traditional definition, *color* was the primary object of vision, a surface appearance which encapsulated the visual aspect of the original object in its entirety.[100] Lucretius' example from the theatre, then, is halfway between example and analogy in vindication of his theory of *simulacra*. The *simulacrum* reproduces both the colour and the form of the original object. The awnings make the features of the theatre undulate with colour in the same way that they themselves undulate (*fluitare*). The *color* of the awnings reproduces itself in hue and form on the theatre.

Lucretius' theatrical spectacle was an innovative example, and one not readily available to Epicurus himself. The Roman theatre appears to have been undergoing something of a revolution in the first century BC and the awning formed a popular and familiar visual motif.[101] The colours were vivid, but cheap. *Luteus* was a basic 'yellow' popularly used for the dresses of women, *russus* was a coarse red, and *ferruginus* a cheap imitation of *purpureus*; all these textile colours were paraded here on an unprecedented

99 Epicurus, *Ep. Hdt.* 49–50.

100 Cf. 4.265–8, where Lucretius argues that, when we touch a stone, we do not feel just the *extremus summusque color* but the combined effects of the inner layers of the stone. Here *color* very clearly denotes that external *simulacrum* (rather than what we mean by 'colour'). See also Long and Sedley (1987) 77.

101 Mentioned again by Lucretius at 6.109; see also references in Prop. 3.18.13; 4.1.15. The *uela* are a typical example of imperial *luxuria* at Plin. *HN* 19.23–5.

scale.[102] The importance of the imagery featured in this passage is also underpinned by the setting of the theatre, where image and imitation are native concepts; the *species scaenai* (the *display* of the stage, 79) reminds us aptly of the performance culture fostered here, and the clever games of Lucretius' own literary and linguistic performance. The theatre too was the location for aesthetics and spectacle, the place to learn about the world through perception and analysis.

Summary

Lucretius held the senses (including the perception of colour) to be a basis for truth and knowledge. This assertion is made in the face of the far-reaching contemporary scepticism of the New Academics, closely echoing Epicurus' attack on modes of scepticism that were around in his own day (4.469–521).[103] Lucretius' argument: we must have some infallible standard for truth and falsehood, and what standard can be more certain than sensation? Reason cannot refute the senses, since it arises from them.

It can be argued that Lucretius' philosophy of perception follows the orthodox Epicurean doctrine, and may not take into account contemporary developments in thinking. However, the *De Rerum Natura* was produced at a time when diverse philosophical schools were converging in Italy, and readers are likely to have compared and contrasted other schools of thought, particularly the New Academics and the Stoics. Its doctrine considered *color* (alongside other qualities) to be a secondary feature triggered by the shape, size, arrangement and movement of atoms. It was, then, a by-product, and (so Lucretius implies) more subject to interpretation and error than form.[104] This doctrine however differed from Democritus, in implying that *color* was a real, and finite, feature or 'accident' of atom position and location, rather than simply a subjective interpretation. Lucretius set *color* as the primary object

[102] For references, see André (1949) 84 (*russus*); 107 (*ferruginus*); 151–3 (*luteus*).
[103] See Sedley (1998) 85–7.
[104] Though at 4.324–78 more of the optical illusions are to do with form rather than with colour.

of sight (just as he dealt with heat, sound, taste and smell as the sensations of other sense organs). It was the visible property of an object, and therefore – as Lucretius sometimes means it – the outward appearance (*simulacrum*) of the object.

Lucretius exploits various poetic forms and techniques (inventing verbs like *nigro*; exploiting similes and metaphors of dyeing, veiling and cosmetics; describing the surface of the sea simultaneously as *niger*, *caeruleus*, *marmoreus* or *canus*) to demonstrate the transitory nature of *color* and underwrite its secondariness as a by-product of atomic arrangement. By writing in epic hexameter, he was in an ideal position to explore Epicurean doctrine about perception: creative and imaginative expressions of colour were well suited to verse, and this medium allowed Lucretius to explore provocatively the epistemological difficulties of colour perception and the fluidity of colour as a measure of things. This said, colour was not entirely in the mind, and the trained observer could use it as a source of information about the world. Atomic films, for example, *touched* the eye, and (because *color* is a product of the shape of atoms) Lucretius felt able to claim that some colours are objectively pleasing or displeasing, depending on how offensive the shapes of the atoms are that penetrate the eye. In the examples he chooses to illustrate this point, it is clear that *color* can refer to the general visual 'aspect' of an object (e.g. the *color* of a cock scaring the lion, the *color* of awnings undulating over the theatre). Although Lucretius emphasised the difficulties inherent to colour discrimination, he recognised that sensation channelled in the right direction was the only way of reaching the truth. Lucretius sometimes described the world in theatrical terms, where the spectator can look upon the inscrutable colours of the ocean and the Roman theatre, and the strangeness of the lion and the cock, and (with Epicurean guidance) use these examples as a kit for working out the fundamentals of nature.

3

PLINY THE ELDER AND THE UNNATURAL HISTORY OF *COLOR*

Colour is a dominant feature of Pliny's *Natural History*. As well as being a fundamental component of philosophical epistemology (in which Pliny himself was deeply interested), it is also a central characteristic of atmospheric phenomena, botanic chlorophyl, species of livestock, bodily malfunctions, earths, minerals, stones and so on. This chapter will examine how some of the principles and themes arising from the philosophical study of colour perception were translated into a different genre of Roman literature. As well as providing a commentary on imperial Rome's advanced state of material cornucopia and all the difficulties of classification that brought with it, Pliny's *Natural History* wrestled with the ethics and morality of contemporary art and the relationship between the Roman viewer and the natural world. Pliny's discussion of coloured marbles, which exposes a number of these themes, has received some detailed attention in recent years. This chapter will summarise this research, and then focus on two underexploited sections of the *Natural History* in which Pliny examines the role of colour: first, his treatment of artistic pigments in book 35, and secondly his extraordinary discussion of gemstones in book 37, which concludes the work.

While traditional archaeological and art-historical scholarship envisaged the *Natural History* as a patchwork of awkward and incoherent digressions, recent years have seen a sequence of publications reinstating Pliny's work in its own right as a coherent and comprehensible view of nature in the service of man.[1] Pervading the *Natural History* (published in AD 77) we can detect a nexus of

[1] See for example *CHCL* 2:670–2; Norden (1909) 314 on Pliny's tortuous style; Lloyd (1983) 136–49. 'Modern' assessments of Pliny start with Gros (1979); Locher (1986); Isager (1986) and (1991); Beagon (1992); De Oliveira (1992); Healy (1999). More recently, Carey (2003); Sinclair (2003); Murphy (2003) and (2004), arguing for the vast literary debt of the work. On Pliny's career, Beagon (1992) 6–10; Maxwell-Stuart (1996).

related social, political and moral themes which themselves intersect with a long tradition of natural philosophy dating back to the Pre-Socratics, Aristotle and Theophrastus.[2] His Stoic ideas about the divinity of Nature work hand in hand with a typically Peripatetic empirical approach to natural historical investigation.[3] Furthermore, some have interpreted Pliny's style and appropriation of themes as displaying complex subtleties, satires and cynical subnarratives.[4]

The chapters on the history of art (books 33–37) have – unsurprisingly – attracted the most attention, both from the old critical commentaries and the new redemptive scholarship. The central themes in these books, and indeed in the work as a whole, have been the relationship of Man (the inventor and artist) and Nature, and the use and abuse of art – particularly by good and bad emperors (often simplified to anti-Neronian/pro-Flavian). Isager (1991) offered a compelling thematic framework for reading these books: invention and luxury; private and public; Greece and Rome; rise and decline. Pliny's central thesis was that man may exploit nature within moral limits or to immoral excess, but that Nature exists for the benefit of man.[5] For Pliny, *luxuria* – excesses in wall-decoration, furniture, clothes, gems, perfumes, slaves etc. – is a site for moral attack on the grounds that it constitutes on the part of mankind an abuse of nature in rivalling her variety and power. In this anthropocentrism, Pliny finds precedence in the theories of the Peripatetics, and even the theory of Lucretius that man uses the environment to make sense of the world. He contemplated nature as a *spectaculum*, something to look at and learn from.[6] He also offers evidence for, and is himself symptomatic of, a rich specialised tradition of literary discourse on

[2] Which is not to say, as does the *OCD*³, that Pliny was not a philosopher. For a full treatment of the philosophical background to the *Natural History*, see Marchetti (1992).

[3] Healy (1999) 58–60 on whole sections of Theophrastus' *De Lapidibus* translated verbatim. He also made full use of Aristotle's *Meteorologica* 1–3 and 4, as well as Posidonius' works on the formation of stones. On the arrangement and exposition of knowledge in the *Natural History* as part of a broader representation of Roman imperial culture, see Murphy (2004).

[4] For example, De Oliveira (1992) esp. 343.

[5] On Pliny's culture–nature dichotomy, see Wallace-Hadrill (1990).

[6] Beagon (1992) 76–9 (abuse); 47, 153–6 (*spectaculum*).

artistic culture that had developed since the early third century BC. This discourse reveals a sophisticated appreciation of the role of colour in artistic ekphrasis, and a philosophical polemic about the mismatch between perception and truth in contemporary art.[7]

Marbles

Pliny remarked that in his day (the 70s) the types and appearances of marble (*marmorum genera et colores*) were well known.[8] He casually describes marble from Sparta (*marmor Lacedaemonium*) as 'verdant' (*uiride*) – it is, he explains, more lively than all other marbles (*cunctis hilarius*). He goes on to specify that Egyptian *porphyrites* 'blushes' (*rubet*). Pliny's epistemological handbook of geology, however, is most concerned with connecting *color* (what one *sees*) with *genus* (what the material fundamentally *is*). Virtually all locations around the world (he goes on) had *suum marmor* – their own trademark marble (*quoto cuique enim loco non suum marmor inuenitur?*), and he devotes significant sections of book 36 to classifying and describing these marbles. By fusing the imperialist vocabulary of marble provenance with creative associations of colour, Pliny sets the intellectual benchmark for the educated elite of the early Empire. Marble-watching was a complex and highly sophisticated process that evoked a wide range of aesthetic, cultural and ethnographic associations.

At the same time, Pliny (like his contemporary Seneca) expresses a certain amount of discomfort with this contemporary fascination with marbles – a characteristic lunacy (*insania morum*), as he puts it.[9] Opening book 36, he imagines mountains as joints (*compages*) holding together the bowels (*uiscera*) of the earth; quarrying them and carving them into a thousand types of marble (*mille genera marmorum*), removing nature's boundaries (*termini*) and transporting mountain ranges across the sea was the height of cultural perversity (1–2).[10] He goes on to lament that 'men do such things – even put up with

[7] See Rouveret *et al.* (2006) 9 and Prioux (2006) on this theme.

[8] Plin. *HN* 36.55.

[9] Ibid. 36.1.

[10] Pliny's idioms in this section are aggressive – conquering, smashing, slicing away (*domare, frangere, caedere*). The association of marbles with imperial conquest, technology and phenomenal effort is a typical theme: see Strabo 12.8.14 and Bradley (2006a) esp. 2–5; cf. Maugan-Chemin (2006).

them – for no other use or pleasure than to recline amid the stains (*maculae*) of marbles, just as if these delights were not taken from them by the darkness of night which makes up half of each man's life' (3).[11]

In addition to berating the displacement of mountain ranges to satisfy the aesthetic fancies of Roman connoisseurs, Pliny elsewhere expresses his frustration at the Neronian trend for painting patterns onto marble surfaces (*lapidem pingere*): 'a plan was discovered to give variety to unity by inserting 'stains' (*maculae*) that were not present in the marble patterns, so that Numidian marble might display oval lines and Synnadic marble might be picked out with sea-purple dye – just as contemporary pretensions would have them be naturally (*ut ouatus esset Numidicus, ut purpura distingueretur Synnadicus, qualiter illos nasci optassent deliciae*)'.[12] Not only were parts of the earth being displaced and reconstituted in entirely unnatural contexts, but the very patterns and colours that made those surfaces recognisable were being manipulated and altered: *uarietas* replaced *unitas* in the form of stains (*maculae*), egg shapes and patches of purple dye. Contemporary material culture was bombarding the senses with a series of contradictory messages and this aesthetic saturation challenged the ability of vision to understand the world around it. Pliny demonstrates that describing and discussing marble could be as hotly contested as talking about geography, imperialism or morality. The challenge the natural historian of imperial Rome faced, then, was to educate his readers to identify all these stones and appreciate them for what they really were.

For the purpose of this exercise, 'colour' (i.e. what the stone *looked like*) was something of an intellectual red herring, subject to misuse and the flimsy world of aesthetic connoisseurship. The

[11] Cf. *HN* 36.46 on *uersicolores maculae* on marbles, and Dworakowska (1973).

[12] *HN* 35.3. Cf. Vitr. *De arch.* 7.5.1 on painters imitating the variations and arrangements of marble inlays (*crustarum marmorearum uarietates et conlocationes*). Cf. the architectural trend in Africa, Sicily, Sardinia and Italy of arranging marble/glass *tesserae* to imitate single marble tiles of *giallo antico*, *rosso antico*, *cipollino*, various granites and even red porphyry: see Michaelides (1985) 155–6; Bianchi *et al.* (2002); Falzone (2002) 171–5 and 464–70 for illustrations. For various aspects of the use of paint on marble sculpture, see Bradley (2009a).

aesthetic illusions of one particular polished stone in the *Domus Aurea* caught the eye – and the critical tongue – of Pliny (36.163):

Nerone principe in Cappadocia repertus est lapis duritia marmoris, candidus atque tralucens etiam qua parte fuluae inciderant uenae, ex argumento phengites appellatus. hoc construxerat aedem Fortunae quam Seiani appellant, a Seruio rege sacratum, amplexus aurea domo; quae etiam foribus opertis interdiu claritas ibi diurna erat alio quam specularium modo tamquam inclusa luce, non transmissa.

During Nero's principate there was discovered in Cappadocia a stone as hard as marble (*lapis duritia marmoris*), shining white (*candidus*) and, even where 'yellow' (*fuluae*) veins occurred, translucent – for this reason it was called 'phengites'. Of this stone, Nero rebuilt the temple of Fortune, known as the shrine of Sejanus, but originally consecrated by King Servius and incorporated by Nero in his Golden House. In the daytime it was as light as day there, even when the doors were shut; but the effect was not that of glass (*lapis specularis*), since the light was, so to speak, trapped within rather than allowed to pass through.

That a type of stone used in the *Domus Aurea* could project an illusion of daylight, could make inside seem like outside, was one more example of Pliny's frustration at the sensory bedlam at work in Neronian Rome.[13] This *lapis* was a sensational medium for *Domus* architecture which not only imported a real bit of Cappadocia all the way into Rome, but also upset some of the common categories of perception (daylight indoors, both *fuluus* and *tralucens*, 'glassy' and yet light-absorbent). Its perceptual complexity complemented the monument's difficult history. This stone was anathema even to specialists like Pliny who were familiar with minerals such as *lapis specularis*; furthermore, the hazy and difficult categories *candidus*

[13] Cf. Luciani and Sperduti (1993) 50 on *phengites*: 'utilizzata nella *Domus Aurea* per filtrare e colorare la luce diurna all' interno delle stanze' and Ward-Perkins (1956) 215; Sen. *Controv.* 2.1.12. The illusory and contradictory deployment of coloured surfaces and materials by Nero and his regime is a recurring topos throughout the *Natural History*: cf. 19.24 on Nero's temporary amphitheatre covered by awnings that were *colore* caeli, as well as *stellata*; 33.90 on Nero's circus spectacles, where the sand was sprinkled with a type of gold dust and the emperor as a charioteer dressed in a golden mantle. This theme is also exploited at Cassius Dio 62.3.4–6 on Nero's reception and crowning of Tiridates in a specially adorned theatre, where the readers' senses are saturated with images of gold and gilding (ἐκεχρύσωτο ... χρυσῷ ἐκεκόσμητο ... ἡμέραν χρυσῆν), sea-purple awnings (ἁλουργα) and an embroidered figure of Nero driving a chariot, with golden stars (ἀστέρες χρυσοῖ) gleaming (ἐπέλαμπον) all about him.

and *fuluus* failed to express fully its appearance. *Phengites* was a visual anomaly – another barrier for Pliny's essential project to connect perception and geological knowledge. This material (or one very similar) also used to line the walls of Domitian's colonnades so that he could see in its brilliant surface the reflections of what happened behind him.[14] Phengites lent itself to visual manipulation, one of the trademarks of a corrupt ruler.

Pliny was not alone in finding the aesthetics of marble challenging and problematic. His contemporary Seneca, a spokesman for Stoic approaches to the material world, considered marble-watching a childish pursuit, a deceitful drug for the eyes (*Epistle* 115.8–9):[15]

> [Children] are pleased by the smooth and variegated pebbles (*calculi leues et aliquid habentes uarietatis*) which they pick up on the beach, while we take delight in the spots (*maculae*) of enormous columns brought either from Egyptian sands or African deserts to hold up a portico or a dining room large enough to contain a population; we admire walls veneered with plates of marble (*tenue marmor*), although we know what sort of material is being concealed. We cheat our own eyesight, and when we have overlaid our ceilings with gold, what else is it but a lie in which we take such delight? For we know that beneath this gold there lurks some rotten wood.

Elsewhere, Seneca contrasts the dark, simple bath-house of Scipio Africanus with the typical contemporary establishment; pools lined with *Thasius lapis* (once, Seneca reminisces, a *spectaculum* even in a temple), *marmora Alexandrina* set off by *marmor Numidicum*, all 'embroidered' (*praetexitur*) by difficult patterns and variegated like paintings (*operosa et in picturae modum uariata circumlitio praetexitur*).[16] This discourse – aesthetic *qua* aesthetic – was a childish one, non-functional, non-didactic. Seneca's exegesis highlights a second dimension to this perceptual decay: marble veneering was an expanding phenomenon, and one that gave the illusion of solid marble. Marble plating (*tenue marmor*), claims Seneca, was

[14] Suet. *Dom.* 14.4: *e cuius splendore imagines quidquid a tergo fieret prouideret.*

[15] Part of an examination of the relationship between literary style and moral character, written towards the end of 64 (see Préchac (1914) 232; Morford (1968) 175–7).

[16] Sen. *Ep.* 86.6. Cf. Suet. *Ner.* 31.2 on all parts of the *Domus Aurea* 'smeared' with gold (*cuncta auro lita*).

(like gilding) a visual lie (*mendacium*) – one cannot really believe what one sees; all that lies beneath marble and gold, he elsewhere argues, is slavery (*seruitus*).[17] A generation later, Juvenal pictures one Umbricius leaving the polyglot and corrupt city he has come to loathe (*Satires* 3.17–20); he describes the valley of Egeria and its caves as surreal (*dissimiles ueris*) and longs for green grass (*uiridis herba*) by the river, rather than the foreign *marmora* that insult the native rock (*ingenuum tofum*).[18]

Imperial marbles, then, offered contemporaries a fertile playing field for exploring the relationship between colour, matter and culture. Marble had become one of the most evocative manifestations of empire and luxury, and it is little surprise that Pliny devotes so much space and moral reflection to it. How his aristocratic peers classified and described those marbles, and how far those classifications and descriptions did justice to the inherent nature of the material, was a central concern. Colours, patterns and metaphors characterised the language of contemporary aesthetics, and (as Pliny's account of Neronian *phengites* or Seneca's spotty marble columns demonstrate) this language was lacking in didactic purpose or function. Taken to its extreme, this fad could cheat one's eyesight: Pliny's painted marbles and Seneca's marble veneering both gave false impressions, interfering with what both considered the proper objective of the senses. Marble and colour had an uneasy relationship.

[17] *Ep.* 90.10; cf. 90.45 talking about earlier generations: *illi quidem non aurum nec argentum nec perlucidos lapides in ima terrarum faece quarebant*. They were also free from *uestes pictae*. On Seneca and marble, see Pensabene (2000). His father had also explored similar themes at *Controv.* 2.1.12–13, where he attacks the contemporary fad for gilding private roofs (*infusum tectis aurum*), as well as floor mosaics and varied panels of marble (*uarius lapis*) cut in order to conceal (*tegit*) walls with a thin exterior (*tenuis frons*): such base imitations (*praua imitamenta*), he argues, are no substitute for the real thing (*uera*). He goes on to connect the imitation of *montes siluaeque* in wall-paintings in order to conceal rotting houses, as well as *uiridia*, *maria* and *amnes* amid the gloom and smoke (he can scarcely believe the owners have ever actually seen real woods or fields that are 'green with grass' (*uirentes gramine*)). The same theme of gilding, veneering and deception is explored by Lucian; see Gassino (2002) esp. 173–4. On veneers and chromatic deception in Classical Greek art, see Duigan (2004) 81. Some of the issues surrounding descriptions of the Roman countryside and the representation of colour in contemporary garden-paintings are explored at length by Trinquier (2006).

[18] See Edwards (1996) 125–9.

Pigments

Book 35 of the *Natural History* is an essay on the history of painting, as well as the exploitation of nature to acquire a wide range of pigments. It follows two books documenting the cultural use and abuse of metals in Greco-Roman art and architecture. For Pliny, colour lay at the heart of the visuals of painting and belonged properly to the discourse of earth sciences, minerals and pigments. Book 35, then, is a technical manual, packed with technical categories of pigments, real earths and dyes from real places, produced using often complex and expensive methods. Like Lucretius, Pliny had set out to provide an explanation and interpretation of the *spectacula* of the world – one can enjoy a painting of verdant greenery, but one must aim to understand both what that 'greenness' represents and how it is produced.

The ethical background to book 35 was the contemporary decay of art in imperial Rome, the elaboration of painting, and the replacement of simple wall-paintings with extravagant embossed metals and engraved marbles (35.2–3). The abuse of resources, the influence of Nero, the disrespect shown to natural *spectacula* – Pliny quickly sets the agenda. The painted ancestor-masks (*imagines*) of old Roman *uirtus* have been replaced with expensive and artificial portraits of strangers (4–5). After a sketchy Roman history of portraits in public places, Pliny moves on to the subject of painting: an Egyptian invention passed on to the Greeks, he suggests sceptically. He then imagines (15) an evolutionary (or devolutionary) history of painting where outline drawings were succeeded by monochrome (*monochromaton/singuli colores*), and then by the more elaborate (*operosior*) style of polychrome.

Pliny's introduction of *color* as an artistic medium makes it clear that he believes form to precede colour. This reproduces feelings voiced by Aristotle (*Poetics* 1450b) and Vitruvius (7.5) that drawing was more fundamental than colour, and that brilliant colours are no substitute for craftsmanship. The image can exist without the *color* (line-drawing itself lacks *color*). Pliny then proceeds to describe early line-drawings that were simply filled in with the *color* of powdered earthenware (the formulation of *color* as pigment is commonplace in the *Natural History*).[19] He goes on (17–28) to trace the rapid development of painting in Etruria and Rome (mentioning the Fabius *Pictor* clan who first painted in the temple of Salus in 304 BC). In Rome, Pliny observes, paintings appear to have served as trophies (*trophaea*) and *spectacula* for a sequence of ambitious politicians and conquerors.

Then at 29, Pliny begins his treatment of pigments proper. He had, he reminds us, already in book 33 (discussing metals) touched upon the use of *minium*, a prized red pigment discovered in silver mines, for monochrome paintings.[20] This was for the old Romans a sacred pigment (*sacrum pigmentum*, 33.111) used to highlight the face of the statue of Jupiter Optimus Maximus, along with triumphing generals, added to unguents at festivals, and the ritual pigment prescribed by censors for paintings of Jupiter. Book 33 recounts how the *Aethiopes* also coloured (*tingi*) their leaders and their gods entirely with *minium*. This was their *color*, he states explicitly (*hunc ibi deorum simulacris colorem esse*, 112). The purest type of *minium* is found in the Cilbian territory beyond Ephesus, where the sand has the *color* of the kermes insect (*harena cocci colorem habente*, 114). The production of the finest *minium*, he claims, is a long and arduous process; he goes on (115–16) to claim that he is not surprised that such importance was attached to this pigment (*auctoritatem colori fuisse non mirror*). 'Red earth' (*rubrica*) was valued as far back as Trojan times, as Homer testifies when he recommends it for ships. This the Greeks call *miltos*, and *minium* they call '*cinnabar*' – the source of *error* (Pliny asserts), since 'Indian cinnabar' (*Indica cinnabar*) is in fact the name of the gore of a snake crushed by the weight of dying elephants, when the blood of each animal is thoroughly mixed together; there is no other *color*, he asserts, which properly represents blood in a painting.[21] This suspiciously cool digression on the production of 'Indian cinnabar' is one of many accounts in Pliny of far-fetched techniques employed in the creation of artistic materials; some

[19] Cf. 35.57, 64 ([Zeuxis] *pinxit et monochromata ex albo*).

[20] By focusing on *minium* in a book on metals, Pliny effectively re-situates the pigment in its natural place of origin. On Pliny's discussion of *purpura* in book 9 (on aquatic biology), see below pp. 193–7.

[21] On *miltos* as a Classical Greek cosmetic, see Hannah (2004).

scholars have observed sustained levels of cynicism in Pliny's work at the extent to which man will go to reproduce appearances.[22] Nevertheless, the implication is that the reader should recognise that each *color* in painting has a story behind it, and only through learning from Pliny and appreciating the origin and nature of the pigments can one achieve a true understanding of what one sees. Furthermore, the principle that particular pigments should be used to reproduce particular features in painting is especially significant (e.g. a pigment containing blood used to depict blood): Pliny's didactic manual, therefore, performs an important function for the accurate appreciation of art. The distinctions between the categories of pigment, however, are subtle ones: one should aim to appreciate the difference between *rubrica*, *minium* and *Indica cinnabar*, but perhaps not take the distinctions too seriously. Roman material culture was over-sated with diversity.

Back to book 35. Introducing his catalogue of pigments, he claims that some *colores* are 'sombre' (*austeri*), and some 'florid' (*floridi*). This depends either on their *natura* (i.e. the natural substance which forms them) or their *mixtura* (the artificial processes out of which they are derived). Precisely what the categories *austeri* and *floridi* mean is unclear, although the short list of the latter – *minium, Armenium, cinnabaris, chrysocolla, Indicum* and *purpurissum* – suggest (particularly in the light of what Pliny goes on to say) that they all fall under the category of what we might call 'bright reds'.[23] *Colores austeri*, on the other hand, are more subdued and more conservative. This division at least appears to be an aesthetic one; pigment identification in this artistic register performs little function. But then Pliny gets down to basics and offers a further set of divisions: some *colores* are natural (earths occurring naturally with that *color*) and some are artificial (*ex omnibus alii nascuntur, alii fiunt*, 30).

Pliny begins his description of pigments with an account of Sinopis, a basic red iron oxide from Pontus that often replaced *minium*. He describes it: lumps of Sinopis carry their own *color*, but

[22] Pliny also mentions *minium* could be adulterated by goat's blood. On the theme of cynical sub-narratives, see De Oliveira (1992), esp. 343.

[23] On *colores floridi/austeri* and the imprecision of their use, see Brécoulaki (2006) esp. 36–9.

are speckled on the outside (*glaebis suus colos, extra maculosus*). The meaning is not easy: Pliny is suggesting that its distinctive *color* – what *makes* it Sinopis – is essentially the visual property of the substance itself. He goes on to observe that the ancestors used to use it to create splendour (*hac usi sunt ueteres ad splendorem*); in other words, its artistic trademark was its potential to represent light and luminosity. There are three types of Sinopis, he says: 'red' (*rubra*), 'less red' (*minus rubens*) and somewhere in the middle (*inter has media*). It is hard to decide if Pliny here was exploiting technical trading categories, or if these were colour observations in more general circulation, but the pigment appears to be represented in artistic gradations of redness based on brightness or intensity. This makes sense for viewing the painting in which the pigment is used: what one is looking for in a lump of Sinopis is the glow of blood or blush.[24] One further type – the 'chickpea' variety – is 'redder' than the rest (*magis ceteris rubet*). What Pliny broadly classifies as *rubrica*, then, is an earth pigment used in art and linguistically tied up with its capacity to reproduce in artistic images things where one would expect *rubor*.

Next Pliny deals with 'white pigments' (*candidi colores*, 36–40). The first type he describes is *Paraetonium*, again a category of provenance and reportedly a product of hardened sea-foam (*spumam maris esse dicunt soldatam*). Here, Pliny demonstrates a need to situate pigments categorically within the natural materials from which they are derived. He writes 'this is the most greasy (*pinguissimum*) of all the *candidi colores*, and the most tenacious (*tenacissimum*) for plaster on account of its smoothness (36)'. The adjective *pinguissimum* is a clear indication that Pliny's *color* is here synonymous with *pigmentum* (he goes on to describe the weight of colours: *nec sunt alii colores maioris ponderis*, 40). Like *rubrica*, Pliny henceforth uses the substantive *candidum* to describe his pigments, a reminder to his readers that he is drawing upon an artistic register, where *color* is a real thing valued for its capacity to produce a particular visual effect. This type of category, however, is not always reliable: Pliny proceeeds to describe how

[24] On '*rubor*', see Bradley (2004). Hannah (2004) discusses the use of '*miltos*' as a skin colorant, perhaps used to reproduce a healthy tan on males.

one of the whites, *cerussa*, when burnt, changes colour and is called 'purple' (*purpurea*), used for producing shadows. One need not let colours mislead, however. This purple *cerussa* is one of a number of man-made pigments formed by mixing and changing chemically natural pigments, which Pliny describes as *facticii* or 'artificial' (a rare word which occurs only once outside Pliny). Pliny teaches his readers to identify *colores* for what they really are.

Next, the black pigment '*atramentum*' (41–3), also a *facticius color* according to Pliny (because it is mostly achieved by burning materials such as resin, pitch, dried wine lees etc.). Painters, he notes cynically, have been known to dig up charred remains from violated graves to supply it – although this method is inconvenient (*inportuna*) and a new fad (*nouicia*); there are many more straightforward ways to obtain it. He goes on to describe other types of black pigment. The lees of excellent wine, he notes, is distinctive for reproducing the appearance of indigo (*Indicum*): *Indici speciem id atramentum praebere*. One special *atramentum* was burnt ivory (*elephantinum*), a pigment patented by Apelles. Even within the artistic repertoire of black pigments, Pliny argues, there are significant distinctions to be learned on visual, moral, economic and historical grounds.

Only now does Pliny introduce *purpurissum* (44–5), by which he means the pigment used for painting rather than the cloth-dye.[25] Nevertheless, it derives from the same source: 'of the remaining *colores*, which we said are supplied by patrons on account of their high cost, *purpurissum* is number one. Silversmith's earth is stained together with purple cloth, and the earth drinks up that *color* more quickly than the wool (*creta argentaria cum purpuris pariter tinguitur bibitque eum colorem celerius lanis*)'. Pliny appears to mean that *purpura* (sea-purple dyed cloth) is combined with the ground white earth (and a little water) and the earth displaces and soaks up the dye, forming a painter's pigment called *purpurissum*. This section describes an interface between different registers of *color*, the familiar *purpura* which is the passive colour inseparable from the textile (he proceeds to discuss the

[25] For more on sea-purple used in Roman wall-paintings, see Salvadori (1998). Cf. Vitr. *De arch.* 7.13 on *ostrum* (discussed below, pp. 192–3).

expensive purples, *pretiosissimae purpurae*, from Tyre, Gaetulia and Laconia), and the superlative *purpurissum* which is the active pigment derived from it. A superior form of the pigment, Pliny goes on, is produced straight from the raw treatment (*rudia medicamenta*) of the cauldron, presumably the raw dye derived from the seashells.

Pliny then talks about the manipulation of this colour by painters (45): 'applying a coat of *sandyx*, painters then add a layer of *purpurissum* mixed with egg and produce the gleam (*fulgor*) of *minium*. If they prefer to produce the *fulgor* of *purpura*, they lay a coat of *caeruleum* beneath and then add a layer of *purpurissum* mixed with egg.' Here, Pliny documents some empirical methods for replicating certain prestige colours, as well as teaching his readers to discern like pigments and question the categories they use. Both *purpura* and *minium* are *colores* with their own type of *fulgor* – this is what makes them, presumably, *colores floridi*. The mixtures described here are perhaps familiar ones to us: purple + yellow = red; purple + blue = violet. However, the implication of the mixtures for artistic and aesthetic understanding is for Pliny an epistemological problem: for our 'red', read *minium*; for our 'violet', read *purpura* (sea-purple). The mixtures imitate substances which they are not, so that viewers see *minium* and *purpura* where no such pigments exist. Our 'red' can easily be composed of 'purple' and 'yellow', but *minium* has no such genesis. This is where the *color* – colour relationship starts to disintegrate: pigment and shade are not the same thing.

Pliny's next, origin-specific pigment is *Indicum* (46). This is, Pliny spells out, a product of India, the next best pigment after *purpurissum*. In its true form, Pliny describes vividly, it is a slime that adheres to the scum of reeds (*harundinum spumae adhaerescente limo*). He then dissects its *color* – when it is sifted out, it is black (*nigrum*) but when diluted it yields a marvellous mixture of *purpura* and *caeruleum*. However, it (i.e. the category *Indicum*) is also apparently attributed to the scum of sea-purple dye (*purpurae spuma*), floating on the surface of pans in the purple dye-shops. Pliny's account makes hard work of the artist's palette: the scum of *purpura* (a different 'colour' from *purpura* itself, he would have us believe) fits under the artistic category of *Indicum*, even when it is not indigo from India. The aesthetic complexity is dragged out: if it is genuine (*sincerum*), it gives off an outstanding flame of *purpura* and, while it smokes, a smell of the sea (i.e. like *purpura*[26]).

Pliny then sketches two novelty *colores* circulating in Rome which he describes as excessively cheap (*uilissimi*). The first is a type of 'green' (*uiride*) called *Appianum* which counterfeits malachite (*chrysocollam mentitur*). Pliny complains that there are more than enough spurious varieties of it already (*seu parum multa ficta sint mendacia eius*). The second colour, a form of 'white' (*candidum*) called *anulare*, was used to brighten the complexion of women in paintings (*quo muliebres picturae inluminantur*) and made from a mixture of earth and glass stones from the rings of lower classes (*e uolgi anulis*). That a colour had its origin in the pretentious jewellery of the lower classes, and its destination in the vain images of female portraits is a clear indication of the ethical mismatch between pigment (*anulare*) and 'colour' (*candidum*). Pliny's description is a bold and morally embittered attempt to show all these colours for what they really are.

Pliny's concluding thoughts on pigments (49–50) epitomise his attitude towards the polychromy of contemporary Roman art. The encaustic (*quae inuruntur*) application of paint, he says, had been a familiar method for colouring naval ships (*classibus familiari*). Now this had spread to be used even for cargo vessels (*onerariis nauibus*) and road vehicles. Little surprise, he goes on, since even funeral pyres were painted and gladiators rode glamorously (*speciose*) to the scene of their death. Pliny takes it as axiomatic that the diverse array of colours (*tot colorum tanta uarietate*) employed in contemporary art was a profoundly symbolic reminder of the moral superiority of the past. He sums up:

> Four *colores* only were used by the illustrious painters Apelles, Aetion, Melanthus and Nicomachus to execute their immortal works – of white (*alba*), *Melinum*; of 'yellow ochre' (*silacia*), *Atticum*; of red (*rubra*), Pontic *Sinopis*; of black (*nigra*), *atramentum* – although their pictures each sold for the wealth of a whole town. Nowadays when *purpura* finds its way even onto walls and when India contributes the mud of her rivers and the gore of her snakes and elephants, there is no such thing as a noble painting (*nobilis picture*). Everything in fact was superior back

[26] See below esp. pp. 194–7.

when resources were scantier. The reason for this is that, as we have said before, it is now materials (*res*) and not minds (*animus*) that are being coveted.

The four *colores* described here are not white, yellow, red and black, although this is a tempting connection to make. *Alba*, *silacia*, *rubra* and *nigra* are artistic categories of earth. The *colores* Pliny means are *Melinum*, *Atticum*, *Sinopis* and *atramentum*. *Color* in this context is pigment. Had Apelles used two types of *alba*, two types of *silacia*, two types of *rubra* and two types of *nigra*, Pliny would have said he used eight *colores*. Pliny's *color* is a single specific pigment derived from a particular substance. This simple tidy scheme, a neat solution to the complexities of colour discrimination, is blurred only by the Roman fad for imitating and bastardising these *colores*.

Pliny's utopian world of art employed a small handful of accessible and inexpensive colours, from parts of the Mediterranean with which people were familiar. Its cultural foil was a world that used pigments from the slime of Indian river-reeds and the mashed entrails of elephants and snakes. Pliny's didactic efforts trained his readers to reinforce that connection between colour and object. The obsession with expensive and outlandish prestige colours, and the debasing cheaper colours which imitated expensive prestige colours, were emblematic of the social decay which underlies most of Pliny's work.[27]

Gems

Pliny devotes the whole of book 37 to *gemmae*, and *color* is a defining feature (37.1). The word *color* occurs 113 times in book 37, twice that of book 35 on pigments. *Color*, then, is the basic index for the structure of his discussion of primary gems.[28] This is

[27] This said, one should perhaps not place too much credence in Pliny's statements about the preferability of the four-colour palette and the decay of contemporary art (*ars moriens*, *HN* 35.2); on this theme, see Brécoulaki (2006) esp. 31. On Pliny's angst at the displacement of simple pigments by precious materials, see Naas (2006).

[28] Pliny's grudging and difficult catalogue of gems by *color* is loose and not consistent. Many are colour-grouped only by conjecture, rather than by explicit classification, and Pliny seems reluctant to commit himself to umbrella colour-categories. His early examples (18–84) appear to be structured principally by value – an index Pliny cynically

unsurprising to modern sensibilities: gems were pure aesthetic, classified and evaluated according to their appearance. What is surprising, however, is how this very principle of classification by colour is scrutinised and problematised in Pliny's account, and the following section will examine the epistemological difficulties encountered by Pliny in his evaluation of gemstones.

Introducing book 37, Pliny complains that for the present-day Roman a single gem qualifies as a complete and ideal *contemplatio* – snapshot – of nature (*plerisque ad summam absolutamque naturam rerum contemplationem satis sit una aliqua gemma*, 37.1). One striking example of this philosophical outrage occurs in his description of the emerald (*smaragdus*, 62–73).[29] Much to his dismay, it was no longer the case that grass was always greener. We might *greedily* look at plants and leaves to get our fill of 'green' (*uiridis*), he later writes, but emeralds (*smaragdi*) are aesthetically one step ahead – they 'glow green more greenly' (*nam herbas quoque silentes frondesque auide spectamus, smaragdos uero tanto libentius, quoniam nihil omnino uiridius comparatum illis uiret*). The emerald, then, is more than just an alibi for nature – it is *hyper*-nature. It is a serious challenge to the verdant roots of *uiridis*. Pliny rounds off this section, as he does many of his narratives on the abuse of nature, with Nero. This eccentric emperor, he observes, actually used to watch the gladiatorial games through an emerald (*Nero princeps gladiatorum pugnas spectabat in smaragdo*). The soothing properties of *uiridis color* for the eyes had been outlined by Vitruvius and Seneca (as well as others),[30] but Pliny was more concerned with the ethical implications of this paradigmatically counterfeit *contemplatio* than with the medical ones.[31] Nero's

imagines being dictated by a female Senate (*hactenus de principatu conuenit mulierum maxime senatusconsulto*, 85). After this, he talks of *rubrae* (92–106) *uirides* (107 *caeruleae* (119–20), *purpureae* (121–5), *aurei/fulgentes* (126–8), *candidae* (129–34). At 138 Pliny concludes: *expositis per genera colorum principalibus gemmis reliquas per litterarum ordinem explicabimus*.

29 This episode is discussed briefly by Meadows (1945).

30 Vitr. *De arch.* 5.9.5; Sen. *Dial.* 5.9.2 on *uirentia* as remedies for *confusi oculi*. Cf. Cic. *Att.* 2.3.2, '*uiridariorum* διαφάνεῖ ... *suaues*'; Ulp. 7.1.13.4; 33.7.8.1 on *uiridiaria* as pleasure gardens. Some of these issues are discussed by Trinquier (2002) esp. 114–27.

31 Cf. Sen. *Controv.* 2.1.12–13 on the imitation of *montes siluaeque* in contemporary *domus*, as well as *uiridia, maria* and *amnes*. Cf. Sen. *Controv.* 5.5.1–2.

subversion of perception was a neat analogy to his subversive politics and morals.

In spite of the 'greenness' of emeralds, their *color* for Pliny is often something a little different (so later, describing the stone *sandastros*, he says it is the *color* of the apple or of *uiridis* oil (102) – but its *color* is not 'green'). Ethiopian emeralds are rarely *concolores*, giving out a homogeneous *color* – although they are fiercely green (*acriter uirides*, 69). Persian stones have a fault (*uitium*) in that they have the colour of gall or strong oil (*fellis colorem aut acris olei*, 70). Another type of emerald has a dull *color* (*surdus colos*, 67). One is *liquidus color* (66), which – to Pliny's surprise – sends out *color* but receives sight into its interior (*colorem expellat, aciem recipiat*). Here Pliny is endorsing the usual doctrine that an object expels *color* from its surface, but this (so he observes) is something of a paradox when the eye can perceive beneath the surface of an emerald. Another type were the *smaragdi* of Chalcedon (72–3) which had had an unfixed (*incertus*) *color*, changing their 'light' (*lumen*) according to the angle of viewing, like the feathers of a peacock's tail or a dove's neck which are 'verdant' (*uirentes*).[32] *Color* is something Pliny would expect to be consistent and categorical (on the sardonyx, he asserts that no *color* must be broken by another in its own layer (*sedes*), 89); some of these gems, however, break the rules of vision, confounding the accurate understanding of the natural world and adding further fuel to sceptical interpretations of perception. Those of Pliny's stones that are pointedly 'multicoloured' reflect this in their contrived nomenclature.[33] Pliny's coloured rocks pose a giant epistemological challenge, and emeralds – in spite of their characteristic 'greenness' (*uiriditas*) – sit alongside the sceptics' traditional examples in possessing a range of *colores* that defy philosophical logic as well as perceptual optics.

Other gems possessed *colores* that titillated, confused and deceived human vision. *Myrrhina* (18–22), a precious material from the East, used by Romans to produce expensive drinking

[32] For more on the peacock's tail or dove's neck as classic colour 'problems' see above pp. 79–80 and below pp. 113–14.

[33] See 167: *hexecontalithos, in parua magnitudine multicolor – hoc sibi nomen adoptauit*; cf. 178: *panchrus fere ex omnibus coloribus constat*.

vessels, had a *color* so unusual that it was thought to be formed from a liquid solidified underground. Pliny's *myrrhina* was a hallmark of wealth (*diuitiae*) and luxury (*luxuria*),[34] exploited and displayed extensively by Nero (37.19–20). Its worth (*pretium*) resided in its variety of colour (*uarietas colorum*) – its spots (*maculae*), as they revolve, vary from *purpura* to 'bright white' (*candor*) with an intermediate (*ueluti per transitum coloris*) Pliny tortuously reconstructs as a 'fiery purple' (*ignescens purpura*) or 'blushing milk-colour' (*rubescens lacteus* [*color*]). The processual participles help corroborate Pliny's implied metaphor that these *colores* are in the process of being forged. So visually complex are its reflections of colour (*repercussus coloris)* that Pliny is prompted to compare it to the rainbow. For some, he goes on, *myrrhina* is at its best when it has 'thick stains' (*pingues maculae*) and 'spots and warts' (*sales uerrucaeque*), which are mostly flattened like warts on the body. Pliny's angst, then, is that Rome is full of people who pass their time in aesthetic appreciation (*laudent, placent*) of what are effectively the blemishes of precious stones. For Pliny, a natural history of gems based on the senses can only constitute a cultural history of other perceptibles, and the connections he draws frequently constitute a *reductio ad absurdum* of this aesthetic obsession. Pliny later attempts an account of opals (80–4), but the description becomes a tangled web of colour associations – they are like fiery boils (*carbunculi*), the *purpura* of the amethyst, the sea-green (*uirens mare*) emerald, *color Armenius* (Azurite), burning sulphur, ignited olive oil, a *color* between 'air' (*aër*) and *purpura*, or the *color* of wine. Pliny's imagination, his didactic manual of sensory discrimination, is pushed to breaking point.[35]

Pliny goes on (under the general heading of *gemmae*) to offer an extensive treatment of amber (*sucina*, 40–51), a delight for women

[34] 37.18: *et crescit in dies eius luxuria.*

[35] Cf. 87 on the *plures colores* of sardonyx which include suggestions of *caeruleum*, *minium* and *purpura*, all specific materials described elsewhere by Pliny. Cf. 114 on the etymologous mallow-coloured malachite (*non tralucet molochitis; spissius uiret ab colore maluae nomine accepto*), 115 on the sky-blue Persian *aërizusa* and 149 on the *batrachites* ('frog stone') which bears a similar colour to the frog (*ranae similem colore*), (183) the *thelycardios* which has the *color* of the heart (*color cordis*); 162 on *galactitis ex uno colore lactis*; the stone *heliotropium* having a *porraceus color* (leek colour). At 119 a type of *iaspis* earns the name *cyanos* owing to its *color caeruleus*.

(*deliciae feminarum*) and archetype of *luxuria* and Greek vanity (*uanitas Graecorum*). This material is made all the worse because it is useless – it has no *causa*. Pliny catalogues all the objects and phenomena it is thought to resemble: the sun (when described as *electrum*), wax (*cerei coloris*) and *lyncurium* (one of Pliny's sources is convinced that amber is formed from lynx-urine).[36] Pliny, exploring this possibility, digresses on the different *colores* of lynx-urine. The colour comparisons, however, are not able to constitute for Pliny the simple abstract properties they might for us (i.e. we would be satisfied that amber is 'yellow'): at 37.36 he relates various traditions in which amber not only *resembled* phenomena such as the sun or fire, but (like lynx-urine) was thought to have its origins in them. In Plinian epistemology, the object a colour-name denoted (wax, fire etc.) retained its grip on the category, wherever it might be used. On some points, however, Pliny yields to abstraction. In describing the aesthetic pecking order of ambers, he says, the attraction was its likeness to fire (*imago ignea*), not fire itself. 'Falernian' amber won high praise (*summa laus*), deriving its name from the *color* of a wine, and distinguished by its soft glow (*fulgor*), transparency (*perspicuus*), and the smoothness (*lenitas*) of heat-softened honey. Precious materials, then, were valued for their *imago*, a capacity to imitate the perceptual qualities of something familiar, and the ethical problem Pliny faces is that a *color* often signals something other than the object it qualifies. No surprise that he discovers Nero at the heart of amber abuse: by describing Poppaea's hair as 'amber-like' (*sucini*), the emperor had set a fad among high-society *matronae* for a third hair *color*. No vice, he concludes, lacks a precious name (*pretiosum nomen*). Furthermore, amber could be artificially dyed (*tinguere*) with a range of botanic pigments, or even stained with *conchylium*, a form of *purpura*, or in fact any *color* (51) to produce artificial gems such as amethyst (*gemmis quae sunt tralucidae adulterandis*). Pliny's account becomes a satire on the sensory bedlam at work in contemporary material culture.

In a passage towards the end of book 37, Pliny shows his exasperation with his catalogue of gems (191):

36 On the optical attractions (and complexities) of amber, see Causey and Shepherd (2004).

colos appellauit drosolithum herbaceus, melichrum melleus, cuius olura genera, melichlorum geminus, parte flauus, parte melleus, crocian croci similitudine quadam spargente, polian canitie, spartopolian rariore. rhoditis rosae est, melitis mali coloris, chalcitis aeris, sycitis fici.

Colores lend their names to stones – *herbaceus* to the 'dew stone', *melleus* to the 'honey-coloured stone' (of which there are many types – *melichlorum* has two *colores*, partly *flauus*, partly *melleus*), *crocias* from a certain similarity to saffron, *polias* is sprinkled with 'hoariness', and *spartopolias* a more dispersed sprinkling. The 'rose-stone' is *color rosae*, the 'apple-stone' is *color mali*, the 'bronze stone' is *color aeris*, and the 'fig-stone' is *color fici*.

Pliny is almost out of breath. He claims (195) there is no 'end of names' (*finis nominum*), and it is the Greeks' fault (*ex Graeca uanitate*). *Multiplex color* attributes different names to stones, even when they contain the same matter (*eadem materia*). Pliny's etymologising list of stones asserts the principle that in a world of such rich material diversity, one needs to classify a stone principally by its *color*. All too often this *color* is an imitation of something that the stone is not (grass, honey, saffron, blond hair, white hair, bronze, roses, apple and figs). In book 35, pigments normally carried their own distinctive *color*, and colour-associations, when they were used, were frequently part and parcel of the paint's *causa*: to represent in paintings those phenomena their colours evoked. Pliny's 'colour-stones' on the other hand had no such *causa*. Their *color*, stolen directly from something else, was their *raison d'être*. Nor did these stones (in spite of their classification by *uiridis, rubidus, caeruleus* etc.) reproduce the individual colours of an abstract spectrum (the account actually includes a rainbow stone – *iritis*, 138). Pliny's catalogue of gems is a contrived and confusing alignment of *colores* and objects, a cameo of the perceptual hazards inherent to the rich material aesthetics of Neronian Rome.

Neronian Rome

To some extent, Pliny's engagement with – and frustration towards – elaborate and ill-considered uses of colour represented a trend in contemporary evaluations of material culture in early imperial Rome, and in particular of Rome under Nero. Pliny picked up where the Augustan elegists had left off, and merged his own research with the critical ruminations of the younger Seneca and even the satirical voice of Petronius. Roman artistic and material culture in the mid first century was a moral minefield, and colour was a useful tool for exploring this territory. As well as the well-documented and manifold difficulties posed by polychrome marbles following their proliferation under Augustus, the moral and ethical dangers of gold (and things that looked like gold), as well as the contradictions inherent to the idea of a 'Golden Age' and Sun-God iconography, became classic topoi in criticisms of the principate, particularly under Nero.[37] Gems and precious stones likewise had long been symptomatic of luxury and moral decadence: Pliny, with his keen eye and parodic sub-narratives, gave shape and logic to these associations. He identified and explored the disjunction that existed between the aesthetic value of gems and their actual function within society; 'colour' (what they *looked like*, as opposed to what they *were*) was a defining characteristic of these materials, just as it was a defining feature of artistic appreciation in Neronian Rome.

Counterfeit realities and cosmic imitations were also a classic hallmark in the art and architecture of the *Domus Aurea*, and particularly in critiques of the palace.[38] Pliny (35.120) describes Fabullus, the official painter appointed to decorate the Golden House, as a representative of those artists whose colours were serious and strict (*graues ac seueri*), and yet who was famous for his *colores floridi*.[39] One critic has read into Fabullus' habit of

[37] Plin. *HN* 33.90 on gold-sprinkled sand and costumes in Nero's circus spectacles; 19.24 on cosmic imagery in the Games. Cf. Sen. *Ep.* 115.12–14 on the contemporary Golden Age devoted to material splendours. On this alternative *aureum saeculum*, see also Hor. *Epist.* 115.12–14; 90.5–10. On Sun-God imagery and greed for gold, see Sen. *Ep.* 115 cites Ov. *Met.* 2.1–2 and 107–10, discussed by Préchac (1914) 233–5. For Nero as Sun-God, see Luc. 1.33–46; Calp. 1.4.7; Suet. *Ner.* 53; Gagé (1955), esp. 650–8 on the Roman cult and the title 'Nero Helios'. Nero was the first living emperor to be shown wearing the radiate crown of the Sun-God in coin portraits, Griffin (1984) 217–18. Cf. Hemsoll (1990) 30. On Ptolemy III Euergetes, Mark Antony and Caligula, and Sun-God imagery, see Grant (1970) 161–75.

[38] I have discussed some aspects of this in Bradley (2002); see also Carey (2003) 116–17. On more technical aspects of Domus Aurea architecture, see Ball (2003), esp. 258–76 on the *personae* of Severus and Celer.

[39] Pliny claims Fabullus was remembered for being *floridus* and *umidus* (there is some confusion in the manuscripts). On *colores floridi* in Pliny, see above p. 96. Fabullus was also responsible for a statue of Minerva which faced the spectator at any angle (*huius erat Minerva spectantem spectans, quacumque aspiceretur*).

working in a plain toga a symbolic response, an 'attitude réactionnaire' to the elaborate 'fourth-style' commissions he received for the Golden House: in any case, for Pliny, this gesture further illustrated the artistic contradictions inherent to Nero's palace.[40] In the end, Fabullus' garish *colores* in the *Domus Aurea*, according to Pliny, stigmatised his artistic reputation: the *Domus Aurea* was the prison of his art (*carcer eius artis domus aurea fuit*). It is no accident that Pliny juxtaposes to Fabullus the more familiar and subdued artists Cornelius Pinus and Attius Priscus who, as it happens, painted the temples of Honour and Virtue as part of Vespasian's restoration programme. Seneca (*Epistle* 51.12) imagines the Republican Cato preferring to live in a military camp rather than a villa of lakes, roses and barges painted with diverse colours (*uarii colores*). Seneca, like Pliny, had identified a contemporary infatuation with colours, and took it on himself to expose these superficial aesthetics: gold leaf, marble veneer, painted landscapes – all misled the senses away from appreciating the physical reality of the world. It is within this literary and historical context that we must understand Pliny's complex evaluation of marbles, pigments and gems.

Nevertheless, Pliny's assessment of colour in contemporary material culture reiterates a set of principles, debates and responses that characterised discussions of colour and vision across Greco-Roman antiquity. Colour was a principal tool of vision, a *sine qua non* for the appreciation of the natural world. At the same time, human perception was susceptible to weaknesses, and colour could be confused, abused and misunderstood. Pliny's mammoth task was both to expose these weaknesses and to teach Roman senses how to accurately perceive the world around them.

Summary

For Pliny, *color* was a key index for the classification of the natural world. That perception was a means of acquiring knowledge is an idea that runs throughout various branches of Pre-Socratic, Peripatetic, Epicurean, and most significantly Stoic philosophy.

[40] Dacos (1969) 8.

For Pliny, nature was a *spectaculum* and, with the correct guidance, one could learn from it. The *Natural History* (like Lucretius' *De Rerum Natura*) was an educational manual by which this could be achieved. At the same time, colour could be a difficult, contested and misleading tool for understanding the natural world, and Pliny's account of marbles, pigments and gems devotes as much space to the paradoxes and pitfalls of contemporary classifications and aesthetics as it does to the possibilities.

Pliny's '*color*' could mean several different things. It could be a pigment (particularly when it was used substantively, such as *rubrica*, *candidum*): such pigments could be *austeri* or *floridi*. A pigment's name could reflect its utility rather than its actual appearance (*cyanos*, not necessarily 'cyan' or even 'sky blue' but a pigment suited for use outdoors; *marmorosum* used as a paint to imitate marble; *purpurissum* used to imitate sea-purple cloth; *lucidum* used to represent light; *anulare* made from cheap rings; *color Graecanicus* of Corinthian bronze etc.).[41] It could refer to categories of clothes ('dark' and 'light', 'whites' and 'colours') or hair (Poppaea's 'amber-coloured' (*succini*) hair). It could be the *appearance* of marbles or gems ('green', 'red') as distinct from its material identity ('Lacedaemonian marble' or 'Chalcedonian emeralds'): as such, it offered a convenient – if rather limited – index for grouping marbles and gems. Elsewhere, Pliny used *color* in the sense of 'visible character' (e.g. that of liver, apples, honey, Egyptian leaders etc.). A unitary definition of *color*, then, is not forthcoming from a reading of Pliny's text.

However, Pliny tended to refer to *colores* as real inherent properties of matter, or materials that existed in their own right as pigments. Pliny's *color*, then, was both optically and ontologically more complex than our 'hue'. The *color* of *minium*, therefore, was formulated as much by expressions of light – *nitor* / *splendor* – as it was by 'redness'; two of the four *colores* of *caeruleum* were *crassior* ('coarser') and *tenuior* ('thinner'). The vocabulary Pliny used in describing these pigments was a further indication of their active qualities of pigmentation – e.g. Sinopis is *rubens*, it 'blushes' red, and also paints things red. Pliny appears on a number

[41] Cf. Hannah (2004) 103–4, where red '*miltos*' is a scented ointment as well as a colorant.

of occasions to embrace the optical theory that an object sends out its *color* to the viewer.

Material culture in the mid first century, and contemporary tastes and fashions, had begun to undermine and complicate the accuracy of these classifications, and it is this challenge to the exercise of natural history that most troubled Pliny. In particular, pigments acquired or produced artificially (what Pliny described as '*fucatus color*' or 'fake colour') made identification and understanding a tricky business. It is in the minutiae of artificial pigments and the means by which they are derived (crushed elephants and snakes, goats' blood, plebeian rings, slime, urine and the like) – as well as the vocabulary of staining and infection (*inficio*, *maculae, carbunculi*) – that one can best observe Pliny's subtle parody of contemporary aesthetics and the saturation of the senses by early imperial art. Furthermore, many of Pliny's categories counterfeited a *color* one would expect to find elsewhere (e.g. *rubrica* used for blood and blushing, *purpurissum* used to paint *purpura*). For Pliny (echoing sentiments already expressed by Plato[42]), this was one of the problems inherent to painting and the reason why one should admire art that was simple and monochrome. Above all for Pliny, *color* needed to have a *causa*, an inherent logic and purpose. As a natural historian, Pliny was committed to mapping out links between matter (*res*) and the human mind (*animus*) by offering an accurate and comprehensive account of the sensible world. His art-history books demonstrate, and themselves participate in, the process of extending familiar *colores* to make sense of new materials, while at the same time offering a cautionary thesis about the intellectual dangers of mis-perceiving this world.

[42] See above pp. 71–2.

4

COLOR AND RHETORIC

It was not only the worlds of philosophy, natural history and material culture that struggled with the identification and evaluation of colour, and all the moral and ethical difficulties these processes generated. This chapter will study the development and evolution of a use of '*color*' that is normally relegated to discussions of Latin rhetoric: *color* in the sense of the 'gloss' or complexion put on an argument, sometimes extended to refer to a speaker's personal 'character', behaviour or demeanour. It will aim to reintegrate rhetorical *color* into the broader study of colour and perception in the ancient world, and will argue that this use of *color*, far from being an isolated and specialist register, was symptomatic of a distinctively Roman development in the historical discourse of colour in antiquity. This chapter will first examine discussions of *color* in various philosophical and rhetorical works of Cicero in the mid first century BC, and will then consider the evolution of this concept of *color* within the oratorical treatises of the elder Seneca and Quintilian a century later, as well as contemporary dramatic texts.[1]

It is the aim of this chapter both to explore how ancient approaches to colour formulated and shaped rhetorical *color*, and to assess the extent to which a study of this concept can enrich our understanding of ancient colour. As we have seen, this register was not altogether a Latin novelty: *chrōma* and *chroia* had already been employed to refer to impressions of character and public performance in Classical Athens.[2] However, I will argue that, side by side with the use of *color* in a more literal sense, educated Romans in the late Republic and early Empire intensively exploited these

[1] Some of these issues are discussed under the aegis of art theory by Lichtenstein (1993), who argues that a reconciliation of ancient differences between rhetoric and painting is evident in seventeenth-century art and thought, although with certain misconceptions about the discussion of colour in ancient philosophy.

[2] See above pp. 69–70.

registers of rhetorical and dramatic *color* and incorporated them into a much broader set of debates about the relationship between perception and knowledge. Contrary to the line adopted by C. Lévy that *color* was a concept restricted to changing rhetorical fashions, this chapter will argue that physical and rhetorical *color* developed and evolved in tandem, with uses that frequently overlapped, linking perception (what somebody actually *looks* like) and ethics (what sort of person that individual is).[3]

Cicero

Cicero's philosophical texts contain our earliest surviving discussions of rhetorical *color*.[4] Cicero was a product of the philosophical boom of first-century BC Italy. He studied under Epicurean, Academic and Stoic teachers and his works display and combine interests and theories from all three schools, as well as engaging in Aristotelian and Peripatetic questions.[5] Above all, then, he aimed to provide the Romans with a philosophical language and literature that matched that of the Greeks.[6] His rhetorical and philosophical treatises were as much concerned with continuities as with innovations, and his discussion of colour (both real and rhetorical) were deeply embedded in earlier debates about perception.

Two texts offer us brief points of entry into the interpretation of colour perception in the world of Cicero: *Academica* 2 (entitled 'Lucullus') on epistemology and the criterion of truth and *Tusculan Disputations* 1 on the characteristics of the soul. These demonstrate that Cicero was very much in touch with earlier philosophical debates about optical theory and the relationship between perception, knowledge and understanding – the same

[3] Lévy (2006).

[4] It is likely that rhetorical *colores* had been the explored by earlier lost works: see Wiseman (1979) 4. Cicero's contemporary Philodemus was certainly employing this vocabulary to refer to literary style in general.

[5] On Cicero's philosophy in general, Liscu (1937); Douglas (1965); for a controversial view of Cicero's allegiance to a particular school of philosophy, see Glucker (1988).

[6] Cf. *Div.* 2.150 on the appeal of giving unprejudiced consideration to different theories before approving *simillima ueri*. Elsewhere he claims (*Orat.* 12, *Tusc.* 2.5, 4.47; *Att.* 4.16.3) to be most heavily influenced by the Academy. See Henderson (2006) on classicising elements in Ciceronian philosophy.

criteria that governed contemporary interpretations of *color* in rhetoric and public performance. They also demonstrate the prevailing intellectual emphasis laid on the versatile role of the soul and individual character in identifying and evaluating colour.

Academica 2 treats the views of the New Academy (particularly Carneades) on the impossibility of attaining certain knowledge.[7] The statesman Lucullus defends the cause of the Old Academic Antiochus by attacking scepticism and the arguments of Carneades, and then Cicero attempts to defend these latter arguments. On the subject of the senses (30), Lucullus argues that the senses give material for knowledge and science: *est maxima in sensibus ueritas*. Artistic training (*exercitatio et ars*), he goes on, demonstrates the power (*uis*) of the senses – eyes sensitive to paintings, ears to singing and so on. The acute vision of trained painters perceives the world even when it is in shadows (*umbra*). The truth is out there to see. Carneades had argued that the senses were misleading, but Lucullus responds by saying the senses are the only evidence we have: 'How can you maintain that something is self-evidently white (*perspicue albus*) if it can possibly occur that a thing which is black (*niger*) may appear white, or how can we say that the things in question are visible or accurately imprinted (*impressa*) if it is uncertain whether the mental experience is true or unfounded?' (34). Later at 45, Lucullus claims that Epicurus had drawn attention to the importance of separating opinion (*opinio*) from self-evidence (*perspicuitas*), but did not succeed in separating them, because he believed so many falsehoods.

Cicero, replying in defence of scepticism, suggests that all philosophers are really sceptics. The Stoic Chrysippus (75) was the author of 'many arguments against the senses' (*multa [argumenta] contra sensus*). The Cyrenaics (76) believed that nothing external to themselves was perceptible, neither *color* nor sound (*sonus*), but that they only felt things that affected them internally such as pain and pleasure. Cicero reminds Lucullus that the bent oar and dove's neck were only two of the many arguments scepticism had presented (79), and they do indeed stand: the oar is a false perception, and in the case of the dove multiple *colores* are seen

7 On Stoic epistemology and the senses in *Academica* 2, see Hankinson (2003) 82–4.

when there is not more than one *color*. He then quotes the arguments of Carneades' leading follower Clitomachus that the claims of the Academy regarding sense-perception are not so absolutist (103) – those who say that the Academy robs us of our senses are deluded (*itaque ait uehementer errare eos qui dicant ab Academia sensus eripi*): the claim is not that colour, taste and sound do not exist, but that they do not amount to a mark of truth and certainty (*ueri et certi notam*) which is found uniquely in true impressions (*in iis propriam quae nusquam alibi esset*). The upshot of this is that the wise man (*sapiens*) 'witholds his assent', sees only appearances, and does not rely on the senses unless absolutely necessary. Cicero draws a fundamental distinction between Lucullus' vocabulary of 'perceiving' (*percipi*) and 'grasping' (*comprehendi*), and the Neo-Academic 'appearing' (*uideri*). He ends this topic with a case-study (105):

> That sea which now, as the West Wind rises, looks 'purple' (*purpureus*), will seem the same to our wise man, and yet he will not assent to the sensation, because even to ourselves it appeared blue (*caeruleus*) just recently, in the morning it will look grey (*rauus*), and because now where it lights up with the sun it whitens (*albescit*) and shimmers (*uibrat*) it is unlike the part immediately adjoining, so that even if you are able to explain why this happens, nevertheless you cannot maintain that the appearance which was presented to your eyes was true.

The surface of the sea was a classic example of the difficulty of pinning down *colores*, and Cicero here exploits it for all it is worth.[8] The sceptical New Academic will admit that an object may *appear* to fall under a certain colour category at any moment, but will not accept that the sea is inherently *purpureus* or *rauus*. Colours do exist, but they are not reliable routes to knowledge. For Lucullus, perception and knowledge were arguably the same thing; for Cicero, on the other hand, they are quite different. The fluidity of certain coloured phenomena offered the sceptic a compelling argument against the reliability of perception.

[8] On the difficulties of identifying the colours of the sea in ancient – principally Greek – literature (and with some tenuous solutions), see Christol (2002). See also Lucr. 2.801–9 on the neck of a dove and the tail of a peacock as classic sites for difficult colour discrimination (discussed above pp. 79–80).

A second passage on colour optics picks up these same arguments. The *Tusculan Disputations* reinstate the position of the soul – the *animus* – in perception (1.45–6). It is not the eyes that discriminate but (as physicians and doctors teach us) the *animus*, by means of passages (*uiae*) connecting the *animus* to the eyes, ears and nose. The sense organs are windows to the soul (*fenestrae animi*), but the mind (*mens*) has to be active and attentive to perceive anything through them. Cicero then asks why, with the same mind, we grasp things so utterly different as colour, taste, heat, smell and sound (*color*, *sapor*, *calor*, *odor*, *sonus*): the sense organs, he claims, are five 'messengers' (*nuntii*), and the soul the only judge (*iudex*). He finishes by claiming that earthly perception is rendered imperfect by the physical body, which is a barrier of earthly particles (*terrena concretaque corpora*). In death, when there is only *animus*, perception will access the true nature of everything. Human perception, then, is unreliable and subject to interpretation, although the trained mind can use the senses to assist the search for knowledge.

Later in the same work (4.52), discussing the futility of anger, Cicero asserts that a shifting *color*, voice, eyes or breathing does not indicate a sound mind. Here, *color* means something quite different. In fact, instances of *color* in the writings of Cicero are dominated by references to facial expression, character, disposition and behaviour.[9] This is not (just) a metaphor: these *colores* were somewhere on the line between real facial colour (embarrassed blush, frightened pallor, flush of anger, ill health etc.) and expressions of the sort of person one was at a particular moment in time. The trained politician should understand both how to analyse and interpret these colours, and how to produce them himself. He should also, as with the discrimination and evaluation of physical colours in philosophical debate, be aware of the limitations and dangers inherent in relying too much on appearances. *Color* of this type was most often used of public speakers, when their real faces and rhetorical dispositions were pointedly on display.[10]

[9] Lévy (2006) 185, who has observed more than twenty occurrences of rhetorical *color* in Cicero.

[10] The technical usage of *color* to label specific argumentative strategies in declamation may have had its origins in the employment of *chrōma* by the acolytes of the rhetorician Hermagoras (c. 150 BC) as a shorthand for 'shift of cause' (*metathesis tēs aitias*). On *color*

obrepsisti ad honores errore hominum, commendatione fumosarum imaginum, quarum simile habes nihil praeter colorem.

You snatched at political distinctions as a result of men's mistakes, on the recommendation of the smoke-stained masks (*imagines*) of your ancestors, with whom you have nothing in common except your *color*. (Cicero, *In Pisonem* 1)

Piso had an un-Roman swarthy complexion.[11] In this, he shared his *color* with the soot-stained *imagines* of his ancestors in the Piso atrium.[12] Therein lies Cicero's joke. By *color*, he means Piso's dark facial complexion, but also more pointedly a superficial external appearance that was out of place and evoked staining, neglect and decay. In addition, by referring to Piso's *color*, Cicero draws attention to his opponent's reliance on his outward persona, and consequently to his lack of moral substance.

Elsewhere, Cicero freely employs *color* as a term on this ambiguous line between the perceptible and the ethical. In the *Pro Scauro*, he imagines the unimaginable – a coherent set of witnesses with one *color* (19). Writing to Atticus in 54 in the aftermath of Gabinius' acquittal, Cicero claimed the state had lost all its old *color* and demeanour (*species*).[13] On his return from exile, Cicero complains that while people hoped he would recover from his ordeal, nobody had any regard for his strength or *color* (he goes on, in a metaphorical flurry, to compare himself to an unfinished Venus of Apelles).[14] On gentlemanly conduct (*De Officiis* 1.130), Cicero offers advice on posture and gesture while standing and walking: one should avoid finery and elaborate gestures (the sort one finds in gymnasts and actors), but also one's bearing (*dignitas formae*) is protected by a healthy complexion (*bonitas coloris*). This *color* is achieved through exercising the body, a colour as real and visible as a 'healthy flush'. But at the same time, all these

and rhetoric, see Matthes (1962) 25–30; cf. Fairweather (1981) 166–7; Russell (1983) 48–9. Bonner (1949) 20–31 and Fairweather (1981) 124–31 argue that Roman declamation took on this distinctive terminology in the 40s or 30s BC. More recently, see Lévy (2006) esp. 198–9, who argues that *color* was part of a highly specialised register of rhetoric.

11 So we learn from *In Pisonem*, fr. viii, with Nisbet (1961) 52–3.

12 On the wax images becoming blackened with soot, see Juv. 8.8 *fumosos equitum cum dictatore magistros*; Sen. *Ep*. 44.5.

13 Cic. *Att*. 4.18. 14 Cic. *Fam*. 1.9.15.

instances of *color* denote a particular moral or ethical quality. *Color* to the educated perceiver marked character.[15]

The *De Oratore*, *Brutus* and *Orator* – the three major works representing Cicero's contribution to the theory of Latin rhetoric, and grouped by Cicero himself with his philosophical works – contain more extended descriptions of the role of *color* in public speaking. The development of this concept is symptomatic of a more general shift of emphasis in Ciceronian rhetoric away from the more technical aspects of Greek rhetorical theory over to knowledge of literature, philosophy and general culture, and the qualities of character required of the ideal Roman aristocrat.[16]

In the *De Oratore*, Marcus Antonius the orator argues that wide reading is instrumental to good oratory (2.60). He compares a walk in the sun which, while taken for different reasons, results in a suntan (*ut colorer*); similarly, reading books means that his public speaking is, as it were, 'coloured' (*sentio illorum tactu orationem meam quasi colorari*). In book 3 (96–100), Crassus lays out the rules for an ornate style of rhetoric: this is achieved, he argues, by a sort of inherent *color* and *sucus* ('sap'). It needs 'polish' and 'sensation' (*ut polita, ut sensus*), and 'blooms of words' (*flores uerborum*). This must not be overdone – things which most strongly gratify our senses are also the things which most quickly repel us when we have had too much of them. He pointedly reverts to an example of real colours – the *colores* of new paintings impress us more than those of old paintings (98). Just so, a monotonous poem or speech cannot hold attention for long, however brightly it might be painted with *colores* (100). Crassus drags out the metaphor: because *animus* plays such a vital role in the evaluation of oratory, the curls (*cincinni*) and make-up (*fucus*) of the orator offend much more than do the responses of the senses (*sensus*) to unpleasant or excessive sensations.

Towards the end of book 3 (199), Crassus concludes his discussion of ornate rhetoric with a summary of the 'dress' (*habitus*) and – as it were (*quasi*) – *color* of oratory. It should exhibit a certain

15 According to Lévy (2006) 186–7, this use of rhetorical *color* was medical in origin.

16 Most recently on this theme, see Dugan (2005). Specifically on the Roman context of the *De Oratore*, see Fantham (2004).

color of charm – not something smeared on with make-up (*fucus*) but diffused in the very blood of the speech (*his tribus figuris insidere quidam uenustatis non fuco illitus sed sanguine diffusus debet color*). He later explains (216–17) that every emotion (*motus animi*) has its own face, sound and gesture (*uultus*, *sonus*, *gestus*), like the varieties of musical notes and tones – these, he suggests, are the *colores* available to the actor, as they are to the painter, for achieving variety (*hi sunt actori, ut pictori, expositi ad uariandum colores*). Rhetorical *color* was an ambiguous category – Cicero's use of *quasi* and the extended metaphors of painting or cosmetics (or the *color* of sunburn) remind us that *color* was not sufficiently established in its new rhetorical role to be used independently of its primary meaning as a perceptible quality. However, one development this flags in the Roman conceptualisation of *color* was that the word was becoming connected more and more explicitly with human appearance and character.

Cicero's *Brutus* pictures the orator C. Sulpicius Galba, accused of malpractices in the Jugurthine war, approaching his defence with a *color* that made it look like he had already completed it (87). Cicero later describes the orator Crassus, all of whose speeches exhibited the *color* of truth, and one free from 'make-up' (*fucus*, 162). Crassus possessed '*color*', but it was never such that it painted over the truth. On Latin orators (170–2), Cicero claims that their rhetoric has in the past been identical to that of orators from the city of Rome, except that it was not – as it were (*quasi*) – coloured by a certain *urbanitas* (*non est eorum urbanitate quadam quasi colorata oratio*). What is *color urbanitatis*, asks Brutus? Cicero replies that this *color* was a certain intonation and quality which was characteristic of the city. Towards the end of the *Brutus*, Cicero imagines the Elder Cato as a skilled painter with rudimentary materials (298): nothing in his artwork (*liniamenta*) was lacking except the flower (*flos*) and *color* of those pigments which he had not yet discovered.

Finally, the *Orator*, a work produced alongside the *Brutus*, dealt with more technical points of rhetorical style. On the rhythm of prose (168–9), Cicero comments on the contemporary importance of cadences and ornate binding words; to those who argued that this was not so important in the past, he replies: suppose somebody delights in a painting of few *colores* rather than perfected modern art – must we return to ancient art and reject the moderns? And yet earlier, on the epideictic rhetoric of Isocrates (42), a style which had been criticised as sophistic in origin and grounded in the gymnasium, Cicero comments that such roots offered nutrition (*nutrimenta*) for eloquence until it takes on its own *color* and vigour (*se postea colorat et roborat*). Sophists *per se*, he goes on (65), use ornaments for purposes of pleasure rather than *necessitas*; they wander from the subject, introduce stories (*fabulae*), and use words out of place (i.e. metaphors), arranging them as painters do combinations of *colores*: *uerba altius transferunt eaque ita disponunt ut pictores uarietatem colorum*. Rhetorical *colores* in Cicero, then, were expressions of character and behaviour; at the same time, Cicero relied on and exploited (by comparison with painting, cosmetics or other metaphors) a fundamental connection with registers of colour that were real and visible.

It remains now to chart the development of *color* as an expression of rhetoric and character in the decades after Cicero, using as a central hinge the works of Dionysius of Halicarnassus, the Elder Seneca, the Younger Seneca, and Quintilian.

unumquodque autem genus [dicendi], ut diximus, cum caste pudiceque ornatur, fit illustrius, cum fucatur atque praelinitur, fit praestigiosum.

Moreover, each of these styles [of speaking], as I have said, becomes more brilliant when it is adorned chastely and modestly; when it is painted and plastered over, it becomes full of deceitful tricks. (Aulus Gellius, *Attic Nights* 6.14.11)

Women painted their faces, men painted their words. As we have seen, the cultural ambiguity of cosmetics and 'ornamentation' came to be appropriated to define styles of writing and speaking.[17] Cicero, in a well-known letter to Atticus (2.1) in June 60 BC, compares Atticus' simple and unadorned sketch (*commentarius*) of his consulship with his own book which he describes, in a

[17] Cf. *Orator* 78–9 rejecting artificial *ornamenta*, which resemble the cosmetic *medicamenta* of *rubor* and *candor*. Cf. Clarke (1953) 94; Wiseman (1979) 8. Cf. Fronto, *De Eloquentia* 4.7; Phocas, *Life of Vergil* 9–12 praising Clio's simple language (*sola fucatis uariare dictis / paginas nescis*). Fantham (1972) 166 n. 27 observes that this analogy was never as popular in Greek as in Latin.

sustained metaphor, as using up all the perfume-cabinets (*myrothecia*) and scent-boxes (*arculae*) of the elaborate Asiatic schools of rhetoric, and even some of Aristotle's rouge (*pigmenta*): the result is so 'ornate' that he has outperformed even the most creative of his Greek contemporaries. Cicero was being only partly self-deprecating: it was one of the innate paradoxes of rhetoric that a style without *color* was bland and ineffective, but a style full of *color* could be described as crafty, subversive and risqué (the same paradox dominated discussions of cosmetics, see Chapter 6). Adornment which displayed the traditional female qualities of chastity and modesty (*castitia*, *pudicitia*) was considered by Aulus Gellius the most desirable – such moderation provides rhetoric with a suitable 'polish' (*illustrius*). Further painting (*fucatio*) and plastering was to display the vices of excessively conspicuous women. The metaphor was quickly applied also to prose, and by the end of the first century BC, *chrōma* and *color* had become common terms for literary style in general. Around this time, the dysphemistic vocabulary of artificial painting (*fucus*, *fucare*) began to gain popularity in similar contexts, connecting the imagery closely with the realm of cosmetics and the body's 'colour'.[18]

Dionysius, Seneca and Quintilian

The *color* of Cicero's day, then, was a general term for 'cast' or 'tone' of style, although its metaphorical connotations were often explicitly spelled out.[19] Such was also the case in discussions of rhetoric by Dionysius of Halicarnassus: at *Isaeus* 4.1, he articulates the difference between Lysias and Demosthenes' teacher Isaeus with a painting simile (he explicitly tells his reader that he is using a simile: εἰκόνι χρήσομαι τῶν ὁρατῶν τινι). Lysias resembles older paintings with simple colours (χρώμασι ... εἰργασμέναι

[18] Cic. *De or.* 2.188; 3.199; *Brut.* 162; Quint. *Inst.* 8.3.6; Lucian *Hist. conscr.* 8 (comparing the use of poetic embellishment in history to painting an athlete's face and dressing him up like a harlot). Cf. Fantham (1972) 168–75.

[19] Quint. *Inst.* 2.2.3; cf. 3.8.44 – '*colores*' were also used in *suasoriae*. On the discursive currency of rhetorical *color*, see Goldberg (1996) 276–7; Sussman (1978) 41; Bonner (1949) 137. '*Color*' was very distinct from the '*quaestio*', '*defensio*' or the argumentation itself. For a very detailed and analytical account of '*colores*', see Fairweather (1981) 166–78.

ἁπλῶς) without any subtle blends but clear in outline: these possess the greater charm (χαρίς). Isaeus, on the other hand, resembles later paintings, not as well drawn but with more subtle use of light and shade and a great many nuances in the mixtures used. Dionysius goes on to explain that Isaeus had a reputation for trickery and deception, Lysias for genuine expression.[20] Elsewhere, assessing the rhetoric of Demosthenes, Dionysius compares the intricate principles of musical *chrōma*, which Demosthenes painstakingly observed in the composition of his elaborate orations.[21] He also uses *chrōmata* to describe the styles and moods adopted in the work of Thucydides.[22] Dionysius, then, appeals to various different registers of rhetorical 'colour' (artistic, musical, literary) that were rooted in earlier scholarship; he demonstrates that the concept, while not widely understood in its own right, was developing a certain currency in rhetorical circles.

A generation after Cicero, *color* had become institutionalised as a technical term in rhetoric. At least by the start of the first century AD, a well-educated Roman boy studying rhetoric from the age of about fourteen would practise the *controuersia*, arguing one or the other side of an imaginary case set up and negotiated by his tutor. He was allowed, even encouraged, to introduce any supplementary material he saw fit to shape and shade the facts of the case to favour his own interpretation; in the world of rhetoric, this technique of applying a 'complexion' to the facts, had become known as *color*. This might involve attributing a less dishonourable motive, recasting an opponent's derogatory expressions ('extravagance' as 'generosity', 'avarice' as 'sophistication' etc.), directing his expression, voice and manner to enlist favour or elicit sympathy, even arousing emotion with a plea for mercy, provided it was convincing and consistent.[23] The Elder Seneca's *Controversiae* set out a range of

[20] On *chrōma* in Dionysius of Halicarnassus, see Lévy (2006) 189–90.

[21] Dion. Hal. *Dem.* 48.7.

[22] Dion. Hal. *Thuc.* 24: χρώματα δὲ αὐτῆς τό τε στριφνὸν καὶ τὸ πυκνόν, καὶ τὸ πικρὸν καὶ τὸ αὐστηρόν, καὶ τὸ ἐμβριθὲς καὶ τὸ δεινὸν καὶ τὸ φοβερόν, ὑπὲρ ἅπαντα δὲ ταῦτα τὸ παθητικόν. This passage is discussed briefly at Lévy (2006) 189–90.

[23] Sen. *Contr.* 2.1.37 ('[Iunius Otho] *solebat hos colores, qui silentium et significationem desiderant, bene dicere*'); cf. 2.1.33 where Otho's approval of *colores ... qui non possunt coargui* is outlined by Seneca as a pernicious tendency. Iunius Otho was in fact the author of four books on *colores*, now lost.

exemplary (and counter-exemplary) *colores* for legal cases.[24] *Color* meant a type of invented discourse (*inuentio*), rather than the 'embellishment' (*ornatus*) that featured in Cicero's discussions of the term: 'l'axiologie de l'imaginaire', as one scholar has recently described it.[25] For Seneca, a rhetorical *color* was a line of argument, often represented by a particular kind of demeanour: indignation, innocence, grief, horror, etc. Sometimes, such *colores* could border on the ridiculous: at 1.3, Seneca describes the strange case of an unchaste woman who, after appealing to Vesta, had survived the fall from the Tarpeian Rock.[26] The question is, should she pay the penalty again? Seneca presents several *colores* used to resolve this difficult question, some of which (deliberately, no doubt) expose and explore the weaknesses of this system of rhetorical argumentation: these include that the woman's body had been hardened by poisons (*ueneficiis corpus induruit*, 11) and therefore bounced off the rocks unharmed (*saxa reuerberet inultum*); another speculated that the woman's body was *durius saxo*, another that she was a priestess good at leaping (*uirgo desultrix*); another that the priestess' clothes billowed out and acted as a parachute. Junius Otho, much to Seneca's contempt, had even imagined that she took thorough lessons in falling (*cadere condidicit*). Like Cicero, then, Seneca acknowledged and embraced the importance of creativity and imagination in rhetoric, and expressed this in terms of 'colour'; but he also had a critical eye for excessive, unreasonable and ill-suited *colores*. He treated with scepticism, for example, any appeals to dreams, visions, portents, gods and the like; this he called the 'colour of superstition' (*color religionis*, 1.1.16). One speaker mixed up all these colours (*omnes colores miscuit*), a process viewed sceptically by Seneca as an adulteration of the principles of *color* (4.6 ext.). For Seneca,

[24] On rhetorical fabrication of *colores* in the imaginary case of Cicero's executioner Popillius (Sen. *Contr.* 7.2.10–13), see Roller (1997).

[25] On Senecan *color*, see Lévy (2006) 190–4. Lévy attributes to contemporary declamatory schools 'une imagination plasticienne'.

[26] The declaimers even make out that the *incesta* could be a Vestal (although this is never specified). See Winterbottom (1974) 88. This appears to have been a well-known 'case-study' for practising *controversiae*.

'toning down' (*temperare*) *colores* and making them straightforward (*simplices*) was an important element of the rhetorical technique.[27]

For Quintilian, *color* could be a substitute for *forma* (moral 'shape' or integrity) where it was lacking. It was an essential element of Roman rhetoric, a technique to be emulated (6.2.7), but at the same time it could be a tool of deception and distraction.[28] Quintilian notes that persons on trial must have 'the appearance of anxiety' (*color sollicitudinis*), and must appear to have this *color* whatever their actual feelings.[29] One would expect that *color* to be consistent. Later he asserts that a speaker must maintain a certain *color* throughout his speech, in order to appear not just to speak, but to speak truly (*toto colore actionis, ut id eum non dicere modo sed etiam uere dicere appareat*, 11.1.58). Quintilian clearly recognised the ethical difficulties caught up with the formation and assumption of rhetorical *colores* that were not automatically and inherently there, and to tackle these difficulties advocated consistency in one's rhetorical complexion, so that the qualities designated by that *color* might retain their credibility. Elsewhere (4.2.88), describing types of 'false narrative' (*falsae expositiones*) in cases, Quintilian mentions the importance of involving embarrassment, even if the speaker feels it: he adds that he thinks this is why such pretence is called a *color*. This is a playful exploration of the metaphor, and a reminder that rhetorical *color* was not straightforwardly a specialist register among rhetoricians, but a category that invited connection and association with physical somatic colours.[30] At 2.5.12, Quintilian, considering the lessons to be learned from reading bad speeches, compares the advantages of watching individuals who pay too much attention to adorning their bodies, so that their *color* is anything but their own (*non suo colore*).[31] The suggestive connections between rhetorical presentation, physical appearance and cosmetics are integral to

[27] See Fairweather (1981) 172.
[28] On the complexities of truths and falsehoods in rhetoric, see Quint. 2.17.19–20.
[29] *Inst.* 11.1.49; cf. 81, 85 for further examples of real *colores*. Cf. *color ignorantiae* in Frontin. *Aq.* 105.
[30] For a discussion of some of the implications of this passage, see Lévy (2006) 196–8.
[31] On this passage, see Reinhardt and Winterbottom (2006) 131–2.

Quintilian's interpretation of *color* and *ornatus*, drawing on and exploiting a long-standing literary tradition in which complexion and identity were set side by side: at 8.3.6, Quintilian reiterates that rhetorical *ornatus* must be manly, strong and carefully controlled (*uirilis et fortis et sanctus*) and should not favour effeminate smoothness (*effeminatam leuitatem*) or a *color* fabricated by cosmetics (*fuco ementitum*).[32] A similar relationship is evoked by Tacitus at *Dialogus* 20.2, where Marcus Aper defends contemporary preferences for attractive and engaging rhetoric, including – among other things – the *color* of emotions (*sententiae*): both audible and, one would assume, visible.

Rhetorical *color* beyond rhetoric

Rhetorical *color* was a register not restricted to the rhetoricians. Seneca's contemporary, Ovid, had confessed that no *color* could defend the crimes which had sent him into exile.[33] At the beginning of the *Satyricon* (2), Petronius' Encolpius attacks the intellectual damage caused by the tricks and set-pieces of contemporary rhetoricians, the legacy of Asiatic influences on Greece: rhetoric, literature and art alike had suffered and, in an extended metaphor of painting, he complains that even poetry no longer glowed with a healthy *color* (*ne carmen quidem sani coloris enituit*), and every art form, nourished by the same food, failed to reach old age. The tenuous, dangerous, even absurd nature of *colores* is parodied by Juvenal: an adulterous wife, caught in bed with her lover, appeals to Quintilian for a *color* to defend her behaviour (*dic, / dic aliquem sodes hic, Quintiliane, colorem*).[34] Apuleius observes that the wealthy assume the *color* of poverty when they wish to seem down-to-earth (*Apologia* 19). We also find the term '*color insaniae*' as a recurring formula in the Digest, meaning a 'plea of insanity'.[35]

[32] Cf. 2.15.25 on similarities between rhetorical affectation and slave-dealers painting their slaves for a profit (*colorem fuco ... mentiantur*); 8 pr. 19 (*fucata*). For comparable references in earlier Latin verse, see Reinhardt and Winterbottom (2006) esp. 131–2.

[33] Ov. *Trist.* 1.9.63.

[34] Juv. *Sat.* 6.279–80; this example features in Sen. *Controv.* 2.1.34–6.

[35] *Dig.* 5.2.5; cf. 5.22 pref.; 47.14.1.4; *Inst. Iust.* 2.18.

Unsurprisingly, the concept also featured in the language of the theatre. In Plautus' *Curculio* (230–5), for example, the sick pimp Cappadox is difficult to recognise, because his *color* is unfamiliar: 'Who is this person with the pot belly and the grassy eyes? His shape is familiar, but I can't tell from his *color*' (*quis hic est homo / cum collatiuo uentre atque oculis herbeis? / de forma noui, de colore non queo / nouisse*). By *color*, the speaker is referring both to Cappadox's state of health, and the colour physically expressed in his theatre mask.[36] In a study of characterisation in Senecan tragedy, Hook (2000) tied *color* in with the idea of a character role, the 'spin' of impersonation, specifically a mask (Greek *prosōpeion*, Latin *persona*), which (in rhetorical circles) was often very familiar and predictable.[37] The category found expression in the texts themselves. In the last act of the Younger Seneca's *Thyestes* (903–7), Atreus orders his servants to unbolt the palace doors and reveal to Thyestes the bodies of the children he has just feasted upon. What Atreus wants to see is the emotions he displays (*quos det colores*).[38] Those schooled in rhetoric (presumably most of the elite in Seneca's audience) would recognise, Hook argues, a double meaning in the use of *color*. '*Quos det colores*' could mean either 'what complexion he shows' or, perhaps, 'what face he puts on this'. On the dramatic stage, the colour of the mask was a powerful and institutionalised index of character and disposition. Indeed, Thyestes' response to his horrific banquet had become something of a rhetorical cliché: Seneca's father, in one of the *Controuersiae*, had already represented burning anger as a distinctly Thyestean '*color*'.[39]

[36] It is now generally accepted that Greek and Roman theatre always used masks, and that there were recognised typologies based on hair and skin colour. See Wiles (1991) esp. 129–49. Plautus has here, in a typical comedic manoeuvre, mutated the established pattern of masks.

[37] On the relationship between rhetoric and dramatic character, see Goldberg (1996) 279; Boyle (1997).

[38] On this, see Goldberg (1996) 276. Seneca had elsewhere stereotyped the *color uersus* of a madman – *De Ira* 1.1.3–4; cf. 2.19.5, people who are '*flaui*' and '*rubentes*' are particularly *iracundissimi*; *Ep*. 58.12.

[39] Sen. *Controv*. 1.1.21. Cf. Hor. *Epod*. 5.86; *Ars P*. 2.3.91; Cic. *Tusc*. 4.77 (Thyestes as the personification of *ira*).

Summary

The hundred years or so from Cicero to Quintilian witnessed the development and institutionalisation of a relatively new semantic register of *color* in Latin literature and rhetoric. *Color* played an increasingly important role in the repertoire of public performance (particularly oratory), referring in general terms to the 'face' that a character assumed, a rhetorical slant or an instrument of persuasion. By the first century AD, rhetoricians had developed a more technical repertoire of *colores* which were the specific spins or glosses one could attach to an argument or *controuersia*.

Rhetorical *color* was never entirely divorced from physical *color*, even though some have argued that it was a specialised register of Latin rhetoric. It was formulated as something one detected in an individual's face, and therefore was often semantically interchangeable with 'complexion' (the blush of embarrassment, the pallor of fear etc.). This nuance emerged partly out of the metaphorical conceptualisation of speech (or text) as body, and appears also to have been connected to (or even deriving from) the idea of *chrōma* in early Greek music. In the texts of Cicero, rhetorical *color* was normally qualified by metaphors or similes referring to painting or cosmetics. By the mid first century AD, dramatists and rhetoricians seem to have felt more confident in applying it directly and without qualification – although the rhetoric-as-painting metaphor still held a certain amount of currency.[40] Contemporary theatre appears to have exploited this rhetorical concept of *color* as an expression of dramatic *persona*, probably complementing its colour-coded masks.

For the orator, *color* was a hotly contested moral and ethical quality which could be made to represent 'character'/'flair'/'polish', as well as more controversial aspects of rhetorical argumentation such as overstatement or deception. The moral tensions

[40] Wiseman (1979) 8 argues that cosmetic imagery persisted at the centre of Roman concepts of rhetorical *color*: 'What the pupil of rhetoric did was to "slant" the story in a way favourable to his own case; but what *he* saw himself doing was painting its face with convincing colours'. *Contra*, Bonner (1949) 55 and Lévy (2006) esp. 198–9, who argue that rhetorical *color* was quite separate from the stylistic uses found in (for example) Cicero.

inherent to rhetorical *color* were widely recognised, discussed and exploited by rhetoricians, and these problems were frequently framed in terms of make-up and cosmetic adornment, an area of Roman life that was a traditional subject for debate and controversy (see Chapter 6). *Color* was a weapon in the competition for rank and status that was integral to the social dynamics of declamatory performance: it was an essential component of rhetorical refinement, but it could also be reformulated as artificial *fucus* or paint that concealed the truth and misled the audience.

The rhetorical discourse in which this type of *color* was most often applied had – at face value – little in common with the philosophical discourse that had traditionally monopolised discussions of *chrōma*. However, the development of *color* as a category to qualify emotion, ethics and character perhaps emerged out of contemporary Academic and sceptical concerns that downplayed the significance of optics and viewed the senses more as a negotiable expression of, and impression upon, the soul. *Color* was an active quality marking some individual characterising trait that communicated information about an individual. The orator who was not orating did not have *color*, nor did the actor who was not acting, and so on. At the same time, *color* retained its essentially associative properties – to conceptualise someone's *color* was to conceptualise what created it (embarrassment creates the 'red' face, fear creates the pale face etc.). The relationship between perception and understanding was as important in this context as it was in philosophical debates about the epistemology of vision. For the educated and vigilant Roman, *color* – an evocative feature of the human body – was a powerful index of character, behaviour and disposition.

5

THE NATURAL BODY

This chapter addresses the classification and evaluation of skin, hair and eye colours on the bodies of individuals in and around the city of Rome in the early Empire. *Color*, in the form of natural skin, hair and eye colour, blushing and blanching, as well as cosmetics, hair dyes and wigs, and dyed clothes, played a fundamental role in late Republican and early imperial literature on physical self-display and public performance. Personality (or *persona*) was most clearly signalled by one's external appearance, and Latin *color* (like Greek *chrōma*) was the primary category by which one would classify this external appearance. This connection was most evocatively represented by the Hellenistic science of physiognomy, the art of detecting from individuals' physical appearance their character, disposition, or their destiny. This branch of thought about the external manifestation of ethics and morality exerted influence on a wide range of Latin genres such as historiography, philosophy, satire and elegy.[1] This in turn was linked to connections that were being drawn between somatic colour and health in ancient medical texts, a subject that has recently been discussed by L. Villard.[2] Colour (as well as other perceptual categories) was certainly significant in the development of ancient medicine and physiognomic science, but these branches of thought were in turn important to the development of ancient concepts of colour. This chapter will consider the importance of natural body colours for constructing meaning about character and behaviour in the late Republic and early Empire, as well as the formative role that somatic appearance played for the discrimination and evaluation of colours in contemporary literature.

[1] There have been some excellent recent studies of ancient approaches to physiognomy: see in particular Barton (1994a) ch. 2 and Swain (2007).

[2] Villard (2002b).

The previous chapter argued that from the first century BC, particularly in Latin rhetorical circles, '*color*' developed semantically as an index of personality and behaviour alongside what we consider to be true 'colours' (pigments, blushes, pallor) – and that in contemporary discourse the two could exist symbiotically. *Color* – what one *looked like* and how one came across – took on considerable currency as a tool for character evaluation in a wide range of genres. It was also a pressing concern for contemporary moralists that *color* – this discursive semiotic code – could be manipulated. As well as embellishing and fabricating their rhetoric, Romans could tan their bodies, 'cross-breed', dye their hair, wear wigs, and apply to their faces a rich assortment of cosmetics; they could further complicate their somatic *colores* with an increasingly elaborate repertory of costume dyes and fabrics. Imperial Rome pooled pigments, dyes, hairs and complexions into one small environment on a gigantic scale, a process that generated great visual complexity, and one that inevitably undermined the straightforward relationships that had been established in Rome between *color* and meaning, between one's appearance and one's origins, character and behaviour.

In order to address these issues, this chapter will examine the principal ways the body can achieve *color*. It will take as its starting point the use of colour categories in ancient medical diagnosis, examining the origins of this practice in the Hippocratic corpus and its development in the works of Celsus in the early first and Galen in the late second century: in this context, *color* performed a vital role in epistemological enquiry, where external manifestations of the body were explicitly thought to represent a person's state or condition. It will also examine the central role of colour as an index of meaning in the related science of physiognomy. The chapter will then focus more broadly on Roman literary interpretations of natural *colores* – those colours naturally present and perceived in the skin, hair and eyes – and chart the development of a register of colour categories which distinguished the familiar, indigenous, Roman body from that of the outsider in early imperial Rome. I will finish by examining Roman representations and evaluations of blushing and blanching, and the ways in which *rubor* and *pallor* could temporarily supplant natural skin *color* as tell-tale signs of personality on the surface of the body. This closing section will discuss the deep-seated relationship between the 'colour red' (*rubor*) and the blushing face, and it will also explore how Romans negotiated the phenomenon of colour change within a system that prioritised static ethical codes of *color*.

As the second part of the investigation, Chapter 6 will move on to discuss those somatic colours that were generated artificially. This will begin with accounts of cosmetics in Roman literature, particularly the extensive treatment of the subject in several poems of Ovid. This section will explore the tensions inherent in the Roman concept of '*cultus*' ('culture', but also 'adornment'), and will aim to connect this familiar moral and ethical discourse to traditional debates about the epistemology of vision. I will demonstrate that the problems inherent in viewing and understanding the Roman body – what it meant to see someone's 'true colours' – was a riddle that was wrestled with by elite *cognoscenti* in a range of literary and rhetorical contexts. The maxim that the senses *could* penetrate reality still carried a great deal of intellectual weight, and this principle appears to have been a driving force behind many of the discussions of cosmetics and other somatic accessories. This chapter will briefly consider the use of wigs and the register of hair colour types which became fashionable among high-society ladies of the early Empire, which will lead on to a treatment of some aspects of costume colour in early Latin literature and examine how costume dye elicited a complex vocabulary of new colour terms that itself fuelled satirical interpretations of contemporary material culture.

Medicine and physiognomy

The relationship between colour and meaning on the ancient body was explored in several cultural contexts: descriptions of the female body in elegy and epic; ethnographic accounts of barbarian appearance; self-presentation in public oratory. But perhaps the most compelling and immediate use of colour as a signifier of meaning is to be found in the context of ancient medicine, where experts worked hard to clarify and classify the relationship between colours found on the surface of the body (as well as inside it) and the individual's underlying disposition, state of health and ailments.

The Hippocratic authors of the fifth and fourth centuries employed creative and sophisticated methods to identify and describe the colours of the skin, eyes, excretions and internal organs in order to diagnose a wide range of maladies.[3] For these pioneers of ancient medicine, the correct and precise deployment of perception and the perceptual categories which signalled particular conditions was crucial to the development of their skills, and (it has been argued) medicine may also have contributed to the enrichment and sophistication of ancient colour vision.[4] Colour descriptions in Hippocratic texts could be very subtle, and demonstrated a high level of precision: here we find compounds of different categories (e.g. *ōchro-leukos, eruthro-chlōros*), prefixation (e.g. *hup-ōchros*), and even combinations of the two (*hupo-chlōro-melas*).[5] In order to facilitate correct diagnoses, these doctors sometimes employed allusion or comparison to a familiar object (*orōdēs*, 'whey-coloured'; *galaktōdēs*, 'milk-coloured' etc.). Furthermore, detecting *changes* in colour was central to medical expertise, and therefore the categories used often evoked chromatic change.[6] Epistemology, then, was a fundamental principle of colour perception in Hippocratic texts: colours were *signs* of particular physical states, often connected to the humours of the body, and therefore accurate observation of colour was a crucial aspect of medical expertise.[7] The physiological foundations of colour in this context, it has been argued, can be demonstrated by the flexible meanings of *chroiē* and *chrōma*, both of which can be used to refer to

[3] So Hippoc. *The Art* 9.3 on the manifestations of disease: ἐστι δὲ τὰ μὲν ἐξανθεῦντα ἐς τὴν χροιὴν ἢ χροιῇ. The use of colours was particularly developed in gynaecological treatises.

[4] Villard (2002a) 8. Cf. Clarke (2004) 137, who uses the prevalence of χλωρός in the Hippocratic corpus to denote jaundiced patients (as opposed to fresh growing plants) as an example of the development of multiple distinct meanings for single colour terms, marking a move away from 'the gravitational centre of the word's meaning'.

[5] In addition, the same colour could be described differently, according to diagnosis: so, 'pale yellow' could be *hupochlōromelas* or *hupōchros*.

[6] Hippoc. *Epidemics* 6.4.22: καὶ χροιὴ ἐπὶ τὸ κάκιον ἢ ἄμεινον ἐπιδιδοῖ. See also 7.11.5; 7.24.2.

[7] Colours that were mixed (e.g. in vomit) were considered a bad sign, implying that the humours were all jumbled up: see Villard (2002b) 55. Cf. Christol (2002) esp. 119–21 on the medical origins of the pervasive relationship between ancient 'green' and humidity, connected to theories of humours.

'skin' and to 'colour'.[8] This extraordinary sensitivity towards different colours on the human body and their associated properties was, of course, a highly specialised skill developed and guarded by a set of trained medical experts. This said, these experts were widely educated and highly literate individuals: in order to formulate their observations and develop their language of diagnosis, they creatively exploited the rich categories traditionally used by poets, and their discussions of sense categories suggest that they were very much in touch with contemporary philosophical theory.[9] Furthermore, many of the categories employed (e.g. 'whey-coloured', 'lentil-coloured' etc.) were drawn from everyday experiences,[10] a suggestion that the target audience for this perceptual learning may not necessarily have been restricted to specialists.

The Hippocratic corpus was seminal to all later medical practice in the Greco-Roman world. By the time of Hadrian its various treatises had been collected into a canon of works by Artemidorus Capito, and the late second-century physician Galen (with his four-humour theory of physiology) embraced Hippocratic medicine and did a great deal to update and adapt it to suit the technology and demands of the Roman Empire. Most of the prominent medical experts were Greek, the majority of their literature written in Greek. One exception was Cornelius Celsus, a polymath during the principate of Tiberius who composed eight books *De Medicina* in Latin which dealt with such matters as Greek medical theory, pathology, treatments, surgery and anatomy. Celsus also wrote lost works on agriculture, military science, rhetoric and philosophy, and his medical works have sometimes been discounted as basic and amateurish. Nevertheless, his technical and anatomical knowledge and surgical experience suggest that he was very much in touch with Greek medical theory, and his works demonstrate a sensitivity to the identification of physical colours for medical diagnosis. Describing the warning signs of a serious malady, Celsus

[8] Villard (2002b) 46–7. See also above p. 69.

[9] Villard (2002b) 63. Cf. Villard (2006), where she explores the interdisciplinary development of 'chromatisme' in contemporary intellectual, scientific and artistic discourses, exemplified by the development of the category ἀνδρείκελον which (she argues) was symptomatic of a heightened sensitivity towards the discrimination and representation of colours, particularly on the human body.

[10] Villard (2002b) 62 'des réalités quotidiennes'.

comments that vomit is particularly alarming when it is green or black (*uomitus ... peiorque, si uiridis aut niger*, 2.4.7) or if urine is reddish (*subrubra*) or – even worse – if it is thin and white like flower petals (*quasi folia quaedam tenuia atque alba*) or resembling fine clouds composed of bran (*si tamquam ex furfuribus factas nubeculas repraesentat*). His discussion of bodily excretions carries on along the same vein, drawing on prefixation, compounds and metaphors to clarify the precise nature of the symptoms to be identified. Later, describing battle wounds, a *color pallidissimus* is a sign of a punctured heart (5.6.8), and blood and pus changes in its colour and texture according to the severity of the wound (5.6.20, where comparison to everyday substances is repeated, and colour, texture and heat are used side by side for diagnosis). Colour is an important indicator of the state of a healing wound (*considerandus color est*, 5.26.27): one that is livid, pallid, patchy or black (*liuidus aut pallidus aut uarius aut niger*) is a dangerous sign – better to be white or glowing red (*album aut rubicundum*). Elsewhere, Celsus lists the complex *colores* of carbuncles (5.28.1), ulcers (5.28.13–15), rashes (5.28.17b[11]), and other skin conditions (6.5), all the time employing sophisticated compound categories and similes to associate the complaint with objects and matter familiar to his readers. Similarly, he describes conditions of the eye using rich colour terms (7.7.14): cataracts the colour of sea water or glistening steel (*colorem ... marinae aquae uel ferri nitentis*) and suffusions the colour of the sea or like gold (*color caeruleus ... aut auri similis*). Unlike the Hippocratic authors or Galen, Celsus does not explicitly connect colours to humours, although he does at one point connect the colour of the pupil to the type of humour contained within it: *quasi concretus umor, ex cuius colore pupillae color uel niger est uel caesius* (7.7.13c). Celsus stops short of engaging with the elemental theories of the Greek medical texts, focusing instead on the more practical elements of contemporary medicine; nevertheless, it is clear that the use of colour perception (along with the other senses) is crucial for his methods of diagnosis.

11 Here a particular type of rash is described as *rubrica* ('*rubrica cognominatur*'), because it resembles red ochre.

Galen, an influential Greek physician and polymath in the court of Marcus Aurelius and a pioneer of ancient medical tradition, was much more concerned with the theoretical aspects of medicine, as well as drawing connections between medicine, philosophy and ethics. Like the Hippocratic authors and Celsus, Galen considered accurate visual perception to be central to medical diagnosis, and adapted Aristotelian optical theories for his purpose. In particular, Galen appears to have followed Aristotle (*De Sensu* 436b-437a) and other Greek thinkers in considering colour the primary object of vision.[12] He considered the eyes to be the judges of colours (ἡ δε χρωμάτων ἐστιν διαγνωστική).[13] Furthermore, Galen's optical theory allowed for an almost infinite variety of colours; the poverty of the existing colour vocabulary, therefore, was deceptive, and it was the responsibility of the trained doctor to develop a repertory of categories that allowed for accurate diagnosis and understanding. Like the Hippocratic texts, Galen plotted out a close relationship between somatic colours and the colours of the humours.[14] Galen's four basic colours – white, black, red, yellow – formed the basis of the eight 'dispositions' which were signalled by the colour of hair, skin and eyes; this four-colour palette, he argued, also corresponded to the four humours (blood, phlegm, yellow bile and black bile).[15] It has also been observed that Galen drew close connections between visual and olfactory perception in medical diagnosis, again based principally on the physiology of the four humours (as well as qualities such as hot – cold).[16] For Galen, odours and colours were normally manifestations of somatic *change* and he identified particular sequences of colour change in illnesses (red to black to yellow, for instance); in addition, disorders could often be remedied by exposing the patient to particular types

[12] For a comprehensive discussion of Galen's theory of sense-perception, see Siegel (1970); cf. Boudon (2002) 67: 'voir c'est donc d'abord voir des couleurs'.

[13] Galen, *The art of medicine* 8.6 = Kühn 3.640.2.

[14] On which, see Boudon (2002). On diseases and symptoms in Galen, see Johnston (2006).

[15] See Boudon (2002), esp. 73–4 Galen specifies as hair colours ξανθαί, μέλαιναι, πολιοῦνται and πυρραί (*The art of medicine* 6.12; 7.1; 8.1; 8.7), as well as more subtle shades (ὑπόπυρροι, ὑπόξανθοι); as skin colours εὔχροια and ἄχρουν (8.2, 8.6); and as eye colours γλαυκοί, μέλανες and λάμποντες / λαμπρόν / αὐγοειδές (9.4). Galen's eight dispositions do not include the ideal 'intermediate' disposition.

[16] On this theme, see Boehm (2002). Galen, *De Usu Partium* 7.6 observes that the olfactory nerve is immediately below the optical nerve.

of odours and colours. At the heart of Galen's theory of sense perception is the principle that colours, like odours, are tied to particular objects.[17]

Closely connected with theories and interpretations of colour in ancient medicine was the tradition of physiognomy.[18] Physiognomy became a popular intellectual pursuit in the Hellenistic period, but drew on themes and ideas that were already circulating in philosophy, medicine, ethnography and astrology.[19] The first extant treatise on physiognomy, the third-century BC *Physiognomica*, lists the physical features of the body which constitute signs (*sēmeia*): movements, shapes, colours (*chrōmata*), features appearing on the face, hair, smoothness of the skin, voice, the condition of the flesh, the parts and the general character of the body.[20] Physiognomy continued to be influential for late Republican and early imperial Roman thought, although some considered it to be a controversial and unreliable philosophical discipline.[21] In particular, it came to be associated with sophistic argumentation and the more controversial aspects of rhetoric.[22] Nevertheless, physiognomic principles (in the form of 'colour symbolism') found expression in various literary contexts: Vitruvian architecture, Senecan philosophy,[23] Pliny's natural history,

[17] This is most clearly articulated at Galen, *De Praesagitione ex Pulsibus* 3.6 = Kühn 9. 367: ὥσπερ τῶν ἄλλων ὀνομάτων ἕκαστον ἴδιον δηλοῖ πρᾶγμα παρὰ τοῖς Ἕλλησι πᾶσιν, οὕτω καὶ κατὰ τῶν ὑποπιπτόντων ταῖς αἰσθήσεσιν ἔθεντο προσηγορίας τινάς.

[18] Barton (1994a) c. 2 offers an excellent introduction to ancient physiognomy. The close developmental relationship between medicine and physiognomy is explored by Sassi (1993) and by Barton (1994a) esp. 97–8 (who also plots out connections with astrology). See also De Temmerman (2007) 238–40.

[19] Arist. *An. Pr.* 70b7, for example, discusses the relationship between the body and the soul, and moral types among animals manifested by physical appearance are explored in the *Historia animalium*. The discipline of physiognomy stretched back to the Mesopotamians, although in its early form it was normally prophetic rather than focused on nature and *mores* (as in Greco-Roman practice): see Barton (1994a) 100–1.

[20] [Arist.] *Phgn.* 806a26–33.

[21] Thompson (1989) 104–9; Snowden (1983) 100–1; Cracco Ruggini (1979) 113–14. It was, for example, the profession of a dangerous *ancilla* in Petronius' *Satyricon* (126.3), and Pliny (in spite of Aristotle and Trogus) is dismissive of the possibility of finding clues about one's life on the surface of the body (*praescita uitae in corporibus ipsis*, *HN* 11.274). This said, physiognomy is treated with respect at Sext. Emp. *Pyr.* 1.85.

[22] In particular on this theme, see Gleason (1989) and (1995) esp. 76–81; Barton (1994a) 128–31.

[23] Sen. *Ep.* 58.12. establishes 'genus' divisions of humans with *albi*, *nigri* and *flaui*. Laughton (1948) 110 suggested that this may be reminiscent of established stage convention, where old men wore white wigs, young men black, and slaves red. In fact, it is

and so on (see below pp. 142–3). Connections between bodily appearance, climate, behaviour and morality appear to have been a recurring intellectual exercise across antiquity, stretching back at least as far as the Hippocratic *Airs, Waters, Places* which explored the effects of the physical environment on bodily appearance.[24] The relationship between skin, hair and eye colour and character type was also a familiar feature of ancient drama, where painted theatre masks evoked particular characteristics (red-haired barbarian slave, pale noblewoman, tanned peasant, etc.): this tradition, which (some have argued) became more sophisticated in Hellenistic and Roman theatre was inevitably informed by – and itself contributed to – the discourse of physiognomy.[25] R. Förster's *Scriptores physiognomici Graeci et Latini* (1893) demonstrate that there was an institutionalised tradition that connected external physical features with ethical qualities: stiff woolly hair signalling cowardice, excessively black hair as cowardice and greed, straight hair (especially blond) as stupidity, red hair beastliness, coarse hair bravery, particularly black complexion cowardice and craftiness, particularly white as stupidity, dark olive skin as cowardice, gluttony and irascibility, pale white skin as effeminacy, red skin as fox-like deceit, blue eyes as savagery, black eyes as cowardice, dark-brown eyes as strength and spirit, and so on.[26]

Physiognomy was championed by a series of highly influential individuals at key stages in late Republican and early imperial intellectual development (and not just during the 'Second Sophistic'): the Stoic philosopher Posidonius appears to have written a description of mankind (now lost) from a physiognomic perspective; in the early second century, the prominent sophist and imperial crony M. Antonius Polemo composed an important study of physiognomy

not unusual for individuals to be recognised exclusively by the hair colour, as if it were a synecdoche – for example, Plaut. *Capt.* 648; *Miles* 792; Ter. *Heaut.* 1061; Hor. *Carm.* 2.11.23; 3.14.21; *Sat.* 1.2.31; Suet. *Aug.* 79.

24 Galen and (it is thought) Rufus of Ephesus wrote commentaries on this text: see Barton (1994a) 206 n. 17.

25 On schematic colours on dramatic masks, see Wiles (1991) esp. 71, 74–80 (a useful summary of Pollux's catalogue), 165–6; see also above p. 125. On physiognomy and 'characterology', see Barton (1994a) 110–11.

26 Summarised by Thompson (1989) 104–7. On the pervasiveness of these connections across different genres and contexts, see Evans (1969), esp. 17–28 on philosophy and medicine, 28–39 on drama. See also Evans (1950).

based on the physical features of his contemporaries;[27] and Galen too is sometimes credited with merging a theory of humours with physiognomic characteristics.[28] Figures writing in other areas of Roman literature also adopted physiognomic interpretations: besides Vitruvius, Seneca and Pliny the Elder, Cicero engages in physical evaluation of the protagonists in his speeches,[29] and Suetonius demonstrated an interest in the principles of physiognomy in his imperial biography.[30] The observation and interpretation of colour on the human body, therefore, was a popular intellectual pursuit in Rome that cut across medicine, physiognomy, ethnography and rhetoric, as well as finding expression in Latin biography, historiography and verse. The remainder of this chapter will examine in detail several contexts in early imperial literature in which colour performed a central role in the reflection and formulation of group and individual identity and meaning.

Color, origin and identity

This section will examine the classification and evaluation of natural skin, hair and eye colour in early imperial literature concerned with the theme of ethnography and identity. It will assess the discursive currency attached to the surface of the body for deriving information about the individual's social and cultural *persona*. In the first-century cosmopolis, the range of somatic *colores* one might experience generated complex conceptual difficulties for those concerned with the ethics of perception, and an expanding literarature emerged that engaged with and problematised the visible differences between body types. One of the strategies for dealing with a complex cultural medley of faces was to develop a

[27] On Polemo's work, see Förster (1893) 1.75. For an evaluation of Polemo, see Barton (1994a) c. 2 esp. 102–5. Gleason (1989) 389 and (1995) 55 describes second-century Rome as a 'face-to-face society'; most recently, see Swain (2007).

[28] On Galen and humoral theory in physiognomics, see Evans (1941) 287–96, esp. 291–2; Evans (1945).

[29] See Cic. *Rosc.* 7.20; *Pis.* 1.1 (and above pp. 115–16); Caecin. 10.27; *Red. sen.* 6.13; *In Vatinium* 2.4; *Verr.* 2.2.108; *De or.* 2.46.266; Barton (1994a) 112–13.

[30] See Evans (1935) esp. 57–70; Wardman (1967), also on personal appearance in Plutarch; Barton (1994b) esp. 56–8 on Suetonius' description of Nero. Cf. also Plut. *Sull.* 2.1 on the relationship between Sulla's facial colours and his frightening behaviour.

system of classification based on *colour* and not just on race, and this section will examine the intellectual distance that sometimes emerged between colour and race, as well as some of the tensions that existed between these two forms of classification. The intricate dynamics of Roman 'colour racism' have been well documented in the twentieth century,[31] and it is the purpose of this section to draw out and examine the bigger implications these might have for understanding concepts of colour in early imperial Rome.

It is wrong to suppose that ancient Rome was full of people with black hair and swarthy complexions. Roman somatic homogeneity finds little expression in contemporary literature – appearances were diverse, and this diversity mattered.[32] Ovid's *Amores*, however, manages to take a familiar elegiac tradition that scrutinised and adjudicated the merits of different feminine *colores*, and throw its rationale to the winds (2.4.37–44):

> candida me capiet, capiet me flaua puella;
>   est etiam in fusco grata colore uenus.
> seu pendent niuea pulli ceruice capilli,
>   Leda fuit nigra conspicienda coma;
> seu flauent, placuit croceis Aurora capillis:
>   omnibus historiis se meus aptat amor.

A fair-skinned (*candida*) girl will captivate me, a blond (*flaua*) one will captivate me; there is a pleasing attraction in a swarthy colour (*fuscus color*) too. If dark (*pulli*) locks hang down over a snow-white (*niuea*) neck, then you would say 'Leda was a stunner with her black (*nigra*) hair'; if they are blond (*flauent*), 'Aurora looked lovely with her saffron locks (*crocei capilli*)'. My love adapts itself to all these interpretations.

Ovid is happy to flirt with women of all colours – *candida, flaua, fusca, niuea*, ones with hair that is *pullus, niger* or *croceus*. This mixed bag of *colores*, as far as Ovid is concerned, is insubstantial and the poet parodies the importance conventionally attached to them by noting that the sophisticated male can make just about any

[31] Among the most significant works are Thompson (1989); Balsdon (1979); Snowden (1970), (1983); Nadeau (1977); for general treatments of the subject, see Franklin (1968); Portmann and Ritsema (1972); cf. Barton (1994a) 119–24 on physiognomy and 'the alien'. Most recently, stressing 'proto-racism' and imperialism in antiquity, see Isaac (2004).

[32] Isaac (2004) esp. 82–163, with an emphasis on physiognomic science.

color into a virtue.[33] He veers between *colores* that describe the skin (*candidus, fuscus*) and *colores* that describe the hair (*flauus, croceus*).[34] All are presented as synecdoche, shorthand for the female as a whole, as if they really mattered. They all have their own *historiae*, narrative precedents for feminine beauty, although Ovid makes it clear that he pays little heed to them individually. They are first elevated and then trivialised.[35] The vocabulary of body colour is also shown to be a fluid one: *pullus* can be *niger*, and *flauus* can be *croceus*. In the Augustan cosmopolis this language carried high currency, but it could also be undermined, blurred and fractured. Personal information based on *color* is hazy and negotiable. Ovid's parade of colour *qua* colour, where 'fair', 'blond', 'swarthy' are aesthetic categories divorced from intellectual context, is familiar to our sensibilities. For Ovid, however, this deliberate collapse of the relationship between colour and meaning was a playful parody on the traditional values of elegiac description.

The premise upon which Ovid could play these games was that the discriminating somatic *color* was a pervasive and important topic for the literary elite of early imperial Rome. Imperial expansion and inter-national migration created a demand for a perceptual register that could distinguish slaves, freedmen, merchants and so on according to their origins.[36] The 'black' face was the most common of these ethnic signposts, although the term most frequently used was *Aethiops* (etymologically a 'sun-darkened face' as well as denoting a more specific geography). This category specifically created somatic and cultural distance. Roman descriptions commonly suggested that this skin had been 'coloured' by the sun: *ustus, perustus, coloratus* were regular categories and offered pertinent information about the individual's customary behaviour

[33] So Lucr. 4.1159–62, e.g. *nigra 'melichrus' est … caesia Palladium.*

[34] Némethy (1907) on these lines suggests wrongly that Ovid is speaking of women who in complexion range between '*candida*' and '*fusca*', with '*flaua*' as an intermediate stage. Cf. Oost (1968) 39, who claims that *flaui* and *xanthoi* refer to 'little yellow men'. Laughton (1950) 88–9 argues that '*fuscus*' refers not only to a dark complexion, but also presupposes black hair. On female flesh in *Am.* 3.1, see Wyke (2006), esp. 202–3 on colour terminology.

[35] Ovid uses a similar argument at *Her.* 15.35–40.

[36] See Balsdon (1979) esp. ch. 14, pp. 214–22.

and background.[37] However, such terms could also sometimes be applied (with a certain amount of cultural sneering) to over-bronzed Italians (Martial's *colorati Etrusci*, for example), and even certain Britons.[38] *Fuscus* – the one surprising category in Ovid's throwaway list – was a euphemism for the black African face, as well as denoting those who were excessively tanned.[39] There prevailed the notion that such *color* was not natural and was the result either of barbarian origin, or of unnatural exposure to the sun.

It is no accident, then, that Juvenal could describe a child fathered upon upper-class women by humble blacks as *decolor* ('off-colour'):[40] he recommends that one husband terminate his wife's pregnancy in case he ends up the father of an *Aethiops*, and an 'off-colour heir (*decolor heres*), never visible in the morning light (*numquam tibi mane uidendus*)' should inherit his estate. Juvenal's joke that such a face cannot be seen in the morning light is ironic: the invisible black face is the visible index of illegitimacy. *Color* was the first port of call in this process of recognition. For the fourth-century poet Claudian, a similar union would create a *discolor infans* (*De Bello Gildonico* 188–95). These examples suggest that facial *color* was an evocative code in the context of Roman heir recognition, an expression of identity as a whole. Ovid, while arguing that in the matter of love one should not take skin colour too seriously, elsewhere observes that Andromeda was swarthy (*fusca*) with the *color* of her homeland (*color patriae suae*).[41] Martial (6.39) claims to be able to identify the fathers of all

[37] Verg. *G.* 4.293 (*coloratis amnis deuexus ab Indis*); *Elegia in Maecenatem* 57; Sen. *Med.* 484 (*a perustis Indiae populis*).

[38] Mart. 10.68.3; cf. Tac. *Agr.* 11 (*colorati Silures*). Both are significantly framed as colours out of place; Tacitus uses the latter example as part of his argument that the Silures must have immigrated from Spain.

[39] On the use of *fuscus* to describe blacks, see Snowden (1983) 8 and n. 16 (p. 112), 77. Cf. *Rem. am.* 327; *Ars am.* 2.657. Cf. 1.513 where he advises young Roman men, as part of their *cultus*, *fuscentur corpora Campo*. Mart. 4.42.5–6 imagines the ideal catamite, from Egypt but whiter than snow (*sit niue candidior*) since that *color* is held in higher esteem because of its rarity in a swarthy (*fuscus*) land: *sit niue candidior: namque in Mareotide fusca / pulchrior est quanto rarior iste color*). See Moreno Soldevila (2006) 312 on this passage.

[40] Juv. *Sat.* 6.597–601. '*Decolor*' was an adjective regularly used to describe a colour that was out of place. See André (1949) 126, where '*decolor*' is presented as a subcategory of 'le brun'.

[41] Ov. *Her.* 15.36. He goes to make the point that *albae columbae* readily mate with birds of *uarii colores*, and the *niger* turtle-dove finds love with the *uiridis auis* (the parrot).

Marulla's seven children who had each been born to a different member of her husband's cosmopolitan slave household, just by looking at their heads – one a Moor with curly hair, another with a face that is *candidus*, another black (*nigra*), another red-haired (*rufa*) and so on. Along with flat noses, long ears and bleary eyes, these *colores* were accurate tell-tale features that betrayed the children's origins. Such intellectual connections fuelled Cicero's recurring jibes at Piso's unusually dark *color* in the *In Pisonem* – a swarthy complexion which brought the homeland into contempt (*qui colore ipso patriam aspernaris*, fr. 2), and a servile complexion (*seruilis color*) which imitated Piso's smoke-stained ancestor masks (*fumosae imagines*) (1).[42] Cicero implies that his contemporaries associated a darker complexion with Greek or African slaves.

Of course the Roman *Weltanschauung* demarcated 'whites'/'blonds'/'red-heads' as barbarians or non-Romans just as much as it did the *Aethiopes*.[43] What this meant was that the Romans exploited no simple ascending scale of whiteness (as northern European cultures have tended to do). Instead, categories of ethnic colour can be seen to gravitate around an intermediate Roman *color*. Accordingly, literature on somatic *color* shows little interest in how one might classify that intermediate *color*: rather, the focus was on those whose skin, hair and eyes looked out of place.[44] The Roman observer could use the categories *Aethiops*, *niger*, *fuscus* as well as blond (*flauus*), red-haired (*rutilus*), pale (*pallidus*) etc. as gauges for recognising those who did not belong to the Roman community, or who were on the edge of civilisation.[45] One would

[42] See Nisbet (1961) 52, 58–9 and above pp. 115–16.

[43] See particularly Plin. *HN* 4.88; 6.53; 7.9–12; Strabo 4.5.4. Cf. Sherwin-White (1967) 57–8; Balsdon (1979) 60–1, 216.

[44] On the principle of Rome setting an intermediate *color*, see Vitr. *De arch.* 6.1.3–11. Cf. Ptol. Tetr. 2.2.56; Firm. Mat. 1.2.1 on the contrasting stereotypes of black Africans on the one hand, and pale-faced (*candidi*) Germans and Saxons on the other.

[45] Mart. 6.61.3 on irresponsible *flaui Usipi*; Synesius, *PG* 66.1092–7 on the problem of Germanic palefaces blending socially (if not physically) among native Romans; Tac. *Germ.* 4 *caeruli oculi, rutilae comae*; Sil. *Pun.* 4.200 on Gallic *flaua caesaries*. On red skin/hair and dark complexions in 'Caucasian' women, see Juv. 13.162–6; Sen. *De Ira* 3.26.3; Petron. *Sat.* 102; Mart. 1.62.5; 4.62.1; Hor. *Epod.* 2.411.

find Thracian slaves with the names Rufus or Rufio.[46] Juvenal points out that it is common knowledge that blue eyes (*caerula lumina*) and blond hair (*flaua caesaries*) are the proper features of the Germans who display them.[47] He is perhaps echoing a point that had already been made in Seneca's *De Ira* (3.26.3): 'amongst his own people the *color* of an *Aethiops* is not notable, and amongst the Germans red hair gathered into a knot is not unseemly' (*non est Aethiopis inter suos insignitus color, nec rufus crinis et coactus in nodum apud Germanos uirum dedecet*). These examples demonstrate that, at least among the literary elite of the early Empire, certain *colores* were commonly associated with the ethnic groups that possessed them. In one of his many attacks on the luxuries of contemporary banquets, Seneca (*Epistle* 95.24) professes his shock at the troops of perfumed boys drawn up according to nation and *color* (*agmina exoletorum per nationes coloresque discripta*): here, *nationes coloresque* is meant as hendiadys, the latter constituting the means by which the former is distinguished. Around the same time Pliny the Elder, with a little extra imagination, used elemental theory to take this principle to its inevitable conclusion: nobody doubts, he asserts, that *Aethiopes* are burnt by the heat of the nearby sun and are born with a scorched appearance and curly beard and hair, and that in the opposite region of the world the races have white frosty skins with blond hair that hangs straight; he goes on to point out that Romans in the middle have well-moderated complexion (*color temperies*), and other features that pertain to a moderate *natura*.[48] Vitruvius, introducing his section on the influence of climate upon architecture (6.1.3–4), had also noted the same polarity in bodily appearance at different ends of the earth: the big well-watered northerners whose moisture (*umor*) is not drained from their *colores* and so have a pale complexion, straight red hair and bright blue eyes (*candidi colores, derecti capilli et rufi,*

46 Balsdon (1979) 215.

47 Juv. *Sat.* 13.164–5: *caerula quis stupuit Germani lumina, flauam / caesariem et madido torquentem cornua cirro?*

48 Plin. *HN* 2.189: *namque et Aethiopas uicini sideris uapore torreri adustisque similis gigni barba et capillo uibrata non est dubium, et aduersa plaga mundi candida atque glaciali cute esse gentes flauis promissis crinibus.* Elsewhere (7.51) he mentions a woman whose father was an *Aethiops* but who was *nihil a ceteris colore differente*, who then gave birth to an *Aethiops*. On Pliny and ethnography, see Murphy (2004) ch. 3.

oculi caesi) and a lot of blood, versus the burnt and parched little southerners with their swarthy complexions, curly hair, black eyes (*fuscus color, crispi capilli, oculi nigri*) and thin blood. These subjective exercises in ethnic physiognomy were popular among the cosmopolitan Roman elite of the the early Empire: Seneca in the *De Ira* observes that people who are blond (*flaui*) and ruddy-faced (*rubentes*) are particularly prone to anger (*iracundissimi*) because such people have by nature the *color* that everyone else shows when they are angry, since their blood is thin (*mobilis*) and stirred up (*agitatus*).[49] Vitruvius, Seneca and Pliny were heavily influenced by Hellenistic physiognomy and the theories of ancient medicine (see above pp. 130–7), and were keen to adapt these ideas to make sense of the manifold races of the Roman Empire, as well as the multi-ethnic populations that had swarmed to the imperial metropolis. The impetus was clearly there to connect *color* and race by more than just conjecture: certain *colores* were generated by degrees of heat or degrees of moisture, connections that had also been observed at length in Greek medical texts.

In the early years of the second century, Juvenal stated as a paradigm that one could condone a 'white man' (*albus*) mocking a 'black man' (*Aethiops*) just as one could condone a straight-legged man mocking a cripple (*loripedem rectus derideat, Aethiopem albus*).[50] This rare example of a Roman contemplating a racial white-black (i.e. Roman – African) polarity appears to have its origins in an existing proverbial contrast of *albus* and *ater* which was not concerned with skin colour. A famous two-line ditty of Catullus (poem 93) reads 'I have no great desire, Caesar, to make myself liked by you, nor to know whether you are a "white" (*albus*) man or a "black" (*ater*) man (*nil nimium studeo, Caesar, tibi uelle placere, / nec scire utrum sis albus an ater homo*)'. The precise meaning of Catullus' categories *albus* and *ater* is debated; it has been suggested

[49] Sen. *De Ira* 2.19.5. Cf. Sen. *Ep.* 58.12 on *albi*, *nigri* and *flaui* as three human *genera*. Laughton (1948) 110 suggested that this example is reminiscent of established stage convention, where old men wore white wigs, young men black, and slaves red. Cf. Claudianus Mamertus, *De statu animae* 1.20 (referring to the hair, the eyes and the complexion): *nam si de quopiam quale sit corpus eius inquirimus, sic uidelicet qualitas corporis indicatur: flauus est ille, oculatus* [or Engelbrecht '*coloratus*'] *est, pallet ille uel niger est.*

[50] Juv. 2.23. For a detailed consideration of this passage, see Thompson (1989) 33–5.

that they are transferred onto people from the register of white/red wines, hair colour, or perhaps white and black sheep, or a metaphor drawn from the bright/grim polarity of the sort represented by 'black days' (*dies atrae*) and 'white days' (*dies candidae*) in the calendar.[51] Most commentators now agree, however, that Catullus' reference is unlikely to be grounded in skin colour; there are no precedents in earlier literature for these categories being used to describe ethnic colour.[52] This abstract idiom persisted. Horace (for example) stereotypes the man who cannot keep a secret as *niger* ('black' but clearly not 'dark-skinned').[53] However, it appears that a register evolved fairly early on in which one might use the general terms *albus* and *ater* as labels of racial identity.[54]

This is highly significant for our understanding of the relationship between colour and information in the literature of the early Roman Empire. It would be an easy conjecture (for us) to claim that being 'black' – *niger*, *ater*, *fuscus*, *Aethiops* – was to belong to a whole discursive network of typically negative stereotypes.[55] Black day, black night, black dog, black Dis ('*Dies atra*', '*atra nox*', '*canis ater*', '*niger Dis*') – the pejorative clichés of blackness and darkness were, it seems, deeply embedded in Roman cultural discourse.[56] However, on the whole, Roman literature appears to be unconcerned with the ramifications of having a 'black' face, or the connections one might draw between such ethnic *colores*, and other objects or

[51] The same categories are used at Cic. *Phil.* 2.16.41 (Caesar's henchman) and Apul. *Apol.* 16. Quint. *Inst.* 11.1.38 alludes to this poem of Catullus without remembering who wrote it, and it is adapted (without the colours) at Mart. 1.32. For commentaries on Catullus 93, see Ellis (1889) 371 (who considers it to refer to Caesar's appearance); Ferguson (1985) 295; Godwin (1999) 205 (who takes *ater* and *albus* as 'bright' or 'gloomy'); Garrison (1991) 158; Thomson (1978) 523–4. Campanile (1975) esp. 36–9 on the absence of an equation *albus* = 'good' and *ater* = 'bad' but challenged by Ingemann (1981–2). Cf. Posch (1979), who suggests the categories are external rather than moral in nature. Quinn (1970) 430 prefers an idiomatic translation: 'nor am I especially keen to know you from Adam'. Cf. Fitton Brown (1962), who gets himself into an awful muddle in trying to make sense of 'white' and 'black' wine in Plautus' *Menaechmi*.

[52] Catull. 39.12 *Lanuuinus ater* might refer to a tanned complexion, but is clearly loaded with more general negative connotations.

[53] Hor. *Sat.* 1.4.85, 91, 100.

[54] Varro appears to have been the earliest to do so, *Ling.* 8.38, 41; 9.42, where the distinction is between *albus* and *Aethiops*.

[55] For the importance of these connections in modern colour symbolism, see Thompson (1989) 110 and 211 n. 96.

[56] On the cultural semantics of *ater* and *niger*, see André (1949) 43–59.

concepts one might describe as 'black'. Juvenal's story of the black heir never visible in the morning light (*numquam uidendus mane*), is one exception. Elsewhere, Martial (1.115) jokes about the possible connections one might draw – he claims that a girl whiter than a swan, than silver, than snow, than a lily, than privet (*candidior cycno, argento, niue, lilio, ligustro*) desires him, but that *he* is infatuated with one blacker than night, than an ant, than pitch, than a jackdaw, than a cricket (*nigrior nocte, formica, pice, graculo, cicada*). Here, *candidus* and *niger* are formulated in very abstract terms where white or black skin share similar wavelengths with other white or black objects, but Martial is of course parodying the poetic licence of visual metaphor in elegy, a *reductio ad absurdum* of what happens when one takes the principle of chromatic comparison to its logical conclusion.[57] Later Roman literature, on the other hand, appears to have made these connections more freely;[58] in the first century, however, an abstract 'colour black' in place of *color Aethiopis* was a bold and imaginative poetic venture.

Some of the difficulties of maintaining that vital connection between *color* and the individual are paraded by Martial in a poem (10.12) about Domitius' tanning vacation: he urges Domitius to drink up the sun with his greedy skin (*auida cute combibe soles*) so that on his return he will be unrecognisable (*non cognoscendus*) to his 'white friends' (*albi amici*) in Rome and his cheeks the envy (*liuebit*) of the pale crowd (*pallida turba*). But, he goes on, Rome will quickly steal the *color* that his journey has given him, even if he comes back *niger* with a Nilotic face (*Niliacum os*). Martial pokes fun at contemporary obsessions with complexion, as well as the transience of *color* acquired artificially. But he also pokes fun at the pale city-dwellers, whose own *color* is defined by their

[57] Cf. 1.72.5–6 (*sic dentata sibi uidetur Aegle / emptis ossibus Indicoque cornu / sic, quae nigrior est candente moro / cerussata sibi placet Lycoris*); 4.62; 7.13.

[58] On *Aethiops*-night connections, see *Anth. Lat.* 182 and 183 (a black slave as *custos Ditis*); cf. Juv. 5.52–4; *PG* 69.1188 (Cyril of Alexander on *Aethiopes* lacking divine light). On *dies Aegyptia* = *dies atra* by the fourth century, see *TLL* 1.963. On *Aethiopes* in Christian mythology and iconography, see Thompson (1989) 108–9, 112–13, 123–4. Cf. Luxorius 67.6–14 (= *Anth. Lat.* 353.6–14) on the black gladiator Olympius: *nil tibi forma nocet nigro fuscata colore*, nor does it do so to ebony, *purpura*, violets, sombre gems, black pepper etc.

yearning for a tan (they are only 'white' because they contrast themselves with the swarthy Domitius); furthermore, the envy they feel paints their faces, both physically and emotionally (*liuebit*). And Rome *steals* the *color* back from Domitius, along with his new identity. Martial's satirical jibe parodies Roman attempts to manipulate their skin colour, as well as the contemporary infatuation with appearances. The logical problems bound up with colour change are a recurring topic for satire in Martial: at 7.13, he describes a certain Lycoris as a woman of swarthy (*fusca*) complexion driven by the dictates of contemporary fashion to seek a lighter complexion. She has heard that at Tibur ivory is bleached in the hot sun – the unfortunate result of her following suit, however, is that she turns *nigra*. Martial's Lycoris does suggest that there was some kind of Roman somatic spectrum (at least for women) in which darker colours were less desirable, and one should strive to be *candida*.[59] But his poem also suggests that contemporary society's obsession with the aesthetics of *color*, and with arbitrary connections made between surfaces that *looked* similar, was a ripe topic for debate and satire.

A catalyst for the prioritisation of colour *qua* colour, what it was about blackness, whiteness, blondness *per se* etc. that was so significant, was the development of artificial means of achieving those colours. The sun-tan is just one example. Ovid, playing the seducer, points out that everybody ought to adapt their natural *color* in order that their character fits the bill (*Ars am.* 1.723–32): *candidus* for a sailor is a shameful *color*, he ought to be *niger* from the waves of the sea and the rays of the sun; a pale *color* is also shameful for the farmer who also must toil beneath the open sky; so too the athlete with a fair body (*candidum corpus*) is an anomaly. But then he gets to the point: let every lover be pale – this is the *color* appropriate to the lover (*palleat omnis amans: hic est color aptus amanti*). This is what suits the lover (*hoc decet*), he goes on,

[59] The traditional attractiveness of this kind of complexion is well documented – cf. Prop. 2.3.11–12; Ov. *Am.* 2.5.33–42; 3.3.5–6, *candida, candorem roseo suffusa robore, / ante fuit: niueo lucet in ore rubor*; *Her.* 20.120; *Met.* 3.422–3; Plin. *Pan.* 48.4 on *femineus pallor*. On artificial means of achieving *candor*, with references, see Grillet (1975) 33–6; Howell (1980) 274 on Mart. 1.72.6. This aesthetic on men was considered a sign of effeminacy – see Mart. 4.42.5.

citing '*pallidus Orion*' and '*pallidus Daphnis*' as literary prototypes. For Ovid (in this context) the appropriate/established *color* (like emaciated limbs) could be an accessory to the desperate lover, a means of expressing through the face the depths of one's feelings. Ovid's account is of course a parody of tell-tale facial *colores* – they can be calculated and deliberately manipulated in order to achieve the desired effect. Other writers could be sceptical about such changes: Petronius parodies Roman ingenuity at reassigning one's identity by a change of *color*, in an episode featuring Encolpius and his lover Giton (*Sat.* 100–3) plotting to escape from a ship where numerous affairs and intrigues have prompted murderous feelings. Encolpius suggests that they use black ink (*atramentum*) as a solution (*remedium*) to change their *colores* from their hair to the tips of their fingers – with this new appearance they will resemble 'Aethiopian slaves' (*serui Aethiopes*) and will take in their enemies with their transformed (*permutatus*) *color*. Giton is not convinced; *color* alone cannot transform the *figura* – they need hideously thick lips (*labra ... tumore taeterrimo*), curled hair, bowed legs and scars on their forehead to make a good lie. Besides, *atramentum* might stain one's appearance permanently, or come off on the clothes. *Color* generated artificially befouls one's body, but does not change it (*color arte compositus inquinat corpus, non mutat*). This passage is an adaptation of the conventional anti-cosmetic traditions, parading the principle that the careful Roman observer can see through *color* achieved artificially (*color arte compositus*): the absurdity of this particular colour-change plan allows Petronius' satire to expose contemporary obsessions with altering one's appearance. This episode, then, toes the difficult line between Roman *color* proper (what an *Aethiops* looks like) and our 'colour' ('black' skin or 'black' ink) and explores the tensions between the two for contemporary issues of perception and aesthetics.

These questions and difficulties are brilliantly articulated in a short second-century declamation by Calpurnius Flaccus, examining from both sides the hackneyed case of a lady who, having given birth to an *Aethiops*, is accused of adultery (*matrona Aethiopem peperit. arguitur adulterii*).[60] The wife has proffered the hopeless

[60] Calpurnius Flaccus 2, with Sussman (1994).

argument, in the face of patriarchal traditions of heir recognition, that children are not always born like their parents (*non semper similes parentibus liberi nascuntur*). The husband states in response that every race has its own tell-tale appearance (*sua cuique genti etiam facies manet*), such as the red facial hair (*rutuli uultus*)[61] and blond locks (*flaua proceritas*) of Germany and the Spaniards who are not all tinged with the same *color* (*non eodem omnes colore tinguntur*[62]) – and reasserts the maxim that, in spite of the diverse races of man, nobody is dissimilar to his own race (*nemo tamen est suo generi dissimilis*). The eye does not deceive. The defence's response directly sets out to undermine the prosecution's logic: birth is a violent and difficult process – when you see skin that is scorched by a fault in the blood (i.e. bruising) you suppose that is the baby's *color* (*uides sanguinis uitio perustam cutem; colorem putas*). The defence then claims that bruising has darkened the skin (*infuscatam cutem liuor infecit*), and the *color* will disappear with time (the unusual participle *infuscatus* undermines the traditional ethnic notion that *fuscus* is the inherent property of black/*Aethiops* skin). There are other examples that blur and problematise simple logical connections between *color* and race: for example, snow-white limbs are normally darkened by the sun and paleness leaves the body (*niuea plerumque membra sole fuscantur, et corpori pallor excedit* – where the category *fuscus* is again playfully abstracted); secondly, the defence argues that although limbs might be naturally dark, shade makes them turn white (*quamuis naturaliter fuscos artus umbra cogit albescere*). Just as tanning and staying indoors to turn pale are transient and temporary colorations, the jury ought to grant enough time as they think nature needs to turn the baby '*albus*'. This latter argument is a typically sophistic one, its reassignment and renegotiation of conventional categories and logic a bold challenge to the ethnic epistemologies of skin colour. In addition, by presenting an array of far-fetched and unlikely rhetorical *colores* for the defence,

[61] If *rutuli* is correct in the manuscript, it must refer to hair colour rather than to skin colour. See André (1949) 85–8.

[62] This sentence appears to be corrupt.

Calpurnius Flaccus also exposes the weaknesses and vulnerabilities of systems of meaning based on *color*.

This section has argued that natural hair, skin and eye colour categories constituted an important and established register through which early imperial writers could classify individuals and groups based on their origin. These categories orbited a discursive somatic system of colours at whose centre the Italian face and body constituted the typical (and therefore rarely articulated) appearance. This system represented a very general somatic polarity – with *Aethiops*, *niger*, *ater*, *fuscus* on the one side describing 'southerners' (mainly Africans as well as Egyptians and Asians), and *candidus*, *flauus*, *rutilus, caeruleus, pallidus* on the other describing Nordic races (Gauls, Germans, Britons). In early imperial literature, these categories were principally ethnic signposts and until the later period there is surprisingly little interest in the consideration of what the colours might mean in abstract (the ramifications of black-night-underworld, for example).[63] There is some evidence that physiognomic rules encouraged the consideration of 'colour symbolism' (red = beastly; black = cunning, etc.), but in philosophical circles this was considered something of an anti-intellectual pursuit, and Stoics like Seneca preferred to see the relationship between *color* and ethos as an objective physiological one, grounded in the humour-theories of ancient medicine. Perceptual intelligence in the form of natural colour, however, was coming under attack from several quarters: *color* was no longer considered an uncontroversial index of identity and character. The conceptual and ethical question mark over *what it meant* to possess a certain *color* appears to have been triggered partly by the immersion of a wide range of different skin colours in the city of Rome – cosmopolitan trends which called for the discrimination and evaluation of 'Romans' of different colours (the *decolor heres*, for example, or Ovid's many-hued girlfriends), and partly by the

[63] One exception to this rule was the conventional Roman aesthetic of the *candida puella* which was a well-established cliché of Latin love elegy, and which carried only the most conjectural connection with Nordic skin. The ardent epistemologist might draw connections between ideal feminine behaviour and exposure to the sun, but *candidus* – in the context of feminine beauty – was (as Ovid points out, above) an aesthetic category with very little substance. See Plin. *Pan*. 48.4 on *femineus pallor*, for example.

development of a fashion for artificially manipulating one's *color* to achieve a different appearance. At least in the literary circles of early imperial Rome, the epistemology even of natural *color* was hot intellectual property.

Blushing and blanching

According to Pliny, the African Mesanches tribe was so ashamed of its black complexions (*ater color*) that its members smeared themselves all over with red clay: *hi pudore atri coloris tota corpora rubrica inlinunt* (6.190). This act not only hid their black skin, but also counterfeited the blush: the Mesanches could not demonstrate shame (*pudor*) through the proper channels, so they cheated. Pliny's imaginative interpretation of this people's unusual cosmetic habit is a reassertion of the normality of 'redness' (*rubor*) as a signal of *pudor* on the Roman face, as well as the ethical shortcomings of having a black skin, and a jarring comment on the use of cosmetics by those who were discontented with their natural *color*. They smear it (*inlinunt*) over their whole bodies, an extreme case of artificial colouring. That Pliny's red-painted negroes are being made to play this Roman cultural game – to look 'embarrassed' rather than to be 'red' for any other reason – is a pertinent reminder of the intellectual currency that was attached to maintaining solid ties between colour (*rubor*) and object (*pudor*). Pliny's readers are given a valuable – if somewhat culturally nuanced – epistemological map for the interpretation of the colours they see on the bodies of foreigners.[64]

Back in Rome, '*rubor*' – redness – was what painted the faces of antiquity's blushing brides. *Rubor* was the proper signal that an individual possessed a sense of shame (*pudor*). The embarrassed face, then, was a quintessential site for locating the Roman colour 'red'. Today, blushing is often presented from the sufferer's point of view as a physiological condition that may warrant medical treatment.[65] It is a physiological or psychological phenomenon,

64 Cf. Darwin (1872) 321 for contemporary views of Australian aborigines, who were sometimes considered incapable of blushing.

65 See Bradley (2004) 117.

with a change of colour as a secondary effect. In antiquity, the blush was deeply institutionalised and normalised, a means by which a viewer could derive information about the nature and character of the blusher. This section will examine the position of *rubor* (and its cognates *rubens, rubidus, rubicundus* etc.) as a semiotic code in Roman descriptive literature, the implications that colour *change* has on perceptual intelligence and the evaluation of the individual, and the extent to which concepts of 'redness' could be separated from concepts of 'blush'.

Antiquity's most talked-about blush has to be the blush of Lavinia. Lavinia has become the centre of attention in the epic struggle between the Trojans and the Italians, and both princes are fighting for the maiden's hand in marriage. Her blush is so famous because it is so ambiguous and because, many have argued, there is so much at stake in its ambiguity.[66]

> Lavinia received her mother's speech with tears, bathing her burning cheeks; intense redness (*plurimus rubor*) cast fire over her and ran through her heated face. As when someone violates (*uiolauerit*) Indian ivory with bloody purple (*sanguineo ... / ... ostro*), or when white lilies mixed with many roses grow red (*mixta rubent ubi lilia multa / alba rosa*), such *colores* the maiden produced in her face. Love agitates [Turnus] and he fixes his face on the maiden; he burns for arms all the more. (Virgil, *Aeneid* 12.64–71)

Lavinia never speaks a word in the *Aeneid*. Her only contribution is her *rubor* – a *color* that drives Turnus back into battle, forces the final duel to secure Rome's dominion, and gets him killed. Lavinia has almost become a specimen of modern psychology – critics have detected in her *rubor* an 'apology', a hint of appropriate self-policing, repentance, submission, appeasement and so on. Yet ambiguity, if we accept it, is a contradiction of the Roman principle that one's *color* should be an aid, rather than an obstacle, to knowledge and clarity. Rather, Virgil's reader was able to draw upon an existing code of blushing – a poetic aesthetic of beauty, along with the proper ethics of shame (*pudor*): it would be somewhat unusual if she did not blush.

[66] Todd (1980); Lyne (1983); Dyson (1999); Cairns (2005). Cf. Baran (1983) 355–6. More broadly on the complexities (and centrality) of vision in the *Aeneid*, see Smith (2005).

This passage demonstrates at least three important points. First, *rubor* is not there to start with; it comes from somewhere, signals change, and carries meanings. *Rubor* actively casts fire over her, and runs through her bones – it is an active argument, hence the '*tales colores*' on Lavinia's face remind the reader of the rhetorical *colores* of contemporary oratory (see Chapter 4). From this comes a second point: blushing is not the product of intention. Lavinia, the premature blushing bride, has no control over it. The involuntary blush makes her a genuine object of attraction. Finally, as is frequently the case, the poet is able to draw upon colour metaphors (sea-purple dye – *ostrum/purpura* – staining ivory, roses reddening lilies) to flesh out some of the possible implications of this gesture. The blush is at its most informative when it is superimposed upon a face that is naturally pale (*candidus*), the sort of colour transformation epitomised by dyeing ivory with *purpura* or combining roses and lilies. Here and elsewhere, blushing metaphors are represented as a stain or 'violation' (*uiolauerit*) on a pure and unblemished surface.[67] So at *Amores* 2.4.33–50, Ovid's errant girlfriend is able to dispel his rage with her *purpureus pudor*, which he compares to (among other things) ivory dyed with purple. Virgil's *purpura*-stained ivory and Ovid's *purpureus pudor*, then, are not *just* references to the way a blush can look 'purple': both use sea-purple dye to clarify the role that the blush performs on the blusher – a signal of personal violation and weakness as well as special and distinctive beauty.[68] The aesthetic comparison of colour to colour ('red' to 'purple') is clearly a factor in the choice of blush metaphor, but more prominent is the comparison of object to object (blush to sea-purple).

Romans blushed far more than Greeks. Nobody ever blushes in Homer, and, if we are to take surviving literary sources as our guide, it took nearly a whole century of Athenian democracy before anybody found the nerve to blush in classical Greece.[69] Antiquity's famous blushers emerged out of Hellenistic interests in physiognomy,

[67] See Lateiner (1998) 183–8; Barton (2001) 202–69.

[68] For more on such uses of *purpureus*, see below pp. 190–1.

[69] On instances of ἐρευθός, see Lateiner (1998) 169. I thank Alan Sommerstein for drawing my attention to a fragment of Ion of Chios (*FGrH* 392 F 6, preserved at Ath. 603f), which is perhaps the earliest classical blush.

what the surface of the body could tell you about a person's place in society. By the heyday of Rome, the blush was round every corner. The Roman blusher was someone to look at.[70]

Seneca *Epistle* 11 is the earliest surviving discussion of the blush. He begins by describing a young acquaintance whom he caught off guard in an intellectual conversation, overwhelmed by an uncontrollable blush (*suffusus est rubor*): a good sign (*bonum signum*) in a young man. The *rubor*, says Seneca, came from deep within (*ex alto*); it was ingrained (*infixum*) and innate (*ingenitum*). Neither maturity nor wisdom can ever conquer it, as it is one of the natural vices (like trembling knees, chattering teeth, faltering tongues and quivering lips). Youths are particularly affected by it because they have more body heat (*calor*) and a soft exterior (*tenera frons*). Like the *rutilus* and *flauus* of hot-tempered northerners, Seneca grounds this *color* in an inherent physiology.[71] *Rubor* was the proper sign of the immature youth. But Seneca proceeds to describe how even old men are affected by blushing, adding that, like the dictator Sulla, 'some are never more terrifying than when they redden (*cum erubuerint*), as if they were pouring forth all their modesty (*uerecundia*)'. He switches between *rubor* and blood (*sanguis*): Sulla was at his most violent when blood had invaded his face (*cum faciem eius sanguis inuaserat*). So for Seneca even what we might term 'flustering' was equivalent to blushing (he considered both to be physiologically identical, and therefore the *color* pointed in each case to the same quality). *Rubor* and shame were intertwined.[72]

Seneca then describes the supremely 'soft' (*mollis*) face of Pompey, which always grew red at the popular assemblies, and the witness Fabianus, who blushed in front of the senate, and won over his audience by his display of *pudor*. There follows a scientific explanation for blushing: these people cannot help it – they do not have good blood (*bonus sanguis*). It is stirred up and fluid (*incitatus et mobilis*) and quickly rushes up into the face. This is a natural

70 On shame and visibility in Rome, see Barton (2002).

71 On the physiological basis of the emotions in Aristotle, see Konstan (2003) 104–7.

72 On this connection, see Barton (2001) esp. 223–5. Cf. De Temmerman (2007) 243 on Artaxerxes' blush interpreted as a mark of shame (ᾐδεῖτο) at Chariton, *Callirhoe* 6.3.1. On the visual complexities of *pudor*, see Kaster (2005) 28–65.

weakness, quite involuntary; it cannot be forbidden or summoned. Seneca's blush is a condition from birth (*condicio nascendi*), a crucial physiological sign of the individual's character. He ends with a motif from the theatre: the blush, a colour which found its roots *inside* the body, was the inverse of the painted theatre mask. The theatre-actor (*artifex scaenicus*) could put on fear, sadness, a downcast face and so on, but the blush is neither summoned nor repressed (*rubor nec prohibetur nec adducitur*).[73] Seneca's letter cites examples of appropriate and inappropriate blushers: the innocent, embarrassed young man overwhelmed by Seneca's intellect, Sulla the furious, Pompey the effeminate, and Fabianus the genuinely modest witness – but what mattered in each case was that *rubor* yielded useful and accurate information about character. For Seneca, a man deeply troubled by the moral implications of contemporary society's absorption with material culture and artificial *colores* (see above pp. 92–3), *rubor* was a refreshing change. The blush allowed the Romans to see each other in their true colours.

Displaying *rubor* was all about displaying a changed colour.[74] '*Mutatio coloris*' was how Cicero described the guilty look of a criminal under trial.[75] *Rubor* only made sense as a coloration which contrasted or stood out against the *color* it superseded. A further contrast could be provided by the phenomenon *pallor*. *Pallor* and *rubor* were often described side by side. Cicero, speculating on the visible symptoms of a criminal after his crime, nominates alternating blushing and blanching (*pallor rubor titubatio*).[76] Horace describes the same configuration on the face of a nervous lover (*Carmina* 3.10.14). Alternate blushing and blanching could occur in the same sequence, providing a binary semiotic code for the onset of personal distress, or beauty.[77] What *rubor* and *pallor* have in common, then, is a change of colour, an unsteadiness in the *persona*. Propertius, for example, theorizing on the cause of his

[73] On masks and *personae*, see Wiles (1991) esp. 129–49. More recently (and with an emphasis on reception and adaptation) see Wiles (2007). See also above p. 125.

[74] De Temmerman (2007) argues that the blush is a recurring 'variable physical feature' used as a literary tool to mark the development of Callirhoe's character (particularly as a manipulative blusher) in Chariton's *Callirhoe*. This is in marked contrast to the typical form of characterisation in Greek novels, which favours static, idealised and heavily delineated characters rather than changing and evolving ones.

[75] Cic. *Clu.* 53; cf. Prop. 1.18.17–18. [76] Cic. *Top.* 52. [77] See Rhorer (1980).

girlfriend's scorn, identifies as a possibility his own failure to produce a change in complexion (*mutatus color*) to demonstrate his infatuation with her (1.18.17–18).

Whereas the Roman blush tended to be a temporary, harmless display of innocence and shame, *pallor* was often an unhealthy indication of innocence destroyed, powerlessness, or lovesickness. Ovid tells us that *pallor* was a *color* particularly suited to those sick with love: *palleat omnis amans: hic est color aptus amanti* (*Ars Amatoria* 1.729).[78] It was a defining feature of the underworld and the terminally ill.[79] In Ovid's *Metamorphoses* (9.471), a work devoted to the dynamics of change, Byblis blushes (*erubuit*) when she first imagines making love to her brother, but develops *pallor* when she is rejected. Although it is not difficult to conjecture its affinity to colour in our terms, *pallor* was principally and persistently a somatic phenomenon. It was its relationship to *rubor* and other *colores* that informed the viewer about the individual's behaviour or character, a relationship that prompted Martial to compose a physiognomic satire (1.77):

> pulchre ualet Charinus et tamen pallet.
> parce bibit Charinus et tamen pallet.
> bene concoquit Charinus et tamen pallet.
> sole utitur Charinus et tamen pallet.
> tinguit cutem Charinus et tamen pallet.
> cunnum Charinus lingit et tamen pallet.

Charinus is of splendid health, and yet he grows pale. Charinus drinks sparingly,[80] and yet he grows pale. Charinus has good digestion, and yet he grows pale. Charinus enjoys the sun, and yet he grows pale. Charinus paints his skin, and yet he grows pale. Charinus performs cunnilingus, and yet he grows pale.

Only in the final line do we encounter a scenario that would prompt a Roman to blush. The preceding lines describe physical efforts by Charinus to put 'colour' into his face and avoid looking ill with *pallor* – good health, alcohol avoidance, good food, plenty of sun, even face paint. All fail – Charinus is pathologically *pallidus*. It is perhaps the ultimate Roman social stigma, though, that even his

[78] For more on pallor as a sign of lovesickness, see also p. 9.

[79] Luc. 5.628; 7.129.

[80] This must be the meaning of *parce*, although one might expect alcohol to promote redness in the face. Martial is perhaps suggesting that Charinus avoided the *pallor* associated with hangovers.

shameful sexual habits cannot produce a blush. This crucial internal mechanism for representing *pudor* is lacking. Colourful faces and colourless faces hit the viewer with a barrage of social and cultural ramifications. Martial demonstrates that facial *color* is preconceived, a set of informative categories dependent on memory and cognition. This is a satire on face-colour, both an attack on the philosophy that one can always read a person through their face, *and* an attack on a person whose face is illegible. Charinus was of course not the only example that Martial had witnessed of such 'bare-faced cheek'.

If Lavinia is antiquity's most famous blusher, then Domitian must be its most infamous.

> Under Domitian it was a particular feature of our miseries to see and be watched, when our sighs were noted down, when that savage face and its redness with which he protects himself against shame, was enough to mark out so many men's pallor (*denotandis tot hominum palloribus sufficeret saeuus ille uultus et rubor, quo se contra pudorem muniebat*). (Tacitus, *Agricola* 45.2)

As far as Tacitus was concerned, the notorious *maiestas* (treason) trials ought to have been the fastest trigger for *pudor* – for a display of shame – in Domitian. However, he points out, the usual channel for this expression was closed off, since Domitian's face was *always* red. One could never tell when he was blushing. Domitian's permanent blush was (in Tacitus' interpretation) a permanent expression of guilt. Like many other aspects of contemporary Roman life, Domitian had turned the blush upside down. Colour change did not come into it. His victims, on the other hand, displayed in their faces quite the opposite. Their *pallor*, a natural expression of their fear and a symbol of senatorial powerlessness, became the tell-tale sign which crafted their doom. The senators were predictably and appropriately *pallidi*, but Domitian's face was an epistemological red herring. Tacitus plays the two colours against each other, and examines the dangers and traps under Domitian of seeing and letting oneself be seen. *Rubor* and *pallor* were important social signposts, but in this political climate one could not rely on the directions.

Tacitus was not alone in drawing attention to Domitian's *rubor*:

> Horror and menaces were encountered at his doors, and equal fear for those who were admitted and those who were turned away; on top of this, he himself, terrible

> to meet and see: arrogance on his forehead, anger in his eyes, feminine pallor (*femineus pallor*) on his body and on his face shamelessness, covered over with redness (*impudentia multo rubore suffusa*). (Pliny, *Panegyric* 48.4)

Domitian shows us how ambiguous redness could be. His face was permanently angry, and permanently blushing, so that no one could tell when he was angry or repentant.[81] He was '*im-pudens*' because the colour of his face did not let him show *pudor* – even though (Pliny's language cleverly plays up the paradox) this *color* was its usual signal. And his *femineus pallor* both contradicted and underpinned the *rubor* in its characterisation of a perverted emperor. He became a dramatic showcase of *color* gone wrong. Suetonius in his physiognomic section on Domitian (18) does not miss the joke: he claims the emperor's modest face (*uultus modestus*) was full of redness (*ruboris plenus*), and goes on to record that he was so proud of his modesty (*uerecundia*) that he boasted to the senate (without really blushing, of course) 'up to this point, to be sure, you have approved of both my mind and my face' (*usque adhuc certe et animum meum probastis et uultum*). One of the paradoxes of Domitian's *rubor* is that he was able to bypass the spontaneity of the blush, and so (as it were) 'make faces' at the status quo. Blush and character were offline.

One of Cicero's treatises had rejected the idea of a 'painted-on blush' (*rubor fucatus*) in oratory (*Orator* 79); Quintilian on the other hand asserted that pretend *rubor* was a must in public speaking (12.5.4).[82] Both examples veered between using *rubor* as the physical perceptible blush, and *rubor* as florid, made-up oratorical style – but both were drawing attention to the possible inversion of what had always been a genuine sign of emotion and character. The significance of this inversion, of the idea of *rubor* set in stone, is highlighted by an imaginative description of another set of social misfits in Ovid's *Metamorphoses* (10.238–42). Here, the obscene girls of Cyprus (*obscenae Propoetides*) who denied Venus became the first prostitutes, their *pudor* disappeared and the blood set in

81 Cf. Philostr. *VA* 7.28 who connects Domitian's redness with anger. See also Helmbold (1950).

82 For pejorative remarks on the use of rouge to achieve artificial *rubor*, see Plaut. *Mostell.* 261, 275; *Truculentus* 294; Tib. 1.8.11; Grillet (1975) 36–40.

their faces (*sanguisque induruit oris*) – their metamorphosis into hard rock (*in rigidum silicem*) then came with little noticeable change (*paruo discrimine*). As myth, this example draws a primordial connection between the blush and humanity. Prostitutes do not blush. Similarly, Myrrha's power to blush deserts her as she is about to sleep with her father (10.458–9): *fugitque / et color et sanguis, animusque relinquit euntem*. For Romans of the early Empire, the blush was an essential part of the package of facial *colores* that formed a prerequisite for the civilised human condition.

Lavinia's *rubor* and Domitian's *rubor* were hardly the same thing. We would say that Lavinia *blushed* or 'went red', and that Domitian was ruddy. Although for us these phenomena are only very loosely connected, for the Latin speaker, both characters elicited the same category. Both types of *rubor* told the viewer something about the wearer's relationship with *pudor*. This Latin red did not just 'symbolise' shame; it was *the* shame colour. The cheeks – the 'seats of shame' (*sedes pudoris*) – says Pliny the Elder, were where one would find *rubor* (11.157). *Rubor* could often be used figuratively for a sense of shame or embarrassment.[83] Cicero (*De Re Publica* 4.6) explains why '*ignominia*' was the name of the punishment dished out by the censor – it offered virtually no recrimination except the blush, except *rubor*. The conceptual differences, then, require us to acknowledge that there was no easy strategy at this period in Roman history for abstracting *rubor* as a 'colour' (a category that could be transferred neutrally to a blush, a rash, flowers, rocks etc.). Instead, *rubor* is better understood as the proper visible expression of *pudor* – the means by which one would recognise and evaluate an individual's sense of shame. *Rubor* is 'blush' not 'redness'. We know that people turn red not only from embarrassment, but also from things like exercise, fever, anger, drinking, sex and good health. Ruddiness, flustering, flushing are all (in our terms) easily united by an abstract colour we recognise as 'red' – but for the Roman viewer these were often anomalies, extensions, inversions or distortions of a category that was identified as 'blush'. Finally, a study of blushing in ancient Rome demonstrates that *rubor* occupied an awkward and contested

[83] Liv. 4.35.11; Val. Max. 6.3.7.

position between being a fixed, innate somatic colour that communicated important moral and ethical information about an individual's character, and being a signal of character change, instability and inscrutability. As a particular concern of Roman literary discourse, *rubor*, then, was symptomatic of the patterns and rules of rhetorical *color* (and was often cited as one of them), as well as the moral and ethical debates that emerged around the display and interpretation of an individual's *colores*.

Summary

This chapter has argued that human skin, hair and eye colour performed an important role in the formulation and discussion of meaning in early imperial literature, and that this was connected to modes of enquiry and systems of knowledge from ancient medicine and physiognomy. As a point of reference in the imperial metropolis, *color* became a key ethnographic tool, not only signalling where an individual or group came from, but also likely patterns in behaviour, personality and disposition. Roman discussions of natural colour (black skin, tanned skin, pale faces, red hair etc.) were principally concerned with the recognition and evaluation of non-Romans. *Color* also became a useful tool in the analysis of character and ethics (the pale *matrona* who stays indoors, the blushing youth, etc.), and in this sense had a lot in common with rhetorical *color* (see Chapter 4). Above all, *color* was a medium for information about an individual, and Roman thinkers normally connected it directly to the individual's background, climate, physiology and disposition. The categories of *color* themselves (*Aethiops*, *rubens*, etc.) were evocative indices of identity.

At the same time, *color* was not always static, and its meaning was frequently negotiable. The ethical and philosophical debates on the relationship between colour, perception and knowledge found a rich discursive home on the Roman body. Even without the complication of cosmetics, wigs and clothes (see Chapter 6), individuals could tan, bleach, interbreed and manipulate their blushes, and the significance of *colores* could also be hotly contested and debated. The manipulation of one's natural appearance could be controversial, particularly in contexts where *color* recognition was highly significant such as the determination of a child's paternity or the evaluation of political character, and invective and satire were often directed at individuals who engaged in this activity. The blush (*rubor*) was perhaps the most complex of colour changes. It marked a temporary shift in one's natural *color* (a '*mutatus color*'), considered by thinkers such as Seneca to be a natural and involuntary signal that an individual possessed a sense of shame (*pudor*). Any self-respecting Roman was capable of blushing, and it was only those on the edge of civilisation (Pliny's dark-skinned Mesanches, Ovidian prostitutes, Domitian) who were not. For some, *rubor* (and *pallor*) were manifestations of internal physiological changes based on character and disposition, and firmly situated in the blood of the face. Alongside the natural colours of the skin, hair and eyes, the 'blush', therefore, was considered a fundamental and reliable *color* for observing and understanding an individual's character and identity. Nevertheless, even the blush (as well as other types of redness that were classified as '*rubor*') could be an ambiguous and controversial site for relating colour and meaning, and accounts of blushing appear to have been as interested in debating and questioning its significance as they were in reasserting it. The epistemological difficulties of *color* found expression in, and were themselves fuelled by, a wide range of early imperial literature which asserted, reasserted, corrected and parodied the meanings that were attached to the surface of the human body.

6

THE UNNATURAL BODY

Chapter 5 examined the way the elite literary circles of early imperial Rome described, evaluated and debated the colours that were inherent to an individual's skin, hair and eyes, as well as the significance attached to colour changes that took place on the body (tanning, blushing/blanching, illnesses, etc.). This chapter addresses colours that were artificially applied to the body in the form of cosmetics, wigs, dyes and clothes, the new identities these colours bestowed on the individual, and the intense moral and ethical debates that such colour manipulation generated, particularly in the context of the female body. The *ars ornatrix* ('cosmetic art') was an established Hellenistic and Roman literary genre of its own, implicated in a literary tradition concerned with female concealment, trickery and seduction, and was a theme that dominated early imperial discussion of the female body.[1] The question of visual epistemology was therefore very much at stake in this discourse.[2] The relationship between a woman's natural inherent *color*, and the *color* she applied to her face (in terms of make-up), to her hair (in terms of dyes/wigs) and body (costume dyes) was hotly contested and debated by the literary intelligentsia of the early Empire.

[1] For details of several lost Greek works devoted to cosmetics, see Henriksén (1998) 187–8; Grillet (1975) 97–114; Rosati (1985) 9–20. In Latin, Pliny and Apicius provided occasional recipes for cosmetics, and cosmetic *cultus* was a popular topos: see, for example, Liv. 4.44.11; Plaut. *Mostell.* 258–95; *Truculentus* 289–95; *Poen.* 214–31 (cosmetics as a frivolous vanity); Columella, *Rust.* 12 (pref.). The disapproval of cosmetics in love elegy was a classic topos – cf. Prop. 1.2; 1.15.5–6; 2.18.23–4; Tib. 1.8.15. Galen 12.446–7 (Kühn) recalls a work by Criton (doctor to Trajan's wife Plotina) dedicated to female cosmetics and hair dyeing. The classic treatment of cosmetics in antiquity is Forbes, *Stud. Anc. Technol.* 3.1–50. For a discussion of deceptive colours on the Greek body (with an emphasis on art), see Duigan (2004). On veiling and the Greek female body, see Llewellyn-Jones (2003).

[2] On the female body and 'the eye of the lover' (although not directly concerned with cosmetic colours), see Bartsch (2006) ch. 2, esp. 58–66 on the significance of ancient optical theories.

Cosmetics

Ovid, suggesting cures for lovesickness ('*remedia amoris*'), advises his infatuated male reader to make a surprise early-morning visit to his mistress, before she has had chance to put on her face:

> We are carried away by the art of adornment (*cultus*); everything is covered by gems and gold: the real girl is the least bit of herself (*pars minima est ipsa puella sui*). Often you ask *where is it*, that thing you love, among so many things. With this aegis, rich Love deceives our eyes. So arrive unforeseen, catch her unarmed (while *you* are quite safe): that unlucky girl will collapse under her vices (*uitia*). But it is not safe to trust in this rule too much, for a fine appearance (*forma*) tricks many men without skill (*ars*). So when she is smearing all those concocted poisons (*composita uenena*) on her face, go right up to your mistress' face (do not let *pudor* stand in your way). You will find pots of make-up (*pyxidae*) and stuff in a thousand colours (*rerum mille colores*), and lanoline grease that has melted and run down into her sweaty cleavage (*fluere in tepidos oesypa lapsa sinus*): those drugs (*medicamina*) reek from your tables, Phineus, and not just once has this stirred my stomach to nausea. (*Remedia Amoris* 343–56)

Ovid's passage on the typical *cultus* ('adornment') of the Augustan lady creates and explores a dialogue between perception and knowledge. If one really wants to *see* what one is looking at, one should visit the lady before she has applied her *colores*. Even then, Ovid warns, beauty (*forma*) without *ars* can be dangerously alluring, but at least this is the real thing. Ovid's objective is similar to that of Pliny (see Chapter 3) – as the master of his skill (*magister artis*), he aims to train Roman perception in the sphere of the female body. His description is a potent reminder of precisely what it is the besotted male admirer is seeing: the girl's persuasive *colores* belong not to her but to 'stuff' (*rerum*). This stuff is strange and outlandish, not easy for a Roman to pin down and identify: it belongs to a world of Greek vocabulary and Greek ideas, with cosmetics in a vast array of 'perfume-boxes (*pyxidae*)' accompanised by lanoline grease (*oesypum*), reminding Ovid of the legendary stenches of the Harpies' dinner table.[3] These cosmetics are literally – as well as visually – drugs (*medicamina*) and calculated

[3] On the connection between cosmetics (practitioners and language) and Greekness, see Griffin (1976) 92–4.

poisons (*composita uenena*). This is the *cultus*, Ovid claims, that deceives the eyes (*decipit ... oculos*). Ovid wages war (*aegide ... inermem ... excidet*) on this visual trickery, and to beat it his reader too must be unforeseen (*improuisus*). For the shrewd lover, perception still remained the key to understanding, and Ovid trains his reader to recognise that hardly any of what he sees is the girl herself (*pars minima est ipsa puella sui*). This intellectual anathema betrayed a key cultural problem with cosmetics: it was a deeply embedded principle of Roman intellectual thought that one's *colores* should be inherent properties. If one's natural *color* were an index of character and personality, how could perception function properly when that internal *color* was replaced by external *colores rerum*? What was the best way of observing the female body?

Cultus, then, was a Roman Pandora's Box. But (at least by the early Empire) it was also a *sine qua non* for the Roman body, male and female alike. As well as cosmetics, it could also refer to daily cleansing, spotless clothes, suitably fitting shoes, manicures, fresh breath, regularly trimmed hair, a healthy tan – all involved some level of artificially re-imaging the body. Neglect of *cultus*, particularly by women, was (in spite of the virtues of naturalism) reminiscent of barbarians, or wild beasts.[4] Ovid takes this equation between *cultus* and civilisation as the premise for his cosmetic advice in *Ars Amatoria* 3: 'ugly is a bull without horns, ugly a field without grass, a plant without leaves, or a head without hair' (*turpe pecus mutilum, turpis sine gramina campus, / et sine fronde frutex, et sine crine caput*, 249–50). It is also with this idea that he begins his *Medicamina faciei femineae* (3–7): '*cultus* commanded the sterile ground to produce wheat, and the devouring briers to perish, *cultus* improves the bitter juice of fruit, and the tree when split gains adopted value. What is cultivated gives pleasure (*culta placent*).' For any self-respecting aristocratic male, however, it was best to keep *cultus* minimal: Ovid for example considered that (in contrast with his women) a neglected appearance was most fitting

4 See Liv. 2.23.4. On the contrast between *cultus* and *rusticitas*, see Myerowitz (1985) esp. ch. 2. Further, see Verg. *G.* 2.461–6; [Tib.] 3.3.16; Hor. *Carm.* 2.18.1. For examples of the female *toilette* in visual arts (esp. funerary monuments), see Wyke (1994) 142–4 and figs. 1–5.

for men (*forma uiros neglecta decet*).[5] As Ovid goes on to explain, an elaborated appearance was a threat to one's integrity and *uirtus*: anything beyond eliminating bad breath and body odour, let only promiscuous girls practise, and anyone who is so unmanly as to seek men himself (*cetera lasciuae faciant, concede, puellae et siquis male uir quaerit habere uirum*, 523–4). The Elder Seneca prefaces his first *Controversia* by deploring his contemporaries who sacrifice the honourable practices of men, particularly oratory, because they devote all their time to sordid feminine fineries: braiding their hair, refining their voices to womanly pleasantries (*ad muliebres blanditias*), emulating feminine physical traits (*mollitia corporis*), and cultivating (*excolere*) themselves with the most inelegant forms of elegance (*inmundissimae munditiae*).[6] Perceptual un-truth – a very old problem in the discourse of understanding the female through her body – is, Seneca concludes, now the *specimen* of young Roman men.

A classic example of the ethical debates triggered by female *cultus* was the controversy surrounding the *lex Oppia* of 215 BC. As an emergency wartime measure to deal with a perceived moral decay in the state, the *lex Oppia* ruled that no woman could carry more than half an ounce of gold, wear multicoloured clothes (*uestimenta uersicoloria*) or ride in private carriages in the city. Twenty years later, while the city's women besieged the Forum, Livy pictures Cato and Lucius Valerius engaged in a heated debate over Valerius' proposal to repeal the law (34.1–8). Both accepted that women were socially and morally inferior beings, unable to comprehend civic responsibility, and that this female inferiority found expression on the surface of the body. Cato argued that women will readily initiate insurrection against the state for trivial material reasons, so that they might glow in gold and purple cloth (*ut auro et purpura fulgamus*). The consequence as far as Cato was concerned was far from trivial: they end up imitating *triumphatores* (*uelut triumphantes*), blurring the deeply embedded significance of the materials that cover them. He twits the women's arguments: 'when everybody's *cultus* is made alike, why should any one of you be afraid that she is not conspicuous in herself? … Why am I

[5] Ov. *Ars am.* 1.509. [6] Sen. *Controv.* 1.pref.8–9.

not conspicuous, marked out by gold and purple? (*sic aequato omnium cultu quid unaquaeque uestrum ueretur ne in se conspiciatur? ... cur non insignis auro et purpura conspicior?*).'

For Cato, female identity was rooted in *cultus per se*, rather than any 'true' information lying behind that *cultus*. Valerius agrees that women are *mulierculae* – weak and petty. However, although *cultus* might be classified as trivial and superficial, Valerius points out that elegance, decoration and adornment (*munditiae et ornatus et cultus*) are the hallmarks of women (*insignia feminarum*), and physical self-cultivation is all they have. This ambivalence (whether or not it was really on the lips of Romans at the turn of the second century BC) was well-suited to the moral and ethical questioning of Augustan society to whom Livy was marketing his histories. *Cultus* operated within a nexus of opposed interpretations: on the one hand it could be deceptive and dangerous, on the other it was (on women at least) an essential marker of culture. *Color* – both in terms of the colour categories with which we are familiar and which were part of the cosmetic repertoire, and in more general terms of the physical and ethical 'mask' that resulted from the use of cosmetics – evoked the same ambiguity between cultivated adornment and deceptive entrapment.[7]

Ovid's *Remedia Amoris* was an exercise in unweaving and revealing the raw truths of seduction and sex-appeal, in order to allow the vulnerable lover a greater awareness and understanding of feminine *colores* (both literal and rhetorical), and therefore greater defences against them. In contrast to this, Ovid composed two poems, the *Ars Amatoria* and the *Medicamina Faciei Femineae*, which explicitly lay out the mechanisms for sexual manipulation, the latter being specifically concerned with cosmetics.[8] The *Ars Amatoria* emphasises the importance of *cultus* for women who wish to attract men. This poem systematises deception and entrapment, and the strategies through which women can counterfeit those *colores* they do not naturally possess. Ovid first directs women on various suitable hairstyles, then on the types of

[7] So Batchelor (2000) who explores the antagonistic system of 'chromophobia' versus 'chromophilia'.

[8] On these two poems, see Rimell (2006) chs. 1 and 2.

dress available. His third site for *cultus* is the use of cosmetics (3.199–208).

> scitis et inducta candorem quaerere creta:
>   sanguine quae uero non rubet, arte rubet.
> arte supercilii confinia nuda repletis,
>   paruaque sinceras uelat aluta genas.
> nec pudor est oculos tenui signare fauilla,
>   uel prope te nato, lucide Cydne, croco.
> est mihi, quo dixi uestrae medicamina formae,
>   paruus, sed cura grande, libellus, opus;
> hinc quoque praesidium laesae petitote figurae;
>   non est pro uestris ars mea rebus iners.

You know how to achieve whiteness (*candor*) with an application of chalk; moreover she who does not blush with blood, blushes with skill. With skill you fill in the crude outlines of an eyebrow, and a little patch of leather covers the cheeks so that they appear unblemished. Nor is there any shame in marking the eyes with a little ash, or with saffron born near you, shining Cydnus. I have a book, a small work, but the product of great care, in which I have spoken of treatments for your appearance – from this also go and seek protection for impaired beauty. For your part, my skill is not lazy.

Ovid is playing the '*magister artis*'.[9] He is complicit in a female cultural conspiracy to mislead the senses of the male admirer. He draws attention to his handbook of cosmetics as a source for deriving material knowledge about the pigments that will help the Roman lady to achieve her objectives. His description is masterfully satirical: *candor* is counterfeited by chalk, the blush by cosmetic skill, smooth cheeks by leather patches, and so on. The surface of the body is no longer what it seems. The traditional objective relationship between blush (*rubor*) and blood (*sanguis*) is collapsed by Ovid's skill. Ovid's assertion 'nor is there any shame' (*nec pudor est*, echoing the *nec rubor est* of 167) is therefore deeply ironic. His poem both educates the women in the material *colores* that will counterfeit feminine beauty, and simultaneously trains and cautions the male observer, encouraging him to think twice before believing his eyes, to look harder before drawing that connection between *color* and object. A careful reader of Ovid will not be

[9] As *Ars am.* 3.812.

caught out. There is *ars* in the generation and application of cosmetics, but there is also *ars* in their observation and discrimination. Ovid's stance – and the poem itself – makes it difficult to position oneself in relationship to cosmetics. Ovid parodies the methods and objectives of *ars*, but he also shows how unacceptable a Roman world without *ars* would be.[10] Cosmetics and poetics, therefore, were closely connected; Ovid and his well-groomed Roman lady were united in their mastery of subversive *colores*.

Ovid goes on to remind his female addressee that her appearance (*facies*) is a product of the art of pretence (*ars dissimulata*)[11] – and (as a twist on his advice to the male lover in *Remedia Amoris*) she should take care that the *amator* does not catch her in the act, or see the cosmetic pots (*pyxidae*) that are the source of her appearance. He describes the substances before they become integrated into facial *colores* in graphic detail – 'dirt smeared on the face' (*faex inlita uultu*, 211), 'stinking wool-grease' (*oesypa quid redolent*, 213), 'blended deer-marrow' (*mixtas ceruae ... medullas*, 215). He notes that these things may create beauty (*forma*), but at the same time (like Seneca's *inmundissimmae munditiae*) those same things will be ugly (*deformia*) to look upon.[12] For the purpose of cosmetics, Ovid emphasises the separation of the image created from the actual object being perceived. The finished result is one thing, but the truth is in the making – therefore it is more appropriate for the observer to observe after the last touch has been given (*aptius a summa conspiciere manu*, 226). The cause of the *candor*, he stresses, is best left unknown (*cur mihi nota tuo causa est candoris in ore?*) – although Ovid has already made it quite clear

[10] See Nikolaidis (1994) on the incongruity of Ovid's approaches to cosmetics; Fränkel (1956) 63, 204 n. 4 on possible differences in readership. See Habinek (2002) 50–1 on *cultus* and cornucopia; cf. Watson (1982). On the connection between Ovid's poetics and cosmetic imagery, see Gibson (2002) 33–4, 176. Cf. Gibson (2007) esp. ch. 3, who argues that *Ars am.* 3 advocates a 'middle way', contrary to the Augustan polarity of *meretrix* and *matrona*.

[11] On the traditional association of *dissimulatio artis*, the imitation of nature, and rhetorical training, see Gibson (2002) 183; Stroh (1979) esp. 122; Wiseman (1979) 3–8; Wyke (1994) 144–5.

[12] *Faex* commonly refers to the dregs of wine. It was normal in anti-cosmetic commentaries to picture the moment when cosmetics are made to run through tears or sweat – e.g. Plaut. *Mostell.* 273–8; Ov. *Rem. am.* 353; Hor. *Epod.* 12.9–11: *neque illi / iam manet umida creta colorque / stercore fucatus crocodili*; Petron. *Sat.* 23.5; Mart. 2.41.11–12. Cf. Henriksén (1998) 187–8 on the comparatively 'heavy' make-up used in antiquity.

that he does know.[13] In an analogy that would be exploited at some length by Seneca sixty years later, he compares this to the golden images (*aurea signa*) set up in the theatre:[14] close inspection (coupled with Ovid's information) will reveal that these are in fact gold foil (*brattea*) concealing wood – but the *populus* does not see the theatre until it is finished. Ovid's poem is a clever commentary on the mismatch between what one sees at the surface and what is actually there beneath the surface. Both city and body could be represented in this fashion. The aesthetics of early imperial Rome had the power to trick the senses, but Ovid (like the expert thinkers after him) could empower his readers to see beyond the tricks.

Ovid's *Medicamina*, an exercise in the practicalities of cosmetic *cultus*, is a difficult poem.[15] It is made up of two sections very different in style, content and function, and should be considered an adaptation and subversion of an established theme. Ovid's embrace of *cultus* in the first half of the poem sits uneasily with the technical epistemology of distasteful cosmetic ingredients in the second half.[16] He opens by describing the *cultus* of tilled fields, gold-embossed buildings, marble veneer, fleeces dyed with sea-purple, and worked Indian ivory – such 'masks', he claims, are a necessary ingredient of culture, precisely what (as Ovid puts it, 11–16) the women of early Rome had lacked. Then he plays devil's advocate (17–22): today's tender girls (*tenerae puellae*) desire golden clothes, perfumed hair, gems (*inauratae uestes*, *odorati capilli*, *gemmae*) and all types of exotic jewellery. But Ovid intercedes: this is not undignified (*nec tamen indignum*). It is the job of women, and of *cultus* to please (*sit uobis cura placendi*) men.

[13] This is echoed at Prop. 3.24.7–8 when Propertius recognises that Cynthia's *candor* is a sham (*et color est totiens roseo collatus Eoo, / cum tibi quaesitus candor in ore foret*). Cf. 1.2.19 (*falso ... candore*).

[14] Sen. *Ep.* 115.9; on this passage, see above pp. 92–3. On *aureus* and *auratus* in verse, see André (1949) 155–6.

[15] Its literary complexity is exacerbated by the belief that the poem is incomplete: Green (1979); Green (1982) 426; Rosati (1985) 43–5; also Nikolaidis (1994) 102 n. 18 and Gibson (2002) 179–80. Cf. Watson (2001) who nevertheless points out that the truncated poem is still thematically and stylistically coherent. Cf. Wilkinson (1955) 118 and Leary (1988) 140–2, who consider the truncation possibly deliberate. Ovid's *Medicamina* is discussed at length in Rimell (2006) ch. 1.

[16] On this aspect, see Heldmann (1981).

Nostra saecula, this Augustan Golden Age, even fosters elegant men (*compti viri*) who themselves follow the law of women (*lex feminea*), by 'polishing' (*poliuntur*) their appearance, often with greater success than their brides. Even farmers are doing up their hair (*rure latent finguntque comas*) while hiding behind their rustic identities. Ovid on the one hand embraces *cultus*, then challenges and complicates it; his very analogies of justification (gilded buildings, marble veneer, purple clothes, ivory) were the classic examples that veered awkwardly between cultural sophistication and urban decadence. Ovid goes on to assert that one must not confuse *cultus* and 'black magic'.[17] *Cultus* is far more effective at procuring *amor* than the terrible art (*terribilis ars*) of the mage, herbs and Marsian incantations.[18] But he then claims that *facies* is best preserved by character (*mores*), mind (*ingenium*) and honesty (*probitas*), broad and idealised ethical values that (Ovid suggests) can be expressed through the honest face. The logical implication is that his poem is addressed to those who lack *probitas*, and therefore need Ovid to tell them how to counterfeit it.[19]

Then, in a glaring non sequitur, he gets down to business. The second half of the poem exercises Ovid's own *terribilis ars*, describing in some detail a handful of tricks, recipes and drugs – *medicamina* – which can be used to achieve *cultus*. The style now is informative, a bland set of instructions and ingredients for making the face look different. Many of the ingredients have un-Roman roots – barley from Libya (53), cummin seed from Etruria (65), iris from Illyria (74), honey from Attica (82) and African spice (94). Ovid's description, like Pliny's discussion of pigments (see above pp. 94–101), succeeds in displacing these cosmetics as far as possible from the faces which they make up. The actual ingredients – a rigid prescription which involves plant and animal products – are far removed from the effects they render. The juxtaposition of 'white face' (*candida ... ora*) and 'barley' (*hordea*, 52–3), and remedies from the nests of birds alongside spot treatments (*addita de querulo*

[17] See Watson (2001) 463–6.

[18] Cf. Tib. 1.5.43–4 *non facit hoc uerbis* (i.e. magic incantations), *facie tenerisque lacertis / deuouet et flauis nostra puella comis*; 1.8.24 *forma nihil magicis utitur auxiliis*.

[19] Contrary to Lilja (1965) 130, 152; cf. Rosati (1985) 35 who believes that Ovid's approval of *cultus* is deliberate. Cf. Watson (2001) 466.

uolucrum medicamina nido / ore fugant maculas, 77–8), for example, illustrate the semiotic leap Ovid is making. The effect these recipes (*tali medicamine*) have is described in terms of 'polish': the subject's face can shine brightly (*candida ... possint ora nitere*) and the result is skin that will glow smoother than her own mirror (*fulgebit speculo leuior*).[20] The face-masks of Ovid's *Medicamina* often entail in turn the removal of skin from the ingredients – barley stripped of its chaff (*tegmina*), narcissus bulbs without their skins (*sine cortice*), gum stripped of its bark (*dereptum cortice*). These exploited, flayed and adulterated features of *natura*, Ovid concludes, will produce a strong colour (*multus color*), which will 'stick' to your whole face (*haerebit ... toto in ore*). The last two lines of the surviving poem describe the ground-down and disintegrated (*contereret*) poppies that are then synthesised and re-integrated to become a mask (*illineret*) for the girl's face. Ovid ends the *Medicamina* by parading the susceptibility of the soft face and tender cheeks (*mollis uultus ... tenerae genae*) to receive new *color* – a familiar ethical vocabulary connecting weak personalities with unstable appearances. A theme of the *Medicamina* is (in a very specific way) 'abstraction', the reinvention of unlikely natural products as a counterfeit *color* for the human face, so that what they essentially are is no longer of relevance to where one sees them. Ovid parodies this problem in his poem by playing the proponent, the critic, the devil's advocate and the establishment in his treatment of *cultus* – demonstrating the ambiguity inherent to any interpretation of the use of cosmetics. This was the paradox explored by Pliny the Elder two generations later: the age-old anxieties about women as consumers developed hand in hand with a celebration of imperial cornucopia, and the discrimination and evaluation of *color* performed a central role in this cultural clash.

Intellectual strategies were developed to resolve the ethical tensions inherent to cosmetics. In the late second century, Galen, following in the footsteps of Greek diatribes against the deceptive artifice of cosmetics, distinguishes between good and bad cosmetic

[20] The *speculum* was a classic source of illusion and visual distortion (far different from our mirrors which return a near-perfect image). So Sen. *QNat.* 1.17 and Wyke (1994) 134–51.

arts, between the male-instigated medical practice of preserving the body's natural beauty (τὸ κοσμητικὸν τῆς ἰατρικῆς μέρος) and women's bag of tricks, cosmetics which whitened the face, and dyed or curled the hair, bestowing an unnatural, acquired beauty (described as *to kommōtikon*).[21] Other doctors, committed as they were to the accurate observation of the body, looked down on the female infatuation with cosmetics: Celsus, writing shortly after Ovid, describes the treatment of pimples and spots as a waste of time (*paene ineptiae sunt*), but add that women cannot be torn away from caring for their looks (*sed eripi tamen feminis cura cultus, sui non potest*).[22] The five surviving recipes of Ovid's *Medicamina* might arguably be classed among Galen's *to kosmētikon* (i.e. medical treatments to restore the body's natural appearance), but Ovid typically challenges and reworks any attempt to simplify cosmetics. Both in the *Medicamina* and in the *Ars Amatoria*, he argues on a number of occasions that *ars* may compensate for *natura*.[23] The moral implications of transforming one's appearance (and therefore one's identity) with cosmetics, however, appear to have persistently challenged thinkers for a long period of Greco-Roman antiquity.[24] Martial takes this idea to the extreme in a hyperbolic epigram (9.37) about the old woman Galla, whose *cultus* makes her almost entirely a cosmetic construct.

> cum sis ipsa domi mediaque ornere Subura,
>   fiant absentes et tibi, Galla, comae,
> nec dentes aliter quam Serica nocte reponas,
>   et iaceas centum condita pyxidibus,
> nec tecum facies tua dormiat, innuis illo
>   quod tibi prolatum est mane supercilio,
> et te nulla mouet cani reuerentia cunni,
>   quem potes inter auos iam numerare tuos.
> prommittis sescenta tamen; sed mentula surda est,
>   et sit lusca licet, te tamen illa uidet.

[21] Galen 12.434–5 (Kühn). For the background to the argument, see Grillet (1975) 11–18. Cf. Rosati (1985) 20.

[22] Celsus, *Med.* 6.5. He nevertheless proceeds with a lengthy description of available concealers and treatments.

[23] This in spite of Rosati's claim (1985, 26–7) that Ovid remains within the bounds of 'naturalismo, le colonne d' Ercole dell'estetica antica', an idea taken on by Gibson (2002) 175–6.

[24] Foucault (1985) 160–3; cf. Rosati (1985) 11.

> Although you are at home yourself, Galla, you are made up (*ornere*) in the middle of the Subura. Your hair is created far away from you, you lay your teeth aside at night just like your silks, and you lie stored in a hundred cosmetic pots (*pyxidae*). Your face (*facies*) does not sleep with you, you ogle with an eyebrow that is brought out for you in the morning, and no respect for your hoary cunt (*canus cunnus*), which you may now count among your ancestors, touches you. However, you promise any number of things; but my dick cannot hear you, and one-eyed as it may be, it still sees you.

Martial's metaphorical penis is impotent to Galla's attempts at seduction but, in a cutting satire on the abuse of cosmetics (particularly by the older lady[25]), it *sees* Galla (*te tamen illa uidet*) for who she is. Once again, the poet sits in a position of epistemological superiority, identifying with technical precision each of the elements (the make-up, the wig, the eyebrow, the teeth) that make up Galla's *cultus* (or in fact make up *Galla*, as Martial jokes). Galla is an old woman shamelessly – and unsuccessfully – trying to appear young. Her make-up is cheap (purchased in the Subura), excessive, un-Roman (*pyxidibus*) and above all synthetic. It fails to enhance the woman beneath; instead it transforms her. It takes on a life of its own, and the 'real' Galla is nowhere to be seen. One true *color* that does remain on Galla, Martial jokes, is that of her white-haired vagina (*canus cunnus*), but a *color* so forsaken by her (like that of her white-bearded ancestors, presumably) that it bears witness to her lack of *reuerentia*. Instead, the Galla that everyone recognises is buried inside a hundred pots of make-up (*centum condita pyxidibus*), to the extent that Martial can joke that her *facies* does not sleep with her. Her eyebrow too is '*prolatum mane*', either lengthened by soot or a patch of the sort that became fashionable in the first century.[26] This poem is a *reductio ad absurdum* of an established theme, a brilliant didactic exercise (and one hot on the lips of first-century ethical thinkers) in training the viewer to see accurately the made-up female. And it is highly significant that it does not construct a

[25] On the wearing effects of old age on the body, and the heavy make-up so often applied to conceal it, see *Anth. Pal.* 11.66; 11.310; 11.374.1–2 and 11.408.

[26] Cf. Petron. *Sat.* 110.2; 126.15; Ov. *Ars am.* 3.201; Juv. 2.93; Forbes, *Stud. Anc. Technol.* 3.40.

repertoire of abstract colours (as we might classify cosmetics), but a repertoire of the things that made up these colours.

Other writers missed no opportunity to parody the materials that made up the beautiful lady. Juvenal's early second-century satire on the monstrous and promiscuous race of women includes a description of the face-packs, the *medicamina* which hide the adulterous wife's face while she is with her husband (6.461–73): 'but after it has been coated over and treated with so many transformed remedies (*tot mutata medicamina*) and received lumps of cooked and moistened dough (*offae coctae et madidae siliginis*), shall it be called a face (*facies*) or an ulcer (*ulcus*)?' Only for her lover does she achieve the final stage of transformation and become beautiful (*formosa*) – only then does she reveal her face (*aperit uultum*), peel off the upper layers (*prima tectoria*), and approach her lover with her skin finally cleansed (*lota ... cute*). Juvenal's Roman wife is a figure of metamorphosis and masks. Similarly, Pliny the Elder pulls no punches in his catalogue of the unlikely and unpleasant ingredients that make up these cosmetics. To achieve *candor*, ass's milk (*lac asininus*) is applied religiously (28.183), along with the boiled-down bones of a white bull-calf; both remove wrinkles (*erugari*) from the face and make the skin tender with whiteness (*tenerescere candore*). Pliny apologises for the frivolous character (*friuolum*) of these recipes, but says they are necessary to keep the women happy (*non tamen omittendum propter desideria mulierum*). On *rubor* it is a point of debate, Pliny goes on, whether rubbing (*inlini*) bull's dung on the face, or crocodile dung makes the cheeks rosier (*malas rubescere*) – a revolting recipe for the much sought-after blush. Other facial treatments include oil and gum, vinegar, sulphur, calves' genitals, ass's urine, various types of gall, suet, cheese, grease, marrow and ash. As Pliny puts it, this process normally consists of the removal ('*erugari*', '*tolluntur*', '*erugatio*', '*emendat*', '*tollit*' and so on) of some surface defect, some *macula*, followed by the application, the 'smearing on' ('*tenerescere*', '*inlito*', '*inlitum*', '*praestare*', '*rubescere*') of some counterfeit *color*. Pliny's cold, scientific cosmetic education may on some level be a practical didactic one, but it also manages to collapse – and parody – the social and intellectual currency that was attached to the surface of the female body.

First-century thinkers working in a range of genres – Ovid, Pliny, Martial and Juvenal – recognised and paraded the cultural difficulties posed by cosmetics to the correct evaluation and understanding of character, behaviour and identity. Each performed a diagnostic role, identifying with precision the ingredients that the disgruntled husband has to observe. *Cultus* – the care and enhancement of the body – was a deeply embedded feature of civilised Roman life in the early Empire, but at the same time it set a serious logical challenge for the prevailing ethics of perception, the premise that vision could penetrate reality. Colour – both the pigments that achieved *cultus*, and the resulting 'impression' of the face – was a central part of this discourse. In the modern West, make-up is usually classified by colour. To respond to the epistemological problems posed to perception by cosmetics in ancient Rome, contemporaries appear to have been more concerned with classifying artificial colours by ingredients and origin, and thereby exposing them for what they really were. The result was a deeply pertinent contribution to the evaluation of cosmetics as a manifestation of feminine deception, and the role of perception in the correct understanding of contemporary somatic colours.

Hair

A similar dialogue existed in the artificial coloration of the female hair.[27] One fragment of an elegy by Propertius, a typical anti-cosmetic treatment, closely connects make-up and hair dyes (2.18.23–30):[28]

> nunc etiam infectos demens imitare Britannos,
> ludis et externo tincta nitore caput?
> ut natura dedit, sic omnis recta figurast:
> turpis Romano Belgicus ore color.
> an si caeruleo quaedam sua tempora fuco
> tinxerit, idcirco caerula forma bonast?

[27] Much has been written about the potency of the hair as a focal point for female sexuality – see for example Sensi (1980–1); Sebesta (1994a).

[28] For the difficult manuscript history of this fragment, see Camps (1967) 138 and Heyworth (1995) esp. 168–71.

illi sub terris fiant mala multa puellae,
quae mentita suas uertit inepta comas!

Do you even now madly imitate the painted Britons, and play at dyeing your head with a foreign sheen (*nitor*)? Every figure (*figura*) is best just as nature made it: Belgian *color* is shameful on a Roman face. Or if some woman dyes her forehead with a sea-blue dye (*caeruleus fucus*), for that reason is a sea-blue appearance (*caerula forma*) a good one? In hell below many evils befall that girl who stupidly changes her hair to deceive.

The question of deception (*mentita*) through manipulation of one's *color* is high on Propertius' moral agenda. The transformation of *color* to which he refers is synecdochic – *externus nitor* and *Belgicus color* refer to the lady's entire complexion (*caput, os, tempora*).[29] *Belgicus color* comprises everything that makes the individual perceptibly Belgian and un-Roman (the confusion generated is brilliantly represented by the word order – *Romano Belgicus ore color*). On a Roman, this *color* is disgraceful (*turpis*) and unnatural (*contra naturam*). Propertius suggests that even the artificial disguise is second-hand: even the Britons who typically use woad are 'infected' by it (*infecti* – i.e. their *color* does not belong) and the Roman girl plays (*ludis*) at being dyed (*tincta)* with a sheen that does not belong (*externo*).[30] Layers of visual falsity underlie this passage – being barbarians who cannot manage their true colour (*uerus color*) is bad enough; imitating them is madness (*demens*). Propertius then cites one example of an outlandish *color*: *caeruleus fucus*, used to dye women's heads blue. This pigment – generally understood as 'woad' – had by Propertius' time become emblematic of exotic cosmetics. It coloured the whole bodies – skin and hair – of Gauls and Britons, and was imported to Rome to be used more selectively by Roman ladies as a hair colour and eye liner; nevertheless, Propertius playfully invites the reader to imagine an entirely blue body (*caerula forma*). The language of dyeing

29 Some commentaries (e.g. Butler and Barber (1933) 222) aim to identify Propertius' references with more specific products (for example, *Belgicus color* as the *sapo* mentioned at Plin. *HN* 28.191, and identical with *spuma Bataua* in Mart. 8.33.20 and 14.26). Propertius, however, is being deliberately more open and suggestive than this.

30 So Caes. *BGall.* 5.14.3: *omnes uero se Britanni uitro inficiunt, quod caeruleum efficit colorem, atque hoc horridiores sunt in pugna aspectu.* Cf. Mart. 11.53.1; Pomponius Mela, *Georgics* 3.51 (*incertum ob decorem an quid aliud*); Sil. *Pun.* 17.416.

and adulteration forms a tautology in this passage: *infectos*, *tincta*, *fuco*, *tinxerit*, *mentita* ... *uertit*. Propertius' didactic elegy demonstrates that hair and face were both important sites for self-expression through *color*, and that the manipulation of this *color* was a popular playing field for moral debate. He also demonstrates that hair colour in particular was an evocative index of ethnicity, and that its transformation therefore constituted a serious breach of cultural identity.

Wigs and dyes were part of the package of cosmetic *colores* identified and satirised in love elegy, but (in the hands of bad emperors) they were also recurring instruments of state deception. Suetonius describes Caligula's plans for a sham triumph, apparently over Germany,[31] in which he forced the tallest of the Gauls whose hair had been dyed 'red' (*rutilare*) to pretend to be Germans (*Calig.* 47).[32] *Rutilus* was the category that denoted the red hair of Nordic barbarians, the rare verb form *rutilare* an evocative expression of the chromatic manipulation – linguistic as well as physical – in which Caligula was complicit.[33] Transforming one's hairstyle was, as this example suggests, principally a matter of changing its colour.[34] Domitian too was later accused of similar arrangements.[35] Bad emperors could control and manipulate reality by controlling and manipulating vision.[36] Only the expertise and keen eyes of contemporary historians and poets stood in their way.

The Roman lady's hair is the first of Ovid's sites for examining *cultus* in the *Ars Amatoria*. Here, he lays stress on individual decorum for the choice of hairstyle and avoids too much emphasis on traditional stereotypes.[37] Most of the account focuses on the arrangement of hair into diverse styles (3.135–58) but his final comments (159–68) concern hair colour:

31 This is not clear: see Hurley (1993) 170.

32 Cf. Pers. 6.46–7 on Caligula's wife preparing *lutea gausapa* for the captives.

33 On *rutilus* as principally 'red-haired', see André (1949) 85–8. Cf. Varro, *Ling.* 7.83, which creatively interprets a difficult example of colour-usage in Accius in which *rutilare* is used to describe Aurora: he asserts here that *rutilus* was a category of hair colour.

34 As Dar.-Sag. 172 s.v. '*coma*' suggests.

35 Tac. *Agr.* 39.1 *emptis per commercia quorum habitus et crines in captiuorum speciem formarentur.*

36 So too Domitian with his blush: see above pp. 156–7.

37 See Gibson (2002) 32–5, 150.

O how indulgent is nature to your decorum (*decus*), ladies whose blemishes can be atoned for in so many ways. We men are shamefully uncovered (*detegimur*), and our hair, snatched away by time like leaves shaken off by the North Wind, drops out. A woman stains her white hair (*canities*) with plants from Germany (*Germana herba*), and with skill (*ars*) a colour better than the real thing is sought out (*et melior uero quaeritur arte color*). A woman walks around laden with hair that she has purchased (*densissima crinibus emptis*), and with cash replaces her own hair with somebody else's. Nor is there *rubor* in the buying – openly we see [the wigs] coming forth before the eyes of Hercules and the virgin band.

Here, Ovid pursues his project to isolate the female body as a unique *specimen* for the male observer. With men one sees the bare bones,[38] but women are able to take advantage of *natura* to remedy their appearance. The older woman, stereotypically, has white hair (*canities*) – but in Rome she can escape this stereotype by dyeing (*inficit*) it with *Germana herba*. As in the passages on make-up, Ovid lays his emphasis on the ingredients, rather than on the particular colour that is being achieved: one is invited to assume that *Germana herba* produces hair that is red (*rutili*) or (*flaui*), like the hair of native Germans. Nevertheless this *color*, he jokes, is aesthetically preferable to the real thing (*color melior uero*). Then wigs: a comedic *densissima crinibus emptis*, the butt of many jokes in Greek and Roman literature.[39] All this – the visual and material separation of lady and hair – is the achievement of *ars*, *cultus*, and of course money (*aes*). The contrast between one's own looks (*suis*) and beauty acquired from others (*alios*) is common in the anti-cosmetic tradition, but Ovid plays it cool rather than being overtly critical.[40] One final dig in this section is Ovid's note that – whereas the hair *color* might change – there is no *rubor* detected in the wig-buyers, in spite of the presence of the Vestals near the *porticus Philippi* where the wigs are purchased. The made-up lady

38 But see Mart. 6.57 on a certain Phoebus who *paints* hair onto his bald head.

39 Myrinus, *Anth. Pal.* 11.67.4; Lucilius, *Anth. Pal.* 11.68, 69, 310; Lucian, *Anth. Pal.* 11.408; Mart. 3.43; 6.12; 12.23; 14.26; 14.27. Note also Eumolpus' *capillorum elegidaria* at Petron. *Sat.* 109.9–10. Further on the use of wigs, see Leary's introduction to Mart. 14.26; Bartman (1999) 38–9.

40 Not so at *Am.* 1.14, where Corinna finds *rubor* when Ovid comments on her wig, which has 'reinvented' her as a Sygambrian woman. Even the authenticity of the blush is ambiguous (*protegit ingenuas picta rubore genas*). Further on this ambiguity, see McKeown (1989) 384. There appear to be no parallels for *pictus* used to describe blushing.

has mastery of *colores*, and one needs both astute vision and Ovidian expertise to beat her. As far as Martial was concerned, males too could be implicated in this visual manipulation (3.43):

mentiris iuuenem tinctis, Laetine, capillis,
  tam subito coruus, qui modo cycnus eras.
non omnes fallis; scit te Proserpina canum:
  personam capiti detrahet illa tuo.

You simulate youth, Laetinus, with your dyed hair, so suddenly a raven, you who just now were a swan. You do not fool everybody. Proserpina knows you are hoary (*canus*) – she will drag that mask (*personam*) from your head.

This rare example of a Roman man dyeing his white hair black is, like so many of these satires, a reassertion of knowledge in the face of attempts to manipulate vision. Laetinus counterfeits (*mentiris*) a young man, but both Martial and Proserpina know (*scit*) who Laetinus really is and that his real *color* is hoary (*canum*). The use of *coruus* and *cycnus*, perhaps contemporary idioms for the younger and older Roman man, underpin the idea that physical escapism is the objective of this *cultus*. Martial's poem is a parody of the euphemisms of colour change: by taking black and white into the abstract (via ravens and swans) one is coaxed into overlooking what these *colores* actually signify (old hair – young hair). The achievement of Laetinus' *cultus* is a new *persona*: his *color* gives him a new identity, but not one that deceives the keen eye of the satirist. Martial does not stop at hair: such is the contemporary fad for cosmetics that one should expect that the woman with black teeth (*nigri dentes*) has her own, whereas the woman with snow-white teeth (*niuei dentes*) has bought them (5.43). The educated observer of the early Empire knew not to take the colours of the human body at face value.

Clothes

While costume might be considered a somewhat less personal medium for colour expression than cosmetics or wigs/hair dyes, the coloured surfaces it created for the body were no less evocative as expressions of identity and tapped into a comparable discourse of imitation and deception. Here, too, colour was an essential index of meaning. As the Oppian Law demonstrated (above pp. 164–5), the materials and colours of female clothes were considered the traditional site for moral criticism and ethical debate. By the early Empire, well-off women had access to a wide range of cloth-dyes, a far more extensive repertory of colours than was available to paint the face.[41]

Alongside hairstyle and make-up, an established technical prose tradition emerged that described and discussed cloth-dyes. Dress choice was also a subject traditional to didactic verse, and the powers of attraction inherent to clothes was a familiar topic in elegy. Most literary efforts, however, were concerned with the relationship between costume, avarice and promiscuity, and the discourse of persuasiveness and deception.[42] Even the art of dyeing itself did not escape criticism.[43] In the early second century BC, Plautus' *Epidicus* staged an extended campaign against the courtesan population (*meretricum numerus*) in the city of Athens, all heavily adorned (*ornatae*) and snaring men with their trappings. Their costume colours were elaborate and fanciful, generating a complex repertoire of unique and contrived categories (but one clearly familiar to Plautus' Roman audience):

***Periphanes*:** quid erat induta? an regillam induculam an mendiculam?
***Epidicus*:** inpluuiatam, ut istaec faciunt uestimentis nomina.
***Periphanes*:** utin inpluuium induta fuerit?
***Epidicus*:** quid istuc tam mirabile est?

quasi non fundis exornatae multae incedant per uias.
at tributus quom imperatus est, negant pendi potis;
illis quibus tributus maior penditur, pendi potest.
quid istae, quae uesti quotannis nomina inueniunt noua?
tunicam rallam, tunicam spissam, linteolum caesicium,
indusiatam, patagiatam, caltulam aut crocotulam,

[41] For Roman women's clothing, see Wilson (1938) 146–72; Sebesta (1994b); Bartman (1999) 40–6; Cleland *et al.* (2005) 113–53. On colours and dyes, see Blümner (1875) 238–53; Wilson (1938) 6–13; André (1949) 293–6; Forbes, *Stud. Anc. Technol.* 3.98–127; Healy (1999) 136–41.

[42] References connecting costume and dyed fabrics with *luxuria* and moral/social degeneracy are extensive; for a full list, see Gibson (2002) 162–3.

[43] Cf. Ath. 15.686b; Clem. Al. *Paedagogus* 2.108; Plut. *Mor.* 228b (Lycurgus banned dyes outright from Sparta, considering them to be 'flattery' (κολακεία) of the senses).

subparum aut subnimium, ricam, basilicum aut exoticum,
cumatile aut plumatile, carinum aut cerinum – gerrae maxumae.
cani quoque etiam ademptumst nomen.

Per.: What did she have on? A princess's tunic or a beggar's?
Ep.: The 'sky-light', as those women call their clothes.
Per.: You mean she was wearing a skylight (*inpluuium*)?
Ep.: What's so remarkable in that? As if lots of women weren't parading the streets decked out with estates. But when taxes are levied, they deny they're able to pay up. The heavier tax levied by those women – that can be paid all right. What are those women up to, who invent new names for their clothes every year? The 'loose-woven' tunic, the 'close-woven' tunic, the 'little blue linen cloth', the 'under-tunic', the 'gold-edged tunic', the 'marigold' or 'crocus' tunic, the 'under-petticoat' or the 'under-greatcoat', the 'mantilla' headcloth, the 'royal' or the 'exotic', the 'wavy' or the 'downy', the 'nutty' or the 'waxy' – all utter nonsense! A name has even been taken from a dog!

Plautus, *Epidicus* 223–34

This arduous list of fashionable dress types contains several we could describe as colours (*linteolum caesicium*, *patagiatam, caltulam*, *crocotulam, cumatile, carinum, cerinum*). However, the categories Epidicus uses, and the joke within this passage, refer principally to the effects of these garments in imitating some other natural phenomenon or object; on the clothed female body, perception and classification lead the observer to contemplate things that have very little to do with what one is seeing.[44] Abstract colour categories would be one way (for us) of dealing with this, but the categories available to Romans of Plautus' day evoked an ever-expanding repertoire of flowers, luxuries and aesthetic fancies.[45] Periphanes' bafflement at the terminology underpins the kinds of contemporary philosophical problems connected to the increasingly elaborate resources and techniques of Roman *cultus*. This said, one might inadvertently discover levels of verism in the technical vocabulary: being '*inpluuiata*' might refer not to a garment with the same shape or *color* as an *inpluuium*, but the familiar slur that women carried whole estates on their back.

44 Wilson (1938) 153–5 and Sebesta (1994b) 66–7 use this passage as a primary source for clothing styles and colours.

45 On the idea of abstract colours as a logical response to rich chromatic environments, see Clarke (2004) 132.

Epidicus' joke is loaded with philosophical frustration. 'Utter nonsense' (*gerrae maxumae*) is Epidicus' final expression of dismay at the vocabulary and the heavily abstracted aesthetics that generated it. The development of *cultus* that went hand in hand with early imperial expansion had created a great deal of ethical and political fuss (the *Epidicus* probably co-dated the repeal of the *lex Oppia*), and one way of expressing this moral discomfort was to focus on the relationship between language, perception and knowledge. Plautus demonstrates that this fuss, and the logical problems associated with 'perceiving' the cloth-dye, were familiar enough at least to be paraded on the mid Republican comedic stage.

Nearly two hundred years later, Ovid was less confounded by the diverse dress types than was Periphanes or Epidicus. But it was against this literary and ethical background that Ovid undertook his account of dress colours, in which he carefully and systematically advised the Roman lady on the dress types and colours most appropriate to the seduction of men. Roman female costume is the second site for *cultus* in *Ars Amatoria* 3, and Ovid presents a clever parody of the female obsession with imaginative *colores*, a satire on the halucinogenic potential of the materials and pigments newly available to the Roman consumer, and a shrewd contribution to the association of bright colours, courtesans (*meretrices*) and sexual promiscuity (3.169–92):[46]

> quid de ueste loquar? Nec uos, segmenta, requiro
> nec te, quae Tyrio murice, lana, rubes.
> cum tot prodierint pretio leuiore colores,
> quis furor est census corpore ferre suos!
> aeris, ecce, color, tum cum sine nubibus aer,
> nec tepidus pluuias concitat auster aquas:
> ecce, tibi similis, quae quondam Phrixon et Hellen
> diceris Inois eripuisse dolis;
> hic undas imitatur, habet quoque nomen ab undis:
> crediderim nymphas hac ego ueste tegi.
> ille crocum simulat: croceo uelatur amictu,
> roscida luciferos cum dea iungit equos:

[46] Gibson (2002) 162–3. suggests that this passage deliberately sidesteps moral criticism, and offers nothing more than pragmatic advice to women. Cf. Gibson (2006), esp. 127–9, where he argues that Ovid rises above the traditional polar stereotypes of *meretrix* and *matrona*.

hic Paphias myrtos, hic purpureas amethystos,
albentesue rosas, Threiciamue gruem;
nec glandes, Amarylli, tuae, nec amygdala desunt;
et sua uelleribus nomina cera dedit.
quot noua terra parit flores, cum uere tepenti
Vitis agit gemmas pigraque fugit hiemps,
lana tot aut plures sucos bibit; elige certos:
nam non conueniens omnibus omnis erit.
pulla decent niueas: Briseida pulla decebant:
cum rapta est, pulla tum quoque ueste fuit.
alba decent fuscas: albis, Cephei, placebas:
sic tibi uestitae pressa Seriphos erat.

What shall I say about clothes? You, trimmings I have no need of, nor you, wool, who blush (*rubes*) with Tyrian sea-purple (*murex*). When so many *colores* walk around at a lighter price, what madness it is to carry your incomes on your body! See there the *color* of the sky (*aëris*), when the sky is cloudless and warm Auster does not stir up rainy showers. See there a *color* like you, who once are said to have rescued Phrixus and Helle from Ino's wiles; this *color* imitates the waves (*undas imitatur*), and from the waves it takes its name – in this garment I could believe the nymphs were clad. That *color* counterfeits saffron (*crocum simulat*): in a saffron robe (*croceus amictus*) the dewy goddess is veiled when she yokes her light-bearing steeds. This pretends to be Paphian myrtle, this purple amethysts (*purpureae amethysti*), or white roses (*albentes rosae*), or the Thracian crane. Nor, Amaryllis, are your chestnuts lacking, nor your almonds, and wax (*cera*) has given to fleeces its own name. As many as are the flowers the fresh earth produces, when the vine in warm spring drives forth its jewels (*gemmae*), and sluggish winter flees, so many juices (*suci*) the wool drinks up, or more. Choose the right ones, for not all of them are suited to everyone. Dark (*pulla*) suits snow-white girls (*niueas*); dark used to suit Briseis – when she was carried off, even then she wore a dark robe. White (*alba*) suits tanned girls (*fuscas*); you, Cepheis, were delightful in white: for you clothed in this way Seriphus was suppressed.

R. Gibson begins his commentary of this passage by claiming that Ovid's catalogue of cloth-dyes 'includes two shades each of blue, grey and yellow, one green and one amethyst, two browns and perhaps one light pink', although (he concedes) other interpretations are possible. To some extent, to align Ovid's *colores* with a modern set of abstract colours is to miss the point of what this passage is about. Like other aspects of feminine *cultus* (but to a far greater degree), these dyes engage in a discourse of artistic imitation and imagination. The *colores* that Ovid describes are expressed in terms of natural phenomena which they counterfeit:

aëris color, undas imitatur, crocum simulat etc. This catalogue, with its recourse to mythological characters, is an exercise in diverting attention (or highlighting diverted attention) away from consideration of the woman herself. Female costume colours (even more so than make-up or false hair) carried the viewer somewhere else. The poet himself indulges in these imaginative aesthetics, and his poetry is carried away by metaphor and abstraction: besides the mythical digressions, the purple 'blushes', grapes are 'gems', the wool drinks 'juices', the girls best suited to dark clothes are 'snow-white', and so on.

The sheer variety of innovative *colores* available to the female body causes Ovid (and perhaps Plautus) to avoid discussing sea-purple dye (*purpura*), which had become institutionalised as a dress-colour and a familiar hallmark of decadence (see Chapter 7). For Ovid's purposes, *purpura* was a rather costly way for women to achieve *cultus*; as he imaginatively demonstrates, cheaper colours could spark the imagination more successfully. Ovid throws in a small joke to pre-empt the more elaborate colour comparisons and red herrings he is about to employ: the wool *blushes* (*rubet*) with Tyrian *murex*. This colour signalled shame as much as it signalled wealth.

It is crazy to carry whole estates on one's back; there are, Ovid playfully suggests, lighter/cheaper (*leuiores*) *colores* walking around out there. Drawing out his joke, he suggests that sky-colour (*color aëris*) is one of the lighter ones. Ovid gets carried away with the implications of this celestial comparison, and steers his thoughts into the realm of mythology with a second *color* – that of the cloud-goddess Nephele/Nubes who rescued Phrixus and Helle. The simple contrast of a cloudless sky *color* followed by a cloudy *color* is offset by Ovid's casual reference to the tricks (*doli*) of Ino, a passing reminder that female entrapment is the subject of the whole poem.

Ovid's next colour imitates waves (*undas imitatur*) and takes its name from waves. The implication (and selling-point) is that girls who wear it resemble sea-nymphs, an entirely new fantasy persona: *crediderim nymphas hac ego ueste tegi.* This *color* (which may correspond to the *cumatile* of the *Epidicus*), then, finds meaning through its resemblance to waves and cognate watery phenomena, evoking a much broader visual paradigm than 'sea-blue (green) shade', as Gibson translates it.[47] Ovid's point hinges on the strange dye's imitative and illusive properties. Its power to lead vision astray also finds expression in the syntax of Ovid's lines. These dyes are individually stamped agents of women's skill (*ars feminea*): they are the ones that take names from other objects (*habet quoque nomen ab undis*), 'walk around' (*prodierint*) and carry out the imitating and counterfeiting. The next *color*, an established dye for Greco-Roman costume and deeply embedded in the mythopoetic repertory of colours: the one that counterfeits saffron (*ille crocum simulat*).[48] Ovid imagines the predatory goddess Aurora clothed in a saffron garb (*croceo uelatur amictu*), another suggestive reference in the deceptive and manipulative context of the poem. Even the saffron is counterfeit (*simulat*), substituted by a cheaper alternative.[49] Ovid's verse pursues a strong tautology of imitation and deception, his rich interpretation of colours unveiling truths and allusions that simultaneously reinforce and expose his female clients' *ars amatoria*.

Ovid then packs four dyes into two lines, and with each reference the reader needs to supply the verb *simulat*: *hic Paphias myrtos, hic purpureas amethystos, / albentesue rosas, Threïciamue gruem*. The myrtle here is chosen as a point of reference not because of its shade of green, but because of its deep-seated association with Paphos and Venus' temple.[50] The provocative sexuality of the wearer is simmering beneath the surface, its semiotic associations far more relevant for Ovid than saying the garb's colour is simply 'green'. Then 'sea-purple amethysts' (*purpureae amethysti*), a dye that evoked and

47 Gibson (2002) 166. For the prominence of 'wave' over 'blue', cf. Nonius p. 879 L. = 548 M. *cumatilis aut marinus aut caeruleus; a graeco tractum, quasi fluctum similis; fluctus enim graece* κύματα *dicuntur.* Varro (Nonius p. 278 L. = 189 M.) mentions *undulatae togae*; cf. Plin. *HN* 8.191. Cf. also *thalassina uestis* at Lucr. 4.1127, referring to sea-purple.

48 For the various yellow colorants of antiquity, see Blümner (1875) 242–3; André (1949) 151–5; Forbes, *Stud. Anc. Technol.* 3:122–6. Women could wear the *crocota* or *crocotula* – cf. Plaut. *Epidicus* 231; Cic. *Har. resp.* 44; *Ciris* 252; *TLL* 4.1215.18–27.

49 André (1949) 309–10 notes that this is the only verse instance of the verb *simulare* used of colour-imitation.

50 Ovid accepts a gift of Paphian myrtle from Venus at *Ars am.* 3.53–4; cf. Verg. *G.* 2.64. Risqué myrtle-coloured clothes are mentioned at Petron. *Sat.* 21.2. For types of green dye used, see Blümner (1875) 252–3; Sebesta (1994b) 70.

counterfeited two prodigiously expensive luxuries at the same time (there is something desperately self-seeking about amethysts that have to be qualified by 'sea-purple').[51] Then *albentes rosae* – roses that are 'white' or 'pale red/pink' (as the commentators debate), although one suspects the precise shade of colour here is less important than the fact the garment is imitating a floral paradigm of female beauty.[52] Finally, the ashen Thracian crane (*Threiciam gruem*), an unlikely *color* to imitate perhaps, but nevertheless a familiar feature of Callimachean and Virgilian verse, appealing to the intellectual snobbery of the contemporary literary elite.[53] This last, far-fetched, comparison adds a deliberate element of bathos to Ovid's exercise – a *reductio ad absurdum* of the extent to which Ovid's females will go to reproduce alien experiences on the surfaces of their bodies. Similarly, *glandes* (chestnuts) and *amygdala* (almonds) can give their *color* to female costume, and *cera* (wax) gives names to fleeces (i.e. *cereus, cerinus*).[54] These examples demonstrate the lengths to which *ars* could go to reproduce reality. Ovid was well aware that the *colores* of dyes were developing a technical register of their own, but in this passage, he was eager to reunite them with their referents and explore/invent/parade the ramifications and possibilities of these connections.

Ovid then (185–6) compares the available cloth-dyes to a proverbially infinite set of natural phenomena, namely the diverse array of flowers that both set the paradigm for diverse *colores*, and also provided the raw ingredients for many dyes.[55] In a humorous hyperbole, Ovid qualifies his metaphor: so many juices does the wool drink up, or even more (*lana tot aut plures sucos bibit*, 187). *Sucus* was a word often used in poetic contexts to describe a medicinal liquor or potion, a subtle reminder (echoing the *Medicamina*) that there was a force more sinister at play here

[51] A similar contrived etymology ('*Tyriamethystinus*') is parodied by Pliny in his discussion of purple dye: see below p. 196.

[52] Sebesta (1994b) 68 on the chromatic possiblities here; cf. *TLL* 1.1490.3–10.

[53] Call. *Aet.* prol. 13; Verg. *G.* 1.120; *Aen.* 10.265. Cf. André (1949) 294.

[54] On *cereus/ cerinus*, see Plaut. *Aulularia* 510; *Epidicus* 233; Nonius p. 880 L. = 548 M. *cerinum, a cerae colore*. André (1949) 157–8.

[55] For the conventional *uarietas colorum* associated with spring, see Verg. *G.* 2.319–45; Ov. *Met.* 1.107–12; *Fast.* 1.149–60; 4.125–32; Hor. *Carm.* 1.4, with Nisbet and Hubbard (1970).

than simply attractive *colores*. The *suci* available rival and even excel the natural colours of flowers – this is powerful *ars*.[56]

Only now does Ovid reveal that his colourful exhibition of *suci* is not supposed to be worn by all women, but they should observe the principle of individual decorum.[57] The fashionable girl must choose her weapon carefully (*elige certos*), for not every one is appropriate (*conueniens*) for every girl: dark (*pulla*) suits snow-white girls (*niueas*) and white (*alba*) suits dark-skinned girls (*fuscas*). Ovid's antagonistic system of colour coding underpins his more pervasive intellectual point that all these artificial *colores* are alibis/concealers/foils to the girl's real *color*.[58] In order to make this agenda clearer to his reader, Ovid illustrates his two simple examples of colour-coding with two literary heroines, Briseis and Cepheis (Andromeda), both institutionalised troublemakers whose beauty manipulated the course of Greek mythology. *Color* and *ars feminea*, then, could be a recipe for disaster.

Ovid's passage on female clothing raises several points. First, *color* is the most important element in the choice of garment. Secondly, this *color/sucus* performs a powerful function in the construction of the female *persona*, to the extent that the female beneath becomes almost subsidiary to the dress she wears. This argument was one of the cornerstones of the anti-cosmetic tradition, and is heavily exploited by Ovid. Dress colour, in a far more developed and sophisticated way than cosmetics and hair dyes, tapped into the visual imagination and allowed Ovid (like the infatuated male observer he is imitating) to be carried away by a flurry of elaborate visual comparisons and paradigms drawn from the literary clichés of the natural world. At the same time, Ovid's rich allusions test the limits of the aesthetic imagination and, in subtle and sophisticated ways, expose the methods and agenda of the *ars feminea*. It is also significant, as we have seen in discussions of make-up and hair dyes, that elite Romans of this period were uninterested in classifying cloth-dyes (as we tend to do) by abstract colour categories ('blue', 'yellow', 'green') but rather by the objects the dyes imitated

[56] Similarly, Mart. 2.46.

[57] Cf. Ov. *Ars am.* 135–6, *nec genus ornatus unum est: quod quamque decebit / eligat.*

[58] On *niueus* = female skin, see André (1949) 39–40, 324–5; also McKeown (1989) on *Am.* 2.1.24. On the difficulties involved in the use of *fuscus* here, see Gibson (2002) 171.

(sky, saffron, myrtle). These *colores* actively concealed and imitated (*similis, imitatur, tegi, simulat, uelatur*), distracting the viewer away from the actual identity of the female wearer onto a series of exotic images and mythical stories. There are plenty of instances of such critical diatribes on the ethics of *cultus* outside Ovid, but the *Ars Amatoria* manages to play intellectual games with this literary tradition. Ovid makes a case for the use of artificial *colores* on the female body, but he also shows the moral and ethical weaknesses in this case. He plays the enchanted, starry-eyed male observer who is carried away by the *colores* he admires, and he plays devil's advocate by drawing repeated attention to the frivolities and nonsense of the connections one might make.

Summary

Ovid's account of *cultus* in *Ars Amatoria* 3 has been shown to be heavily dependent structurally and stylistically on Virgil's account of natural products in *Georgics* 2.[59] His list of hairstyles mimics Virgil's list of trees and vines, and his list of cloth-dyes echoes Virgil's list of the products of the earth. *Georgics* 2, however, was not just a literary time-saver for Ovid. The contrast between Virgil's inherently natural landscape where features were precisely and properly visible in their place, and Ovid's unnatural cityscape where the Roman female was the carrier of a host of artificial *colores* that were very unreal and out of place, draws attention to contemporary concerns about the relationship between the natural world and the world of *cultus*, of artificial human adornment. The adorned female body was a classic site for contemplating colour in abstraction, and occupied a central position in early imperial discussions of *cultus*: make-up, wigs and clothes reworked and reinvented the viewer's conception of reality, complicating the relationship between the perceptible surface of the body and the nature and character of the person beneath. At the same time, *cultus* was an essential ingredient of culture and civilisation, and the unadorned, unenhanced female body was an object of mockery. The

[59] Gibson (2002) 155, 169; Watson (2001) 461–2. *Georgics* 2 appears also to have been a paradigm at *Ars am.* 2.267–8.

moral and ethical debates this paradox generated dominated discussions of the female body in early imperial literature, and in this context the relationship between colour and meaning was frequently explored, negotiated, collapsed and parodied.

Cosmetics (in the form of make-up, wigs/hair dyes and dyed clothes) dominated discussions of somatic *color* in early imperial literature, precisely because they transformed and manipulated moral and ethical information and meaning on the human body. The rich material cosmetic culture of early imperial Rome revived and developed the established literary theme of feminine concealment, deceptiveness and trickery, by exploring the relationship between the visible woman and the underlying character. Discussions of artificial *colores* applied to the body were principally concerned with the identity and provenance of those pigments and dyes (*faex, oesypum, pane, purpura*, etc.), rather than with the system of abstract categories familiar to the modern West (scarlet, lilac, revolution pink, royal blue, etc.). By identifying these colorants as a sequence of exotic and unusual animal, plant and mineral products, the trained observer could highlight the discrepancy between body colour and body. This discursive pattern was symptomatic of a broad intellectual resistance to colours that were out of place (white lead on the face, German hair on a Roman head, etc.); educated Romans imagined that their worst emperors were complicit in this cultural conspiracy (Domitian's permanent *rubor*, or Caligula's pretend-blond Gauls). Even costume dyes were steeped in the language of imitation and deception. An extensive repertory of categories emerged to deal with the manifold dyes that were available from the earliest documented stages of Roman history, which were expressed and discussed principally in terms of what natural phenomena they imitated (rather than what 'colour' they happened to be). This contrived and misleading visual semiotics was often treated with derision or bafflement, although the literature itself transformed these cloth-dyes – as it did with make-up – into constituents of a colour code through which one could recognise the dangerous female *meretrix*. Through the very act of describing cosmetics, the educated male *cognoscenti* of the early Empire could beat the *meretrix* at her own game and train their readers to understand correctly what they were seeing.

7

PURPLE

Purpura may not have made it into Ovid's list of dress-colour sensations, but for many writers it was visually and conceptually the most distinctive and versatile dress colour available. It was perhaps the fastest and most expensive dye in antiquity, extracted in tiny quantities from a marine snail of the genus *murex* which could be found off the coasts of modern-day Turkey, Lebanon, Israel, Greece and southern Italy.[1] The way its crystals sat on the surface of the fabric caused it to refract light so that the garment appeared to shimmer and glow. The dye itself (as well as the effects it generated) came in a diverse array of colours depending on the species of *murex* used, methods of production and the dyeing process.[2] For the imaginative Greek and Roman observer, this dye could evoke the appearance of the sea, blood, gems and marbles, even swans and rainbows. It was the single most talked-about colour in Greco-Roman antiquity.[3] It is also the colour term that best affords us the opportunity to chart changes and developments in the description and evaluation of colour across Roman antiquity, and it is the purpose of this chapter to study interpretations

[1] On the zoology of the purple snail in the ancient Mediterranean, see Longo (1998b). On the extraordinarily high production costs of *purpura*, see Bridgeman (1987) 159 and n. 5. On the technical details of purple dye production, see Lowe (2004).

[2] On the chemical make-up of the dye and its chromatic variability, see Giacometti (1998), esp. 38: 'tinture ancora più variate, mimando le strade della natura'; on chromatic variation, location and manufacturing process, see Lepschy (1998), esp. 64 for a diagram illustrating the dye's colour range. Lepschy also discusses the significance of linguistic differences and descriptive contexts. Further on these themes, see Ziderman (2004).

[3] The fullest account of this dye in antiquity is Reinhold (1976); on the dye in late antiquity, see Bridgeman (1987) and Steigerwald (1990). Longo (1998a) collects a diverse range of short essays on the literature, art and science of purple from antiquity through to the early modern period. Of these, the most useful for this study is Bessone (1998), who (closely following Reinhold) offers a detailed historical synopsis of the evolution of purple as a status symbol from regal times through to the Late Empire. More recently, and useful for the technical aspects of the dye, see Edmonds (2000).

of one particular colour in detail, as well as to explore changing patterns in colour usage across time.

The colour purple

Purpureus (Greek *porphureos*) was, as we have seen, a highly versatile category of colour. From Homer onwards it was used – principally in verse – to describe a wide range of objects, materials and phenomena that were far removed from sea-purple dye. However, to understand these manifold references as abstract descriptions of things that shared similar wavelengths with sea-purple dye (as we might do with our colour 'purple') is to ignore the underlying connections that existed between the colour category and all the physical, economic and political properties of the material to which that category referred. To ignore these connections is also to overlook or misunderstand the rich nuances and allusions that existed in the colour usage of early imperial ekphrasis. I have argued (above pp. 48–50), for example, that Propertius' difficult *purpureus arcus* (3.5.32) does not simply refer to the appearance of the rainbow, as some have argued, but rather evokes a metaphor of fine and exquisite poetic embroidery. Verse descriptions of 'purple sea', 'purple marble', 'purple swans', 'purple Cupid', 'purple Spring', 'purple snow' etc. likewise invoke the object (luxury artefact) and all its social, cultural and historical associations as much as they invoke the colour.[4]

To take an example, one recurring colour formula of Greek and Latin verse – 'purple blood' – evokes several sets of aesthetic associations: not only do purple dye and blood share similar wavelengths, but the formula evokes fluidity, poetic embroidery, and the widely acclaimed staining power of sea-purple dye.[5] Blood this colour is simultaneously picturesque, precious, violent and irreversible – physically and metaphorically staining everything around it.

[4] Some have argued that the category πορφύρεος may have a double etymology: the reduplicated verb πορφύρω ('heave', 'surge') and the purple murex πορφύρα: see Cestuignano (1952); Perotti (1984); Stulz (1990) 155–67; Clarke (2004) 136.

[5] On the lasting relationship between purple and blood in Western literature, see Longo (1998c).

So it is that Horace considers the Sicilian sea stained *purpureus* with Punic blood as an unfit topic for lyric poetry, Ovid's *Tristia* describes the purple blood (*purpureus sanguis*) of a sacrificial bull spilling onto Roman soil, and the nurse in Seneca's *Agamemnon* pictures the angry river Simois rolling forth waves that are *purpurei* with Trojan bloodshed.[6] Purple blood, the stuff of poetic ekphrasis, stained in a striking and dramatic way. These associations also found expression in the creative prose of the Greek novel: Achilles Tatius, describing Kalligone's stunning purple wedding-dress (2.11), engages in a lengthy digression on the initial discovery of Tyrian purple by a fisherman's dog which bit into the shell of a murex snail and released the dye – described as the snail's 'blood' (τὸ αἶμα) – leaving a permanent stain (ὑφαίνει ... τὴν πορφύραν) on the dog's lips. The fisherman believed his dog was wounded and bloodstained (ᾑμαγμένα), but on discovering the true cause of this colour he used the shell to dye a fleece, which he also observed to appear bloodstained; so it was, the author summarises, that the fisherman first discovered the 'image' (εἰκών) of *porphura*.[7] Ekphrastic descriptions of purple, then, frequently returned to its unlikely origins in the murex snail, its value, and its colour-fast properties as a dye. Exploiting a poetic motif that was used to illustrate the permanence of bloodstains by Homer and Aeschylus, and that would be picked up again later in Senecan tragedy, Shakespeare's *Macbeth* and other contexts,[8] Lucretius (discussing

[6] Hor. *Carm.* 2.12.3; Ov. *Trist.* 4.2.6; Sen. *Ag.* 214; cf. Verg. *Aen.* 9.349 (*purpuream uomit ille animam*); Valerius Flaccus, *Argonautica* 3.107 (*ille purpuream singultibus expulit hastam*).

[7] The precise meaning of εἰκόνα in this context is dubious, and the manuscript has been questioned (there is also some confusion over the role of the protagonists described in the passage): see Vilborg (1962) 49. Whitmarsh (2001) translates 'then it was that he learned how purple may be represented', but this seems clumsy. The category εἰκών more likely describes the image or colour of the dye, which had not been seen before; moreover, its proximity to the verb ᾑμάσσετο, along with the recurring imagery of bloodstains in this passage, suggests that blood was the 'appearance' this dye principally evoked.

[8] Hom. *Il.* 17.360; 21.326–7; Aesch. *Pers.* 316–17; *Eum.* 237–9, 280–1; *Cho.* 1055; Sen. *Phaedr.* 715–16; *Herc. F.* 1321–9; Shakespeare, *Macbeth* 2.2. Cf. Hom. *Il.* 16.330–1, πορφύρεος θάνατος; the twelfth-century Homeric commentator Eustathius of Thessalonica interprets this difficult colour-usage (*Ad Iliadem* 524.43) as a reference to the suddenness of death, comparable to the sudden and violent death that needed to be inflicted on the purple mollusc in order to secure its dye (Eustathius cites Ael. *NA* 16.1 to illustrate his case).

the manner by which some substances blend together naturally) observes that purple dye stains wool irreversibly:

> purpureusque colos conchyli iungitur una
> corpore cum lanae, dirimi qui non queat usquam –
> non si Neptuni fluctu renouare operam des
> non mare si totum uelit eluere omnibus undis.

The purple colour of the sea-snail unites with the substance of wool so that it can nowhere be separated, not if you do your best to restore it with Neptune's flood, not if the whole sea would wash it out with all his waters. (Lucretius, *De Rerum Natura* 6.1074–7)

Lucretius playfully illustrates his mixture theory by drawing upon a distinctive feature of contemporary material culture that would be familiar to his elite Roman readers: the purple dye that comes from the sea binds itself irreversibly with Roman wool, and cannot be reunited with the sea no matter how much water it is exposed to. All these examples, then, show that ancient 'purple' was a versatile and transferable aesthetic category, but they also demonstrate that the physical, social and economic properties of the dye continued to confer value and meaning wherever the category was used.

Both the character and the intellectual currency of the dye were debated across antiquity, and particularly by the literary and artistic elite of the early Empire. In a book discussing architectural materials and colours, Vitruvius includes a short section on *ostrum*, a generic term for sea-purple which could also denote an artistic pigment.[9] Vitruvius' account (reminiscent of his ethnographic account of racial appearances, see above pp. 142–3) attempts to interpret the diverse colours of sea-purple according to geographic principles:

I shall now discuss *ostrum*, which has the most highly prized allure in its appearance, the most splendid out of these *colores*. It is actually (*autem*) obtained from a sea shell (*e conchylio marino*), from which purple dye (*purpura*) is produced, of which there are no fewer admirers than of any other aspect of nature,

[9] On the use, value and production of the pigment *purpurissum* at Plin. *HN* 35.30, 44–5, 49, see above pp. 98–9. Pliny also comments that this was the most valuable pigment used (*ante omnes est purpurissum*, 44). On the use of sea-purple in Roman wall-painting, see Salvadori (1998), who discusses its use to distinguish images of regal figures (i.e. sea-purple dye used to reproduce sea-purple garments).

> since it does not have the same *color* in every region in which it is produced, but is controlled naturally by the course of the sun. And so that which is collected in Pontus and Gaul is black (*atrum*), because these regions are nearest to the north. When you move between the north and the west it is found to be livid in colour (*liuidum*), and what is collected in the equinoctial regions east and west is found to be violet in colour (*uiolaceo colore*). But that which is obtained in the southern regions is produced with a reddish quality (*rubra ... potestate*), and for that reason this sort is also obtained on the island of Rhodes and other similar regions which are nearest to the sun's course. (Vitruvius, *De Architectura* 7.13)

Vitruvius, a polymath with interests in architecture and natural philosopher writing in the early days of the Principate, draws his reader's attention to the value of the sea-purple pigment by focusing on the relationship between its appearance and its provenance. Vitruvius (with a carefully placed *autem*) downplays the significance of its fishy origins, and instead interprets the pigment's various colours as products of the climate in which it is produced, in particular the quantity and character of sunlight to which that climate (and the creatures in it) are exposed. His creative interpretation is reminiscent of the complex mixture theories that accounted for the colours of the rainbow (see above pp. 41–2). *Ostrum* was, for Vitruvius, a versatile representation of light and (like many of his imperial products) a visible expression of the reaches of the Roman Empire.[10] Sea-purple was a classic object of prestige and needed no introduction to Vitruvius' readers, but the architect was faced with the challenge of describing and 'appreciating' a pigment with no fixed colour and no fixed origin (besides the marine mollusc): his solution, then, was to ground its appearance in the light of the sun and to justify its visual diversity by presenting it as a pan-imperial product, worthy (like polychrome marbles) of decorating the elite homes of the metropolis.

Pliny on purple

So versatile was 'purple' in qualifying a whole range of objects and phenomena, and (as Vitruvius demonstrates) so varied was its

[10] Cf. Giacometti (1998) 38: 'tinture ancora più variate, mimando le strade della natura'. See Baran (1983) 357–8 on specific and specialised registers of colour in 'l'époque de Vitruve'.

appearance, that it was easy to lose sight of the object to which it belonged. Pliny the Elder met this problem head on. He begins his lengthy account of *purpura* in the shoals off the Phoenician coast, part of a book not on pigments or costume art, but one which examines the sea, a catalogue of marine phenomena and all the ways Roman *luxuria* had exploited them. Pliny's account of *purpura* (9.125–38) was a typical *reductio ad absurdum*, a potent reminder of precisely where it was that all those senatorial purple stripes, triumphal garbs and emperors' clothes came from.[11]

Pliny's purple-snail, sharing with the dye the name *purpura*, was an ugly and unpalatable life form, nurtured with mud, slime and algae. Fishermen took advantage of its notorious greed (*auiditas*), leaving cockles as bait which would snap shut on the snails' tongues and trap them. Only a few sections earlier (9.104), Pliny had deplored the perils of the Roman appetite for seafood – 'the sea is most harmful for the stomach' (*damnosissimum uentri mare est*) – but, he adds, that is nothing compared to the Roman greed for pearls and sea-purple dye. When it comes to greed, at least for Pliny, the purple snail and the purple Roman had much in common. Pliny then describes the production of the dye (133–4) in gruesome detail. He adds that varying the mixtures and boiling times produced different *colores* and the highest glory goes to that which resembled congealed blood (*laus ei summa in colore sanguinis concreti*).[12] Another method (138) diluted the dye with human urine to produce that highly prized paleness (*ille laudatus pallor*) which meant the dyers could cheat the saturation process (*saturitas fraudata*) and save money. As an afterthought, Pliny adds that the fleeces *devour* (*esuriunt*) this diluted dye. The snail, the fleece, the dyer and the fashionable Roman – all shared this common greed (*auaritia*).

Pliny interrupts his account of *purpura*, the eastern sea-snail, with an account of *purpura* the Roman colour (127):

[11] This is also the emphasis at *De Coloribus* 4, where the author stresses that all dyed things take their colour from what dyes them (τὰ δὲ βαπτόμενα πάντα τὰς χρόας ἀπὸ τῶν βαπτόντων λαμβάνει), and illustrates the case of animal juice dyes with 'sea-purple' (τὸ ἁλουργές) produced from the murex (τῇ πορφύρᾳ).

[12] Pliny goes on to claim that this method is the source of Homer's phrase πορφυρέον αἷμα (*unde et Homero purpureus dicitur sanguis*) at *Il.* 17.361, an imaginative attempt to align a traditional poetic epithet with the technical jargon of purple production.

> [For *purpura*] the rods and axes of Rome clear a path, and it likewise marks the dignity of boyhood (*maiestas pueritiae*); it distinguishes senator from equestrian and it is summoned to secure the favour of the gods. It illuminates (*inluminat*) every garment and on the triumphal robe it is blended with gold. For this reason, even the craze for *purpura* might be excused – but why the price of purple-shells, with the unhealthy stench in their dye, and their grim *color* which resembles a gloomy and angry sea (*sed unde conchyliis pretia, quis uirus graue in fuco, color austerus in glauco et irascenti similis mari*)?

Pliny playfully switches between using *purpura* to mean the dress-colour 'purple', and *purpura* to mean the snail: to really appreciate the former, one must understand the latter. He prefaces his account of *purpura* (105) with an exclamation of his philosophical frustration – 'what connection is there between the sea and our clothing, between the waves and waters and our woollen fabric (*quid mari cum uestibus, quid undis fluctibusque cum uellere*)?' The *Natural History* was a giant demonstration of how one could use perception and sensory categories to classify the world and derive knowledge (further on this text, see Chapter 3). One of Pliny's aims was to reassert and reinstate Aristotelian physics, to demonstrate that traditional epistemology was being undermined by the Roman habit of taking bits of the world – like *purpura* and colourful stones – entirely out of context, and deriving satisfaction from aesthetic appreciation alone. Just as the principles of food are grasped for eating, Pliny will train his readers to have knowledge of the objects that perform such an important visual role in their lives (129). But *purpura* was dysfunctional: the snail was inedible, the cloth perishable (124), and the dye not even particularly attractive (127). Pliny's fundamentalist assessment of *purpura* posed to his elite Roman readers a pertinent rhetorical question: why the obsession?

Pliny's angst is not just that of a conservative on his moral high horse: the processes that were making *purpura* an abstract 'colour' (as opposed to a shellfish) interfered with prevailing philosophical concerns with the epistemology of vision. Purple the colour was a bit of an outcast for Pliny, mentioned only briefly as a component of certain pigments in book 35. One of the reasons underlying its functional complexity, Pliny explains, was that as a colour *purpura* was unstable: it could exhibit a blushing colour (*rubens color*), one leaning towards black (*nigrans/nigricans*), the glint of scarlet (*nitor cocci*), the colour of the amethyst (*amethysti colos*), violet (*uiolacea*) as well as the *color* of a gloomy and angry sea (*glaucum et irascens mare*) and congealed blood (*sanguis concretus*). It was a visual curiosity: as Pliny puts it, blackish at first sight then gleaming when held up to the light (*nigricans aspectu idemque suspectu refulgens*, 135). Shortly after this section, Pliny proceeds more generally to attack Rome's habit of 'readulterating nature's adulterations' (*ipsa adulterare adulteria naturae*) and berate the artificial character of dyes (139). On the dye '*amethystinus*' he comments that it is not enough simply to have stolen the name of a gem (*non est satis abstulisse gemmae nomen amethystum*): *amethystinus* – 'sober-stone' in Greek – can be 'made drunk' (*inebriatur*) with Tyrian purple to produce a twofold luxury (*duplex luxuria*) and the shameless category (*improbum nomen*) '*Tyriamethystinus*'. The contrived nomenclature, alongside the intellectual difficulties posed to perception and understanding by such blends, echoes the parodies on categories (*nomina*) in discussions of cloth-dyes in Plautus' *Epidicus* and Ovid's *Ars Amatoria* (see above pp. 179–87). The point, though, was a serious one for Pliny: categories (*nomina*) represent our understanding of what we perceive, and all these dye names were contrived and synthetic. He does not let the point drop: the derivation '*Tyriamethistinus*' was accidental, the result of dissatisfaction (*paenitentia*) at an unsatisfying *color* (i.e. *amethystinus*) which the dyer fixed with a further layer of Tyrian purple, so that one colour might be concealed by another (*ut color alius operiretur alio*). With this artificial synthesis, how can one tell what one is seeing?

Pliny's objective, then, was first to reinstate *purpura* categorically as genus shellfish, and secondly, with this epistemological premise, to convince the reader that purple was not a particularly appropriate colour for Roman indulgence. Other early imperial writers, for similar reasons, were reinstating this connection between colour and shellfish, and the dye's smell was a potent reminder of where it came from. Martial, satirising contemporary fads for exotic luxuries, described mattresses dipped in strong-smelling Sidonian purple (*Sidone tinctus olenti*, 2.16.3) and, among a list of typical urban nuisances, clothes smelling of murex dye (*olidae ... uestes murice*, 1.39.32); elsewhere (4.4.6) he ranks double-dyed purple (*bis murice uellus inquinatum*) among the foremost foul smells, and jokes (9.63) that the sweaty Philaenis wears purple-dyed garments for their smell, and not for their colour (*delectatur odore, non colore*).[13] Martial's witty repartees and Pliny's sharp cultural commentaries were doing the same thing with *purpura*: both recognised that in the rich material culture of first-century Rome, coloured objects and coloured surfaces were regularly taken out of context and paraded for their abstract aesthetic properties. Pliny, then, was concerned in his description of *purpura* to make perception and object 'fit'. His moral outrage, one might argue, was a result of traditional philosophical epistemology meeting the real world.

Politics and morality

In the real world, *purpura* was a highly versatile and sophisticated medium for perception and recognition. By the late Republic, there is some evidence that the trained eye could decipher one's political character from the shade of *purpura* one chose to wear on the senatorial *toga praetexta*: some politicians were associating light, reddish shades of purple with *popularis* politics, and dark shades with *optimate* politics. One *genus* (probably a lighter, redder shade) could be associated with political immaturity and radicalism: so Cicero assures his peers that age, experience and the passage of time (*aetas*, *usus*, *dies*) would soon mellow the violence, ferocity and stubbornness (*uis*, *ferocitas*, *pertinacia*) of his client Marcus Caelius, along with his 'type of purple' (*purpurae genus*) and the glitter (*splendor*) and shine (*nitor*) that he carried with him.[14] According to Plutarch, the Younger Cato – disturbed by an excessively red (ἐρυθρά) and sharp (ὀξεῖα) shade of purple – accordingly made a point of wearing as dark a shade as possible (αὐτὸς ἐφόρει τὴν μέλαιναν).[15] So institutionalised was this *color* within Roman politics that there emerged a discriminatory vocabulary of light purples, dark purples, Tyrian

[13] See Williams (2004) 79–80.

[14] Cic. *Cael.* 77. Austin (1960) 137 associates this reference (without reason) with the use of Tyrian or Tarentine dye. Cf. *Sest.* 19, where Piso's austere *purpura plebeia ac paene fusca* makes him (falsely) appear *exemplum imperii ueteris, imago antiquitatis*. At *Clu.* 111, Cicero attacks a certain Quinctius for his long, flowing *purpura*; cf. also *Scaur.* 45.

[15] Plut. *Cat. Min.* 6.3.

purples vs. Italian/Sicilian/Greek purples, and double-dyed purples.[16] One might even deduce from the special colour-fast properties of the dye that a '*purpuratus*' was a particularly clean individual, who could wash his clothes regularly without them losing their colour.[17] Even without the fishy aetiologies on which Pliny insists, the Roman observer could derive copious social and political information from the uses and abuses of *purpura* on both the male and female body.

The long-standing status of *purpura* as the epitomy of *luxuria* derived from a common association with the dress of Lydian, Persian and Hellenistic royalty, as well as the iconographic influences of the Etruscans (the Latin category *purpuratus* was often used to describe kings and tyrants). These associations may have been very old indeed.[18] The debate over the *lex Oppia* demonstrates that *purpura* was extensively exploited across the board, worn by low-ranking colonial and municipal magistrates as well as Roman senators, by priests, boys, women as well as Latin allies.[19] According to Polybius in his account of Roman funerals, *purpura* in quantity and quality was very carefully policed and colour-coded (consular *toga praetexta*, censorial *toga purpurea*, triumphatorial *toga picta*), so that this *color* developed a very cogent symbolism

[16] So Plin. *HN* 9.137 (citing Cornelius Nepos) on the criticism P. Lentulus Spinther (cur. aed. 63 BC) received for first using *dibapha Tyria* on his *toga praetexta*: *me iuuene uiolacea purpura uigebat, cuius libra denariis centum uenibat, nec multo post rubra Tarentina. huic successit dibapha Tyria, quae in libras denariis mille non poterat emi. hac P. Lentulus Spinther aedilis curulis primus in praetexta usus inprobabatur. qua purpura quis non iam triclinaria facit?* Bessone (1998) 152–3 observes that Greek vocabulary was generally unable to reproduce the full range of lexical terms and nuances for Roman costume colours, particularly types of purple. Cf. Bessone (1998) 170–1 on the significance of Tyrian double-dyed purple from the late Republic onwards.

[17] As Cicero does at *Flac.* 29.70, with a pun on the double-meaning of *lautus*: *purpuram Tyriam, in qua tibi inuideo, quod unis uestimentis tam diu lautus es.*

[18] Pliny clearly thought so: 9.136, *purpurae usum Romae semper fuisse uideo*; a (corrupt) text of the Twelve Tables limits the use of *purpura* at funerals to one small purple tunic (*Tabula* 10.3 (= Cic. *Leg.* 1.13.27; *Fontes Iuris Romani Antejustiniani* 1.66)). For an example of '*purpuratus*' used to describe royalty, see Flor. 1.4.5 (*ubi frustrate circa purpuratum eius ictu tenetur*). On purple in the ancient Near East, see Mario Fales (1998); on Phoenician and Carthaginian uses of purple see Acquaro (1998), esp. 103 for a map of purple-making centres across the Mediterranean.

[19] Liv. 34.1–8 and above pp. 164–5; Bessone (1998) 161–4. On praetextate garments, and particularly their use as signifiers of inviolability for children (and priests), see Sebesta (2005).

and epistemology of its own.[20] A long catalogue of references suggests that the political turmoil of the late Republic compromised and to some extent fractured this neat political symbolism: the use of *purpura* in anything but the most ritualised political context could betray aspirations to autocracy and anti-establishment sympathies.[21] For similar reasons, its excessive use by women was also treated with suspicion.[22] The epistemology of this dress *color*, then, evolved in tandem with the social and political developments of the late Republic and early Empire; as it changed, the ramifications of *purpura* became increasingly contentious, establishing the dye as a classic medium for controversy, uncertainty and misunderstanding. So potent was this *color* in contemporary thought, that legislation implemented by Caesar ruled that sea-purple clothes (*conchyliatae uestes*) were not to be worn on certain days of the year, except by those whose social or political status demanded them.[23] Dio claimed (perhaps wrongly) that Octavian as *triumuir* in 36 BC enacted legislation which restricted garments of *purpura* to senators holding magistracies.[24] Around the same time, Antony appears to have passed a decree on behalf of the *Hieroneikai* at Ephesus, granting to members of the association the exclusive right to wear purple on special festival

[20] Polyb. 6.53, with Walbank (1957) 739; cf. Liv. 40.6; 45.39.2; [Quint.] *Declamationes* 340.13 on '*Nouicius praetextatus*'.

[21] Plut. *Tib. Gracch.* 14 (the tribune presented with a royal purple robe); Diod. Sic. 36.13 (the *gallus* Bittaches); Plut. *Marius* 17.5; Novius (fl. 95–80 BC), *Atell.* 86; *Rhet. Her.* 3.22.37; 4.6.9; 4.47.60; Cic. *Verr.* 2.72.176; 2.5.31; 5.86; 5.137; 4.26.59; Lucr. 2.34–6 (purple spreads on couches contrasted with *plebeia uestis*); 2.50–2 (*clarum uestis splendorem purpureai* of kings and men of power); 2.501 (*barbaricae uestis*); 5.1423–4, 1427–9 (plebeian garments suffice, in contrast with purple and gold); Cic. *Cat.* 2.5; 4.6.12; App. *Mith.* 117 (Pompey wearing the cloak of Alexander); Cic. *Phil.* 2.67 (accusing Antony of using purple spreads from Pompey's stores as bed covers for his slaves); Luc. 7.227–8; Gell. 15.8.2. For further references (particularly with regard to Caesar), see Reinhold (1976) 45–7. On the recurring exploitation of purple in Ciceronian invective, see Bessone (1998) 168–71. Bessone argues that there was a general shift over time from purple as status symbol to purple as a badge of *luxus*, although he overstates the case.

[22] Varro (Nonnius 538 M.). For Varro's comments on purple, see also *Sat. Men.* 212, 372, 447.

[23] Suet. *Iul.* 43.

[24] Dio 49.16.1. For the difficulties of this legislation, see Reinhold (1976) 46. The move (however it was manifested) appears to have been part of a reaction to Antony's flaunting of sea-purple in the East, in the fashion of the Hellenistic courts (cf. Flor. 4.11.7).

days.[25] Political legislation implemented by several Julio-Claudian emperors also attempted to restrict the use of *purpura* to certain individuals, and at certain times.[26]

In the early Empire, four forces battled with one another: the dye's long-standing vogue as a status colour to signal social rank and economic status; the use of *purpura* for various badges of official Roman positions (priests, politicians, children); the growing nationalistic anti-oriental invective against *luxuria*; and sporadic attempts to (re)institutionalise certain uses of this dye for official Roman status roles.[27] Under Augustus, *purpura* developed a reputation as a discursive foil to the *simplicitas/moderatio/ciuilitas* associated with the new regime.[28] At the same time, Augustan poetry exploited this colour and its associations (particularly in metaphors of fruit, flowers, beauty etc.) to evoke contemporary prosperity and imperial cornucopia.[29] Nevertheless, taking it too seriously as an ethical or political symbol, or giving it too much attention, came to be a familiar topos for attack in Augustan literature. Macrobius' *Saturnalia* (2.4.14), among a list of jokes ascribed to Augustus, describes the *princeps* making a parody of the *color*, satirising the connection so commonly drawn between *purpura* and *cultus*:

> When [Augustus] complained about the darkness (*obscuritas*) of some Tyrian *purpura* which he had ordered to be bought, and the salesman replied 'Hold it up higher and look at it from below', he made this witty remark: 'What? Have I, in order that the Roman people can say that I am suitably civilised (*bene cultus*), got to walk about on my roof?'

Augustus' joke parodied the fad for dark shades of purple that had been given currency by traditionalists like Cato (see above, p. 197),

[25] On this decree, see Reinhold (1976) 46–7; Kenyon (1893) 476; Brandis (1897); *SB* 4224.18. This trend for 'purple licences' became a recurring feature of Roman imperial history: cf. *IG*. 4.586; 606; Lucian, *Anacharsis* 3; *Etym. Magn.* s.v. 'Hellankodikai'; *Anecd. Bekk.* p. 249 (local benefactors granted privilege of wearing purple garments for life, officials at athletic contests allowed to wear purple cloaks).

[26] On Nero, Suet. *Ner.* 32 (*interdixisset usum amethystini ac Tyrii coloris*), with Bradley (1978) 193; cf. 25; Orosius 7.7. On this theme, see Bessone (1998) 177–8. Cf. Reinhold (1976) 49–50 for details of policing under Tiberius and Caligula.

[27] This scheme is noted by Reinhold (1976) 48 (cf. n. 2 here for Augustan examples of all four tendencies).

[28] For example, Hor. *Carm.* 1.35.12 (*purpurei tyranni*).

[29] On this theme, see Bessone (1998) 175–6.

but it also parodied the contemporary emphasis on fashion and the politics of display: the colour *purpura* had become a *sine qua non* for prestige and imperial power and there was considerable social pressure for it to be seen and recognised.

In the Stoic commentaries of Seneca, *purpura* received its most critical press yet, becoming (along with gold and polychrome marble) a standard symptom of *luxuria* and contemporary moral and ethical decline.[30] By the first century, it had become (in spite of its cost and moral associations) a 'must-have' for Roman social climbers.[31] The following century, Artemidorus' *Onirocriticon* considered visions of *porphura* in dreams to be a prediction of office and prestige (1.77).[32] The purple industry was one of the most lucrative businesses of the Roman empire, and documents attest the existence of professional purple-producers (*purpurarii*/*negotiatores artis purpurae*/*uenditores purpurae*/*porphuropōloi*) in both the eastern and western provinces. All of these specialists worked with genuine sea-purple, with a recognised *object* as opposed to an abstract colour.[33]

Pretend purples

Such formulae however were a potent reminder that the dyeing industry was becoming steeped in imitation purples that were

[30] See Sen. *Ep.* 90.41 *sollicitudo nos in nostra purpura uersat*; cf. 16.8; 76.31; 94.70; 114.21; *Dial.* 2.13.2; *De Ira* 1.21.1; *De Vita Beata* 25.2; *Phaedra* 387; *Hercules Oetaeus* 643, 647; *Thyestes* 345 (*uestis Tyriae color*). The persistent Stoic and Cynic polemicism against *purpura* was inherited by the early Church fathers (cf. Tertull. *De Idolatria* 18, where he criticises the practise of dressing statues of the gods with *purpura*); Clem. Alex. *Paedag.* 2.10.108–9, 114–15.

[31] *Purpura* is commonplace in Martial's epigrams – see 1.96.7; 5.8; 5.23; 6.11; 8.10; 10.41; 14.154. Statius uses *purpura* as a *sine qua non* for mythical royalty, goddesses and the Roman senate alike (*Silv.* 2.7.47; 4.1.6; *Theb.* 6.81; 10.60; 12.315; cf. Sil. *Pun.* 15.116. Egyptian papyri attest the open use of *purpura* by private individuals around this time, see Reinhold (1976) 51–2, 60 (public availability of all grades of purple fabrics, as attested by Diocletian's *Price Edict*).

[32] See Kasprzyk (2002) esp. 138–9. Artem. 2.3 juxtaposes πορφυροῦς to ἁλουργίς and implies that the two were quite different shades (although both emblematic of power and prestige).

[33] Documents lay great emphasis on articles dyed with true sea-purple: *P. Oxy.* 520.18 (a white veil with 'genuine' purple adornment); cf. 931.4; 531.14; 114.7; *SB* 9523. For details, see Reinhold (1976) 53 n. 1, 54 n. 3.

manufactured from a range of animal, mineral and vegetable dyes.[34] In the middle of his catalogue of trees, Pliny mentions the 'whortleberry' (*uaccinia*) which he says was used in Gaul in order to reproduce purple dye for the clothing of slaves (*purpurae tinguendae causa ad seruitiorum uestes*, 16.77) – a base counterfeit for a base purpose in a base province. He begins book 22 with an account of vegetable dyes, claiming 'Transalpine Gaul with its plants can dye something Tyrian purple (*Tyria*) and *conchylia*, and all other *colores*' (4). He goes on to argue that there are far more sensible and economical ways of acquiring *colores* for one's costume than seeking murex snails in the depths of the sea, and exposing oneself to sharks – all done, he adds, so that a matron can charm a paramour, and an adulterer someone else's bride. One can stand on dry land and harvest dyes. Although these are not colourfast (*ablui usu*), they can deck out *luxuria* more brightly (*fulgentius*), as well as more safely (*innocentius*). For Pliny, *purpura* signalled expense and decadence, but it also revealed the gratuitous lengths to which Romans might go to acquire this notorious *color*. Imitation purples, then, offered an escape route. This was not so much approval of imitation dyes as a deliberate and calculated dismissal of the inherent value of high-status dress *colores*. And the development of imitation purples demonstrates that to some extent the 'colour purple' (independently of its fishy origins) had itself become the object that was being imitated.

Porphyry

As purple garments became more and more available across the Roman world, their use less and less exclusive, as production became easier due to improved technology and cheap additives, and as imitation purples became a regular feature of the fashion scene, the ties that existed between the colour and the object inevitably loosened, and the 'colour purple' (as opposed to imperial Tyrian sea-purple) gained increasing perceptual currency. *Purpura*/*purpureus* were categories persistently connected to the

[34] On substitute purples, see Renna (1998); Bessone (1998) 182–5.

body, but they too appear to have relaxed and could, with increasing straightforwardness and regularity, be applied to objects (gems and marbles, for example) that were materially quite different from purple garments, but which happened to look 'purple'.[35] The Egyptian stone porphyry (*lapis porphyrites*) was one such object: its literary association with *purpura* evolved alongside its use as a medium for imperial sculpture, and not simply because it happened to share similar wavelengths. From the first century onwards, this stone was used to represent the imperial family in sculpture and used for the most sumptuous pieces of imperial architecture.[36] Like the dye *purpura*, this was an expensive exotic material available in small quantities, carved and transported with great difficulty and expense and, like *purpura*, fell into the category of a material we might describe as 'purple' (in spite of being mottled with white spots).[37]

The quarries probably became imperial property in 30 BC with the annexation of Egypt, although there is no evidence of imperial porphyry statues until the reign of Caligula.[38] By Pliny's time, the connection of colour and stone was suggestive, if not yet particularly explicit. He tells (36.57) how the procurator had presented Claudius with porphyry statues (perhaps of the emperor), but that this novelty (*nouitas*) did not meet with imperial approval. The association between the stone and what later came to be known as 'imperial purple' was in an embryonic stage, and chromatically Pliny can only comment that this stone has *rubor* (*rubet porphyrites in eadem Aegypto*).[39] Pliny goes on to claim that nobody since had followed the procurator's example (*nemo certe postea imitatus est*),

[35] On marbles with this colour, see, for example, Stat. *Silv.* 1.5.38–9 (with Bradley (2006a) 4, 13). On purple gems, see Plin. *HN* 37.121–5.

[36] See Lucan 10.116 (with Berti (2000) 129) on walls of *purpureus lapis* in Cleopatra's extravagant palace (a connection between 'purple', porphyry and imperial luxury that was probably familiar to Lucan's Neronian readers); further on this, see below pp. 219–20. The only detailed treatment of porphyry, with a comprehensive catalogue of literary and archaeological evidence for red porphyry, remains Delbrueck (1932a). On the use of porphyry in medieval Venice, see Lorenzoni (1998).

[37] Although Isid. *Etym.* 16.5.5 later explains: *Porphyrites in Aegypto est rubens candidis interuenientibus punctis. nominis causa quod rubeat [ut] purpura.*

[38] Blake (1959) 3.

[39] Pliny's choice of verb *rubet* is perhaps an expression of Egypt's embarrassment at its ownership of this luxury: see above p. 89.

although Suetonius comments that Nero was buried with a porphyry throne (*solium porphyretici marmoris*), along with an altar of Luna marble and a balustrade of Thasian marble.[40]

A generation later, the connections mapped out were bolder. Statius, describing the palace of Domitian, mentions among the evocative *colores* of the marbles one might find there the shining stone which is envied by Spartan *purpura* and the mixer of the Tyrian cauldron.[41] Porphyry could be compared to sea-purple dye, but this connection still had to be spelled out. At *Silvae* 5.37, Statius is more adventurous: the exquisite baths of Claudius Etruscus are decked out with *purpura*, but (to avoid confusion) this is 'carved from the yellow rocks of the Nomads' (*flauis Nomadum decisa metallis*).[42] Statius was perhaps the first of the poets who toyed so adventurously with the transferability of Latin *colores*, an exercise which became commonplace in the imaginative and descriptive Latin poetry of the later Empire (see below pp. 205–6).[43]

It was only under Trajan that porphyry came to be sold in the open market, without political restrictions. From then on, the stone entered a general vogue and reached its highest production levels in the Hadrianic-Antonine period.[44] Unsurprisingly, the stone became a subject of moral ambivalence. Antoninus' biographer recounts an anecdote of the emperor's visit to a nobleman's house, and the imperial tensions upon seeing porphyry columns (*columnae porphyreticae*) there.[45] According to his biographer, a central feature of Elagabalus' sumptuous palace architecture was a pavement of Lacedaimonian and porphyry stone (*saxa Lacedaemonia … Porphyretica*), a design which irked his subjects so much it was later torn up and destroyed (*eruta et exsecta sunt*).[46] These same materials were later used (with less protest) for palace design under

40 Suet. *Ner.* 50; on the significance of marble types, see above pp. 89–93.

41 Stat. *Silv.* 1.2.150–1 (… *rupesque nitent, quis purpura saepe / Oebalis et Tyrii moderator liuet aeni*).

42 On the complex visual games in these passages, see Bradley (2006a) 3–5.

43 On Statius and ekphrasis, see Newlands (2002) esp. 96–100, 183–4 and 209–11 on marble.

44 Delbrueck (1932a) 19–24; [Aristides], *Aegyptius* 67 (K. 285, 5).

45 SHA *Ant. Pius* 10.8.

46 SHA *Elagab.* 24.6.

Alexander Severus.[47] It was around this time that *purpura* became more explicitly associated with the figure of the emperor,[48] and by the time of Diocletian the stone had become almost exclusively a prerogative of imperial authority. It was the only stone used for the emperor's portraits, and was the material chosen for imperial sarcophagi.[49] By this time, one might argue (and in spite of Pliny's efforts), 'purple' had become a colour in its own right: it could cross the line from being a dye that coloured the clothes of walking, breathing Romans to being the colour of a type of stone. That it had taken so long to share these multiple referents, however, is witness to the relatively intransitory nature of categories of *color* in Roman thought.

By the fifth century, poets could be far more flexible and creative in applying *colores* to objects and phenomena that were quite different from their normal contexts.[50] Prudentius, for example, spurned pagan temples designed with 'green' Sparta (*uiride Lacedaemon*, referring to green porphyry) and insisted that no one should dedicate the purple (*ostrum*) that was innate to stone – i.e. red porphyry – to him: *natiuum nemo scopuli mihi dedicet ostrum*.[51] Half a century later, in an adaptation of Prudentius' verse, Sidonius described a throne for Bellona fashioned out of porphyry cut from the blushing Aethiopian mount where, due to the proximity of the sun, a natural *purpura* has breathed on the seared rocks.[52] Here, *purpura* referred to the light of the sun burning Mons Porphyrites from where porphyry was traditionally quarried; aside from the royal connotations of the throne, this use of *purpura* was certainly more dislocated from sea-purple dye than one would find in early imperial literature.[53] In a

[47] SHA *Alex.* 25.7. [48] For details, Reinhold (1976) 59.

[49] Delbrueck (1932a) 11, 23, 24–6.

[50] More generally on this theme, see Baran (1983) 360–3, 'La "littérature de décadence"'.

[51] Prudent *c. Symm.* 248. The association of *scopulum* and *ostrum* is unusual, and perhaps intentionally derisive.

[52] Sid. Apoll. *Carm.* 5.34–6: *consurgit solium saxis quae caesa rubenti / Aethiopum de monte cadunt, ubi sole propinquo / natiua exustas adflauit purpura rupes*. cf. 22.141 for a similar formula, where porphyry has no place in the splendid baths of Pontius Leontius: *uilior est rubro quae pendet purpura saxo*.

[53] Where the connotations had to be explicitly justified: Luc. 10.116 (with Berti (2000) 129) *purpureus lapis*; Suet. *Ner.* 50 (*solium porphyretici marmoris*); Stat. *Silv.* 1.5.37, cf. Plin. *HN* 36.57, where the stone has *rubor*. See Delbrueck (1932b) esp. 19–24 and Reinhold (1976) 59 on the developing imperial vogue; Raedo (2000).

letter to his friend Domitius, Sidonius illustrates the modesty of his baths by describing all the expensive colourful marbles that one would *not* find there: of the stones that are missing, he conjures up an image of the purple (*purpurea*) surfaces that are dyed with genuine murex dye (*genuino fucata conchylio*) on the Aethiopian crags and that counterfeit sprinkled bran (*furfurem mentiuntur*).[54] Sidonius' creative prose account mimicks Statius' poems on coloured marbles, but it takes the colour associations and metaphors to a further level of abstraction than would have been possible in literature of the first century: what porphyry *looked like* was (at least for these Christian literati) of greater significance than what the material essentially represented. By the later Empire, then, when porphyry (along with *purpura*) had become institutionalised as a feature of imperial iconography, aesthetic 'purple' appears to have been transferred loosely, functioning more as a colour (in our terms) than a specific object.

Re-locating purple: the emperor's clothes

Purpura – what it was and what it meant – of course did matter, and these questions continued to be debated well into the later Roman Empire. In some ways, the imperial monopolisation of *purpura* in the later Empire represented a final stand against the shift towards abstraction and pure chromaticity. While 'purple' continued to be imaginatively exploited by late imperial poets as a descriptive metaphor for a vast range of natural phenomena,[55] the 'real thing' (genuine sea-purple) gradually became established as a badge of the imperial regime. Clothes dyed with genuine Tyrian sea-purple – purple diadem, all-purple silk robe, purple trousers, purple shoes – became in the fourth century formal imperial insignia, and their replication or imitation by would-be usurpers rigorously policed.[56]

[54] Sid. Apoll. *Epist.* 2.2.27: *neque per scopulos Aethiopicos et abrupta purpurea genuino fucata conchylio sparsum mihi saxa furfurem mentiuntur.*

[55] See Bessone (1998) 198–200 and nn. 241–7 for a full list of metaphorical/creative uses of purple in late antique verse.

[56] There are numerous instances, see Reinhold (1976) 63–7. For the relaxation of regulations by Severus Alexander and Julian, see SHA *Alex. Sev.* 40.6–10 and Amm. Marc. 22.9.11. Gradually, silk replaced wool as the quintessential purple fabric; see Bessone (1998) 186–7.

By the beginning of the fourth century, Lactantius was able to state that a purple-dyed garment was for the Romans now a badge of royal distinction (*nunc Romanis indumentum purpurae insigne est regiae dignitatis*).[57] Royal purple (*regia purpura* and πορφύρα βασιλική) became regular tags in political jargon, and *purpura* was frequently used as the substantive for imperial authority: *purpuram sumere* (to take on the position of emperor), *natales purpurae* (the date commemmorating the anniversary of the investiture of the emperor's purple robe), and *diuina purpura* (marking imperial affinity to the divine).[58] From the fourth century, imperial purple was a *sine qua non* for any public appearance; it emblematised both the ceremonial iconography of Hellenistic royalty and the traditions of Persian monarchy, as well as the formal manifestations of Roman *imperium*.[59] To underpin this vital connection, the emperor and his heirs were born and died 'in the purple' – born in a porphyry-walled chamber (hence *porphyrogenitus*[60]) and buried in a porphyry sarcophagus.[61] The Roman eye was trained politically, philosophically and linguistically to connect this dye with the body of the emperor. This reinstated the value of the genuine object (what the dye was/how it was made, rather than just the colour), triggering the development of a complex repertoire of specific dye

[57] Lactant. *Div. inst.* 4.7. For the long-established associations between sea-purple and royalty in the early Near East, Egypt, Persia, the Greek cities and Hellenistic states, see Reinhold (1976) 17–21. *Purpuratus* was a coinage used extensively by Livy (e.g. 30.42.6; 32.39.8; 42.51.2; 45.32.4) to describe Hellenistic monarchs; cf. its use in Curt. Ruf. 3.2.10; 3.8.15; 3.13.13–14; 5.1.37; cf. Quint. *Inst.* 8.5.24; Vitr. *De arch.* 2 pref. 1; Tertull. *De Idolatria* 18. On the connections between purple and the emperor in the late imperial and early Byzantine periods, see Steigerwald (1990).

[58] For examples, see Herodian 1.5.5; 2.8.6; 5.3.12; 6.8.5; Amm. Marc. 15.5.16; 15.8.11; 15.8.15; Lactant. *De mort. pers.* 26, 47; SHA *Quattuor Imperatores* 9.3, 10.1; Euseb. *Vit. Const.* 1.22; 4.66 (on purple at Constantine's funeral); *Oratio ad Constantinum* 5.5; 5.6. On *diuina purpura*, see Wessely (1921) no. XIII, 3: *diuinam purpuram dominorum nostrorum principum*. The early Christian associations of *purpura* with pagan luxury quickly abated as the imperial vestiture was extensively adopted in the iconography of the Church (see Reinhold (1976) 65 fn. 3). Cavallo (1998) 13 argues that *adorare purpuram* was synonymous with *adorare principem*. Further on *purpura* as a metonym for imperial power, see Bessone (1998) 197–8.

[59] Cf. Bessone (1998) 193 on the fourth-century emperor's appearance: 'combinando il cerimoniale del vicino Oriente ellenistico con le tradizioni ataviche del costume persiano, l'imperatore incarica compare in pubblico con diadema purpureo costelato di pietre preziose, veste serica in tutta porpora, brache e calzari purpurei'.

[60] This term also appears as a cognomen of Constantine VII (912–69).

[61] Reinhold (1976) 62; Delbrueck (1932a) 1–21; Alföldi (1935) 51, 57.

discrimination: at least in legal circles, it made all the difference whether one was wearing *conchylium, dibapha, blatta, oxyblatta, amethystina* or *ianthina* (or even various concentrations, combinations or styles of these).[62] Sea-purple workshops along the Phoenician coast became imperial property, and the ritual of '*adoratio purpurae*' started to gain currency in the imperial court.[63] *Adoratio* was a ritualised and institutionalised show of allegiance in which the loyal subject would kneel down and kiss the corner of the emperor's (genuine Tyrian) purple robe. Pliny, remembering the robe's fishy origins, would have seen the irony, but for Roman intellectuals of the later Empire *purpura* had developed a new epistemology as the imperial *color*: its new 'object' was the figure of the emperor.

Summary

Purple would continue to develop and evolve as a marker of political, social and religious authority, as well as an aesthetic category used to qualify and distinguish a wide range of objects and phenomena in literary and artistic circles. In the early Church, various patterns and configurations of purple clothing elucidated the hierarchies of Christian officials (as it had done for pagan priesthoods), and purple was in turn connected to various key features of Christian iconography (divine light, the blood of atonement, incorruptibility, cosmic symbolism, the Holy Spirit).[64] Throughout the Byzantine period, purple continued to be exploited, abused

[62] For the intricate and complex legislation concerning the use of different grades of *purpura*, and on the difference between *sacer murex* and *publicus murex*, see Reinhold (1976) 65–6. Cf. Bessone (1998) 202 on the specific wording of the late fourth-century legislation: one (between 383 and 392) prohibited the dyeing and distribution of any fabric which could be described as *blatta*, *oxyblatta* or *hyacintha*; another (393/395) forbade the imitation of *sacer murex*; another (393) prohibited the use of garments that were '*alethinocrustae*' (perhaps dyed with Coan purple) by actors.

[63] *Cod. Iust.* 50.2.11.7; 11.8.2; Amm. Marc. 14.7.20 on the prosecution of a Tyrian dye manufacturer (and the governor of the province) for replicating an *indumentum regale*; cf. Reinhold (1976) 63, who is doubtful about the extent of the imperial monopoly and policing of *purpura* in the fourth century. For the *adoratio purpurae*, see Amm. Marc. 15.5.17 on Constantius' use of *adoratio* and Avery (1940); Bessone (1998) 188–202. Cf. '*Adoratio*' in *RE* 1, col. 400–1.

[64] For a stimulating discussion of the use of purple in early Christian symbology and monastic life, see Filoramo (1998).

and contested for political and ecclesiastical purposes, and (among the educated *literati*) the imagery of purple appears to have been more creatively extended to other natural phenomena and artistic aesthetics than ever before.[65] Individuals, writers, groups and regimes continued to contest ownership of this prestige colour by attaching it to particular figures, phenomena or ideas, with the result that 'purple' could never be straightforwardly described as a 'colour'.

Purple was, in a number of ways, the most important colour of classical antiquity. It was described, discussed and debated in a wide range of literary, artistic, political and philosophical contexts, and what it was and what it represented were hotly contested issues among the educated elite of the ancient world. This colour, then, entered Roman life as a highly exclusive and controversial marker of status and prestige, a defining characteristic of high political and religious authority, and at the same time a tell-tale attribute of tyranny and eastern decadence. It was a colour that transformed the human body and adopted an almost synecdochic role for the way a viewer would perceive, interpret and understand that body.[66] As such, it occupied centre-stage in many of the Roman ethical debates about cosmetics and *cultus*: what does it mean to wear purple; who should and who should not wear it; how should it be represented and described? Versatile as purple appears to have been as a category of colour, its identification as an expensive, colour-fast cloth-dye produced from the murex snail and worn historically by the rich and powerful of the Mediterranean – so as an *object* rather than simply a colour – appears to have dictated its use and evaluation throughout Greco-Roman literary and artistic culture. The origins, provenance and physical characteristics of this object are recurring features in Roman accounts of purple, and also enrich our understanding of creative literary contexts in which the category 'purple' was applied to other objects (blood, marbles, rainbows, water, etc.). Because 'cosmetic colours' were understood

65 On the production and uses of purple in the Byzantine Empire, see Carile (1998).

66 An individual dressed in purple was frequently described in Latin as *purpuratus*: e.g. Plaut. *Mostell.* 289; Cic. *Cat.* 4.12; *Tusc.* 1.102; Liv. 32.29.8; 37.59.5; 42.51.2; 45.39.2; Vitr. *De arch.* 2.pr.1; Curt. 3.2.10; 3.13.13; 5.1.37; Sen. *Ep.* 76.31; Quint. *Inst.* 8.5.24; Flor. 1.4 (1.10.5).

to be taken out of context – away from their physical roots and onto the human body – discussions of purple frequently reasserted its fishy origins in the eastern murex snail (e.g. Pliny attacking the logic of purple as a Roman status symbol), or established new epistemologies for understanding its significance and appearance (e.g. Vitruvius writing the imperial geography of *ostrum* as a representation of sunlight, or late imperial legislation equating *purpura* with imperial authority). The story of purple in the Roman world is a smart reminder that *color* was deeply implicated in an ongoing ethical and philosophical debate on the relationship between vision and knowledge, and that the Roman body was one of the most important and controversial sites for this debate.

Was *purpura* a paradigm for the formulation of 'abstract colours' in antiquity? The history of purple in the Roman world reveals no neat developmental patterns in the use, evaluation or representation of the colour.[67] It would be wrong, for example, to argue that 'purple' underwent a smooth transition from being an object-based category to being an abstract colour: Homeric 'purple' could describe objects far removed from murex dye, and Tyrian purple cloth remained a distinctive material in the Byzantine period, with many oscillating patterns in the intervening period. However, we can trace a number of interlocking phases in which the recognition and description of purple by the educated elite was connected to particular political developments, literary traditions or philosophical debates: the dye (and its various shades), for example, became a manifestation of the political schisms and tyrannical ambitions of the late Republic, or the material decadence of early imperial Rome, or the exclusive privilege of imperial authority in the late antique period. The competitive traditions of poetic ekphrasis, combined with the increasing sophistication of material aesthetics in the metropolis, meant that 'purple' could be extended more and more creatively to objects and phenomena that shared certain physical, economic or social similarities with sea-purple dye. The relatively small handful of literary windows we have on this colour usage, however, do not allow us to make any sweeping statements about how Roman society *en bloc* shifted in its understanding of purple;

[67] In spite of the ambitious claims of Baran (1983), esp. 325, that it did.

rather, we should think in terms of a series of competing literary and aesthetic contexts or registers in which this colour and its meanings were contested and debated by the privileged Roman literary elite, some of which were related to (and themselves influenced) cultural and historical developments. It can (and should) be argued that purple was extended and applied more flexibly and creatively over time as a result of the competitive culture of literary and artistic aesthetics as well as the expanding sophistication of Roman material culture; however, as with all colours, the appreciation of purple was part of a fluid, subjective and interactive process of recognition and evaluation, and the interpretations themselves constructed its meaning as much as they reflected it.

CONCLUSIONS

COLOURS TRIUMPHANT

The Coronation of Queen Elizabeth II on 2 June 1953 was an elaborately colourful event. Radio broadcasts, newspapers, souvenir guides, and television commentaries went out of their way to evoke the colours of the day and fill in the aesthetic gaps for the benefit of those millions whose experience of the ceremony was limited to black-and-white film and monochrome photography. In the lead up to the Coronation and in the days following, the *Daily Mail* published article after article glossing its black-and-white images with descriptive accounts of the spectacle's striking exhibition of colour.

The Queen's satin gown was the chromatic highlight of the ceremony. As one reporter put it, 'The embroidery is not, as we expected, all gold, but in lovely and delicate colourings. In addition to golden crystals, diamonds and pearls, soft-toned silks are used to embroider pale green leaves, mauve thistles, and the pink Tudor Rose.' The whole effect, the reporter sums up, was of 'silver-white moonlight in colour'.[1] Accounts of the ceremony were principally concerned with the aesthetic beauty of the moment.[2] 'The Queen, still wearing the diadem and crimson robe in which she arrived, is at her Chair of Estate, and the Archbishop of Canterbury, a-glitter in mitre and cope of silver and gold is at the altar … The floor covering is all of glowing gold, very luminous. The throne standing on a dais in the midst of the gold, is covered with roseate pink and emblazoned with the Queen's Cipher.' Even the Queen's natural

[1] Description from I. Ashley, *Daily Mail*, 2 June 1953: 7.

[2] So the title of the article 'The beauty of this moment will ever live in my mind …' by G. Schofield, *Daily Mail*, 3 June 1953: 4. The colours of the ceremony are still vividly recaptured in a description on the Royal Family's official website, www.royal.gov.uk (accessed June 2009).

colours are put to full advantage: after disrobing she is 'a lonely little figure clad in pure white linen … her brown hair simply dressed, a very symbol of humility and service amid so much magnificence'. He concludes: 'so glorious a medley of medieval splendour, of gold and scarlet and silver, can on no other occasion ever be seen.' The aesthetic polychromy of the spectacle, and the diverse layers of colour symbolism underlying it, were top priorities for Coronation-ekphrasis in the mass media of June 1953.

Descriptions often resorted to the clichés of poetic metaphor to evoke the Coronation's brilliant colours: 'above it the rose window [of Westminster Abbey] glimmers upon stone pillars and walls that hold the tones of an autumn woodland, palely lighted … opposite where I sit are the massed rows of the peeresses – some 400 of them stretching back into the farthest gloom. From my distance they looked like a glorious bank of white flowers edged with crimson leafage, drenched in a diamond-dew so rich that when they move it seems like living fire.' Another *Daily Mail* reporter on the same day:

> The multitude of impressions almost drowned in a sea of colour … it is as though an artist were dabbing lumps of colour here and there on his canvas until he has completed a chromatic pattern which has no set design and yet, when completed, is a thing of surpassing beauty … here and there are the wondrous robes of the orders of chivalry – blue for the Garter, green for the Thistle, rose-pink for St Michael and St George, white for the Bath, silver-grey for the British Empire. There is the scarlet of the military, and the two blues of the Navy and the Air Force; the judges in red and ermine, the great Law Officers in their black and gold robes and full-bottomed wigs; the exotic costumes of India, Africa, the South Seas, and every country under the sun; the light, charming colours of ladies' dresses and the glitter of tiaras. (G. Murray in *Daily Mail*, 3 June 1953, p. 4)

Murray demonstrates for us the currency of creative metaphor in twentieth-century popular ekphrasis, as well as the enduring role of the artist's palette in evoking the garish stagecraft of contemporary spectacle.[3] He also shows us that 'colour symbolism' – the means by which abstract colours could be connected semantically to figures, phenomena or concepts – was a popular form of expression in the official jargon of ceremonial costume. Collectively, all these

[3] The official artist Feliks Topolski captured the day in an enormous painting in 14 sections, a work of strikingly ebullient colours measuring nearly 30 metres in total.

rich colours constituted a powerful display of British imperial prosperity.[4]

Lady Glenconner, one of the inner circle of royals at the Coronation, explained the importance of colour in the event's preparations: 'Most of the maids-of-honour were also sent ahead to the Abbey, all of them heavily made-up with super-dark eye-brows and unnaturally bright red lips, because it was the first time that it was going to be televised and filmed in colour'.[5] Indeed, the event stimulated popular interest in the development of colour television:

> *Colour-view 'Much better than TV', says 8-year-old Jennifer.*
> A hundred or more patients of the Great Ormond Street Children's Hospital, London, saw the Coronation Procession in colour television. Three cameras at the top of the Foreign Office in Whitehall gave them a chance to watch the first outside broadcast in colour television ever attempted. Ecstatic sighs came for the pictures of the state coaches glittering brightly with coachmen forming brilliant splashes of colour. The pictures showed the shades of colour of the dresses in the crowds and picked out the red-white-and-blue scarves of the watchers. When the cameras went into close-up, even coloured button-holes could be seen.
> (*Daily Mail*, 3 June 1953, p. 9)

As if to sanction the centrality of colour in the Coronation, the *Daily Mail* the previous day ran an article entitled 'Coronation Rainbow': 'A brilliant rainbow with red and blue its predominant colours arched the London sky last evening after a heavy shower of rain. St. Paul's Cathedral stood precisely under the centre of the arch'. Reds and blues were of course to be central to the ceremony, and the rainbow – a modern paradigm for abstract colours and chromatic symbolism – provided the journalists of 1953 with a compelling prop for exploring the interface between the natural world and British cultural superiority. Polychromy – a defining feature of the most exquisite forms of nature, art and culture – occupies centre-stage in the interpretation of the modern western spectacle.

[4] A different reporter described the spectacle: 'Heavy rain had given way to soft sunshine when the procession, a ribbon of gold and scarlet, of blue and silver – wound from Parliament Square to Whitehall, passing the island cluster of hydrangea and geranium.' On the densely packed crowds, 'colourful uniforms and a variety of complexions told of the diversity of the Queen's territories overseas … but all this was only a minute sample of the galaxy of colour and spectacle.'

[5] Cited in Kiggell and Blakeway (2002) 90.

One would expect the Roman triumph to rival the Queen's Coronation in its exhibition of garish colours. Modern accounts imagine it in similar terms. Garish were the paints used in Pippi's representation of *The Triumph of Titus and Vespasian* (1537), Tiepolo's rendering of *The Triumph of Marius* (1729), von Piloty's *Thusnelda in the Triumphal Procession of Germanicus* (1873) and a long list of more recent artistic depictions. The two triumphs of HBO's television series *Rome* (2005–07) imbued the otherwise bleak and relatively colourless set with striking props and costumes.[6] And textbook descriptions of the triumph, both popular and scholarly, do not miss the opportunity to play up the vivid polychromy of the event.[7] The standard description goes something like this: magistrates and senators led the procession, their white togas and purple stripes gleaming in the dazzling brightness of Mediterranean sunshine, followed by lavishly decorated trumpeters and carriages laden with garish spoils and bright multicoloured depictions of war, and then all the captives, their bodies glittering with strange and exotic colours. After these came the white sacrificial oxen and priests in shining white robes, in sharp contrast to the loud colours of the captive leaders' arms and insignia, and then the captive leaders themselves, doomed to execution and sometimes dressed in black, shadowed by lictors in menacing scarlet costumes. Then, at the centre of attention, the triumphant general, his body sparkling with purple and gold, his face painted red and a golden crown suspended above his head, rode in a chariot drawn by four white horses, carrying a white ivory sceptre and accompanied by his children robed in white. Behind him marched his army, a huge body of soldiers in their military colours, an imposing display of red and flashing metal. The procession was completely surrounded and visibly consumed by an overwhelming sea of white togas, tunics and stolas.

This is probably a good guess as to how a *Daily Mail* reporter might have recorded a Roman triumph. As it happens, while the

[6] Colour and spectacle in HBO *Rome*'s triumphs are discussed by Haynes (2008) 54–7.

[7] Examples include Gibbon (1776–88) 361–401; Payne (1962) 9; Langley and De Souza (1996) 14–15 (a tabloid-style illustrated account of Vespasian's triumph); Connolly (1998) 120–1 (a representation for a young audience); cf. Beard (2007) 81–2, whose deliberately synthetic account of the 'standard triumph' (against the existence of which she argues vehemently) is rather conservative in its use of colour.

historian has a fairly clear idea of triumphal iconography, costumes and insignia,[8] ancient accounts are surprisingly uninterested in the aesthetic colours of this fundamental Roman spectacle. Instead, ekphrasis on the triumph tended to concern itself with the precise and systematic identification and description of the materials, figures and decorations that represented Rome's victory and imperial expansion.[9] Livy (39.52), for example, describes the material richness of Flamininus' triumph of 194 BC, with its display of arms, weapons, bronze and marble statues, astonishing quantities of gold and silver, embossed vases, royal prisoners and hostages. Livy offers a very precise account of the contents of this triumph; he is uninterested in the aesthetic colours of the ceremony. Similarly, Pliny's account of the use of the pigment *minium* (33.111) on the bodies of *triumphatores*, as well as in other key Roman ritual contexts, is concerned solely with the material and its significance, and not with the chromatic effects it produced. Suetonius' vivid description of Caesar's four triumphs uses not a single colour category (*Iulius* 37, 51), and in the triumph of Claudius (AD 44) the *minutiae* of the ceremony are described along with the train of generals who had won triumphal *ornamenta*, all in cloaks of *purpura* except M. Crassus Frugi who had been awarded these honours previously and therefore wore the *tunica palmata* (*Claudius* 17). The fullest accounts were written in Greek, and yet even these refrain from garish descriptions. Josephus' lengthy description of the triumph of Vespasian and Titus over Jerusalem in AD 70 describes the two princes decked out for the ceremony in all the traditional accoutrements, and all the customary followers and paraphernalia in the procession.[10] The triumph itself is described as a 'spectacle' (ἡ θέα, 131, 152) – yet 'colours' play no part in Josephus' narrative. As he put it, it was the possessions themselves (τὰ κτήματα) that mattered (132–3):

It is impossible to give a worthy description of the entire range of the spectacles (θεαμάτα) and the magnificence (ἡ μεγαλοπρέπεια) in every conceivable

[8] See Dar.-Sag. s.v. *triumphus*.

[9] One might compare Trinquier (2006) 217–26 on the relative disinterest in colour terms in descriptions of the Roman countryside (especially among prose writers), where the emphasis instead is on the identification of types of plants or landscape features.

[10] Josephus, *Jewish War* 7.123–57.

aspect, either works of skill or diverse riches or natural rarities; for virtually all the possessions ever acquired (ὅσα ἐκτήθη) one by one by men blessed by fortune – a marvellous collection of resources (παρ' ἄλλοις θαυμαστὰ καὶ πολυτελῆ) – displayed, heaped up as they were on that day, the greatness (τὸ μέγεθος) of the Roman Empire.

Josephus goes on to qualify this cornucopic spectacle by describing gold, silver and ivory 'flowing like a river', tapestries of the rarest sea-purple (ἐκ πορφύρας … σπανιωτάτης) or embroidered (πεποικιλμένα) by Babylonian art with precise imitation of life (εἰς ἀκριβῆ ζωγραφίαν), and transparent gems (λίθοι διαφανεῖς) set in golden crowns, in such quantities that no one could believe they were rare. Images of gods, all kinds of beasts with appropriate trappings (κόσμον οἰκεῖον), attended by men with sea-purple garments (ἁλουργαῖς ἐσθῆσι) decorated with gold, enormous moving ivory and gold stages with magnificent gold-embroidered fabrics, vivid depictions of the destruction of Jerusalem (recounted in great detail by Josephus), and the rich spoils from the Temple. Even among the mob of captives, Josephus points out, none was unadorned (ἀκόσμητον) but the variety and beauty of their outfits (ἡ τῶν ἐσθήτων ποικιλία καὶ τὸ κάλλος) disguised from sight any bodily disfigurement. Titus and Vespasian followed (152), each magnificently adorned (διαπρεπῶς κεκοσμημένος) and mounted on a horse that was a sight in itself (θέας ἄξιον). Josephus' description is extensive, and yet colours and aesthetics are not evoked: the emphasis instead is on the power of spectacle and observation to derive objective meaning about the accumulation of resources, the apparatus of the triumph, the rank and honours of its participants, and the systematic organisation of a victorious imperial state. Plutarch's description of the triumph of Aemilius Paulus (168 BC) is similarly precise and materialistic (*Aemilius Paulus* 32–4): a catalogue of gold and silver acquisitions, attendants decked out in ceremonial costume, Macedonian captives in mourning dress, and the *triumphator* himself wearing the customary purple robe interwoven with gold and carrying a spray of laurel.[11]

[11] This is described as *ornatus Iouis*: Tert. *Cor. Mil.* 13; Liv. 10.7.10; Juv. 10.38. Cf. Quint. *Inst.* 11.1.3, who describes it as the most distinguished set of garments available. For a similar account of the triumph, see Appian, *Pun.* 66.

Even verse accounts of the triumph deploy ekphrasis principally as a source of information. Ovid's description of the triumph of Gaius Caesar imagines the *triumphator*, golden (*aureus* – partly because he is wearing the triumphal *toga picta*), drawn on white steeds behind chained Parthian captives and watched by inquisitive youths who are curious to understand the places, hills and rivers depicted in the procession, and thus the new geography of the extended empire.[12] In a brilliant description (reminiscent of the triumph) of the procession of new magistrates, senators and people on 1 January to the Temple of Jupiter Capitolinus, Ovid's *Fasti* employs the full range of senses (sight, hearing and smell) to evoke the annual renewal of Roman authority and the reassertion of Roman imperial superiority.[13] The poet, his reader, and Jupiter himself are imagined looking over the spectacle, and identifying the precise sights, sounds and smells that reaffirm the Roman people as masters of the world (*populus potens rerum*, 88); colour, nevertheless, is strikingly absent. A century later, Martial wrote a poem (8.65) to celebrate Domitian's triumphal return from his Sarmatian campaign: he remembers Domitian's famous blush emanating 'purple radiance' (*purpureum iubar*), the new triumphal monuments, the elephants and the emperor's golden statue, but the emphasis is on the use of visual categories for recognition and identification, not for their colourful effect. Juvenal, in a satire on luxury and aspirations to greatness, pictures the absurd spectacle of an opening ceremony in the Circus (10.36–46) – a mock-up of the triumphal procession with the Praetor parading in a *tunica palmata* and a Tyrian *toga picta*, a sweaty slave holding behind him a crown so big that no neck could bear its weight, the bird on his ivory staff, the horn-blowers, the column of clients, and the citizens dressed in white (*niuei Quirites*) marching alongside him, bribed by the

[12] Ov. *Ars am.* 1.212–38. He identifies the river gods Euphrates with his forehead fringed with reeds (*praecinctus harundine frontem*), and Tigris with flowing hair the colour of water (*cui coma dependet caerula, Tigris erit*) – their hair-types being the means by which these new members of the empire are identified.

[13] Ov. *Fast.* 1.71–88. Colour categories here are integral to the precise features of the ceremony: the envious, litigious crowd (*liuida turba*) is now dressed in white, the same *color* (*concolor*) as its feast day (a *dies candidus*), and the new *purpura* of the incoming magistrates gleams. In addition, Ovid vividly describes incense burning, gilded temples reflecting the glimmering flames, and the ivory chair of the magistrates.

banquet. For this poet, concerned with the relationship between material extravagance and corruption, it was the ceremonial riches of the spectacle that mattered, not what they looked like.

An even more striking example of visual epistemology at work in ancient spectacle is Lucan's account of the extravagant banquet laid on for Caesar in Cleopatra's palace. The setting provided the epic poet with an outstanding opportunity for a literary *tour de force* on the most exquisite in cultural and visual saturation (10.104–35). Here were luxuries as yet unknown to Rome (*luxus nondum translati Romana in saecula*, 110) – although, by implication, not unfamiliar features of Neronian Rome. Lucan, however, repeatedly emphasises the authentic, genuine nature of Cleopatra's *colores*. Coloured surfaces were accurate and reliable indicators of Egyptian cornucopia: ceilings, for example, covered by a thick layer of gold (*crassum ... trabes absconderat aurum*, 113); walls of solid marble rather than thin veneers (*nec summis crustata domus sectisque nitebat / marmoribus*, 114–15); self-supporting agate and porphyry (*non segnis*, 115–16); rich solid ebony doors to assist and not simply decorate the palace (*auxilium non forma domus*, 117–19) – a sharp contrast to Seneca's contemporaneous invective against the sham veneers of imperial Rome (see above pp. 92–3). There follows a diverse array of stones, gems and covers: ivory, Indian tortoiseshell, emeralds, jasper and drapes dyed intensively and repeatedly with Tyrian dye (*Tyrius fucus*) or scarlet (*coccum*) – all objects specifically and correctly identified and organised by the poet, and all testament to the Egyptian wealth shortly to be inherited by Rome. Even Cleopatra's servants were part of this kaleidoscopic package (127–32):

> Then there was a swarm of attendants, a population to serve the guests. Blood of diverse colours (*discolor sanguis*) differentiated some, age others. One group had the hair of Libya, another had locks so blond (*flaui*) that Caesar said he had never seen such reddish (*rutili*) hair in any of the fields of the Rhine. Some, with scorched blood (*sanguis ustus*), had heads of curly hair (*torta caput*) which receded from their foreheads.

Far from the sham defeated peoples with dyed hair due to parade in the triumphal processions of Caligula and Domitian (above p. 176), Cleopatra's diverse collection of servants were the genuine article. They represented a microcosmic scheme of participating bodies – a scheme which plotted out the edges of the known world, from the scorched blood (*sanguis ustus*) of Africa to the fair hair (*flauus / rutilus*) of the Celts. Lucan's rich ekphrasis carefully and systematically scrutinises the palace and its servants, employing accurate visual categories and informative evaluations in order to reveal the precise extent of Egypt's resources and wealth. There was nothing superficial or artificial here: ceiling panels, walls, supports and doors were composed entirely of the material one would see, and even the servants had their *color* in their blood (*discolor sanguis ... sanguis ustus*). '*Libyci crines*' directed one's gaze to Africans, '*flaui crines*' and '*rutilae comae*' pointed unequivocally to figures from the northern reaches of the empire. In some respects, this spectacle represented a golden age of *luxuria* where every colour told a story, and perception and knowledge existed together in harmony.

The flaw in this argument, and the flaw in any attempt to draw neat dichotomies between the use of colour in ancient Rome and the use of colour in the modern West, is that colour and all the meanings and associations attached to it are always re-packaged and reformulated according to the context in which they are used and the individuals or groups that use them. The cultural historian must resist the temptation to formulate a static and monolithic argument connecting a society and its colours (as has regularly been done in the past), and it would be as wrong to assert that ancient Roman colour usage was straightforwardly objective as it would to claim that modern western colour usage is straightforwardly abstract. The relationship between viewers, the world they perceive, and the categories of colour they use is and was a fluid, interactive and negotiable one. We might, for example, expect the highly educated and literate elite writers of ancient Rome – and their target audiences – to privilege the precise identification of features, objects, groups and individuals over the aesthetic appearance and symbolism of individual and collective colours. At the same time, we have very little sense of how the Roman plebs would have viewed such a spectacle. The 1950s *Daily Mail*, with its overarching populist stance, perhaps demonstrated more interest in the overall aesthetics of the Royal Coronation than the precise history, cost and material identities of the numerous accoutrements and paraphernalia that accompanied the spectacle. That same spectacle for the Lord Chamberlain's Office, on the other hand, must have been viewed and evaluated with great precision as to the materials, fabrics and dyes that made it up, and perhaps differently too when they were planning the event from when they actually experienced it.[14] This book has studied a diverse range of contexts utilised by a very narrow cross section of Roman imperial society in which relationships between colour and meaning were formulated (philosophy, natural history, rhetoric, epic, love elegy, political biography, artistic ekphrasis, etc.), and makes no apologies for the various disjunctions it exposes between patterns of colour usage across different texts and genres, and even within individual accounts. Latin *color* could itself be conceptualised in a diverse range of ways: object surface, pigment, dye, basic unit of vision, character, rhetorical 'spin', and so on. Colour – its significance and its associations – is shaped by a complex web of variables that include the perceiver's culture, memories and experience, the style, aims and objectives of the communication in which that colour experience is transmitted, and the context and target audience of that communication. A well-known discussion in Aulus Gellius of Greek and Latin colour terms (the subject of the *Envoi*, see pp. 229–33) epitomises some of the flexibility and negotiability of ancient concepts of colour, reminding us that the definition and function of colour in antiquity was the subject of considerable debate. Colour, then, is a versatile and multifaceted phenomenon and one must be cautious about making sweeping generalisations.

That said, this book has identified a number of significant patterns that distinguish ancient Roman and modern western colour vision. Colour in both cultures exists on a line between what we might term the 'objective' (i.e. visual categories embedded in and evoking a primary object) and the abstract (categories of colour existing in their own right, irrespective of the object to which they are attached). The modern English-speaking observer can without

[14] Cf. the statement on the Royal Family's webpage, www.royal.gov.uk/RoyalEventsandCeremonies/Overview.aspx: (accessed June 2009): 'Occasions such as the State Opening of Parliament, Trooping the Colour and Garter Day are some of the most colourful and exciting events of the year. But they are not simply spectacular pageants. These official occasions are also full of symbolism, tradition and meaning, and an integral part of The Queen's role as Head of State.'

difficulty employ the latter and describe a rock or a felt-tip pen as 'green', or an eye-liner or a car as 'blue'. On the other hand, statements in which the same categories are applied to grass ('the grass is green') or to the sea ('the sea is blue') more directly evoke the object and its essential qualities. Furthermore, some English categories such as 'rosy', 'orange', 'metallic', etc. are inherently more 'objective' than others and complicate blanket attempts to describe our colour system as 'abstract'. Roman colour also veered between the abstract and the objective: *flauus*, for example, could describe sand, honey and corn, as well as 'blond'; *uiridis* could describe gems, marbles, parrots, as well as plants. Some Latin colours were more transferable than others (e.g. *albus*, *niger*); some on the other hand seldom left the semantic field of the object which they properly described (e.g. *marmoreus*, *aerius*). This model of cognitive reference points with concentric circles of meaning resembles that proposed by M. Clarke (2004) in his study of the early Greek word-hoard (see pp. 16–17), although it replaces Clarke's idea of an *abstract* colour prototype at the meeting point of several cognitive domains (e.g. green/fecund/oozing) with a distinct object ('verdure'). By doing this, the present study situates this linguistic model more coherently within the epistemological debates of classical philosophy and literature, in which visual perception was the principal route to knowledge and understanding of the world, and colour was the essential unit by which the object of vision was perceived and understood. In addition, this book has argued that Latin categories of colour were (on the whole) more closely connected to a primary object than categories in modern English: I have demonstrated, for example, that *flauus* and *uiridis* were semantically less flexible than 'yellow' or 'green' are today, even though some creative writers could use them in ways that were far removed from 'blond' or 'verdant'. We could, then, talk of a 'cultural magnetic force', over and above the specific context or nuance in which the term was used, that kept the Latin colour category much more closely tied to the object. Literary or artistic adventures into more 'abstract' uses of colour, therefore, were often subject to philosophical criticism, and any dissociation between colour and underlying object became a hot topic for Roman moral discourse. An appreciation of these principles helps us to achieve a much more sophisticated understanding of the ways in which poets, artists, orators, philosophers and historians deployed colour categories and formulated the relationship between their art or text, and the world it described.

This book has explored several distinct but overlapping windows onto colour and meaning in early imperial Rome, as well as the currency of colour both in contemporary discussions of the relationship between perception and knowledge, and in moral and ethical debates about Roman material culture and public appearance.

As a starting point, Chapter 1 demonstrated that the rainbow, the classic yardstick by which abstract colours can be formulated, was a significant challenge for Greco-Roman perception and colour-classification. Contemporary thinkers were principally concerned with aligning the physics of the rainbow to its visual categories, but accounts of the rainbow were most at home in imaginative and metaphorical narratives of verse. There is evidence that Greek philosopers exploited existing poetic descriptions of the rainbow for their categories, and paraded the epistemological problems of using such a register. Latin prose and verse authors alike exploited these difficulties in order to privilege a particular philosophical doctrine, expose underlying symbologies, or evoke the divine and the sensational. Seneca offers the most extensive account of the spectrum, a difficult and contrived narrative that explores the ways one could connect the *colores* one sees (*igneus, caeruleus* etc.) to the physics of the rainbow (fire, water). Seneca's very way of describing *color*, therefore, is quite different from that adopted by modern writers and artists approaching the rainbow (*contra* J. Gage, who sometimes assumes that the ancients are trying to do the same exercise he is attempting, but doing it badly). The physical foundations of colour that underpin Seneca's discussion are also visible in other prose and verse treatments, although it is clear that competing genres and traditions utilised a versatile range of perceptual categories, epistemologies and associations and that these are not unconnected to various historical and intellectual developments. Furthermore, it is significant that many accounts exploit metaphors of painting, dyeing and weaving to express the subjectivity (and creativity) inherent to viewing and understanding the rainbow: this interdisciplinary dimension is one that cuts across most of the registers in which Roman colour is seen to operate.

The construction of rainbow *colores* as material phenomena grows out of a traditional philosophical interest in the long-debated relationship between sensory perception and epistemology, and between the physical world and thought. This philosophical background was the focus of Chapter 2, which examined Lucretius' assessment of colour and colour perception in the *De Rerum Natura* against the background of debates in Greek and Hellenistic optics and epistemology (as well as rhetorical, musical and artistic registers of 'colour' which were often very much in tune with these debates). This chapter demonstrated that Seneca's concerns regarding the rainbow as to whether objects possess colour or colour is only a matter of appearance had for a long time been central issues for philosophical epistemology. There were various stances on this subject, but the notion prevailed that, with the correct training, the senses were a sound basis for truth and knowledge. *Chrōma* and *color* appear to have been considered the principal units of vision, and Greco-Roman optical theories generally considered colour to be the visible surface of objects, sometimes emitted in the form of effluences that were carried to the observer's eyes (what happened when these effluences reached the eye, though, was a matter of some debate). All these theories translated into the doctrines of Stoicism and Epicureanism, as well as the 'sceptical' tradition, which appear to have had the greatest influence on Roman thinkers. Lucretius' Epicurean doctrine, in the face of Neo-Academic scepticism, was committed to the idea that colour was a real and finite 'by-product' of atomic position and location. Nevertheless, colour was a transitory phenomenon and Lucretius playfully and creatively exploits poetic forms and techniques to demonstrate its fluidity and secondariness, as well as the limitations of colour perception as an accurate measure of things (the extent to which he does this appears to have gone unnoticed by modern commentators). Nevertheless, with Epicurean guidance, the observer was able to use perception and *color* as a kit for understanding the world.

Chapter 3 explored visual epistemology in Roman material culture by examining the theme of colour in the art-historical books of Pliny the Elder's *Natural History*, which were themselves influenced by the philosophical approaches to perception outlined in Chapter 2. For Pliny, as for Lucretius, *color* was a primary site for the classification of the natural world, but represented an area of human life which was subject to misunderstanding and abuse. In his survey of the marbles, pigments and gems, Pliny both trains his readers to classify and understand the material culture of imperial Rome accurately, *and* (with his subtle and nuanced commentaries) alerts them to the many errors, difficulties and paradoxes of contemporary aesthetics. In particular, Pliny draws attention to the epistemological dangers posed by the manipulation and artificial reproduction of coloured surfaces and materials. This chapter offers an interpretation of the (often puzzling) way Pliny categorises and evaluates *colores* that places colour – as a basic index of contemporary art appreciation – at the centre of Pliny's bigger moral enterprise about decadence, in which the materiality of colour translates into a moral requirement for art to be 'sincere'.

This emphasis on the moral and ethical dimensions of colour – both in perceiving it and controlling it – was even more directly evoked by rhetorical *color* ('complexion', 'spin', 'gloss'), a phenomenon of Latin oratory that is normally considered quite distinct from other registers of colour. Chapter 4 argued that rhetorical *color* both developed out of, and itself influenced, philosophical and artistic discourses of colour that were concerned with surfaces, sense impressions and epistemology. This use of *color* continued to be concerned with linking perception (a person's appearance) and reality (a person's character and ethics) – but became part of a much broader debate on the reliability of those links (the authenticity of the orator's performance, for example). The manifestation of this type of *color* as an expression of character and behaviour in other genres such as drama further reveals the way in which rhetorical *color* and physical *color* could be mutually implicated (for example in Senecan tragedy), and this correspondence between *color* and character was perhaps the most important Roman innovation in the conceptualisation of colour. This chapter also introduces and explores one of the most significant Roman contexts in which colour was discussed and debated, that of personal appearance and its manipulation by cosmetics (a fundamental metaphor for the formulation of *color* in rhetoric).

This idea that *color* was a powerful index of character, behaviour and disposition is pursued in Chapter 5, the first of two chapters examining the display, interpretation and manipulation of colours on the human body. This chapter argued that skin, hair and eye colour performed an important role in the formulation and discussion of meaning in several genres of early imperial literature, and that this was connected to various modes of enquiry and systems of knowledge in ancient medicine and physiognomy. In particular, the emphasis on personal colour as a manifestation of race and gender grounded in such phenomena as climate, behaviour and physiology is reminiscent of the material origins of *color* that are stressed and reasserted in contemporary discussions of the rainbow, gems and pigments. Furthermore, natural colour changes in the form of blushing and blanching (*rubor* and *pallor*) were considered to be manifestations of internal physiological changes based on character and disposition. Much of the literature concerned with the body's natural colours, therefore, was epistemological in nature – both offering guidance in observing and understanding an individual's character and identity, *and* identifying the ways these systems of knowledge could be abused and misunderstood.

Nowhere is the abuse of colour, and the collapse of visual epistemology, better demonstrated than in the manipulation of one's personal appearance by cosmetics (in the form of make-up, wigs/hair dyes and dyed clothes). This phenomenon, which was a popular topic for discussion, debate and parody in early imperial literature, found its most evocative home on the female body, and was connected to a long-established literary discourse about feminine concealment, deceptiveness and trickery. *Color*, then, was an essential index for exploring the relationship between the visible woman and her underlying character, and it is no accident that (as with Pliny's discussion of artistic pigments) the astute and educated male observer frequently – and parodically – rehabilitates the *colores* he sees in the exotic and sometimes unflattering materials and contexts from which they derive. This highly sophisticated discourse transforms these cosmetics and dyes into constituents of a new colour-code through which one could recognise – and beat – the dangerous female *meretrix*.

The final chapter draws together a number of the defining approaches, themes and issues explored in the book by examining the most important, versatile and complex of Roman colours – *purpura* / *purpureus*. Like other Latin categories of colour, *purpura* retained its physical, material connection to the murex dye, along with all the physical, social and economic properties and associations the dye brought with it (so it was an object rather than simply a 'colour'), and this appears to have directed the way it was used and evaluated throughout Greco-Roman literary and artistic culture. This 'achromatic baggage' goes some way to explaining its use as a literary tag for the rainbow and other unlikely objects and phenomena in Greco-Roman verse. Its currency both as aesthetic and as status symbol in imperial Rome prompted Pliny, exercising the same logic he had applied to certain pigments and stones, to re-situate it in the unpleasant fishy origins from which it derived – a powerful (and to us slightly strange) reminder of the lengths to which visual epistemology would go to connect coloured surfaces to the material to which that colour properly belonged. This chapter also examined a number of other attempts to 'rationalise' purple by giving it a more objective frame of reference: Vitruvius' interpretation of the appearance of *ostrum* grounded in the climates of imperial territories and late imperial legislation claiming 'ownership' of the dye represent just two of these. Purple occupied a hotly contested position in Roman literary and political circles; its semiotic flexibility (purple senators, purple emperors, purple sea, purple rainbow, purple stones etc.) demonstrates that – in spite of various efforts to 'place' it – purple had no single 'cognitive reference point', and the history of this colour can go some way towards helping us understand (*pace* Berlin and Kay) the complex and versatile means by which colours develop and evolve.

This book raises a number of significant issues for Roman cultural history. Colour, both in ancient theories of perception and in general literary use, was a highly versatile unit of information. It was the primary visual index for describing an object, a person, a building or a landscape, as well as an evaluative category of 'character' in the broadest sense. Colour is a basic cultural building block by which we can gauge how educated Romans saw the world around them. An appreciation of this principle can enrich our understanding of ekphrasis and other forms of literary description and evaluation. Against this background, the translator and commentator faced with colour categories should be better equipped to appreciate the semantic associations and nuances at work in Latin expressions of colour that do not translate straightforwardly into English. But this must do more than simply colour our views of *color* at work in Latin literature and ancient art: *color*, and all the categories that made it up, contributed to a Roman moral discourse crucially concerned with the ability to distinguish the true from the fake, whether in the context of philosophical epistemology, natural history, love elegy, drama or rhetoric. This book has argued that the questions and debates about what colour is, what function it is supposed to perform, how to discriminate and describe colours, as well as how they could mislead and be abused were fundamental intellectual concerns for a wide range of contemporary Roman thinkers. Colour was so central to these debates precisely because it was so difficult to know, or indicate linguistically, whether it was inherent and the product of what was inside (racial appearance or blushing), or whether it was applied from the outside and existed only at the surface (gilding, cosmetics). Furthermore, the early Empire was at a crossroads in the history of colour and colour categories, where competing literary traditions and the demanding aesthetics of a rich material culture were vying with a conservative intellectual protocol that closely monitored and regulated the correlations between perception, colour and knowledge. In all these respects, *color* is – necessarily and incontrovertibly – the very site at which epistemological and moral concerns meet.

ENVOI

Aulus Gellius 2.26

It would be a mistake to end a book about concepts of colour in ancient Rome without exploring how its findings might help to elucidate one of antiquity's most famous – and most problematic – colour debates: Aulus Gellius' *Attic Nights* 2.26. This *Envoi*, therefore, will attempt to apply some of the principles underlying the perception, description and discourse of colour that have emerged from this study in order to make sense of a difficult and idiosyncratic discussion of colour in early imperial Rome.

Aulus Gellius' *Attic Nights* – a collection of fictitious conversations or debates on a range of topics – offers a sequence of cameos of cultured life in mid second-century Rome.[1] His highly cosmopolitan approach plays out the differences between Latin and Greek, as well as the bigger cultural ramifications at work.[2] While one can detect the rhetorical, philosophical and literary influence of Plato, Lucretius and Cicero on his writings, it is usually claimed that Gellius is weak in abstract independent thinking.[3] He has been described as a champion of the generally educated population against the *grammatici* and the fortress of academia. Nevertheless, there is also a certain disdain for the decline of popular lexical understanding, something triggered by language change and diversity.[4] People forget what words really mean.

Aulus Gellius' commentary on colour derives from one short chapter (2.26) imagining a debate on Greek and Latin colour terms between the flamboyant orator, philhellene and eunuch Favorinus, and his social antitype M. Cornelius Fronto the ex-consul and Latin master, whom

1 See Holford-Strevens (1989) and, more concisely, Baldwin (1975). On Gellius as a champion of parody, paradox and comedy, Beall (2001) 100–5; Vogt-Spira (2000).

2 See most importantly Beall (1997). On the Latin title *Noctes Atticae*, see Vardi (1993). The comparison of Greek and Latin style and vocabulary is a theme of *NA* 2.22, 2.26, 8.2, 17.10.

3 On Gellius' philosophy, see Tarrant (1996); Poignault (1999). Vardi (2001) sees Gellius as an anti-intellectual. Cf. Holford-Strevens (1989) 78, 192–3.

4 An explicit focus of *NA* 4.1. See Holford-Strevens (1989) 128 for some further examples; cf. Collart (1965); Cavaza (1987); Wolanin (1999).

Gellius and Favorinus had visited when he was ill with gout.[5] Favorinus declares that Greek is richer in colour-names than Latin, but Fronto's reply convinces him that Latin is superior in its nuances of certain colours.[6] This colour debate demonstrates the importance of bilingualism in second-century Rome for achieving *urbanitas*; knowledge of Greek is a *sine qua non* for an appreciation of the linguistic achievements of Latin.[7] This conversation is particularly helpful as a point of entry into ancient concepts of colour because, by focusing on linguistic categories of colour (rather than material pigments), it forces the question of *color* into an abstract field as well as integrating it explicitly within a cultural dimension (the sub-text of the conversation is that colour discrimination is mapped onto cultural evolution). It also introduces an ancient register of primary colours, or 'basic colour terms' and allows us to compare the formulation of such a discourse with that developed – for example – by Berlin and Kay (1969).

The discussion immediately establishes a distinction between innate types (*genera*) of *color* and linguistic categories (*uocabula*), and takes it as axiomatic that people see more colours than they can name (*multiplex colorum facies, appellationes autem incertae et exiguae*). Favorinus sets out to demonstrate this with the two 'basic colours' (*simplices colores*) 'red' (*rufus*) and 'green' (*uiridis*) which have many different *species* but just the two Latin categories. Under the category of *rufus*, he mentions fire (*ignis*), blood (*sanguis*), sea-purple (*ostrum*), saffron (*crocum*) and gold (*aurum*). These, he suggests, all give off *rubor* (*rubeat*) in individual ways, but are not individually recognised in Latin because they only borrow names from the things they are describing, like *flammeus*, *sanguineus*, *croceus*, *ostrinus*, and *aureus*. Categories that Latin does employ, such as *ruber* and *russus*, do not indicate unique properties at all. Favorinus then maintains that the Greek terms *xanthos, eruthros, purros* and *kirros* and *phoinix* in contrast mark certain innate differences within the colour red (*rufus*). These differences are expressed in terms of intensification (*augentes*), dilution (*remittentes*) or the mixture of appearances (*mixta quadam specie temperantes*). Favorinus' point seems to hinge on the idea that his Greek colour terms can be used abstractly, whereas his Latin ones are tied to the primary object from

[5] For the characterisation of Favorinus, see Philostr. *VS* 489; Polemo, *De physiognomia*; Beall (2001); cf. Gleason (1995) 3–20. On Fronto, see Holford-Strevens (1989) 93–9.

[6] The conversation has been a classic reference for scholarship on colour categories. See Rowe (1972) 351; Dürbeck (1977) 38–42; Eco (1985) 157–9; Gage (1993) 31; surprisingly, the conversation is not referenced by André (1949). Cf. Baldwin (1975) 22; Holford-Strevens (1989) 47; Fögen (2000) 207–9; Beall (2001) 89. Cf. Baran (1983) 325 and n. 3, arguing that Latin colour vocabulary is in fact richer and more varied than Greek.

[7] See Baldwin (1975) 95–102 for a discussion of this general theme; further on bilingualism/biculturalism in Aulus Gellius, see Swain (2004), esp. 32 on *NA* 2.26.

which they are derived. Favorinus' basic colour chart consigns Latin to the primitive rungs of the colour ladder.

Fronto's immediate response to this is a list of colours which Favorinus has overlooked: *fuluus*, *flauus*, *rubidus*, *poeniceus*, *rutilus*, *luteus* and *spadix*. All these, he claims, are expressions of *color rufus*. Fronto matches and outscores Favorinus' list of Greek terms. Each is a distinct and 'basic' colour category, varying in brightness (*acuentes eum* – an intense *rufus* is 'fiery'), content of green (*uiridis*), darkness (*nigro infuscantes*) or luminous 'verdant white' (*uirenti sensim albo illuminantes*). Different blends of these ingredients create separate and identifiable colours; this is why Virgil (whom Fronto describes as the most diligent poet in his use of words) applies *fuluus* to eagles, jasper, fur caps, gold, sand and lions,[8] whereas *flauus* with its greater white content makes more sense describing blond hair or (even) olive leaves. Once you recognise that *fuluus* and *flauus* are particular configurations of 'basic' *colores*, through careful observation you will see which categories belong with which objects. Language has to keep up with the eye. In the past, Fronto goes on, *flauus* had been used to describe water, and *fuluus* to describe dust. In doing so, Pacuvius was absolutely accurate; one must use the senses to perceive this accuracy.

Fronto moves on to describe *rubidus* (a darker version of *rufus*), and *luteus* (a more di-*lute* form, as he creatively etymologises) and then the richness of the Latin 'green' vocabulary. Under the category of *uiridis* he includes *caerulus* and *glaucus*. The latter, he goes on, was what Virgil chose to describe the 'green *color* of the horse',[9] rather than the former, because *glaucus* was a more familiar Greek word, and *caerulus* an unusual Latin one (especially in this context). Fronto winds up by connecting the Latin category *caesius* with Greek *glaukōpis*. Favorinus admits defeat (ironically quoting two lines of the *Iliad* on competition), and closes the discussion with a new insight into a passage of Ennius describing the 'yellow marble surface' (*flauom marmor*) of the 'blue sea' (*caeruleum mare*). The connection had previously been a puzzle for colour usage, but with Fronto's new mixture scheme (*flauus* = *uiridis* + *albus*) it all made sense.

For Gellius, *colores* existed independently of the linguistic categories which described them. '*Rubor*' actually existed – that is where the category *rufus* came from. And yet, in spite of Gage and others,[10] Gellius was not discussing the artist's palette, and these were not paints but observable phenomena (fire, blood, saffron, sea-purple, gold) where *color* could be found. In this, we detect echoes of the doctrine of the *De*

[8] Fronto adds that Ennius applied the category to *aer*.

[9] Verg. *G.* 3.82 (*uiridis color equi*).

[10] Gage (1993) 31 on the ignorance and uncertainty *NA* 2.26 displays towards basic artistic colours and mixtures. Dürbeck (1977) 39–40 works himself into a dreadful mess through his assumption that Gellius is discussing 'langwelligen Farben', and argues that the incongruities could be explained away as a peculiarity of Roman optical sensitivities.

Coloribus where it was said (792b 16) that colours and colour mixtures (which are real) were based not on pigments but on the observed effects of different illuminations (a principle found also in Plato's *Timaeus* and Aristotle). Gellius also identified *rufus* and *uiridis* as the 'basic colours' (*simplices colores*). In doing so, he demonstrates that Roman thinkers were able to privilege some colour categories over others and think in terms of 'primary' or 'basic' colour terms. Following Fronto's line, a colour was distinct if it denoted a particular and identifiable mixture of ingredients. A good language would have dedicated words (*propria uocabula*) for these colours. Gellius' discussion demonstrates that one could conceptualise Latin categories of colour in abstract terms, divorced from their objects of reference.

NA 2.26 is nevertheless a difficult text. Gellius' subset categories of red and green apparently include what are for us quite separate basic colours, like 'yellow' (*fuluus*, *flauus*, and *luteus*), 'purple' (*puniceus*) and 'blue' (*caeruleus*, *glaucus*). Some of these terms do not transfer easily into our own colour registers – for example, 'gold' as a category of 'red', 'red' eagles, 'green' horses. Favorinus also contrasts Latin 'fiery' (*igneus*, which he argues is too associative to be a real colour category) and Greek *purros*, which he argues constitutes a colour category in its own right (as opposed to being simply 'fiery'). Then *poeniceus* and *spadix*, which Fronto introduces as separate colour categories, he goes on to say are synonyms, and what is more derive from the same source, the fruit of the palm tree. These are reminders (and warnings to those who read Berlin and Kay) that the distinction between a 'basic' and an 'associative' colour category can be a subtle one as much grounded in cultural and developmental nuance as in linguistic morphology.

The precept of Gellius' debate is that the connection between *rufus* and *uiridis*, and all the various Greek and Latin colour categories described, must have been subject to a certain degree of inventiveness. No inherited institutionalised system of abstracts or primaries was available to Gellius. Fronto makes a claim based on little more than empirical observation that categories such as *fuluus*, *flauus*, *luteus*, *spadix* belong properly to a subset of *rufus*. He admits, for example, that *fuluus* can contain more *uiridis* than *rufus*, and he goes on to discuss the variety of the *color flauus*. He also explains *rubidus* as a darker form of *rufus* with *niger* 'burnt on' (*rufus atrior et nigriore multo inustus*). Among these observable ingredients in any coloured object, Fronto also includes fluctuations in texture, brightness (*acuentes*) and intensification (*augentes*, *remittentes*). This theory, then, was not about a mixture of elements (as we find in Empedocles and Democritus) but of colours *qua* colours (more like Anaxagoras' 'portions' or Hering's elemental theory of basic colours).

Favorinus buys it, and Fronto wins, but the debate is a *suasoria*, not a Peripatetic treatise on colour optics. The lesson is taught, absorbed and applied: if we accept that colour A is a mixture of x, y and z, we need to look for x, y and z in an object in order to describe it properly as A-coloured. Fronto's proposal was probably an original one.[11] With its heavy reliance on difficult and creative passages of Latin verse, it is also an imaginative one. Gellius selected these particular excerpts of verse as much for their literary excellence as for their challenging formulations of colour: in citing Pacuvius' 'fair water' (*lymphis flauis*) and 'swarthy dust' (*fuluum ... puluerem*), he sought to discover the aesthetic foundations of colour perception within the traditional Latin literary canon.[12] Gellius' system was just one attempt to reach a coherent doctrine of *color* – to establish a cogent epistemology for a system that was badly in need of intellectual schematisation. 'Basic colours', then, were up for debate.

Dialogue 2.26 also exemplifies the tension in the study of colour perception between the sensibilia of the world and the capacity of language to express them, a tension at the heart of all philosophical discussions of colour (and one of Gellius' central concerns). 'Stuff' (*res*) and words (*uerba*) formed a binary code for the conceptualisation of colour: it is both Fronto's knowledge of things (*conscientia rerum*) and his refined command of words (*uerborum elegantia*) that win the day. By employing contrived etymologies and empirical mixture theories,[13] Gellius argues that difficult connections of colour and objects in early Latin poets such as Pacuvius and Ennius are in fact innately accurate. The difficulty occurs when language-use changes, linguistic categories are not properly applied, and uneducated speakers forget why certain categories belong with certain objects. In the crowded cultural crossroads of the second century, where Greek and Latin linguistic and literary traditions increasingly overlapped and bilingualism was a prerequisite of the educated elite, the historically complex issue of colour discrimination and evaluation needed to find new methods of simplification and standardisation. 2.26, then, is a (re-)learning experience.

[11] Cf. Eco (1985) 171: 'I suspect he [Gellius] was a prisoner of his cultural mish-mash'.

[12] On Gellius' taste for creative Latin verse and 2.26, see Holford-Strevens (2003) 220–1.

[13] For example, one knows what *poeniceus* and *spadix* look like through the etymological connection with the palm tree; *luteus* is *dilutior rufus*; *caesius* derives from *caelius* ('sky-coloured').

BIBLIOGRAPHY

All references cited in the text are listed below. This is by no means an exhaustive bibliography of works that have influenced the book, nor of studies of ancient and modern colour in general, although it is hoped that this list will be of use to anyone pursuing research in this area in the future.

Abellàn, C. (1994) *Estructura semàntica de los adjetivos de color en los tratadistas Latinos de Agricultura y parte de la Enciclopedia de Plinio*. Seville.

Acquaro, E. (1998) 'I Fenici, Cartagine e l'archeologia della porpora', in O. Longo (ed.) *La porpora: realtà e immaginario di un colore simbolico*. Venice: 99–110.

Alföldi, A. (1935) 'Insignen und Tracht der römischen Kaiser', *MDAI(R)* 50: 1–171.

Anderson, W. (1966) *Ethos and education in Greek music: the evidence of poetry and philosophy*. Cambridge, Mass.

André, J. (1949) *Étude sur les termes de couleurs dans la langue latine*. Paris.

rev. E. Laughton (1951) in *CR* n.s. 1: 202–5; G. Messing (1955) in *AJPhil.* 76: 212–14.

(1955) 'Gaulois sapana, latin *sapo*, grec σάπων', *Estudios Clásicos* 7: 348–55.

(1956) *Lexique des termes de botanique en latin*. Paris.

(1958) *Notes de lexicographie botanique grecque*. Paris.

(1967) *Les Noms d'oiseaux en latin*. Paris.

Appleton, J. (1980) *Landscape in the arts and the sciences: inaugural lecture delivered in the University of Hull on 29th October 1979*. Hull.

Arkins, B. (2005) review of Cleland and Stears (2004) in *CR* 55: 490–1.

Asmis, E. (1999) 'Epicurean epistemology', in K. Algra, J. Mansfeld and M. Schofield (eds.) *The Cambridge history of Hellenistic philosophy*. Cambridge: 260–94.

Augusti, S. (1967) *I colori pompeiani, studi e documentazioni*, vol. II. Rome.

Austin, R. (ed.) (1955) *Aeneidos, Liber Quartus*. Oxford.

(1960) *M. Tulli Ciceronis Pro M. Caelio Oratio*. Oxford.

Avery, W. T. (1940) 'The *Adoratio Purpurae* and the importance of imperial purple in the fourth century of the Christian era', *MAAR* 17: 66–80.

Bailey, C. (ed.) (1947) *Titi Lucreti Cari De rerum natura libri sex, edited with prolegomena, critical apparatus, translation, and commentary*, vol. II. Oxford.

Baines, J. (1985) 'Color terminology and color classification: ancient Egyptian color terminology and polychromy', *American Anthropologist* 87: 282–97.
(2001) 'Colour use and the distribution of relief and painting in the temple of Sety I at Abydos', in W. Davies (ed.) *Colour and painting in ancient Egypt*. London: 145–57.
Balaudé, J.-F. (2004) 'La Vérité des images selon Épicure: perception, rêve et désir', *Mètis* n.s. 2 (Dossier: *Phantasia*): 193–215.
Baldwin, B. (1975) *Studies in Aulus Gellius*. Kansas.
Ball, L. (2003) *The Domus Aurea and the Roman architectural revolution*. Cambridge.
Balsdon, J. (1979) *Romans and aliens*. London.
Baltussen, H. (1998) 'The purpose of Theophrastus "*De sensibus*" reconsidered', *Apeiron* 31/2: 167–99.
Baran, N. (1983) 'Les Caractéristiques essentielles du vocabulaire chromatique latin (aspect general, étapes de développement, sens figurés, valeur stylistique, circulation)', *ANRW* II.29.1: 321–411.
Baran, N. and Chişleag, M. (1968) 'Éléments chromatiques chez Lucrèce', *Rev. Ét. Lat.* 46: 145–69.
Barker, A. (1984) *Greek musical writings*, vol. 1: *The musician and his art*. Cambridge.
Barker, D. (1996) '"The golden age is proclaimed"? The *Carmen Saeculare* and the renascence of the golden race', *CQ* n.s. 46: 434–46.
Barnes, J. and Griffin, M. (eds.) (1997) *Philosophia Togata II: Plato and Aristotle at Rome*. Oxford.
Barolsky, P. (2003) 'Ovid's colors', *Arion* 10.3: 51–6.
Bartholin, C. (1703) *Specimen Philosophiae Naturalis*. Oxford.
Bartman, E. (1999) *Portraits of Livia: imaging the imperial woman in Augustan Rome*. Cambridge.
Barton, C. (2001) *Roman honor: the fire in the bones*. Berkeley.
(2002) 'Being in the eyes: shame and sight in ancient Rome', in D. Fredrick (ed.) *The Roman gaze: vision, power, and the body*. Baltimore: 216–35.
Barton, T. (1994a) *Power and knowledge: astrology, physiognomics and medicine under the Roman Empire*. Michigan.
(1994b) 'The *inventio* of Nero: Suetonius', in J. Masters and J. Elsner (eds.) *Reflections of Nero: culture, history and representation*. London: 48–63.
Bartsch, S. (2006) *The mirror of the self: sexuality, self-knowledge, and the gaze in the early Roman Empire*. Chicago.
Batchelor, D. (2000) *Chromophobia*. London.
Beagon, M. (1992) *Roman nature: the thought of Pliny the Elder*. Oxford.
Beall, S. (1997) 'Translation in Aulus Gellius', *CQ* n.s. 47: 215–26.
(2001) '*Homo fandi dulcissimus*: the role of Favorinus in the *Attic Nights* of Aulus Gellius', *AJPhil.* 122: 87–106.
Béarat, H., Fuchs, M., Maggetti, M. and Paunier, D. (1997) *Roman wall painting: materials, techniques, analysis and conservation* (Proceedings of the International Workshop, Fribourg 7–9 March 1996). Fribourg.

Beard, M. (2002) 'Did Romans have elbows? or: Arms and the Romans', in P. Moreau (ed.) *Corps romains*. Grenoble: 47–59.

(2007) *The Roman Triumph*. Harvard.

Beare, A. (1963) 'Color-name as a function of wavelength', *American Journal of Psychology* 76: 248–56.

Berlin, B. and Kay, P. (1969) *Basic color terms*. Berkeley.

Berlin, B., Kay, P., Maffi, L. and Merrifield, W. (1997) 'Color naming across languages', in C. Hardin and L. Maffi (eds.) *Color categories in thought and language*. Cambridge: 21–56.

Berti, L. (ed.) (2000) *M. Annaei Lucani Bellum civile Liber X* (Biblioteca Nazionale, Serie dei Classici Greci e Latini, Testi con Commento Filologico, n.s. 7). Florence.

Bessone, L. (1998) 'La porpora a Roma', in O. Longo (ed.) *La porpora: realtà e immaginario di un colore simbolico*. Venice: 149–202.

Beta, S. and Sassi, M. (eds.) (2003) *I colori nel mondo antico: esperienze linguistiche e quadri simbolici* (Atti della giornata di studio). Siena.

Betts, R. (2007) 'Sceptic optics', *Apeiron* 40: 95–115.

Bianchi, F., Bruno, M. and De Nuccio, M. (2002) 'La domus sopra le sette sale: la decorazione pavimentale e parietale dell'aula absidata', in M. De Nuccio and L. Ungaro (eds.) *I marmi colorati della Roma imperiale* (Exhibition Catalogue, Rome, 28 September 2002–19 January 2003). Rome: 161–9.

Blake, M. (1959) *Roman construction in Italy from Tiberius through the Flavians*. Washington DC.

Blanc, A. (2002) 'Rendre les nuances de couleur en grec: l'emploi du procédé linguistique de la composition nominale', in L. Villard (ed.) *Couleurs et vision dans l'antiquité classique*. Rouen: 11–26.

Blümner, H. (1875) *Technologie und Terminologie der Gewerbe und Künste bei Griechen und Römern*, vol. 1. Leipzig.

Boehm, I. (2002) 'Couleur et odeur chez Galien', in L. Villard (ed.) *Couleurs et vision dans l'antiquité classique*. Rouen: 77–96.

Boigey, M. de (1923) *La Science des couleurs et l'art du peintre*. Paris.

Bonazzi, G. (ed.) (1939) *Le Elegie di Sesto Properzio*. Rome.

Bonner, S. (1949) *Roman declamation in the late republic and early empire*. Liverpool.

Borg, A. (ed.) (1999) *The language of colour in the Mediterranean*. Stockholm.

Boudon, V. (2002) 'La Théorie galénique de la vision: couleurs du corps et couleurs des humeurs', in L. Villard (ed.) *Couleurs et vision dans l'antiquité classique*. Rouen: 65–76.

Bourdieu, P. (1977) *Outline of a theory of practice*. Cambridge.

Boyle, A. (ed.) (1987) *Seneca's Phaedra*. Cairns.

(1997) *Tragic Seneca: an essay in the theatrical tradition*. London.

Bradley, K. (1978) *Suetonius' Life of Nero: an historical commentary*. Brussels.

Bradley, M. (2002) 'Fool's gold: colour, culture, innovation and madness in Nero's Golden House', *Apollo Magazine*, July 2002: 35–44.

(2004) 'The colour blush in ancient Rome', in L. Cleland and K. Stears (eds.) *Colour in the ancient Mediterranean world*. Oxford: 117–21.

(2006a) 'Colour and marble in early imperial Rome', *Proceedings of the Cambridge Philological Society* 52: 1–22.

(2006b) review of Villard (2002) in *Bryn Mawr Classical Review* 2006.08.47: http://bmcr.brynmawr.edu/2006/2006-08-47.html

(2007) review of Rouveret *et al.* (2006) in *CR* 57: 548–50.

(2009a) 'The importance of colour on ancient marble sculpture', *Art History* 32: 427–57.

(2009b) review of Panzanelli (2008) in *Bryn Mawr Classical Review* 2009.04.55: http://bmcr.brynmawr.edu/2009/2009-04-55.html

Brandis, C. (1897) 'Ein Schreiben des Triumvirn Marcus Antonius an den Landtag Asiens', *Hermes* 32: 509–22.

Brécoulaki, C. (2006) 'Considérations sur les peintres tétrachromatistes et les *colores austeri* et *floridi*: l'économie des moyens picturaux contre l'emploi de matériaux onéreux dans la peinture ancienne', in A. Rouveret *et al.* (eds.) *Couleurs et matières dans l'antiquité: texts, techniques et pratiques*. Paris: 29–42.

Bremmer, J. N. (1973) 'Seneca *Phaedra* 651–2', *Mnemos.* 26: 180.

Brenner, A. (1982) *Colour terms in the Old Testament*. Sheffield.

Bridgeman, J. (1987) 'Purple dye in late antiquity and Byzantium', in E. Spanier (ed.) *The royal purple and the biblical blue: Argaman and Tekhelet*. Jerusalem: 159–65.

Brinkmann, V. (1987) 'La Polychromie de la sculpture archaïque en marbre', *PACT* (Journal of the European Study Group on Physical, Chemical and Mathematical Techniques applied to Archaeology) 17: 35–70.

(1994) *Die Friese des Siphnierschatzhauses*. Munich.

(2003a) *Die Polychromie der archaischen und frühklassischen Skulpturen*. Munich.

(2003b) 'Farben und Maltechnik', in V. Brinkmann and R. Wünsche (2003 eds.) *Bunte Götter* (Exhibition catalogue, Munich Glyptothek, December 2003). Munich: 239–43.

Brinkmann, V. and Wünsche, R. (eds.) (2003) *Bunte Götter* (Exhibition catalogue, Munich Glyptothek, December 2003). Munich.

Broackes, J. (1999) 'Aristotle, objectivity and perception', *Oxford Studies in Ancient Philosophy* 17: 57–113.

Broadhead, H. (ed.) (1960) *The Persae of Aeschylus*. Cambridge.

Broadie, S. (1993) 'Aristotle's perceptual realism', *Southern Journal of Philosophy* 31, suppl.: 137–59.

Brück, J. (1998) 'In the footsteps of the ancestors: a review of Christopher Tilley's *A phenomenology of landscape: places, paths and monuments*', in *The archaeology of perception and the senses* (*Archaeological Review from Cambridge* 15:1): 23–36.

Bruno, V. J. (1977) *Form and colour in Greek painting*. London.

Burnyeat, M. (ed.) (1990) *The Theaetetus of Plato*. Indianopolis.

(1996) 'How much happens when Aristotle sees red and hears a middle C? Remarks on *De anima* 2.7–8', in M. Nussbaum and A. Rorty (eds.) *Essays on Aristotle's De Anima*. Oxford: 421–34.

Butler, H. and Barber, E. (eds.) (1933) *The Elegies of Propertius*. Oxford.

Butler Greenfield, A. (2005) *A perfect red: empire, espionage and the quest for the color of desire*. New York.

Cairns, F. (2005) 'Lavinia's blush', in D. Cairns (ed.) *Body language in the Greek and Roman world*. Swansea: 195–213.

Campanile, E. (1975) 'Una struttura indoeuropea a Roma', *Studi e Saggi Linguistici* 15: 36–44.

Camps, W. (ed.) (1966) *Propertius Elegies Book III*. Cambridge.

(ed.) (1967) *Propertius Elegies Book II*. Cambridge.

Capelle, W. (1958) 'Farbenbezeichnungen bei Theophrast', *Rheinisches Museum* 101: 1–45.

Carey, S. (2003) *Pliny's catalogue of culture: art and empire in the Natural History*. Oxford.

Carile, A. (1998) 'Produzione e usi della porpora nell'impero bizantino', in O. Longo (ed.) *La porpora: realtà e immaginario di un colore simbolico*. Venice: 243–69.

Carr, G. (2005) 'Woad, tattooing and identity in the later Iron Age and Early Roman Britain', *Oxford Journal of Archaeology* 24: 273–92.

Castner, C. (1998) *A prosopography of Roman Epicureans*. Frankfurt am Main.

Causey, F. and Shepherd, J. (2004) 'Amber', in L. Cleland and K. Stears (eds.) *Colour in the ancient Mediterranean world*. Oxford: 74–7.

Cavallo, G. (1998) 'La porpora tra scienze e culture', in O. Longo (ed.) *La porpora: realtà e immaginario di un colore simbolico*. Venice: 11–16.

Cavaza, F. (1987) 'Gellio grammatico e i suoi rapporti con l'ars grammatica romana', in D. Taylor (ed.) *The history of linguistics in the classical period*. Amsterdam: 85–105.

Cestuignano, A. (1952) 'Ancora a proposito di πορφύρω/ πορφύρεος', *Maia* 5: 118–20.

Chenciner, R. (2000) *Madder red*. Curzon.

Christol, A. (2002) 'Les couleurs de la mer', in L. Villard (ed.) *Couleurs et vision dans l'antiquité classique*. Rouen: 29–44.

Clarke, J. (2001) 'Colours in conflict: Catullus' use of colour imagery in c. 63', *CQ* n.s. 51: 163–77.

(2002) *Imagery of colour and shining in Catullus, Propertius and Horace*. New York.

(2004) 'Colour sequences in Catullus' "Long Poems"', in L. Cleland and K. Stears (eds.) *Colour in the ancient Mediterranean world*. Oxford: 122–5.

Clarke, M. (1953) *Rhetoric at Rome: a historical survey*. London.

Clarke, M. (2004) 'The semantics of colour in the early Greek word-hoard', in L. Cleland and K. Stears (eds.) *Colour in the ancient Mediterranean world*. Oxford: 131–9.

Cleland, L. and Stears, K. (eds.) (2004) *Colour in the ancient Mediterranean world* (BAR International Series 1267). Oxford.

Cleland, L., Harlow, M. and Llewellyn-Jones, L. (eds.) (2005) *The clothed body in the ancient world*. Oxford.

Coffey, M. and Mayer, R. (eds.) (1990) *Seneca, Phaedra*. Cambridge.

Collart, J. (1965) 'Quelques observations sur Aulu-Gelle, grammarien', *Rev. Ét. Lat.* 43: 384–95.

Conklin, H. (1955) 'Hanunóo color categories', *Southwestern Journal of Anthropology* 2: 339–44.

Connolly, P. (1998) *The ancient city: life in Classical Athens and Rome*. Oxford.

Cook, R. M. (1978) 'The Peplos Kore and its dress', *Journal of the Walters Art Gallery* 37: 85–7.

Cooper, J. (1970) 'Plato on sense-perception and knowledge (*Theaet. 184–86*)', *Phronesis* 15: 123–46.

Coote, J. (1992) '"Marvels of everyday vision": The anthropology of aesthetics and the cattle keeping Nilotes', in J. Coote and A. Shelton (eds.) *Anthropology and Aesthetics*. Oxford: 245–73.

Corbett, G. and Davies, I. (1997) 'Establishing basic color terms: measures and techniques', in C. Hardin and L. Maffi (eds.) *Color categories in thought and language*. Cambridge: 197–223.

Cracco Ruggini, L. (1979) 'Il negro buono e il negro malvagio nel mondo classico', in M. Sordi (ed.) *Conoscenze etniche e rapporti di convivenza nell'antichità*. Milan: 108–33.

Culham, P. (1986) 'Again, what meaning lies in colour!', *ZPE* 64: 235–45.

Dacos, N. (1969) *La découverte de la Domus Aurea et la formation des grotesques à la Renaissance*. London.

Dana, F. (1919) *The ritual significance of yellow among the Romans*. Philadelphia.

Darwin, C. (1872) *The expression of emotions in man and animals*. London.

Day, J. (1997) 'The theory of perception in Plato's *Theaet.* 152–83', *Oxford Studies in Ancient Philosophy* 15: 51–80.

Deacy, S. and Villing, A. (2004) 'Athena blues? Color and divinity in ancient Greece', in L. Cleland and K. Stears (eds.) *Colour in the ancient Mediterranean world*. Oxford: 85–90.

Delamare, F. and Guineau, B. (2000) *Colour: making and using dyes and pigments* (tr. S. Hawkes). London.

Delbrueck, R. (1932a) *Antike Porphyrywerke*. Leipzig.

(1932b) 'Die spätantike Kaiserornat', *Die Antike* 8: 1–21.

Den Boeft, J., Den Hengst, J. and Teitler, H. (eds.) (1987) *Philological and historical commentary on Ammianus Marcellinus XX*. Groningen.

Deng, F. (1972) *The Dinka of the Sudan*. New York.

(1973) *The Dinka and their songs*. Oxford.

Denis, J. and Schiffermüller, M. (1775) *Systematisches Verzeichniss Schmetterlindge*. Vienna.

De Nuccio, M. and Ungaro, L. (eds.) (2002) *I marmi colorati della Roma imperiale* (Exhibition Catalogue, Rome, 28 September 2002–19 January 2003). Rome.

De Oliveira, F. (1992) *Les Idées politiques et morales de Pline l'Ancien (Estudos de Cultura Clássica 5)*. Coimbra.

Descamps-Lequime, S. (2006) 'La polychromie des bronzes grecs et romains', in A. Rouveret *et al.* (eds.) *Couleurs et matières dans l'antiquité: texts, techniques et pratiques*. Paris: 79–92.

De Temmerman, K. (2007) 'Blushing beauty: characterizing blushes in Chariton's *Callirhoe*', *Mnemos.* 60: 235–52.

Douglas, A. (1965) 'Cicero the philosopher', in T. Dorey (ed.) *Cicero*. London: 135–70.

Doumet, J. (1980) *Étude sur la couleur pourpre ancienne*. Beyrouth.

Dowden, K. (2005) 'Héliodore: une esthétique sans couleur', in B. Pouderon (ed.) *Lieux, décors et paysages de l'ancien roman des origines à Byzance*. Lyon: 247–56.

Dubel, S. (2006) 'Quand la matière est couleur: du bouclier d'Achille aux "tableaux de bronze" de Taxila', in A. Rouveret *et al.* (eds.) *Couleurs et matières dans l'antiquité: texts, techniques et pratiques*. Paris: 161–81.

Dugan, J. (2005) *Making a new man: Ciceronian self-fashioning in the rhetorical works*. Oxford.

Duigan, M. (2004) 'Pretending to be what they are not: colour and the deceptive gift', in L. Cleland and K. Stears (eds.) *Colour in the ancient Mediterranean world*. Oxford: 78–84.

Duranti, M. (1997) *Linguistic anthropology*. Cambridge.

Dürbeck, H. (1977) *Zur Charakteristik der griechischen Farbenzeichnungen*. Bonn.

Dworakowska, A. (1973) 'Versicolores maculae (Plinio, *Naturalis Historia*, XXXVI, 6, 5, 46)', *Archeologia Polona* 14: 131–46.

Dyson, J. (1999) 'Lilies and violence: Lavinia's blush in the song of Orpheus', *CPhil.* 94: 281–8.

Eco, U. (1985) 'How culture conditions the colours we see', in M. Blonsky (ed.), *On signs*. Oxford: 157–75.

Edgeworth, R. J. (1979) 'Does *purpureus* mean "bright"?', *Glotta* 57: 281–91.

(1992) *The colors of the Aeneid*. New York.

Edmonds, J. (2000) *Tyrian or imperial purple dye* (Historic Dyes Series no. 7). Little Chalfont, Buckinghamshire.

Edwards, C. (1996) *Writing Rome: textual approaches to the city*. Cambridge.

Ellis, R. (ed.) (1889) *A commentary on Catullus*. Oxford.

Ernout, A. and Robin, L. (eds.) (1962) *Lucrèce: De rerum natura: commentaire exégétique et critique* (3 volumes). Paris.

Evans, E. (1935) 'Roman descriptions of personal appearance in Roman history and biography', *Harv. Stud.* 46: 43–84.

(1941) 'The study of physiognomy in the second century AD', *TAPhS* 72: 287–98.

(1945) 'Galen the physician as physiognomist', *TAPhS* 76: 96–108.

(1950) 'Physiognomics in the Roman Empire', *CJ* 45: 277–82.

(1969) *Physiognomics in the ancient world* (Transactions of the American Philosophical Society 59, part 5). Philadelphia.

Fairclough, H. (ed.) (1932) *Virgil, Aeneid*. London.

Fairweather, J. (1981) *Seneca the Elder*. Cambridge.

Falzone, S. (2002) 'L'imitazione dell'*opus sectile* nella pittura tardo antica a Romane a Ostia', in M. De Nuccio and L. Ungaro (eds.) (2002) *I marmi colorati della Roma imperiale* (Exhibition Catalogue, Rome, 28 September 2002–19 January 2003). Rome: 171–5.

Fantham, E. (1972) *Comparative studies in Republican Latin imagery*. Toronto.

(2004) *The Roman world of Cicero's De Oratore*. Oxford.

Ferguson, J. (ed.) (1985) *Catullus*. Lawrence, KS.

Field, G. (1845) *Chromatics or, the analogy, harmony, and philosophy of colours*. London.

Filoramo, G. (1998) 'Variazioni simboliche sul tema della porpora nel cristianesimo antico', in O. Longo (ed.) *La porpora: realtà e immaginario di un colore simbolico*. Venice: 227–42.

Fitch, J. (ed.) (2002) *Seneca, Tragedies: Hercules, Trojan Women, Phoenician Women, Medea, Phaedra* (Loeb Classical Library). Cambridge, Mass.

Fitton Brown, A. (1962) 'Black wine', *CR* n.s. 12: 192–5.

Fögen, T. (2000) *Patrii sermonis egestas: Einstellungen lateinischer Autoren zu ihrer Muttersprache, ein Beitrag zum sprachbewusstsein in der römischen Antike*. Munich.

Förster, R. (ed.) (1893) *Scriptores physiognomici Graeci et Latini* (2 volumes). Leipzig.

Foucault, M. (1985) *The use of pleasure: the history of sexuality*, vol. II (tr. R. Hurley). New York.

Fränkel, H. (1956) *Ovid: a poet between two worlds*. Berkeley.

Franklin, J. (ed.) (1968) *Color and race*. Boston, Mass.

Furley, D. (1966) 'Lucretius and the Stoics', *BICS* 13: 13–33.

Gagé, J. (1955) *Apollon romain: essai sur le culte d'Apollon et le développement du 'ritus Graecus' à Rome des origines à Auguste*. Paris.

Gage, J. (1981) 'A "locus classicus" of colour theory: the fortunes of Apelles', *JWI* 44: 1–26.

(1993) *Colour and culture: practice and meaning from antiquity to abstraction*. London.

(1999) *Colour and meaning: art, science and symbolism*. London.

Gaiser, K. (1965) 'Platons Farbenlehre', in H. Flashar and K. Gaiser (eds.) *Synusia: Festschrift für Wolfgang Schadewaldt*. Pfullingen: 173–222.

Gale, M. (1994) *Myth and poetry in Lucretius*. Cambridge.

Ganson, T. (2003) 'Alexander of Aphrodisias on the role of color appearances', *Ancient Philosophy* 23: 383–93.

Garfield, S. (2000) *Mauve: how one man invented a colour that changed the world*. London.

Garrison, D. (ed.) (1991) *The student's Catullus*. London.

Gassino, I. (2002) 'Voir et savoir: les difficultés de la connaissance chez Lucien', in L. Villard (ed.) *Couleurs et vision dans l'antiquité classique*. Rouen: 167–77.

Gell, A. (1995) 'On Coote's "Marvels of everyday vision"', *Social Analysis* 38: 18–30.

Gernot, L. (1957) 'Dénomination et perception des couleurs chez les grecs', in I. Meyerson (ed.) *Problèmes de la couleur* (Colloquium, Paris, 18–20 May 1954). Paris: 313–24.

Giacometti, G. (1998) 'Il colore della porpora e la meccanica quantistica', in O. Longo (ed.) *La porpora: realtà e immaginario di un colore simbolico*. Venezia: 29–40.

Giardina, C. (ed.) (1966) *Tragoediae/L. Annaei Senecae*. Bologna.

Gibbon, E. (1776–88) *The history of the decline and fall of the Roman Empire*, vol. II. London.

Gibson, J. (1968) *The senses considered as perceptual systems*. London.

Gibson, R. (2002) *Ars amatoria book 3*. Cambridge.

(2006) 'Politics of moderation in *Ars Amatoria* 3', in R. Gibson, S. Green and A. Sharrock (eds.) *The art of love: bimillenial essays on Ovid's* Ars Amatoria *and* Remedia Amoris. Oxford: 121–42.

(2007) *Excess and restraint: Propertius, Horace and Ovid's Ars Amatoria*. London.

Gilbert, O. (1907) *Die meteorologischen Theorien des griechischen Altertums*. Leipzig.

Gladstone, W. E. (1858) *Studies in Homer and the Homeric age*, vol. III. Oxford.

(1877) 'The colour-sense' in *Nineteenth Century*, 2: 366–88.

Gleason, M. (1989) 'The semiotics of gender: physiognomy and self-fashioning in the second century C.E.', in D. Halperin, J. Winkler and F. Zeitlin (eds.) *Before sexuality: the construction of erotic experience in the ancient Greek world*. Princeton: 389–416.

(1995) *Making men: sophists and self-presentation in ancient Rome*. Princeton.

Glucker, J. (1988) 'Cicero's philosophical affiliations', in J. Dillon and A. Long (eds.) *The question of 'Eclecticism': studies in later Greek philosophy*. London: 34–69.

Goclenius, R. (the Elder) (1613) *Lexicon Philosophicum*. Frankfurt.

Godwin, J. (1998) *Aesthetic ethics in the De rerum natura of Lucretius*. PhD dissertation, Open University.

Godwin, J. (ed.) (1999) *Catullus: the shorter poems*. Warminster.

Goethe, J. W. (1810) *Zur Farbenlehre*. Tübingen.

Goldberg, S. (1996) 'The fall and rise of Roman tragedy', *TAPA* 126: 265–86.

Gombrich, E. and Riley, B. (1994) 'The use of colour and its effect: the how and the why', transcript of radio transmission published in *Burlington Magazine* 126: 427–9.

Gottschalk, H. (1964) 'The *De Coloribus* and its author', *Hermes* 92: 59–85.

Grant, M. (1970) *Nero*. London.

Grant, M. (2004) 'Colourful characters: a note on the use of colour in Petronius', *Hermes* 132: 244–7.
Green, P. (1979) '*Ars gratia cultus*. Ovid as beautician', *AJPhil.* 100: 381–92.
(1982) *Ovid: the erotic poems*. Harmondsworth.
Griffin, J. (1976) 'Augustan poetry and the life of luxury', *JRS* 66: 87–105.
Griffin, M. (1984) *Nero: the end of a dynasty*. London.
(1995) 'Philosophical badinage in Cicero's letters to his friends', in J. Powell (ed.) *Cicero the philosopher*. Oxford: 325–46.
Grillet, B. (1975) *Les Femmes et les fards dans l'antiquité grecque*. Lyon.
Gros, P. (1979) 'Vie et mort de l'art hellénistique selon Vitruve et Pline', *Rev. Ét. Lat.* 56: 289–313.
Gross, N. (1988) *Senecas Naturales Quaestiones: Komposition, Naturphilosophische Ausagen und ihre Quellen*. Stuttgart.
Grossman, M. (1988) *Colore e lessico: studi sulla struttura semantica degli aggettivi di colore in catalano, castigliano, italiano, romeno, latino*. Tübingen.
Habinek, T. (2002) 'Ovid and empire', in P. Hardie (ed.) *The Cambridge companion to Ovid*. Cambridge: 46–61.
Hagendahl, H. (1921) *Studia Ammianea* (Dissertation). Uppsala.
Hahm, D. (1978) 'Early Hellenistic theories of vision and the perception of color', in P. Machamer and R. Turnbull (eds.) *Studies in perception*. Ohio: 60–95.
Hamlyn, D. (1961) *Sensation and perception: a history of the philosophy of perception*. London.
Handschur, E. (1970) *Die Farb- und Glanzwörter bei Homer und Hesiod, in den homerischen Hymnen und den Fragmenten des epischen Kyklos*. Vienna.
Hankinson, R. (2003) 'Stoic epistemology', in B. Inwood (ed.) *The Cambridge companion to the Stoics*. Cambridge: 59–84.
Hannah, P. (2004) 'The cosmetic use of red ochre (*Miltos*)', in L. Cleland and K. Stears (eds.) *Colour in the ancient Mediterranean world*. Oxford: 100–105.
Harris, E. (ed.) (1904) *The Tragedies of Seneca/L.A. Seneca*. London.
Harris, M. (c. 1766) *The natural system of colours*. Licester-Fields: Laidler.
Harrison, S. J. (2003) 'The colour of olive leaves: Vergil *Aeneid* 5.309', *Ordia Prima* 2: 79–81.
Harry, B. (1970) 'Epicurus: some problems in physics and perception', *G&R* 17: 58–63.
Haynes, H. (2008) '*Rome*'s opening titles: triumph, spectacle and desire', in M. Cyrino (ed.) Rome *season one: history makes television*. Oxford: 49–60.
Healy, J. (1999) *Pliny the Elder on science and technology*. Oxford.
Heider, E. (1972) 'Probabilities, sampling, and ethnographic method: the case of the Dani colour names', *Man* 7.3: 448–66.
Heldmann, K. (1981) 'Schönheitspflege und Characterstärke in Ovids Liebeslehre: zum Proömium der *Medicamina Faciei*', *WJA* 7: 153–76.
Helm, R. (ed.) (1965) *Properz Gedichte*. Berlin.
Helmbold, W. C. (1950) 'The complexion of Domitian', *CJ* 45: 388–9.

Hemsoll, D. (1990) 'The architecture of Nero's Golden House', in M. Henig (ed.) *Architecture and architectural sculpture in the Roman empire*. Oxford: 10–38.

Henderson, J. (2006) 'From philosophia into *PHILOSOPHIA*: Classicism and Ciceronianism', in J. Porter (ed.) *Classical pasts: the classical traditions of Greece and Rome*. Princeton: 173–203.

Henriksén, C. (1998) *Martial book 9, a commentary*. Uppsala.

Henry, J. (ed.) (1889) *Aeneidea III*. Dublin.

Hering, E. (1878) *Zur Lehre vom Lichtsinn*. Vienna.

Heyworth, S. (1995) 'Propertius: division, transmission, and the editor's task', *Papers of the Leeds International Latin Seminar* 8: 165–85.

Hine, H. (ed.) (1981) *An edition with commentary of Seneca's Natural Questions, book 2*. New York.

Hochegger, R. (1884) *Die Geschichtliche Entwicklung des Farbsinnes*.

Holford-Strevens, L. (1989) *Aulus Gellius*. London.

(2003) *Aulus Gellius: an Antonine scholar and his achievement* (revised edition). Oxford.

Hook, B. (2000) 'Nothing within which passeth show: character and "*color*" in Senecan tragedy', in G. Harrison (ed.) *Seneca in performance*. London: 53–71.

House, D. K. (1980) 'The life of Sextus Empiricus', *CQ* n.s. 30: 227–38.

Howell, P. (ed.) (1980) *A commentary on book one of the Epigrams of Martial*. London.

Hurley, D. (1993) *An historical and historiographical commentary on Suetonius' Life of C. Caligula*. Atlanta, Ga.

Ierodiakonou, K. (2004) 'Empedocles and the ancient painters', in L. Cleland and K. Stears (eds.) *Colour in the ancient Mediterranean world*. Oxford: 91–5.

(2005) 'Empedocles on colour and colour vision', *Oxford Studies in Ancient Philosophy* 29: 1–38.

Ingemann, V. (1981–2) '*Albus an ater* – a double entendre in C. 93?', *Classica et Mediaeualia* 33: 145–50.

Ingold, T. (1992) 'Culture and the perception of the environment', in E. Croll and D. Parkin (eds.) *Bush base: forest farm. Culture, environment and development*. London: 39–56.

Inwood, B. (2007) *Seneca: selected philosophical letters*. Oxford.

Irwin, E. (1974) *Colour terms in Greek poetry*. Toronto.

Isaac, B. (2004) *The invention of racism in classical antiquity*. Princeton.

Isager, J. (1986) 'Plinio il Vecchio e le meraviglie di Roma', *Analecta Romana Instituti Danici* 15: 37–50.

(1991) *Pliny on art and society*. Odense.

Itten, J. (1961) *Kunst der Farbe*. Leipzig.

James, E. (1995) *Light and colour in Byzantine art*. New York.

(2003) 'Colour and meaning in Byzantium', *Journal of Early Christian Studies* 11: 223–33.

Jarman, D. (1995) *Chroma: a book of colour*. London.

Jenkins, I. (ed.) (2001) *Cleaning and controversy: the cleaning of the Parthenon sculptures 1811–1939* (BM *Occasional Paper* 146). London.

Jenkins, I. and Middleton, A. (1988) 'Paint on the Parthenon sculptures', *BSA* 83: 183–207.

Jocelyn, H. D. (1977) 'The ruling class of the Roman republic and Greek philosophers', *Bull. Rylands Libr.* 59: 323–66.

Johansen, T. (2006) 'What's new in the *De Sensu*?', in R. King (ed.) *Common to body and soul: philosophical approaches to explaining living behaviour in antiquity*. Berlin: 140–64.

Johnston, I. (2006) *Galen on diseases and symptoms*. Cambridge.

Jones, A. and MacGregor, G. (2002) *Colouring the past: the significance of colour in archaeological research*. Oxford.

Jones, C. (1998) 'Interpreting the perceptions of past people', *Archaeological Review from Cambridge* 15:1 (*The archaeology of perception and the senses*): 7–22.

(1999) 'Processional colors', in B. Bergmann and C. Kondoleon (eds.) *The art of ancient spectacle*. Yale: 247–57.

Kader, I. (2003) '"Täuschende Spielereien": kolorierte Abgüsse im 19. und frühen 20. Jahrhunder', in V. Brinkmann and R. Wünsche (eds.) *Bunte Götter* (Exhibition catalogue, Munich Glyptothek, December 2003). Munich: 245–55.

Kasprzyk, D. (2002) 'Les Couleurs du rêve chez Artémidore', in L. Villard (ed.) *Couleurs et vision dans l'antiquité classique*. Rouen: 129–52.

Kaster, R. (2005) *Emotion, restraint and community in ancient Rome*. Oxford.

Kay, P. and McDaniel, C. (1978) 'The linguistic significance of the meaning of basic color terms', *Language* 54: 610–46.

Kenyon, F. (1893) 'A rescript of Marcus Antonius', *CR* 7: 476–8.

Keuls, E. (1978) *Plato and Greek painting*. Leiden.

Kiggell, M. and Blakeway, D. (2002) *The Queen's story*. London.

Kober, A. E. (1932) *The use of color terms in the Greek poets to 146 BC*. New York.

Konstan, D. (2003) 'Aristotle on anger and the emotions: the strategies of status', in S. Braund and G. Most (eds.) *Ancient anger: perspectives from Homer to Galen*. Cambridge: 99–120.

Kranz, W. (1912) 'Die ältesten Farbenlehren der Griechen', *Hermes* 47: 18–42.

(1943) 'Lukrez und Empedokles', *Philol.* 96: 68–107.

Lakoff, G. (1987) *Women, fire and dangerous things: what categories reveal about the mind*. Chicago.

Lamb, T. and Bourriau, J. (1995) *Colour: art and science*. Cambridge.

Landels, J. (1999) *Music in ancient Greece and Rome*. London.

Langley, A. and De Souza, P. (1996) *The Roman News*. London.

Lapidge, M. (1978) 'Stoic cosmology', in J. Rist (ed.) *The Stoics*. Berkeley: 161–86.

Lateiner, D. (1998) 'Blushes and pallor in ancient fictions', *Helios* 25: 163–89.
Laughton, E. (1948) 'Flauus pudor', *CR* 62: 109–10.
(1950) '*Flauus* again', *CR* 64: 88–9.
Lawall, G., Kunkel, G. and Lawall, S. (eds.) (1982) *The Phaedra of Seneca, with a new translation of the Hippolytus of Euripides*. Chicago.
Leary, T. J. (1988) '*Medicamina* recalled', *LCM* 13: 140–2.
Lee, M.-K. (2005) *Epistemology after Protagoras: responses to relativism in Plato, Aristotle, and Democritus*. Oxford.
Lepschy, A. (1998) 'Il colore della porpora', in O. Longo (ed.) *La porpora: realtà e immaginario di un colore simbolico*. Venice: 53–66.
Lévi-Strauss, C. (1970) *The raw and the cooked* (tr. J. Weightman and D. Weightman). London.
Lévy, C. (2006) 'La Notion de *color* dans la rhétorique latine: Cicéron, Sénèque le Rhéteur, Quintilien', in A. Rouveret *et al.* (eds.) *Couleurs et matières dans l'antiquité: texts, techniques et pratiques*. Paris: 185–99.
Lewis, C. and Short, C. (1879) *A Latin dictionary*. Oxford.
Lichtenstein, J. (1993) *The eloquence of color: rhetoric and painting in the French Classical Age* (tr. E. McVarish). Berkeley.
Lienhardt, G. (1960) *Divinity and experience: the religion of the Dinka*. Oxford.
Lilja, S. (1965) *The Roman elegists' attitude to women*. Helsinki.
Linksz, A. (1952) *Physiology of the eye*, vol. II. New York.
Liscu, M. (1937) *L'Expression des idées philosophiques chéz Cicéron*. Paris.
Llewellyn-Jones, L. (2003) *Aphrodite's tortoise: the veiled woman of ancient Greece*. London.
Lloyd, G. (1983) *Science, folklore and ideology: studies in the life sciences in ancient Greece*. Cambridge.
(1991) *Methods and problems in Greek science*. Cambridge.
Locher, A. (1986) 'The structure of Pliny the Elder's Natural History', in R. French and F. Greenaway (eds.) *Science in the early Roman empire: Pliny the Elder, his sources and influence*. London: 20–9.
Lodge, R. C. (1975) *Plato's theory of art*. New York.
Long, A. (1966) 'Thinking and sense-perception in Empedocles: mysticism or materialism?', *CQ* n.s. 16: 256–76.
(1996a) *Stoic studies*. Cambridge.
(1996b) 'Theophrastus' *De sensibus* on Plato', in K. Algra, A. Kiempe, P. Van der Horst and D. Runia (eds.) *Polyhistor: studies in the history and historiography of ancient philosophy*. Leiden: 345–62.
(2006) *From Epicurus to Epictetus: Studies in Hellenistic and Roman Philosophy*. Oxford.
Long, A. and Sedley, D. (1987) *The Hellenistic philosophers*, vol. I. Cambridge.
Longo, O. (ed.) (1998a) *La porpora: realtà e immaginario di un colore simbolico* (Atti del Convegno di Studio, Venezia 24 e 25 ottobre 1996). Venice.
(1998b) 'La zoologia delle porpore nell'antichità greco-romana', in O. Longo (ed.) *La porpora: realtà e immaginario di un colore simbolico*. Venice: 79–90.

(1998c) 'Porpora e sangue: da Omero a Shakespeare', in O. Longo (ed.) *La porpora: realtà e immaginario di un colore simbolico*. Venice: 125–31.

Lorenzoni, G. (1998) 'Il porfido, marmo di porpora in qualche esempio del Veneto medievale', in O. Longo (ed.) *La porpora: realtà e immaginario di un colore simbolico*. Venice: 300–16.

Lowe, B. (2004) 'The industrial exploitation of murex: purple dye production in the Western Mediterranean', in L. Cleland and K. Stears (eds.) *Colour in the ancient Mediterranean world*. Oxford: 46–8.

Luciani, R. and Sperduti, L. (1993) *Domus Aurea Neronis Roma*. Ministero per i beni culturali ambientali (n.s. 20). Rome.

Luck, G. (ed.) (1964) *Properz und Tibull, Liebeselegien*. Zurich and Stuttgart.

Lucy, J. (1992) *Language diversity and thought: a reformulation of the linguistic relativity hypothesis*. Cambridge.

(1997) 'The linguistics of "color"', in C. Hardin and L. Maffi (eds.) *Color categories in thought and language*. Cambridge: 320–46.

Lycos, K. (1964) 'Aristotle and Plato on "appearing"', *Mind* 73: 496–514.

Lyne, R. (1983) 'Lavinia's blush: Vergil *Aeneid* 12.64–70', *G&R* 30: 55–64.

Lyons, J. (1999) 'The vocabulary of color with particular reference to Ancient Greek and Classical Latin', in A. Borg (ed.) *The language of color in the Mediterranean*. Stockholm: 38–75.

Machamer, P. and Turnbull, R. (1978) *Studies in perception: interrelations in the history of philosophy and science*. Columbus.

Mackail, J. (ed.) (1930) *The Aeneid / Virgil; edited, with introduction and commentary*. Oxford.

MacLaury, R. (1991) 'Social and cognitive motivations of change: measuring variability in color semantics', *Language* 67: 34–62.

Maltby, R. (ed.) (2002) *Tibullus, Elegies: text, introduction and commentary*. Leeds.

Manetti, G. (ed.) (1996) *Knowledge through signs: ancient semiotic theories and practices*. Brussels.

Manzelli, V. (1994) *La policromia nella statuaria greca arcaica*. Rome.

Marchetti, S. C. (1992) 'Filosofia e ideologia nella *Naturalis Historia* de Plinio', *ANRW* II.36.5: 3249–306.

Mario Fales, F. (1998) 'Archeologia della porpora nel vicino oriente antico', in O. Longo (ed.) *La porpora: realtà e immaginario di un colore simbolico*. Venezia: 91–8.

Matthes, D. (ed.) (1962) *Hermagorae Temnitae testimonia et fragmenta*. Leipzig.

Maugan-Chemin, V. (2006) 'Les Couleurs du marbre chez Pline l'Ancien, Martial et Stace', in A. Rouveret *et al.* (eds.) *Couleurs et matières dans l'antiquité: texts, techniques et pratiques*. Paris: 103–25.

Mausfield, R. and Heyer, D. (2005) *Colour perceptions: mind and the physical world*. Oxford.

Maxwell-Stuart, P. G. (1981) *Studies in Greek colour terminology*, vol. I: γλαυκός; vol. II: χαροπός. Leiden.

(1996) 'Studies in the career of Pliny the Elder and the composition of his *Naturalis Historia*'. PhD thesis, St Andrews.

McKeown, J. (ed.) (1989) *Ovid, Amores: text, prolegomena and commentary in four volumes*, vol. II. Leeds.

Meadows, J. (1945) 'Pliny on *smaragdus*', *CR* 59: 50–1.

Michaelides, D. (1985) 'Some aspects of marble imitation in mosaic', in P. Pensabene (ed.) *Marmi Antichi: problemi d'impiego, di restauro e d'identificazione* (*Studi Miscellanei* 26 (1981–83)). Rome: 155–63.

Miller, F. (ed.) (1917) *Seneca: Tragedies*, vol. I (Loeb Classical Library). London.

Moonwomon, B. (1994) 'Color categorization in early Greek', *Journal of Indo-European Studies* 22: 37–65.

Moreno Soldevila, R. (ed.) (2006) *Martial, Book IV: A Commentary* (Mnemosyne Supplement 278). Leiden.

Morford, M. (1968) 'The distortion of the *Domus Aurea* tradition', *Eranos* 66: 158–79.

Mourelatos, A. (1970) *The route of Parmenides: a study of word, image and argument in the fragments*. New Haven.

Mugler, C. (1960) 'La Lumière et la vision dans la poésie grecque', *Rev. Ét. Grec.* 73: 40–72.

Müller-Boré, K. (1922) 'Stilistische Untersuchungen zum Farbwort und zur Verwendung der Farbe in der älteren griechischen Poesie', *Klass. philol. Stud.* 3: 5–126.

Muller-Dufeu, V. (2006) 'Les Couleurs du bronze dans les statues grecques d'après les descriptions antiques', in A. Rouveret *et al.* (eds.) *Couleurs et matières dans l'antiquité: texts, techniques et pratiques*. Paris: 93–102.

Murgatroyd, P. (ed.) (1994) *Tibullus, Elegies II*. Oxford.

Murphy, T. (2003) 'Pliny's *Naturalis Historia*: the prodigal text', in A. Boyle and W. Dominik (eds.) *Flavian Rome*. Leiden: 301–22.

(2004) *Pliny the Elder's Natural History: the empire in the encyclopaedia*. Oxford.

Myerowitz, M. (1985) *Ovid's games of love*. Detroit.

Naas, V. (2006) '*Omnia ergo meliora fuere, cum minor copia* (Pline l'Ancien, *NH*, XXXV, 50): matières et couleurs au service d'un discours moral dans la minéralogie de Pline l'Ancien', in A. Rouveret *et al.* (eds.) *Couleurs et matières dans l'antiquité: texts, techniques et pratiques*. Paris: 201–12.

Nadeau, J. (1977) 'Ethiopians again and again', *Mnemos.* 30: 75–8.

Nakhnikian, G. (1955) 'Plato's theory of sensation, I', *Review of Metaphysics* 9: 129–48.

Némethy, G. (ed.) (1907) *P. Ovidii Nasonis Amores*. Budapest.

Newbold, R. F. (1981–82) 'Perception and sensory awareness among Latin writers in Late Antiquity', *Classica et Mediaevalia* 33: 169–90.

Newlands, C. (2002) *Statius' Silvae and the poetics of empire*. Cambridge.

Newton, I. (1671–72) 'New theory about light and colours', *Philosophical Transactions of the Royal Society* 80: 3075–87.

(1704) *Opticks*. London.
Nikolaidis, A. (1994) 'On a supposed contradiction in Ovid (*Medicamina Faciei* 18–22 vs. *Ars Amatoria* 3.129–32)', *AJPh* 115: 97–103.
Nisbet, R. (ed.) (1961) *In L. Calpurnium Pisonem oratio / M. Tulli Ciceronis*. Oxford.
Nisbet, R. and Hubbard, M. (eds.) (1970) *A Commentary on Horace, Odes Book I*. Oxford.
Norden, E. (1909) *Die antike Kunstprosa*. Berlin.
O'Brien, D. (1970) 'The effect of a simile: Empedocles' theories of seeing and breathing', *JHS* 90: 140–79.
O'Hara, J. (2007) *Inconsistency in Roman epic: studies in Catullus, Lucretius, Vergil, Ovid and Lucan*. Cambridge.
Oost, S. (1968) *Galla Placidia Augusta: a biographic essay*. Chicago.
Osborne, H. (1968) 'Colour concepts of the ancient Greeks', *British Journal of Aesthetics* 8: 274.
Paganelli, D. (ed.) (1929) *Properce: Elegies*. Paris.
Panzanelli, R. (ed.) (2008) *The color of life: polychromy in sculpture from antiquity to the present*. Los Angeles.
Pastoureau, M. (1986) *Figures et couleurs: étude sur la symbolique et la sensibilité médiévale*. Paris.
Payne, R. (1962) *Rome Triumphant: how the empire celebrated its victories*. New York.
Pearson, A. (1891) *The fragments of Zeno and Cleanthes*. Cambridge.
Pease, A. (ed.) (1935) *Publi Vergili Maronis Aeneidos Liber Quartus*. Cambridge, Mass.
Pensabene, P. (2000) 'I marmi in Seneca: residenze fastose ed esecrazione del lusso', in P. Parroni (ed.) *Seneca e il suo tempo, Atti del Convegno internazionalie*. Rome: 91–109.
Perotti, P. (1984) 'A proposito dell'aggetivo πορφύρεος', *Prometheus* 10: 205–9.
Phelps, H. (1930) *Die Farbige Architektur bei den Romern und in Mittelalter*. Berlin.
Pinker, S. (1994) *The language instinct*. Harmondsworth.
Platnauer, M. (1921) 'Greek colour-perception', *CQ* 15.155–62.
Poignault, R. (1999) 'Lucrèce chez Quintilien, Fronton et Aulu-Gelle', in R. Poignault (ed.) *Présence du Lucrèce* (Actes du colloque tenu à Tours, 3–5 décembre 1998). Tours: 177–98.
Pokorny, J. (1959) *Indogermanisches etymologishes Wörterbuch*, vol. I. Basel.
Pollitt, J. (2002) 'ΠΕΡΙ ΧΡΩΜΑΤΩΝ: what ancient Greek painters thought about colours', in M. Tiverios and D. Tsiafakis (eds.) *Color in ancient Greece: the role of color in ancient Greek art and architecture 700–31 BC*. Thessaloniki: 1–8.
Portmann, A. and Ritsema, R. (eds.) (1972) *The realms of colour*. Leiden.
Posch, S. (1979) '*Albus an ater homo*. Zu C. c. 93', *Serta Philologica Aenipontana* 3: 319–36.

Prater, A. (2003) 'Streit um Farbe: die Wiederentdeckung der Polychromie in der griechischen Architektur und Plastik im 18. und 19. Jahrhundert', in V. Brinkmann and R. Wünsche (eds.) *Bunte Götter* (Exhibition catalogue, Munich Glyptothek, December 2003). Munich: 257–67.

Préchac, F. (1914) 'Sénèque et la Maison d'Or', *CR Acad. Inscr.* 231–42.

Priestley, J. (1772) *History and present state of discoveries relating to vision, light and colours*. London.

Prioux, E. (2006) '*Materiae non cedit opus*: matières et sujets dans les épigrammes descriptives (IIIe siècle av/J.-C.-50 apr. J.-C.)', in A. Rouveret *et al.* (eds.) *Couleurs et matières dans l'antiquité: texts, techniques et pratiques*. Paris: 127–60.

Quinn, K. (ed.) (1970) *Catullus: the poems*. London.

Racine, J. (1677) *Phèdre: Tragédie*. Paris.

Raedo, L. (2000) 'I porfidi: imagines di potere', in S. Ensoli and E. La Rocca (eds.) *Aurea Roma: dalla città pagana alla città cristiana* (Exhibition catalogue, Rome, Palazzo delle Esposizioni). Rome: 61–5.

Reinhardt, K. (1921) *Poseidonius*. Munich.

Reinhardt, T. and Winterbottom, M. (eds.) (2006) *Institutio Oratoria Book 2 / Quintilian*. Oxford.

Reinhold, M. (1976) *The history of purple as a status symbol in antiquity*. Brussels.

Reiter, G. (1962) *Die griechischen Bezeichnungen der Farben Weiss, Grau und Braun*. Innsbruck.

Renfrew, C. (1987) 'Towards a cognitive archaeology', in C. Renfrew and E. Zubrow (eds.) *The ancient mind: elements of cognitive archaeology*. Cambridge: 3–12.

Renna, E. (1998) 'Ricette per succadenei della porpora in due papyri greci', in O. Longo (ed.) *La porpora: realtà e immaginario di un colore simbolico*. Venice: 133–47.

Reuterswärd, P. (1960) *Studien zur Polychromie der Plastik: Griechenland und Rom*. Stockholm.

Rhorer, C. (1980) 'Red and white in Ovid's Metamorphoses: the mulberry tree in the tale of Pyramus and Thisbe', *Ramus* 9: 79–88.

Riley, C. (1996) *Color codes: modern theories of color in philosophy, painting and architecture, literature, music, and psychology*. Hanover.

Rimell, V. (2006) *Ovid's lovers: desire, difference and the poetic imagination*. Cambridge.

Roberts, M. (1989) *The jeweled style: poetry and poetics in late antiquity*. London.

Roller, M. (1997) 'Color-blindness: Cicero's death, declamation, and the production of history', *CPhil.* 92: 109–30.

Rosati, G. (1985) *I cosmetici delle donne*. Venice.

Rothstein, M. (ed.) (1966) *Die Elegien des Sextus Propertius*. Dublin and Zurich.

Rouveret, A. (2006) 'Les Yeux pourpres: l'expérience de la couleur dans la peinture classique entre realités et fictions', in A. Rouveret *et al.* (eds.) *Couleurs et matières dans l'antiquité: texts, techniques et pratiques*. Paris: 17–28.

Rouveret, A., Dubel, S. and Naas, V. (eds.) (2006) *Couleurs et matières dans l'antiquité: texts, techniques et pratiques*. Paris.

Rowe, C. (1972) 'Conceptions of colour and colour-symbolism in the ancient world', *Eranos Yearbook* 41: 327–64.

Russell, D. (1983) *Greek declamation*. Cambridge.

Sahlins, M. (1976) 'Colors and cultures', *Semiotica* 16 (1): 1–22.

Salvadori, M. (1998) 'Ante omnes est purpurissum: la porpora nella pittura parietale romana', in O. Longo (ed.) *La porpora: realtà e immaginario di un colore simbolico*. Venice: 203–25.

Salvetti, C. (1998) 'Il colore dell'antichità', in A. Donati (ed.) *Romana pictura: la pittura romana dalle origini all'età bizantina* (Exhibition catalogue, Rimini, Palazzi del Podestà e dell'Arengo, Mar. 28-Aug. 30, 1998). Milan: 85–92.

Sandbach, F. (1985) *Aristotle and the Stoics*. Cambridge.

Sassi, M. (1982) 'Xenophan. B 16 e Herodt. 4, 108: una nota sul significato di PURROS', *Rivista di Filologia e di Istruzione Classica* 110: 391–3.

(1993) 'Fisiognomica', in G. Cambiano, L. Canfora, and D. Lanza (eds.) *Lo spazio letterario della Grecia Antica*. Rome: 431–78.

(1994) 'Una percezione imperfetta? I Greci e la definizione dei colori', *L'Immagine Riflessa* 2: 281–302.

(2001) *The science of man in ancient Greece* (tr. P. Tucker). Chicago.

(2005) 'L'esperienza del colore nel mondo greco' in M. Antico Gallina, (ed.) *I Greci: il sacro e il quotidiano*. Milan: 119–29.

Schiesaro, A. (1990) *Simulacrum et imago: gli argomenti analogici nel 'De rerum Natura'*. Pisa.

Schindler, M. (1964) *Goethe's theory of colour*. London.

Schneider, R. (1986) *Bunte Barbaren*. Worms.

Schrivers, P. H. (1992) 'Philosophie et paraphrase: Lucrèce et les sceptiques', in P. Grimal (ed.) *La Langue latine, langue de la philosophie* (Ecole française de Rome). Rome: 125–40.

Schulbaum, S. (1930–31) 'La Symbolique de la lumière et des couleurs chez Virgile', *Eos* 33: 117–35.

Schultz, W. (1904) *Das Farbenemfindungssystem der Hellenen*. Leipzig.

Schwarzenberg, E. (2000) 'Color, light and transparency in the Greek world', in E. Borsook, F. Gioffredi Superbi and G. Pagliarulo (eds.) *Medieval mosaics: light, color, materials*. Milan: 15–34.

Scranton, R. (1964) *Aesthetic aspects of ancient art*. Chicago.

Sebesta, J. (1994a) 'Symbolism in the costume of the Roman woman', in J. Sebesta and L. Bonfante (eds.) *The world of Roman costume*. Madison: 46–53.

(1994b) 'Tunica Ralla, Tunica Spissa: the colors and textiles of Roman costume', in J. Sebesta and L. Bonfante (eds.) *The world of Roman costume*. Madison: 65–76.

(2005) 'The toga praetexta of Roman children and praetextate garments', in L. Cleland *et al.* (eds.) *The clothed body in the ancient world*. Oxford: 113–20.

Sedley, D. (1988) 'Epicurean anti-reductivism', in J. Barnes and M. Mignucci (eds.) *Matter and metaphysics*. Naples: 295–328.

(1989) 'Philosophical allegiance in the Greco-Roman world', in M. Griffin and J. Barnes (eds.) *Philosophia togata*. Oxford: 97–119.

(1992) 'Empedocles' theory of vision and Theophrastus' De sensibus', in W. Fortenbaugh and D. Gutas (eds.) *Theophrastus: his psychological, doxographical and scientific writings*. New Brunswick, N.J.: 20–31.

(1998) *Lucretius and the transformation of Greek wisdom*. Cambridge.

Sensi, L. (1980–81) 'Ornatus e status sociale delle donne romane', *Annali della Facoltà di Lettere e Filosofia, Perugia* n.s. 4: 55–102.

Shackleton Bailey, D. R. (ed.) (1956) *Propertiana*. Cambridge.

Shapiro, A. (1993) *Fits, passions and paroxysms: physics, method, and chemistry and Newton's theories of coloured bodies and fits of easy reflection*. Cambridge.

Sharples, R. (2002) 'Some problems in Lucretius' account of vision', *Leeds International Classical Studies* 1.2 (www.leeds.ac.uk/classics/lics/).

Sharples, R. and Sheppard, A. (eds.) (2003) *Ancient approaches to Plato's Timaeus* (Bulletin of the Institute of Classical Studies supplement 78). London.

Sherwin-White, A. N. (1967) *Racial prejudice in imperial Rome*. Cambridge.

Siegel, R. (1959) 'Theories of vision and colour perception of Empedocles and Democritus; some similarities to the modern approach', *Bulletin of the History of Medicine* 33: 145–59.

(1970) *Galen on sense perception*. New York.

Silverman, A. (1989) 'Color and color-perception in Aristotle's *De anima*', *Ancient Philosophy* 9: 271–92.

Sinclair, P. (2003) 'Rhetoric of writing and reading in the preface to Pliny's *Naturalis Historia*', in A. Boyle and W. Dominik (eds.) *Flavian Rome*. Leiden: 277–300.

Smith, A. (2005) *The primacy of vision in Virgil's Aeneid*. Austin.

Smith, K. (ed.) (1913) *Tibullus: the Elegies*. New York.

Smyshliaeva, V. [Смышляева, В.] (2002) '"Цвет небесный" в языке римской элегии', *Hyperboreus: Studia Classica* 8: 287–93.

Smyth, W. R. (1970) *Thesaurus Criticus ad Sexti Propertii Textum* (Mnemosyne Supplement 12). Leiden.

Snowden, F. M. (1970) *Blacks in antiquity: Ethiopians in the Greco-Roman experience*. Cambridge, Mass.

(1983) *Before color prejudice: the ancient view of blacks*. Cambridge, Mass.

Snyder, J. (1980) *Puns and poetry in Lucretius' De Rerum Natura*. Amsterdam.

Solmsen, F. (1961) 'Αἴσθησις in Aristotelian and Epicurean thought', *Mededelingen der Koninklijke Nederlandse Akademie van Wetenschappen, Afd. Letterkunde* 24 no. 8: 241–62 (repr. in F. Solmsen (ed.) (1968) *Kleine Schriften*, vol. I. Hildesheim: 612–33; and C. Classen (ed.) (1986) *Probleme der Lukrezforschung*. Hildesheim: 484–501).

Sorabji, R. (1971) 'Aristotle on demarcating the five senses', *Philosophical Review* 80: 55–79.

(1972) 'Aristotle, mathematics and colour', *CQ* n.s. 22: 293–308.

Soverini, L. (1998) 'Il cielo di porpora nella litteratura greca arcaica e il linguaggio delle vesti', in O. Longo (ed.) *La porpora: realtà e immaginario di un colore simbolico*. Venice: 111–24.

Spanier, E. (ed.) (1987) *The royal purple and the biblical blue: Argaman and Tekhelet*. Jerusalem.

Sperber, D. (1975) *Rethinking symbolism* (tr. A. Morton). Cambridge.

Steigerwald, G. (1990) 'Das kaiserliche Purpurprivileg in spätrömischer und frühbyzantinischer Zeit', *Jahrbuch für Antike und Christentum* 33: 209–39.

Striker, G. (1977) 'Epicurus on the truth of sense-impressions', *Archiv für Geschichte der Philosophie* 59: 125–42.

Stroh, W. (1979) 'Rhetorik und Erotik: eine Studie zu Ovids liebesdidaktischen Gedichten', *WJA* 5: 117–32.

Struycken, P. (2003) 'Colour mixtures according to Democritus and Plato', *Mnemos*. 56: 273–305.

Stulz, H. (1990) *Die Farbe Purpur im frühen Griechentum*. Stuttgart.

Sussman, L. (1978) *The Elder Seneca* (Mnemosyne Supplement 51). Leiden.

(ed.) (1994) *The Declamations of Calpurnius Flaccus*. New York.

Svenbro, J. (2004) 'Voir et voyant: la perception visuelle chez Empédocle', *Mètis* n.s. 2 (Dossier: Phantasia): 47–70.

Swain, S. (2004) 'Bilingualism and biculturalism in Antonine Rome: Apuleius, Fronto, and Gellius', in L. Holford-Strevens and A. Vardi (eds.) *The worlds of Aulus Gellius*. Oxford: 3–40.

(ed.) (2007) *Seeing the face, seeing the soul: Polemon's Physiognomy from classical antiquity to medieval Islam*. Oxford.

Szidat, J. (1996) *Historischer Kommentar zu Ammianus Marcellinus Buch XX–XXI* (Teil III, Historia Einzelschriften 89). Stuttgart.

Tarrant, H. (1996) 'Platonic interpretation in Aulus Gellius', *GRBS* 37: 173–93.

Taylor, A. (1928) *A commentary on Plato's Timaeus*. Oxford.

Taylor, B. (1719) *New principles of linear perspective* (2nd edn). London.

Thomas, P. L. (1979) 'Red and white: a Roman colour symbol', *Rh. Mus.* 122: 310–16.

Thompson, L. (1989) *Romans and blacks*. London.

Thomson, D. (ed.) (1978) *Catullus: a critical edition*. Chapel Hill.

Tilley, C. (1994) *A phenomenology of landscape: places, paths and monuments*. Oxford.

Tiverios, M. and Tsiafakis, D. (eds.) (2002) *Color in ancient Greece: the role of color in ancient Greek art and architecture 700–31 BC*. Thessaloniki.

Todd, R. (1980) 'Lavinia blushed', *Vergilius* 26: 27–33.

Trinquier, J. (2002) 'Les Vertus magiques et hygiéniques du vert dans l'antiquité', in L. Villard (ed.) *Couleurs et vision dans l'antiquité classique*. Rouen: 97–128.

(2006) '*Quid de pratorum uiriditate...plura dicam ?* (Cicéron, *De senectute*, 57): les couleurs du paysage dans la littérature latine, de Lucrèce à l'époque flavienne', in A. Rouveret *et al.* (eds.) *Couleurs et matières dans l'antiquité: texts, techniques et pratiques*. Paris: 213–59.

Tsouna, V. (1998) *The epistemology of the Cyrenaic School*. Cambridge.

Tuan, Y. F. (1977) *Space and place: the perspective of experience*. London.

Turner, V. (1967) *The forest of symbols: aspects of Ndembu ritual*. New York.

Vardi, A. (1993) 'Why *Attic Nights*? or, What's in a name?' *CQ* n.s. 43: 298–301.

(2001) 'Gellius against the professors', *ZPE* 137: 41–54.

Veckenstedt, E. (1888) *Geschichte der griechischen Farbenlehre*. Paderborn.

Vilborg, E. (ed.) (1962) *Achilles Tatius, Leucippe and Clitophon: a commentary*. Göteborg.

Villard, L. (ed.) (2002a) *Couleurs et vision dans l'antiquité classique*. Rouen.

(2002b) 'Couleurs et maladies dans la Collection Hippocratique: les faits et les mots', in L. Villard (ed.) *Couleurs et vision dans l'antiquité classique*. Rouen: 45–64.

(2006) 'L'Essor du chromatisme au IVe siècle: quelques témoignages contemporains', in A. Rouveret *et al.* (eds.) *Couleurs et matières dans l'antiquité: texts, techniques et pratiques*. Paris: 43–54.

Vogt-Spira, G. (2000) 'Gellius, die römische Komödie und die Kategorie der Imitatio', in E. Stärk and G. Vogt-Spira (eds.) *Dramatische Wälchen: Festschrift für Eckard Lefèvre zum 65. Geburstag*. Hildersheim: 683–96.

Wachsmuth, C. (ed.) (1884) *Ioannis Stobaei anthologium*. Berlin.

Walbank, F. (ed.) (1957) *A historical commentary on Polybius*, vol. I. Oxford.

Wallace, F. E. (1927) *Color in Homer and in ancient art: preliminary studies* (*Smith College Classical Studies* 9). Northampton.

Wallace-Hadrill, A. (1990) 'Pliny the Elder and man's unnatural history', *G&R* 37: 80–96.

Warburton, D. (2004) 'The terminology of ancient Egyptian colours in context', in L. Cleland and K. Stears (eds.) *Colour in the ancient Mediterranean world*. Oxford: 126–30.

Wardman, A. (1967) 'Description of personal appearance in Plutarch and Suetonius: the use of statues as evidence', *CQ* 17: 414–20.

Ward-Perkins, J. B. (1956) 'Nero's Golden House', *Antiquity* 30: 209–19.

Wardy, R. (1988) 'Lucretius on what atoms are not', *CPhil.*: 112–28.

Watson, P. (1982) 'Ovid and *cultus*: *Ars Amatoria* 3.113–28', *TAPA* 112: 237–44.

(2001) 'Parody and subversion in Ovid's *Medicamina Faciei Femineae*', *Mnemos.* 54: 457–71.

Wessely, C. (ed.) (1921) *Studien zur Paläographie und Papyruskunde* XIV. Leipzig.

West, D. (1969) *The imagery and poetry of Lucretius*. Edinburgh.

Westerink, L. (ed.) (1962) *Anonymous prolegomena to Platonic philosophy*. Amsterdam.

Whitmarsh, T. (ed.) (2001) *Achilles Tatius: Leucippe and Clitophon*. Oxford.

Wierzbicka, A. (1990) 'The meaning of colour terms: semantics, colour and cognition', *Comparative Linguistics* 1: 99–150.

Wiles, D. (1991) *Masks of Menander: sign and meaning in Greek and Roman performance*. Cambridge.

(2007) *Mask and performance in Greek tragedy: from ancient festival to modern experimentation*. Cambridge.

Wilkinson, L. (1955) *Ovid recalled*. Cambridge.

Williams, C. (ed.) (2004) *Epigrams Book 2 / Martial*. Oxford.

Williams, R. (ed.) (1960) *Aeneidos Liber Quintus*. Oxford.

Wilson, L. (1938) *The clothing of the ancient Romans*. Baltimore.

Winterbottom, M. (ed.) (1974) *Declamations / The Elder Seneca* (The Loeb Classical Library, vol. 1). Cambridge, Mass.

Wiseman, T. P. (1979) *Clio's cosmetics*. Leicester.

Wittgenstein, L. (1977) *Bemerkungen über die Farben* (tr. L. McAlister and M. Schättle). Oxford.

Wolanin, H. (1999) 'Aulus Gellius and vulgar Latin', in H. Petersmann and R. Kettemann (eds.) *Latin vulgaire – latin tardif: Actes du Vème Colloque international sur le latin vulgaire et tardif Heidelberg, 5–8 septembre 1997*. Heidelberg: 497–503.

Wright, F. (1920) 'A note on Plato's definition of colour', *CR* 34: 31–2.

Wyke, M. (1994) 'Woman in the mirror: the rhetoric of adornment in the Roman world', in L. Archer, J. Fischler and M. Wyke (eds.) *Women in ancient societies: an illusion of the night*. London: 134–51.

(2006) 'Reading female flesh: *Amores* 3.1', in P. Knox (ed.) *Oxford readings in Classical Studies: Ovid*. Oxford: 169–204.

Young, D. (1964) 'The Greeks' colour sense', *Review of the Society for Hellenic Travel* 4: 42–6.

Ziderman, I. (2004) 'Purple dyeing in the Mediterranean world: characterisation of biblical *Tekhelet*', in L. Cleland and K. Stears (eds.) *Colour in the ancient Mediterranean world*. Oxford: 40–5.

INDEX OF ANCIENT PASSAGES DISCUSSED

This index is not a definitive list of ancient references within this book. I have selected references to passages which are discussed in some detail, or which have particular significance for the argument presented.

GENERAL INDEX

This is a selective index of themes, phenomena, persons and categories that are discussed in detail in the book. One of the book's critical arguments is that it is misleading to separate colour categories from the objects they describe, and so it diverges from previous discussions of colour in antiquity in not attempting to draw up a glossary of ancient colour terms. The key categories addressed by this book (which are by no means definitive) are listed below under 'colours, key categories discussed'.

Lightning Source UK Ltd.
Milton Keynes UK
UKOW031120040112

184718UK00001B/45/P

9 780521 291224

Contents

What to Do

Choose a face

Remember the colour you have chosen.

When you see your face on the page, you are the LEADER.

The LEADER reads the text in the speech bubbles.

There are extra words and questions to help you on the teacher's whiteboard. The LEADER reads these aloud.

When you see this stop sign, the LEADER reads it aloud.

You might need:

- to look at the WORD HELP on pages 20–22;
- to look at the LOCATION HELP on page 23;
- an atlas.

If you are the **LEADER**, follow these steps:

1 PREDICT

Think about what is on the page.

- Say to your group:

"I am looking at this page and I think it is going to be about . . ."

- Tell your group:

"Read the page to yourselves."

2 CLARIFY

Talk about words and their meaning.

- Say to your group:

"Are there any words you don't know?"

"Is there anything else on the page you didn't understand?"

- Talk about the words and their meanings with your group.
- Read the whiteboard.

- Ask your group to find the LET'S CHECK word in the WORD HELP on pages 20–22. Ask them to read the meaning of the word aloud.

3 ASK QUESTIONS

Talk about how to find out more.

- Say to your group:

"Who has a question about what we have read?"

- Question starters are: how..., why..., when..., where..., what..., who...
- Read the question on the whiteboard and talk about it with your group.

4 SUMMARISE

Think about who and what the story was mainly about.

When you get to pages 16–17, you can talk to a partner or write and draw on your own.

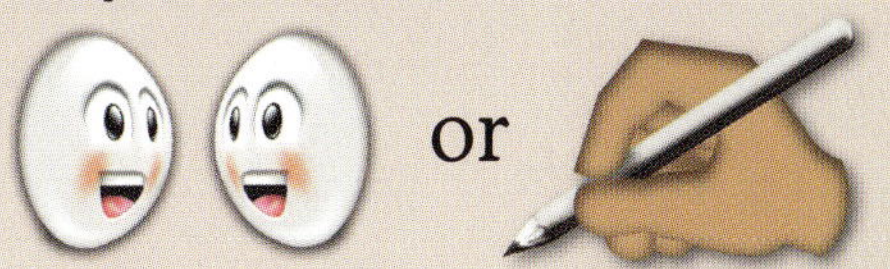

Suma and Edita

I am looking at this page and I think it is going to be about… because...

Suma and Edita are orang-utans. They live in a **rainforest**.

Suma had a baby and so did Edita. However, their babies died.

After a while, Suma had another baby, but Edita didn't.

This was how the **problem** started.

Are there any words you don't know?

Let's check: problem

Who has a question about what we have read?

What do you think the problem will be?

This page was mainly about

fact

fact

STOP

My predictions were right/wrong because . . .

Strange Behaviour

I am looking at this page and I think it is going to be about… because...

Suma's new baby was called Forester.

One day, the **rangers** saw Edita with Forester. They did not know how she had taken him. They could only **guess**. An orang-utan baby had never been taken like this before.

Are there any words you don't know?

Let's check: rangers

Who has a question about what we have read?

How do you think Edita took the baby?

Edita **hangs** from the trees with Suma's baby.

Watching Edita

I am looking at this page and I think it is going to be about… because...

The rangers **followed** Edita in the rainforest. They watched her with Forester.

Forester was **clinging** to her fur. He was **hungry** but Edita had no milk.

The rangers saw Suma, too. She was looking very sad and **lonely**.

Are there any words you don't know?

Let's check: clinging

Who has a question about what we have read?

What do you think the rangers might do?

Forester tries to drink milk from Edita.

A Problem

I am looking at this page and I think it is going to be about... because...

Edita wasn't taking care of Forester very well. But she wouldn't let go of him.

The rangers saw that Forester was very sleepy. Edita was **climbing** high up in the trees. If Forester went to sleep, he might fall down.

The rangers knew that they had to do something.

Are there any words you don't know?

Let's check: climbing

Who has a question about what we have read?

Why do you think Edita didn't want to let go of Forester?

Forester was very tired because he had no milk to drink.

This page was mainly about

fact

fact

STOP

My predictions were right/wrong because . . .

The Plan

I am looking at this page and I think it is going to be about... because...

The rangers knew that they had to get Forester back. They had to think of a **plan**.

Edita loved bananas, so the rangers put some in a cage.

Edita saw the bananas and went into the cage. She ate the bananas. Then, Edita went to sleep. While she was sleeping, the rangers took Forester.

Are there any words you don't know?

Let's check: plan

Who has a question about what we have read?

Why do you think the rangers took Forester when Edita was sleeping?

Edita is happy to be eating bananas.

This page was mainly about fact fact

STOP

My predictions were right/wrong because . . .

A Happy Ending

I am looking at this page and I think it is going to be about... because...

Forester was put in the tree where his mother was. When he saw his mother, he kissed her.

This story had a happy **ending** for Suma and her baby. It had a happy ending for Edita, too. A few years later, she had a baby of her own.

Are there any words you don't know?

Let's check: ending

Who has a question about what we have read?

Why do you think Edita took Suma's baby?

Suma and baby Forester are back together.

This page was mainly about fact fact

STOP
My predictions were right/wrong because . . .

Something to Think About

 or 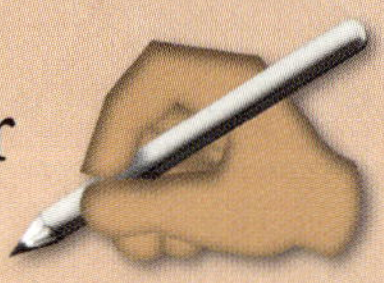

What

What was the problem?

How

How did the problem get solved?

Think about what happened in the story of the orang-utans. Read the questions then talk about your ideas with a partner, or write them down.

What if

What if the rangers had not helped?

Do You Need to Find an Answer?

You could go to . . .

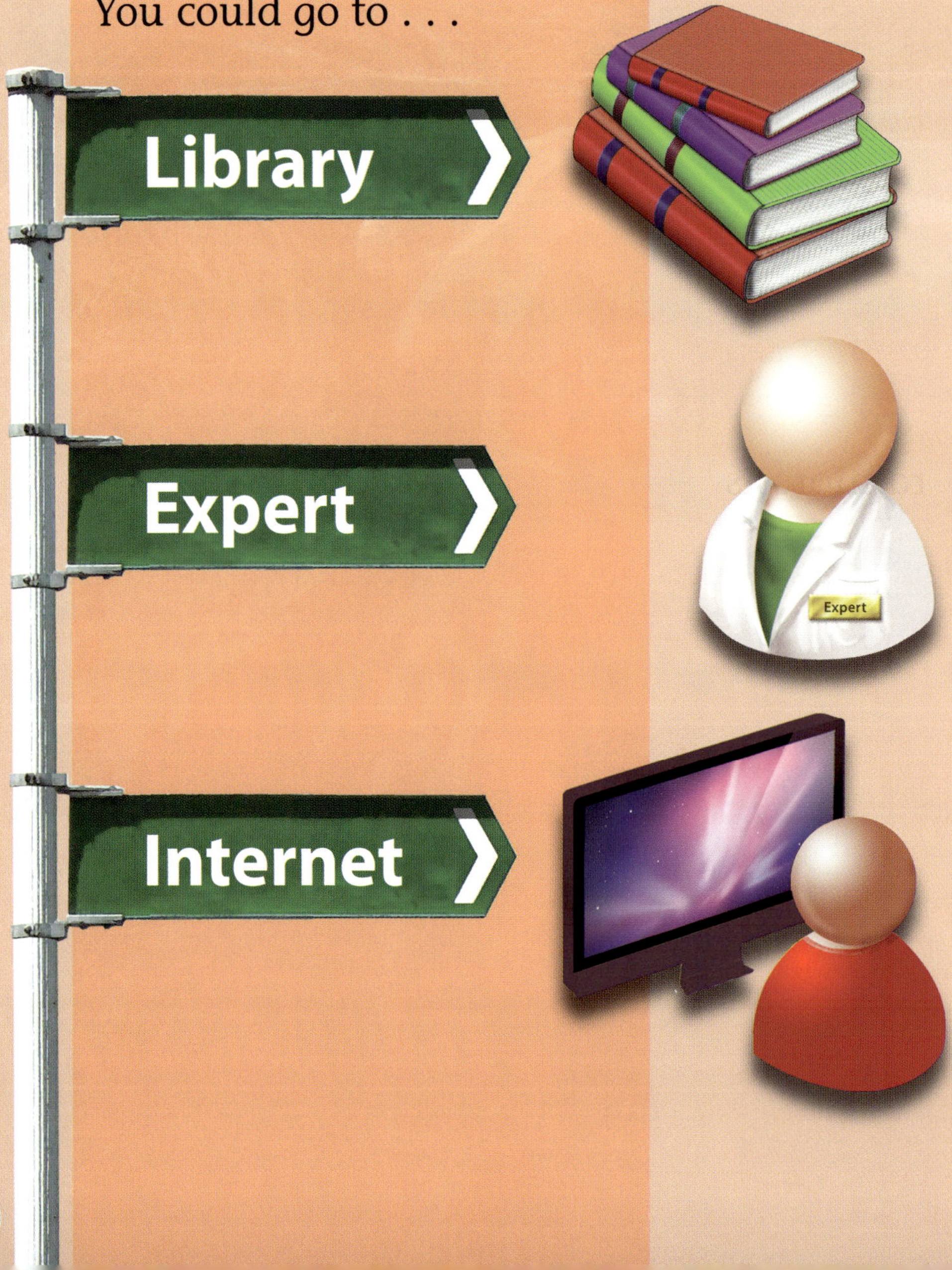

Do You Want to Find Out More?

You could look in books or on the internet. These key words could help you:

- animal babies
- animal mothers
- orang-utan
- rainforests
- rangers
- Sumatra

Word Help

Dictionary

climbing	moving up by using the hands and feet
clinging	holding on tightly to something or someone
ending	the last part of something
followed	went after
guess	to say what you think the answer is when you do not really know
hangs	holds on to something with the feet off the ground
hungry	feeling the need for food

lonely	sad because you are on your own
plan	a way of doing something
problem	something that is difficult to understand
rainforest	a hot, wet place with a lot of trees
rangers	people whose job it is to take care of a park or animals

Word Help

Thesaurus

clinging	holding
fall	tumble
happy	glad, pleased
sad	unhappy
sleepy	tired
taken	stolen

Location Help

Where Suma and Edita Live

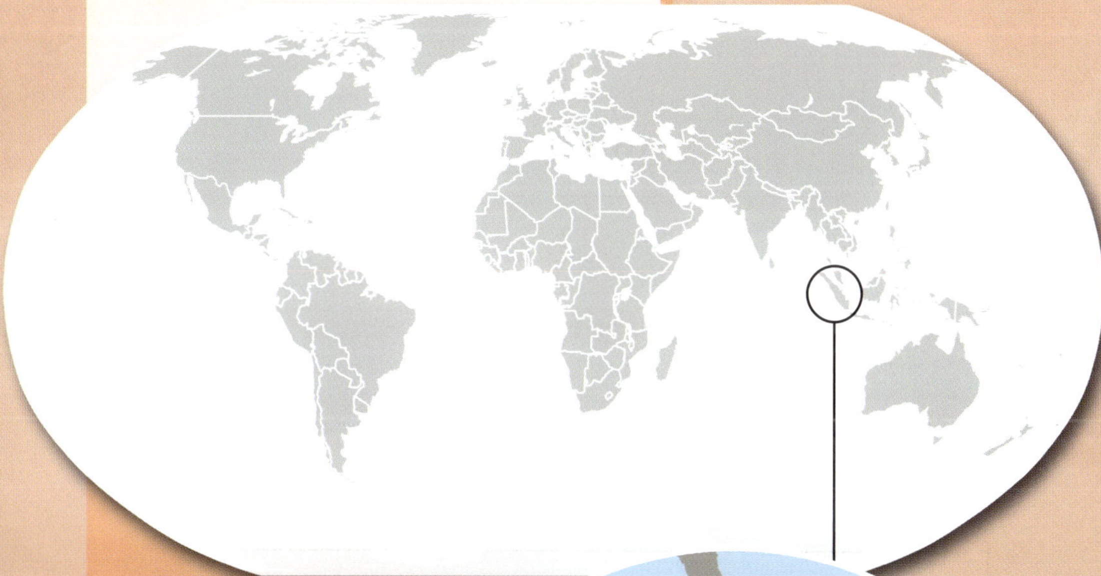

Index